JB Chifley

JB Chifley

An ardent internationalist

Julie Suares

MELBOURNE UNIVERSITY PUBLISHING
An imprint of Melbourne University Publishing Limited
Level 1, 715 Swanston Street, Carlton, Victoria 3053, Australia
mup-contact@unimelb.edu.au
www.mup.com.au

First published 2019
Text © Julie Suares
Design and typography © Melbourne University Publishing Limited, 2019

This book is copyright. Apart from any use permitted under the *Copyright Act 1968* and subsequent amendments, no part may be reproduced, stored in a retrieval system or transmitted by any means or process whatsoever without the prior written permission of the publishers.

Every attempt has been made to locate the copyright holders for material quoted in this book. Any person or organisation that may have been overlooked or misattributed may contact the publisher.

Text design by Phil Campbell
Cover design by Phil Campbell
Typeset by J&M Typesetting
Printed in Australia by OPUS Group

 A catalogue record for this book is available from the National Library of Australia

9780522874709 (paperback)
9780522874693 (hardback)
9780522874716 (ebook)

*Portrait of Prime Minister Ben Chifley,
courtesy National Library of Australia.*

Contents

Acknowledgements	viii

PART 1: ORIGINS OF CHIFLEY'S INTERNATIONALISM

1. 'Mr. JB Chifley … a great friend of India'	3
2. From Bathurst to Canberra	31

PART II: CHIFLEY AND ECONOMIC INTERNATIONALISM

3. Chifley and the Great Depression	73
4. Chifley and the World Economy, from 1941 to 1949	113

PART III: CHIFLEY AND AUSTRALIAN FOREIGN POLICY TOWARDS ASIA

5. Chifley and Post-colonial Asia	143
6. Chifley and Nehru—Fellow Internationalists	181

PART IV: CHIFLEY AND THE ESTABLISHMENT OF A NEW COLLECTIVE POLITICAL–STRATEGIC ORDER

7. The Japanese Peace Settlement	213
8. Chifley and the Cold War	239

PART V: CONCLUSION

9. A Receptivity to 'New Ideas and to the Impact of New Conditions'	273
Bibliography	283
Index	307

Acknowledgements

This book is dedicated to the memory of my dear mother, Leila.

I would like to thank my sister Lyn and my step-father Richard—who voted for Chifley because 'Chifley was *of* the people' and 'he did what he said he'd do'—for their support and their friendship. Thank you to Lyn for putting up with my distracted behaviour and the books littered throughout the lounge-room. She has been a great source of strength to me.

Thank you also to my niece Jessie and her partner Andrew and their children Anna, Jack and Gos for their inspiration and encouragement. Thank you, Anna, Jack and Gos for your cards wishing me the best. I kept them on my desk as I worked. Anna—I will treasure my heart-flower always. Without the love and support—and forbearance—of my family and friends, I would not have been able to complete this book.

Associate Professor Christopher Waters has been extraordinarily generous with his time and his patience. His commitment to archival research is outstanding and a fine example to follow. His belief that I could actually complete this book has been especially reassuring. Associate Professor Helen Gardner has also been very supportive of my work.

To Professor Frank Bongiorno, Emeritus Professor Phillip Deery and Associate Professor Kent Fedorowich, thank you for your contribution to my work. I owe you all a special debt of gratitude.

Thank you also to Professor David Lowe for your support, and to Dr Meg Gurry, for being so helpful with the knowledge that you have shared. Thank you to the Contemporary Histories Research Group at Deakin University for the support it has provided me.

Many thanks to Professor Janice Stargardt and to her son, Professor Nicholas Stargardt, for all the kind assistance they have provided, especially the many details about the life of AW Stargardt, together with a photo of him.

Thank you also to Professor Geoffrey Bolton and to Professor Duncan Waterson, who sadly have passed away, for the information they gave me.

I'm very grateful to Professor Joy Damousi, commissioning editor of the History Series at Melbourne University Press, who invited me to submit a book proposal on Chifley and also Catherine McInnis, the editor of MUP Academic, who has been very helpful to me. My copy editor and indexer, Meryl Potter was an absolute delight to work with, providing me with many useful suggestions.

Thank you to Sarah Brown and the Brown family for their very generous *Philip Brown Award* for research into Australian history entailing the use of primary sources.

To all those friends who have inspired and supported me, sincere thanks to Joe and Julie; Christine and Peter; John and Carole; Sue and Frank; Nadine and Ronald; Colin; Michaela, Alex and Sam; Blair and Cath; Margaret, Ran and Cath; Rick; Stefanie; Dianne; Mark and Fiona; Antony; Barry and Cheryl; Pat and Jenny; John and Jo; Jenny and Peter; Kate; John; Mary and Keith; Phil and Barbara; Phuong, Damien and Max; Michael and Linda; Craig and Nai; Leon; Ken; Kerry and Clem; Ian and Mary; Lis and Peter; Alwyn and Frank; Mary, Margaret and Gabrielle; Dot; Gerard; Glenda and Ken; Helen; Roberta; Joyce, Jim, Mick and Colin; Anne and Greg; Tim and Alison; Ev; Jacinta; Andy; Robert; Travis; Pam and Peter; Julie and Jack; Belinda; Bob and Tim; Robyn and Bruce; Gayle; Greg and Kim; Muffy, Athol and Pam; Suzanne; Micky, Matt and Julian; Wendy and Rhonda. And Craig, thank you for my copy of *Things Worth Fighting For*. Thank you, Marion for my book, *Ben Chifley: A Biography* by LF Crisp.

I would like to thank the librarians at Deakin University Library, and the staff at Deakin Research for their very generous support. I am also grateful to the librarians and archivists at the National Library of Australia, the National Archives of Australia, the State Library of Victoria and the University of Melbourne Archives for all the assistance they have provided. Thank you also to Radhey Shyam, Deputy Librarian and Information Officer at the Nehru Memorial Museum and Library for providing me with a copy of JN Sahni's article on his interview with Chifley.

To my doctor Novreen Rasool, the doctors and nurses at the Ararat Medical Centre and the Ararat Hospital; to the neurosurgeons, anaesthetists, doctors, nurses, workers and volunteers at the Royal Melbourne Hospital—thank you.

Ararat—where I live—is a railway town in regional Victoria. Thank you to the Ararat community for being so welcoming and inclusive.

Part I
Origins of Chifley's Internationalism

AW Stargardt selected and compiled the collection of Chifley's speeches published as Things Worth Fighting For: Speeches by Joseph Benedict *Chifley. Many thanks to Professor Janice Stargardt and to Janice and Wolfgang's son Professor Nicholas Stargardt for their gift of a photo of AW Stargardt and their kind permission for me to use it in my book on Chifley.*

Chapter One
'Mr JB Chifley ... a great friend of India'

In June 1951, a delegation of Indian journalists visited Australia for the opening of the Australian federal parliament and to report on the Commonwealth jubilee celebrations commemorating the fiftieth anniversary of the federation of Australia. Journalist JN Sahni, president of the Press Association of India, was a member of the delegation.[1] His description of this visit provides an intriguing account of an Indian journalist's perceptions of Australia and former prime minister JB Chifley, whom he interviewed on 13 June 1951.[2] After arriving in Darwin behind schedule, inclement weather and thick fog in Sydney forced the delegation to continue their journey to Canberra in a small Australian Holden. Sahni wrote that, travelling through 'rich undulating country, peppered with small towns, villages and scattered farm houses ... thick forests of gum and bush, lent an exotic colour to the landscape'. During this trip to Canberra, Sahni's exuberant comments on the 'picturesqueness' of the countryside met with reserve from his Australian driver, who it turned out was not a native of New South Wales, but a Tasmanian. Sahni noted that 'state loyalties in Australia die hard'. He added:

> You do not have to be in Australia for many hours, or to see many places to realize that it is a rich country, with abundant resources, and has a kindly, affable, prosperous

unpretentious people, a little over-conscious of their kinship with the white races, and slightly over-afraid of an Asiatic infiltration.[3]

The delegation duly arrived in the 'infant Capital city', one that Sahni compared to New Delhi in the mid-1920s, existing 'more in design than in reality'.[4] The capital's major buildings consisted of 'Parliament House, the Secretariat, two shopping centres, a few hotels and hostels'. From Canberra's centre, through 'long open stretches of wild country, dimly lit, but extensive roads … reach out to cottage homes which are springing up rapidly on the periphery of the Capital'. The Indian journalists missed the 'colourful Jubilee ceremony', but were in time for the parade. 'Striped trousers, tail coats, top hats, long flowing dresses indicated the formality of the occasion', even though they were exposed to 'drizzling rain' and 'wet seats'.

That night there was a banquet with 'more tail coats, decorations and speeches'. The delegation of Indian journalists, together with the distinguished visitors, parliamentarians, diplomats and journalists, heard eminent Australian politicians 'trace Australia's story of coming of age'. Amongst them was former prime minister William Morris 'Billy' Hughes, who declared in his speech, 'The time has come for common people to rule, and to ask vested interests and class-minded people to get out'. Sahni expressed surprise because:

> Judging from the formal attire of the guests, the decorative pendants hanging from the collars of some on the main table, and the multiple decorations displayed on the lapels of several others, it almost looked like a body of lords and barons. And yet there was one man, who sat at the end of the main table, wearing a smoky lounge suit, a blue cotton tie, and a simple pastel shirt. He had evidently not had the time to brush back his unruly hair. He smoked the pipe of the common man.[5]

This was Joseph Benedict Chifley, prime minister of Australia from 1945 to 1949, treasurer from 1941 to 1949, leader of the Australian Labor Party, now Opposition leader and, according to Sahni, 'the most powerful man in Australia outside the Government'. Next day, late in the afternoon of 13 June, Sahni interviewed Chifley. It was Sahni's 'last interview of the day' and Chifley's 'last interview for all time'.[6] Over the course of two hours, the wide-ranging conversation explored many subjects, 'from pipe smoking to Yoga'.[7] The journalist described Chifley as having:

> an athletic figure, reminiscent of the early rough life he had led. His sharp, small, dark eyes, shadowed by shapely arching brows, emphasised honesty, frankness, a kindly heart, and an observant mind. There was a ruggedness about his cheekbones, which would have made him indistinguishable in any team of workers in overalls. He spoke the workers' mixture of brogue and cockney, with almost Gladstonian sense of inflexion and emphasis. As I sat there talking to him, smoking our respective pipes, sharing tobacco from a common carton, helpfully offered by my host, I little realized that this man, who combined the toughness of a bricklayer, with the vision and dynamic urge of a great architect of his nation's destiny, was conveying through me his last message.[8]

During this interview, Chifley told Sahni that India had 'a very great leader' in Jawaharlal Nehru,[9] India's first prime minister and foreign minister after it became an independent nation in 1947 until his death in 1964.[10] Nehru, together with Mohandas Karamchand Gandhi, were the leaders of the Indian independence movement in India's long struggle against Britain.[11] Sahni wrote that Chifley insisted on talking about India and repeatedly got up from his desk to study a map of Asia. He was particularly interested in whether Nehru was still convinced that India should remain neutral in the event of war. Sahni replied that despite pressure from the rival power blocs, he thought that Nehru had the courage and tenacity to resist their influence. Chifley urged Nehru to remain neutral—India could do 'a great service to the world … by showing the way to preserving peace'. He then asked about India's 'great leader Gandhi' and his 'methods of international co-operation to pacifically meet the challenge of war'; it was a tragedy that 'so many fine young men should become gun-fodder every five or ten years in every country'. In response, Sahni described the Gandhian creed of non-violent resistance at great length.[12]

Referring to the Indian-Pacific region, Chifley stated: 'we on this side of Asia, from Bombay to Sydney, could do a lot for mutual development, and for helping each other in distress'; he urged a rationalisation of the economies of India and Australia on the 'basis of greater inter-dependence and mutual help'. When asked his opinion of Commonwealth politicians' attitude towards the Indian–Pakistan conflict over Kashmir, Chifley replied he thought it was 'damn impertinent of any outsider to try to dictate a solution to India and Pakistan'. The two countries should be left alone to settle the issue themselves. In Chifley's opinion, if Nehru and Liaquat Ali Khan, Pakistan's prime minister, were not able to settle this problem, 'no outsider can'. He then went on to confide in Sahni something that was not generally known in India: the United Nations Security Council had offered him the position of mediator in the dispute between India and Pakistan over Kashmir, before the position was offered to High Court judge, Sir Owen Dixon. Chifley appreciated the confidence shown by the Indian government in 'two Australians'.[13]

Chifley also explained to Sahni that he did not care for public functions such as the jubilee ball and would not be attending.[14] He mentioned his struggle to 'preserve his right to smoke his pipe, and to wear the clothes of the common man, even in the presence of royalty, and at all formal occasions'.[15] When Sahni said he wanted to discuss Australian affairs, Chifley suggested that the journalist should see more of Australia first, then have lunch with him and discuss his impressions of Australia on his return to Canberra.[16] That night, Sahni described the state ball:

> Representatives of all nations, delegates from Commonwealth countries, men and women from all sections of Australian society, dressed in almost regal formalism, lent splendour to a fantastically decorated Ball room. There was music and dancing! In the supper hall, one saw exhibited a hundred kinds of foods, dressed in a variety of artistic designs, by the deft hands of chefs from all over the world. The Ball was reminiscent of mid Victorian

splendour. And then suddenly a meteor crashed! The waltz music stopped. Powdered faces were wet with tears. Mr Menzies, the Prime Minister, announced that his parliamentary colleague, an honourable opponent, the man who loved his neighbour better than he loved himself, the whimsical philosopher, the man who rose without favour or patronage to the Prime Ministership and he was never far from God, had died suddenly.[17]

Chifley had suffered a heart attack in his room at the Hotel Kurrajong and died that night. Sahni 'felt choked with emotion'. In his articles on his meeting with Chifley—which appeared in a number of English language newspapers in various regions of India, and in four or five Indian language newspapers—Sahni wrote that India had 'lost one of its greatest friends across the seas'. Chifley's last words to the journalist were: 'Tell Nehru not to lose heart, but to carry on, India will still show the way to peace. In him not only you, but the world has a great man'. Sahni declared that with Chifley's death, India had 'lost a great and sincere friend, Pandit Nehru an ardent personal admirer, Australia a leader of great vision, sterling honesty, irrepressible courage and idealism'.[18] He was the leader who 'understood India and her problems as no foreigner ever did'.[19]

JN Sahni's account of his interview with Chifley portrays the former prime minister in a manner not readily recognisable to those accustomed to observing him in the context of domestic politics. It reveals a politician who was an internationalist with a keen interest in India and its leaders. Chifley's admiration for Nehru is very evident in this interview, as is his interest in the Gandhian creed of non-violent passive resistance. It is also clear that he acknowledged and accepted Australia's geographic identity as belonging to the Indian-Pacific region: Australia and India were co-habitants in a common region sharing regional interests and concerns.

India was a source of great hope for Chifley, first, because of future economic opportunities for the two countries, and second, because he saw India as an inspiration in 'showing the way to preserving peace', in a post-colonial Cold War era in which the world was divided into two polarised and competing power blocs. Both Chifley and India's prime minister, Jawaharlal Nehru, were united in their opposition to Cold War politics. Chifley believed that war should be avoided at all cost to prevent the never-ending cycle of young men becoming 'gun-fodder every five or ten years'.[20] This is an aspect of Chifley that has received little attention from historians, many of whom have preferred to situate him entirely within the domestic arena, focusing on such issues as his attempt to nationalise the Australian banks in 1947.

Portrayals of Chifley

There is a considerable literature on Chifley the man and his domestic policy, but less on his attitudes and actions in the international sphere. There are two major biographies of Chifley, by political scientist and public servant, Leslie Finlay (Fin) Crisp and historian David Day, and a brief biography by Scott Bennett, a former student of Crisp.[21] In 1940, Crisp joined the Commonwealth Public Service and worked in the Department of Labour and National Service. In 1942, this became the Department of Post-War Reconstruction, where Crisp worked closely with Chifley, his minister. In 1949 he was appointed director-general of the Department of Post-War Reconstruction. The next year Crisp became the first professor of political science at the Canberra University College. He was also a lifelong member of the Australian Labor Party.[22] Crisp, therefore, wrote as an insider on a personal, work and political level. According to historian Geoffrey Bolton, Crisp's *Ben Chifley* was 'a very good biography, but it might have been even better with a little more shade to the light'.[23] Instead, 'it erred on the side of canonisation'.[24]

Crisp devotes an excellent chapter to observing Chifley on the international stage. He argues that when Chifley became prime minister, 'he was the last man who would have put himself forward as an expert on foreign affairs'. Crisp does note, however, that by 1945, Chifley had practical experience and knowledge, and a 'deep interest in the substance of international economic relations'.[25] It seems that Crisp made a distinction between 'the "high politics" of diplomacy and the "low politics" of economics and trade'.[26] It is intriguing to speculate that Chifley would probably have been very much at home with the present-day dominance of the 'economic dimension' in Australia's international affairs. As historian David Lee states, it would be inconceivable now to 'think of offering an account of Australian foreign policy which did not address both its geo-economic and geo-strategic dimensions'.[27] Crisp writes of the warm relationship between Chifley and Nehru, and his enjoyment of the Commonwealth prime ministers' conferences.[28] Crisp devotes another chapter to Chifley's struggle in 1947 to get the Labor Party caucus to approve the government's ratification of the 1944 Bretton Woods Agreement which would establish a system of rules and institutions to regulate the international monetary system.[29] As a contemporary biographer, Crisp also provides an invaluable insider's view into Chifley the politician, his background and the workings of his government. However, Crisp did not have access to the many primary sources now available to historians.[30]

Historian David Day's *Chifley* is a very large book, but there is little on Chifley in the international arena. The biography provides no extensive analysis of Chifley's ideas on international relations. My main point of departure from Day's account is when he compares the two new Opposition members of parliament, Curtin and Chifley, seated next to each other on the back benches at the opening of parliament on 6 February 1929. Day contrasts Curtin's 'internationalist outlook', gained as a member of the Victorian Socialist Party, with Chifley's 'rural socialism', which according to Day, was more 'pragmatic than ideological'. Day contrasts Curtin's interest in Australia's defence and international affairs after a trip to Europe, with Chifley's political interests, which he argues were 'focused overwhelmingly on domestic issues'.[31] One of the major arguments I make in this book is that Chifley's rural background meant that he was well aware of how the Australian economy was dependent on world trade, and he therefore viewed it within the context of the world economic system. As a small economy, Australia was reliant on its commodity exports, and, as a consequence, it was dependent on the stability of the international economic and financial system. This was a critical factor in the development of Chifley's ideas on the Australian economy and Australia's place in the world. Chifley was not an economic nationalist, he was an economic internationalist, and this was the basis for his 'ardent' advocacy of all international organisations.[32]

There are also very fine short biographies of Chifley by historians Ross McMullin, in *Australian Prime Ministers* (2000), and

DB Waterson, who was the author of the biographical entry for Chifley in the *Australian Dictionary of Biography*. Tom Sheridan, in his study of industrial relations in the post-war years, provides an excellent and well-rounded biographical chapter on Chifley, his background and character, and his approach to politics and government policy.[33] Another account comes from Harold Breen—director of the secondary industries division from 1945 and then director of industrial development from 1947 in the Department of Post-war Reconstruction—who worked closely with Chifley. From very early on, Breen understood and advocated that Australia should 'recognise its relationship to Asia'. An admirer of John Curtin and Chifley,[34] Breen's article on Chifley, which was published in 1974, was an instalment from his unpublished autobiography. Breen provides a fascinating personal portrait of Chifley, describing him as 'the driving force or the initiator' of most of his government's activities at home and in Asia, Europe and the United States.[35]

Australian foreign policy in the 1940s has been written about extensively, but very few historians have focused on the role played by Ben Chifley. The focus is usually on Dr Herbert Vere (Doc) Evatt, Australia's brilliant but abrasive minister for External Affairs, and the secretary of his department, Dr John Burton, who was part of the 'new wave' of university-educated economists who played a major role in influencing the post-war foreign policy of the Australian government.[36] In general, historians have preferred to place Chifley, the former locomotive engine driver and unionist, within the context of domestic politics. Some historians have assumed that Chifley had little or no interest in international affairs, and left the field to Evatt.[37] Historian Neville Meaney has recently argued that for eight years after Evatt was appointed minister for External Affairs in the Curtin and Chifley governments, 'apart from some occasional interventions by the prime minister', Evatt was 'in charge of Australia's foreign relations'.[38] This statement certainly underestimates and ignores Chifley's role in Australia's foreign policy-making. It might be accurate regarding Evatt's involvement with and commitment to Australia and its relationship with the United Nations, but this in turn meant that Evatt was overseas a great deal of the time, especially in his position as president of the third session of the United Nations General Assembly. According to LF Crisp, Chifley was acting minister for

External Affairs for a period of about eighteen months, from July to August 1947; September to December 1947; July 1948 to January 1949; and February to June 1949.[39] During this time, Chifley played a major role in making Australian post-war foreign policy, in particular, towards post-colonial Asia.

Historian David Fettling, in his recent account of Chifley and the Indonesian revolution, has written that there is a lack of 'in-depth analyses of Chifley's contribution to Australian foreign affairs'. In his article, Fettling sets out to make up for this lack by revealing the central role that Chifley played in the Australian government's policy in support of the Indonesian nationalist movement. Fettling makes a convincing case that, from the time of the second military offensive against the Indonesian Republic in December 1948, Chifley was 'running Indonesian policy'.[40] In this book, I will argue, however, that Chifley's influence on Australia's policy towards the Indonesian–Dutch conflict occurred even earlier.

Detailed studies of the Chifley government's foreign policy and economic and security policies have been written by historians Christopher Waters, David Lee, David Lowe and Ann Capling.[41] In the 1990s, there was a great deal of research on the Chifley government's foreign policy towards Asia. Christopher Waters and David Lee argued that the government's post-war foreign policy was a bold and innovative break with the past.[42] According to David Lee, it was based on liberal internationalist principles, shaped primarily by a concern to ensure the economic future of Australia in the post-war world economy.[43] Waters argued that the Chifley government's liberal internationalist approach to foreign policy meant that it had a radically different perception of events in Asia and the instability that was occurring as a result of decolonisation.[44] It did not see this flux and volatility as a consequence of communist inspired insurrection; it was, instead, the result of entrenched poverty and a desire for better living standards and a need to determine one's own destiny. Other historians, such as Peter Dennis, saw post-war foreign policy as unpredictable and in no sense representing a coherent readjustment of Australia's relations with its region.[45] David Lowe, in his study of Australia during the Cold War of the late 1940s and early 1950s, examined the Chifley government's response to East–West conflict and described how the government, at home and abroad, 'resisted the

Cold War as a framework for understanding change'.[46] In her book *Australia and the Global Trade System* (2001), Ann Capling provides detailed coverage of the vital and 'influential' role that Australia played in the establishment of the post-war multilateral trade system.[47]

But, apart from certain intimations from historian Peter Edwards that Chifley, 'a strong Prime Minister', had a 'greater knowledge of foreign affairs than was often realised',[48] and Christopher Waters that Chifley had a 'long interest and deep involvement in foreign affairs',[49] in general, the literature underestimates Chifley's intellectual and practical input to Australia's post-war foreign policy. Also, historians sometimes reveal a wilful blindness to the messy nature of politics and the 'constraints within which politicians act', and the inevitable compromises needed to achieve policy outcomes.[50] This book, in investigating an unexplored topic—the evolution of Chifley's internationalism—aims to situate Chifley, the politician, within the political arena of Australia's foreign policy-making. Despite considerable public and political constraints, Chifley and his government were able to pursue a new and radical approach in Australia's international relations.

A Reluctance to Leave Traces

A major problem for any historian writing about Chifley is the lack of his own writings on both political and personal issues. Chifley did not leave diaries or extensive correspondence from which personal details of his life can be easily ascertained and related to the development of his views. David Day has commented on Chifley's reluctance to leave traces of his life for posterity. According to Day: 'Chifley simply was very reticent about revealing his inner thoughts and feelings and destroyed so much documentation'.[51] Economic historian Marcus Robinson, in his study of the influence of economic ideas on Labor politicians and governments from 1931 to 1949, argued that Chifley was the most influential leader in economic policy matters in the Labor governments of 1941–1949. However, Robinson wrote it was difficult to discern Chifley's attitude on economic policy—there were few major statements on economic theory, and certainly no detailed accounts by Chifley of the major influences on him.[52]

It seems it made little difference whether it was personal or official correspondence, Chifley was reluctant to, or indifferent to, leaving traces. John Dedman, a member of the Curtin–Chifley cabinets who worked closely with Chifley for eight years, reminisced:

> Apart from little notes sent down from his office about some current problem or other and which were not retained, I don't suppose I received more than half a dozen letters from him during the eight years we were together in the Cabinet. Unless one was away overseas, he always made contact by telephone.[53]

According to LF Crisp, Chifley was 'not always mindful of the interest of biographers or posterity'. From time to time he 'had wholesale clear-outs of his old papers'. Consequently, there has only been 'a limited number of his letters available for perusal and those date, for the most part, from the last years of his life'.[54] Crisp later wrote, in a letter to *Sydney Morning Herald* journalist MJB Kenny, who was gathering material for an article on the 'paucity of books on Australian politics and political personalities', that:

> While Chifley had a fairly keen sense of history in some ways, he was not preoccupied with his own place in it and though I had discussed with him two or three times the possibility of his writing some memoirs he just laughed at that sort of thing, so I would say that, from your point of view, he was an extreme case of a man who set no store by personal accumulation of papers for use or contemplation in retirement.[55]

Chifley himself dismissed any idea that 'his life might be a suitable subject for historical study'. When Crisp suggested that he write his memoirs, Chifley's response was: 'Ah, boy, when I go no one will care a damn about me!'[56] According to Crisp:

> If he had lived before the day of the telephone and the postcard, I think we would have had some very interesting literature from him but he, like the rest of us, has been

ruined as a biographical subject by these new-fangled conveniences. Anyway, he was always much more fun face-to-face.[57]

In his review of Crisp's biography of Chifley, Dr John Burton, who was secretary of the Department of External Affairs from 1947 to 1950, and a senior adviser to Chifley, also noted that a major problem for any biographer of Chifley was the 'limits imposed by the absence of material'. He wrote, however, that Crisp had done a fine piece of research within those restrictions. According to Burton, there was 'a Chifley myth', not least because of 'an excellent press relations job', and Crisp's Chifley was the man of the 'myth'. Burton wrote that Chifley was an excellent subject for a myth to be created around him, because of his 'humility, a capacity for hard work, a selflessness which were unusual'. However, Burton said these qualities hid other character traits that made him more 'human' and 'no less attractive'. This included a tendency to 'dominate … small occasions' and a need for the 'undivided attention of the hostess'. One of his great enjoyments was cream, which was banned during the war. He used to welcome any gift of cream 'from some domestic production which did not come under regulations'. Burton added that 'the myth … does not do justice to the person'.[58]

The paucity of private material, such as diaries, memoirs and papers kept by Australian politicians such as Chifley, is a problem that confronts many historians researching Australian history. However, detailed examination of archival material, the most common form of historical research, can reveal much about the ideas and motivations of politicians, providing an opportunity to examine Chifley's attitudes and policies on a number of international issues.

Chifley's Political Rhetoric

As well as official diplomatic correspondence, Chifley's public speeches are used in this book to reveal the mix of experience and reflection that informed his views on Australia's place in the world. These speeches include those made in parliament, as well as speeches given at state and federal Labor Party conferences, and to local political meetings, and those made to Bathurst community groups. The *National Advocate*, one of two daily newspapers in

Bathurst, provides an extraordinarily rich source of material on Chifley, with its wide-ranging coverage of domestic and international politics, and reports of Chifley's speeches in parliament, and to local political and community groups. Chifley's father, Patrick, was a director of the *National Advocate*, and its editor, Hilton West, was a friend of Chifley.[59] After the death of his father, in August 1921,[60] Chifley joined the board of the *National Advocate* in 1922.[61] Because of its telephone and cable connections with Sydney and overseas, the *National Advocate* was able to get the most up-to-date news to country towns in western New South Wales on the evening mail train, some time before the Sydney newspapers could cross the Blue Mountains. A pro-Labor newspaper, the *National Advocate* was a rarity in Australian country towns, and through it, Chifley was able to exert considerable political influence in Bathurst and its region.[62] This book makes extensive use of the *National Advocate's* coverage of Chifley's speeches.

How much can be inferred from Chifley's speeches? As historian David Lowe has commented: 'despite recent (and overdue) recognition by historians in the nation-shaping capacity of political speeches, few academics have taken this approach far in the direction of foreign policy'.[63] One of the historians to focus on political speeches, Phillip Williamson, examines the 'political rhetoric' of his subject, British prime minister Stanley Baldwin. In his book, Williamson argues that he is attempting to bring to light the 'nature and practice of political leadership' through Baldwin's speeches, an approach that has rarely been used in recent historical works.[64] In the Australian context, apart from recent contributions from historians David Lowe, David McCooey and James Curran, little attention has been paid to speeches by Australian politicians.[65] With the exception of Albert Wolfgang Stargardt's collection of Chifley's speeches, *Things Worth Fighting For: Speeches by Joseph Benedict Chifley*, first published in 1952, there has been no detailed analysis of the ideas and assumptions underlying Chifley's speeches, a major omission in the study of Australian political leaders.[66] This will be a very productive way to explore Chifley's core beliefs. In this book, Chifley's speeches or 'political rhetoric' will be used as a way of 'mining' evidence to reveal his thinking and to understand how he viewed the world and Australia's place in it.

In order to do this, a contemporary review of *Things Worth Fighting For: Speeches by Joseph Benedict Chifley*, by political scientist Leicester Webb, published in the *Australian Quarterly* in March 1953, provides an insightful analysis of Chifley's political rhetoric. Webb argued that Chifley avoided theoretical discussions about political issues; instead, he was concerned with immediate economic matters. According to Webb, Chifley was essentially 'a day-to-day thinker'. Webb then asked if we can't discern a 'political philosophy', what prevented Chifley from being a 'mere political opportunist'? Webb argued that we find the answer to this question in Chifley's speeches. In these speeches, we do not find a 'core of political or economic doctrine' revealed. Instead, we find 'an unwavering faith in the moral worth of the Labour movement', a movement dedicated to the protection of the poor and the disadvantaged, and to the eradication of poverty and economic uncertainty. Out of this came Chifley's belief in the vital importance of unity in the party. When considering Chifley's speeches, Webb wrote that the main impression we get is 'integrity' and it was this that made him such a 'transcendent political leader'.[67]

AW Stargardt—who preferred to be called Wolfgang, although some of his Australian contemporaries called him Wolf—selected and compiled the collection of Chifley's speeches published as *Things Worth Fighting For: Speeches by Joseph Benedict Chifley*. Stargardt was a historian whose PhD supervisor was Professor Max Crawford at the University of Melbourne.[68] Stargardt was a 'third generation secular Jewish socialist' who had arrived in Australia in 1939 on one of the last ships to leave Nazi Germany before war erupted. He had grown up in Berlin in a household in which the socialist debates of the 1920s and 1930s were carried on in an era that saw the Nazis rise to power.[69] Stargardt took great pride in the fact that his parents knew revolutionary activists Rosa Luxemburg and Franz Mehring, and 'followed them into the Independent Social Democrats during the World War I as anti-war pacifists'.[70] Encouraged by Professor Crawford, Stargardt had approached the prime minister in September 1949 about putting together a collection of Chifley's major speeches, modelled on a recently published collection of speeches by the British prime minister Clement Attlee. Stargardt's first draft was not completed until a year later, when Chifley was leader of the Opposition. Soon after, Chifley suffered a heart attack. After his recovery, he was able to read the introduction in December 1950. At the end of February 1951, Stargardt had a 'very long conversation' with Chifley about the project when he visited Canberra. Chifley 'emphatically approved' Stargardt's selection of speeches and his introduction.[71]

In March 1951 Stargardt wrote to Professor Crawford that Chifley had recovered quite well from his heart attack the previous year and it seemed he was looking after his health. Chifley had scrutinised the introduction 'line by line' and reminded Stargardt of 'the good old times last year' that he had enjoyed with the professor. He was especially partial to the 'controversial bits in the last part' of the introduction—he was 'emphatic about this and did not mince his words'.[72] In this section, Stargardt wrote that a new generation of party members had grown up in a period of full employment and had not experienced the 'bitter economic struggles of the past'. Preoccupied with power and indifferent to idealism, these people took the achievements of the labour movement for granted and saw 'the struggle too simply in terms of rivalry for organizational control and ideological monopoly'. Chifley feared this would lead to division in the party, because he believed the strength of the labour movement and the Labor Party lay in unity.[73] Stargardt wrote to Crawford that, once again, he came away from his meeting with Chifley, with 'a feeling of boundless admiration and trust'.[74] He retained a lifelong admiration for Chifley and, although based in Cambridge from 1970, he remained an Australian citizen all his life. From 1970 until 1975, Stargardt was a Fellow, with professorial status, at the Cambridge Centre for International Studies in the Faculty of History. From 1976 until 1987, when he retired, he was a Member, again with professorial status, of the Cambridge Faculty of Social and Political Sciences. At the same time, he was a Member of the Management Committee of the Asian Studies Centre, St Antony's College Oxford until his death in March 2000. His major research projects while at Cambridge concerned first, Australia's Asian policies, then the history of Neutrality in Asia and finally, the history of Asian diplomacy.

In Stargardt's introduction, he wrote that in Chifley's speeches, his style was 'plain and unadorned', exhibiting a certain 'earthiness'. However, the concepts Chifley spoke of were somewhat more complex than the words he used. It is worth taking a brief look at excerpts from two speeches given by Chifley in order to explore important themes that he emphasised repeatedly: the inevitability of change and, in Stargardt's words, his sense of the 'emergent future which was ever in his mind'.[75] Chifley understood that momentous change was occurring in the post-war world—that the old colonial order was ending. He realised the need to adjust government policy to these new circumstances to ensure the future prosperity and security of Australia. In an address to the party faithful in 1947, Chifley spoke about Australia's relations with other nations. He emphasised that there was a new order in the world that Australians must adapt to, declaring:

> I do not think that some persons ... fully realize the changed order in the world today. We have a proud history but we must not live in the past. The methods of twenty years ago are no good today ... We have to prepare to build a stronger nation in the Pacific than today, and try to look into the future. Many think just of today or just a year or two ahead.[76]

The concepts of change and 'the emergent future' were ever present in Chifley's thought and speeches. Many of his speeches seem unrehearsed and impromptu. Occasionally, flashes of brilliance will flare unexpectedly, as in this account of the war in Korea, delivered when Chifley was in Opposition. It combines a treasurer's knowledge of facts and figures, together with an understanding of the horror of war, and an awareness that, in war, civilians were as likely to be killed or maimed by allies as by enemies:

> Over 1,000,000 casualties have been caused among the Koreans whilst 2,500,000 of them have been rendered completely homeless under climatic conditions which for many months of the year are appalling. Over 200,000 houses, such as they are, have been burned to the ground and from 75 per cent. to 80 per cent. of Korea's textile production has been destroyed. I need not discuss what happened when the United Nations forces pursued the Communists to the

north. We know of the use of jelly-petrol bombs. When, from time to time, we see pictures in the newspapers of South Koreans fleeing in their hundreds of thousands from scenes of destruction, no doubt in many instances they were fleeing to escape destruction by Allied bombs as well as destruction at the hands of North Korean forces.[77]

In the midst of details regarding casualties suffered, and a description of homelessness in 'appalling' and extreme weather conditions, Chifley notes that from '75 per cent. to 80 per cent. of Korea's textile production has been destroyed'. The 'very earthiness' of Chifley's language reveals that 'belief in the emergent future' that was always present in his mind.[78] A major concern for Chifley was the future viability of the Korean economy. How could a prosperous economy emerge from the terrible destruction of war? In a more general sense, Chifley and other world leaders were confronted at the end of World War II with the same question of how world peace and prosperity could be secured. This concern among world leaders led to a period in which new international institutions, and new rules and new charters regulating international affairs and trade were established, in the hope that future wars and economic depressions could be avoided.

Chifley's Internationalism

The aim of this book is to trace the evolution of Chifley as an internationalist. What made him, as he said, an 'ardent advocate of all international organisations'?[79] What were the influences that shaped Chifley's internationalism? What were his views on the major international issues of the time and what actions in international policy did Chifley implement when he was prime minister and treasurer? A closer look at Chifley's personal experiences, his intellectual influences and the political, economic and social issues he encountered, will shed light on the reasons behind his policy-making decisions. Some of these significant experiential factors include living through two economic depressions and two world wars; his rural background and his trade unionism. These experiences generated Chifley's belief that the only way to avoid war and economic depression was through the establishment of a rules-based international order. He understood that the Pacific war had brought enormous change to the

Asia-Pacific, with the result that European colonial power was in rapid decline in the region. He was convinced that it was only through the creation of a stable international economic order that future generations could 'attain a reasonable and decent standard of living to which every human being, black or white, is entitled'.[80]

This book seeks, first, to establish a genealogy of Chifley's internationalism, from his pre-parliamentary days, his time spent as a member of the Scullin government during the Great Depression of the 1930s, to his period as treasurer in the Curtin government, to when Chifley was both prime minister and treasurer of Australia, and to his time as leader of the Labor Opposition until his death in June 1951. Second, it will consider how this internationalism manifested itself in policy implemented by Chifley and his government in the following areas: the reconfiguration of the post-war international economy; the decolonisation of Asia; the establishment of a new collective political–strategic order; and Chifley's response to the emerging Cold War view of a changing world promoted by Australia's allies, the United States and Great Britain.

According to historian Akira Iriye, internationalism refers to 'an idea, a movement, or an institution that seeks to reformulate the nature of relations among nations through cross-national cooperation and interchange'.[81] Internationalism offered a 'vision of a global order based upon adherence to universal laws and institutions'. It is very different to a world governed by power politics and brute force in which the 'crude exercise of power relations' reigns supreme.[82] For many in the twentieth century, internationalism seemed to be the way to achieve a 'permanent peace'. International relations historian Glenda Sluga writes that the League of Nations and the United Nations were unprecedented experiments in what was sometimes termed 'international government'. The widespread appeal of this new internationalism was spurred on by 'mass literacy', which led to a dissemination of ideas among nations and an acceptance of internationalism by the general public. Support for internationalism was also due to an ongoing fear of war and the evidence of mass war crimes carried out 'in the name of nationalism'.[83] The 'apogee' of this 'new internationalism' occurred at the end of World War II.[84] Paradoxically, the surge in public approval for 'international solutions' took place during a time of war and destruction. This is exemplified by the creation of the United Nations at the conclusion of World War II.[85]

Internationalism takes many forms, including cultural internationalism, legal internationalism and economic internationalism. The last form of internationalism envisages 'a global network of economic exchanges'. The best way to prevent war caused by excessive nationalism was by promoting economic exchange across national borders which would 'strengthen interdependence and peaceful relations among nations'—the answer lay in increased international trade and global economic development.[86] This was very much the path taken by the post-war Chifley government. Historian David Lee argues that the Chifley government was intent on securing Australia's security in the post-war years. But, according to Lee, the government's foreign policy was concerned not so much with potential external threats—Japan and Germany had been defeated—but with ensuring Australia's economic security. The government was also determined that Australia would play a significant role in the reform of the world economy. Lee argues that Australia's foreign policy in the early Cold War years was not 'a single-minded concern with security against external threats, but a search for security which embraced the economic well-being of the country as well as its politico-strategic security'.[87]

Lee notes that this aspect of Australian foreign policy in the early post-war period has been almost totally neglected by historians.[88] Instead, the realist tradition in international relations has tended to dominate Australian studies in this area, in which the main focus of the state's foreign policy is based on a very narrow definition of security, with 'economic issues playing a subsidiary role'.[89] Historians in the realist tradition saw Australia's national interests as 'unchanging' and 'uncontested', in which succeeding governments sought to protect Australia from external threats. As Lee states, this is a 'simplistic' view: there are many contested views of Australia's 'national interests'.[90]

Historians such as Christopher Waters and David Lowe have also argued that the Chifley government was committed to liberal internationalist principles. Liberal internationalism was a concept that assumed conflict between nations could be prevented by promoting economic prosperity and social justice; nations would use international arbitration through the United Nations rather than power politics and force; secret diplomacy would be ended; all peoples would have the right to self-determination which would bring about the end of colonialism and the rule of law would be applied to international relations. An international collective security system such as the United Nations Organization provided an alternative avenue through which a small country such as Australia—whose vulnerability to power politics had been demonstrated during World War II—could exert influence on the major powers in the post-war world.[91]

Chifley's economic internationalism developed very early in his political career. He believed it was vital to set up international organisations through which a rules-based economic order could be established. This was a position he had taken from the early 1930s when, in the depths of the Great Depression, he declared there could be no economic recovery until there was 'a very great change in the monetary and financial policy of the world'.[92] The 'economic dimension' in international relations was of paramount importance for Chifley, whose economic internationalist perspective was gained through his experience of the 1930s depression and his understanding of how the Australian economy was dependent on world trade conditions. This belief carried through to Chifley's later 'ardent' support for 'all international organizations'.[93] Post-war economic recovery was essential to ensure the world's peace and prosperity, and to prevent a return to the disastrous period after World War I when global trade collapsed and the world was plunged into the economic chaos of the Great Depression.

In his speech to parliament on 20 March 1947, when he introduced the bill to ratify the Bretton Woods Agreement, Chifley declared that the agreement was 'a great human experiment … designed to prevent the catastrophes that result from wars and financial and economic depressions'. He went on to say that economic stability was essential in order to improve living standards throughout the world:

> If we have any love for mankind and a desire to free future generations from the terrible happenings of the last 30 years, we must put our faith in these international organizations. Even the youngest member of this House has seen

two world wars, and a world-wide financial and economic depression ... some measure of economic stability must be established in order to enable future generations, if not even the present generation, to attain a reasonable and decent standard of living to which every human being, black or white, is entitled.[94]

Chifley's intellectual affinity with economic internationalism was supported by many of the advisers to the Curtin and Chifley governments, who assisted in the development and implementation of policy, while Chifley advanced it through caucus and cabinet. James Cotton has recently published a history of international relations in Australia, in which he identifies an Australian school which sought to 'accommodate, on the one hand, membership of international organisations and on the other the problematic nature of Australia's place in what was then known as the "Pacific" region'.[95] Cotton looks at eight academics, diplomats, public intellectuals and media commentators, two of whom, Frederic W Eggleston and William Macmahon Ball, acted as influential policy advisers to the Chifley government. Eggleston and Ball were members of an intellectual network with a 'dense web of personal acquaintanceship'.[96] According to Cotton, the 'Australian School' espoused a number of 'ideas or doctrines',[97] including the global 'interdependence' of nations,[98] the need for new international institutions to ensure world peace and economic security,[99] and the need for greater understanding and better relations with Asia.[100] All of these 'ideas or doctrines' were shared by Chifley. The intellectual environment in which Chifley moved is an essential part of tracing the influences on Chifley in his role as prime minister, treasurer and acting minister for External Affairs.

A New View of Chifley
In the five parts of this book, Chifley's speeches and other archival material are mined to reveal the ideas and values that informed his internationalist world-view. A number of case studies are used to illustrate the development of Chifley's internationalism and how it manifested itself in policy implemented by Chifley and his government.

Part I includes a brief biography of Chifley and explores his lived experience in order to understand how his rural background, his deep connections to the labour movement and his experience of war and economic depression influenced his understanding of the world and his policies on world affairs. It then looks at the intellectual and working milieu from which he came, and in which he operated as a member of the Australian Labor Party, as treasurer, prime minister and as leader of the Opposition.

Part II traces the origins of Chifley's economic internationalism by examining the impact of World War I and the Great Depression on him and how this influenced his later policy decisions when in government. The inter-war years are critical in any study of Chifley's political life and the development of his ideas on economic and social policy. During this period, Chifley's ongoing interest in international affairs, and the global economic and monetary system can be traced in the speeches he delivered in parliament, to local Bathurst groups and at political meetings. By examining these speeches and looking at his role as a commissioner on the Royal Commission into the Monetary and Banking System (1935–1937), it is clear that Chifley was developing a coherent form of internationalism during this period. Chapter 4 then considers how this economic internationalism translated into policy implemented by the government when Chifley was treasurer and prime minister in the Labor governments of 1941–1949. Against fierce opposition from his own party, many of whom did not share his internationalism, Chifley played a major role in persuading his party to approve the government's ratification of the 1944 Bretton Woods Agreement, through which Australia became part of the new international financial and economic system.

Part III explores Chifley's role in Australian foreign–policy making. Chapter 5 argues that his government's policy towards post-colonial Asia was a bold and innovative break with the past. It demonstrates that Chifley played a much more significant and influential role in Australia's foreign policy in the 1940s than previously assumed. This chapter also considers Chifley's time as Opposition leader and demonstrates that his long-standing interest in Asia continued into his period in Opposition. Chapter 6 reveals that Chifley was a great admirer of India's prime minister, Jawaharlal Nehru, one of the few prominent Australian politicians to endorse an Asian leader's world-view. Chifley regarded Nehru as 'the most powerful figure in Asian politics, and, indeed, in the Asian world', and quoted him extensively. Chifley's attendance at the 1949 Commonwealth Prime Ministers' Conference is used as a case study and reveals a convergence of world-views of two fellow internationalists.

Part IV deals with the establishment of a new collective political–strategic order. Two case studies are used to explore Chifley's attitudes to the new post-war post-colonial world. Chapter 7 traces Chifley's attitude towards the Japanese peace settlement. Chifley had long held the belief that economic recovery was vital to post-war peace and prosperity. It therefore followed that a policy of revenge against former enemies such as Japan and Germany would be counter-productive. Chapter 8 provides a detailed analysis of the ideas and assumptions underlying Chifley's speeches and his communications to other governments in order to reveal his thinking on the Cold War and its impact on Australia's relations with Great Britain, the United States and its own region. Chifley's response to the Western Union proposal put forward by the British foreign secretary Ernest Bevin and the British Labour government in 1948 is analysed to reveal the deep divide in the two governments' approach to foreign affairs.

Conclusion

Previous accounts have paid little attention to the relationship between Chifley's life experiences, the political, economic and social concerns encountered in his political life and the evolution of his internationalist world-view. This book provides the first comprehensive account of Chifley's development as an internationalist, demonstrating that his internationalism was an 'economic' one. It shows that Chifley's rural background was of major significance in the development of his internationalism. This is also the first time attention has been paid to a statement of the views of the prime minister—available in the Australian National Archives—to support his argument to the Labor caucus that Australia should ratify the Bretton Woods Agreement, under which a new post-war international economic order would be established. This study also demonstrates that, although Dr Evatt, Australia's External Affairs minister, has usually taken centre stage in any study of Australia's foreign policy in the 1940s, Chifley's role in the making of Australian foreign policy has been vastly underestimated.

Notes

I am indebted to Professor Janice Stargardt, Professorial Research Fellow in Asian Historical Archaeology & Geography, Sydney Sussex College and Senior Fellow at the McDonald Institute for Archaeological Research, University of Cambridge, for information about her husband AW Stargardt. I am also very grateful for the information provided by Janice and Wolfgang's son, Nicholas Stargardt, who is Professor of Modern European History at Magdalen College, Oxford.

1. 'Visitor on India's Outlook', *Advertiser* (Adelaide), 22 June 1951, p. 3.
2. Cited by Meg Gurry in *India: Australia's Neglected Neighbour? 1947–1996*, Centre for the Study of Australia-Asia Relations, Griffith University, Queensland, 1996, pp. 18–20. I am very grateful to the author for her assistance in accessing these articles by JN Sahni.
3. JN Sahni, 'Vision, Honesty and Courage Personified: Great Leader that Australia Had', *Sunday Tribune* (Ambala), 1 July 1951, in 'Articles by JN Sahni', Australian High Commissioner, New Delhi to Department of External Affairs (hereafter DEA), 5 July 1951, NAA: A1838, 169/10/1 Part 1.
4. JN Sahni, 'It's Damn Impertinent of Any Outsider to Dictate to India', *Bharat Jyoti* (Bombay), 1 July 1951, in 'Articles by JN Sahni', in ibid.
5. Sahni, 'Vision, Honesty and Courage Personified'.
6. ibid.
7. 'Indian Last Pressman to Interview "Chif"', *Worker* (Brisbane), 2 July 1951, p. 2.
8. Sahni, 'Vision, Honesty and Courage Personified'.
9. ibid.
10. Srinath Raghavan, *War and Peace in Modern India*, Palgrave Macmillan, Basingstoke, London, 2010, p. xxii.
11. ibid., p. 12.
12. Sahni, 'Vision, Honesty and Courage Personified'; 'Indian Last Pressman to Interview "Chif"'.
13. Sahni, 'Vision, Honesty and Courage Personified'.
14. 'Indian Last Pressman to Interview "Chif"'.
15. Sahni, 'Vision, Honesty and Courage Personified'.
16. 'Indian Last Pressman to Interview "Chif"'.
17. Sahni, 'It's Damn Impertinent'
18. 'Articles by JN Sahni', Memorandum, Australian High Commissioner, New Delhi to Secretary of DEA, 5 July 1951, NAA: A1838, 169/10/1 Part 1; Sahni, 'Vision, Honesty and Courage Personified'.
19. Sahni, 'It's Damn Impertinent'
20. Sahni, 'Vision, Honesty and Courage Personified'.
21. LF Crisp, *Ben Chifley: A Biography*, Longmans, London, no date (n.d.); David Day, *Chifley*, HarperCollins, Pymble, NSW, 2001; Scott Bennett,

    JB Chifley, Oxford University Press, Melbourne, 1973.
22   Scott Bennett, 'Crisp, Leslie Finlay (Fin) (1917–1984)', in *Australian Dictionary of Biography*, vol. 17, Melbourne University Press, Carlton, Victoria, 2006, pp. 269–270.
23   Geoffrey Bolton, 'The Art of Australian Political Biography', in Tracey Arklay, John Nethercote and John Wanna (eds), *Australian Political Lives: Chronicling Political Careers and Administrative Histories*, ANU E Press, Canberra, c.2006, p. 4.
24   Geoffrey Bolton, 'Duncan Waterson: A Lapidary Historian', in Paul Ashton and Bridget Griffen-Foley (eds), 'From the Frontier: Essays in Honour of Duncan Waterson', special joint issue of *Journal of Australian Studies*, no. 69, and *Australian Cultural History*, no. 20, 2001, p. 15.
25   Crisp, *Ben Chifley*, p. 275.
26   David Lee, *Search for Security: The Political Economy of Australia's Postwar Foreign and Defence Policy*, Allen & Unwin, Canberra, 1995, p. 2.
27   ibid., p. 1.
28   Crisp, *Ben Chifley*, pp. 275–295.
29   ibid., pp. 198–212.
30   Especially the superb Oral History Collection available at the National Library of Australia.
31   Day, *Chifley*, pp. 235–236.
32   *Commonwealth Parliamentary Debates*, House of Representatives, (hereafter *CPD*, HoR), 20 March 1947, p. 1002.
33   See Ross McMullin, 'Joseph Benedict Chifley', in Michelle Grattan (ed.), *Australian Prime Ministers*, New Holland, Sydney, 2000, pp. 246–268; DB Waterson, 'Chifley, Joseph Benedict (Ben) (1885–1951)', *Australian Dictionary of Biography*, vol. 13, Melbourne University Press, Carlton, Victoria, 1993, pp. 412–420; Tom Sheridan, *Division of Labour: Industrial Relations in the Chifley Years 1945–1949*, Oxford University Press, Melbourne, 1989, pp. 18–29.
34   DP Blaazer, 'Breen, Harold Patrick (1893–1966)', *Australian Dictionary of Biography*, National Centre of Biography, Australian National University, http://adb.anu.edu.au/biography/breen-harold-patrick-9574/text16869 (accessed 5 April 2013).
35   Harold Breen, 'JB Chifley', *Twentieth Century*, March 1974, p. 239. The title of Breen's unpublished autobiography is *The Years After*, available in the National Library of Australia.
36   Christopher Waters, 'The Great Debates: HV Evatt and the Department of External Affairs, 1941–49', in Joan Beaumont, Christopher Waters, David Lowe with Garry Woodard (eds), *Ministers, Mandarins and Diplomats: Australian Foreign Policy Making 1949–1969*, Melbourne University Press, Carlton, 2003, p. 53.
37   For example, Roger Dingman, 'The View from Down Under: Australia and Japan, 1945–1952', in Thomas W Burkman (ed.), *The Occupation of Japan: The International Context*, MacArthur Memorial Foundation, Norfolk, VA, 1984.
38   Neville Meaney, 'Dr HV Evatt and the United Nations: The Problem of

Collective Security and Liberal Internationalism', in James Cotton and David Lee (eds), *Australia and the United Nations,* Department of Foreign Affairs and Trade, Barton, ACT, c.2012, p. 37.
39 Crisp, *Ben Chifley,* p. 276, fn. 2.
40 David Fettling, 'JB Chifley and the Indonesian Revolution, 1945–1949', *Australian Journal of Politics and History,* vol. 59, issue 4, 2013, pp. 518; 519 and p. 529.
41 See Christopher Waters, *The Empire Fractures: Anglo-Australian Conflict in the 1940s,* Australian Scholarly Publishing, Melbourne, 1995; Lee, *Search for Security;* David Lowe, *Menzies and the 'Great World Struggle': Australia's Cold War 1948–1954,* University of New South Wales Press, Sydney, 1999; Ann Capling, *Australia and the Global Trade System: From Havana to Seattle,* Cambridge University Press, Cambridge, 2001; Ann Capling, 'The "Enfant Terrible": Australia and the Reconstruction of the Multilateral Trade System, 1946–8', *Australian Economic History Review,* vol. 40, no. 1, 2000.
42 David Lee, 'Indonesia's Independence', in David Goldsworthy (ed.), *Facing North. A Century of Australian Engagement with Asia Volume 1: 1901 to the 1970s,* Melbourne University Press, Carlton South, Victoria, 2001, pp. 134, 170; Christopher Waters, 'War, Decolonisation and Postwar Security', in Goldsworthy (ed.), *Facing North,* p. 124.
43 Lee, *Search for Security,* pp. 8, 73–74.
44 Christopher Waters, 'Conflict with Britain in the 1940s' in David Lowe, (ed.), *Australia and the End of Empires: The Impact of Decolonisation in Australia's Near North 1945–1965,* Deakin University Press, Geelong, 1996, pp. 80–84.
45 Peter Dennis, 'Australia and Indonesia: The Early Years' in David Lowe (ed.), *Australia and the End of Empires: The Impact of Decolonisation in Australia's Near North 1945–1965,* Deakin University Press, Geelong, 1996, pp. 43–52.
46 Lowe, *Menzies and the 'Great World Struggle',* p. 14.
47 Capling, *Australia and the Global Trade System,* p. 2.
48 Peter Edwards with Gregory Pemberton, *Crises and Commitments: The Politics and Diplomacy of Australia's Involvement in Southeast Asian Conflicts 1948–1965,* Allen & Unwin, North Sydney, 1992, p. 6.
49 Waters, *The Empire Fractures,* p. 113.
50 Nicholas Brown, 'Review of Kim E Beazley's, *Father of the House* and Ashley Hogan's *Moving in the Open Daylight', History Australia,* vol. 6, no. 3, 2009, p. 82.2.
51 David Day, Speech at the National Biography Award Day of Discussion, 23 March 2002, www.sl.nsw.gov.au/about/awards/doc/sessw.pdf (accessed 19 July 2010).
52 Marcus Laurence Robinson, Economists and Politicians: The Influence of Economic Ideas upon Labor Politicians and Governments, 1931–1949, PhD thesis, Australian National University, 1986, p. 129.
53 Letter, JJ Dedman to Crisp, 4 January 1952, Papers of LF Crisp, National Library of Australia (hereafter NLA): MS 5243, Series 5, Folder 3.

54 Letter, Crisp to WR Robinson, 13 August 1953, in ibid., Series 5, Folder 2.
55 Letter, Crisp to MJB Kenny, 22 October 1954, in ibid., Series 1, Folder 4.
56 Day, *Chifley*, p. x.
57 Letter, LF Crisp to Professor RC Mills, 16 April 1952, Papers of LF Crisp, NLA: MS 5243, Series 5, Folder 2.
58 JW Burton, 'Review of Ben Chifley: A Biography by LF Crisp', in *Bulletin of the Australian Society for the Study of Labour History*, No. 2, May 1962, p. 95.
59 Crisp, *Ben Chifley*, p. 18.
60 Day, *Chifley*, p. 170.
61 Crisp, *Ben Chifley*, p. 111.
62 Day, *Chifley*, pp. 182–184.
63 David Lowe, 'Introduction', *Australian Journal of Politics and History*, vol. 51, no. 3, 2005, p. 327.
64 Philip Williamson, *Stanley Baldwin: Conservative Leadership and National Values*, Cambridge University Press, Cambridge, 1999, p. 14.
65 See David McCooey and David Lowe, 'Autobiography in Australian Parliamentary First Speeches', *Biography*, vol. 33, no. 1, 2010, and James Curran, *The Power of Speech: Australian Prime Ministers Defining the National Image*, Melbourne University Press, Carlton, Victoria, 2004.
66 *Things Worth Fighting For: Speeches by JB Chifley*, selected and arranged by AW Stargardt, Australian Labor Party, Melbourne, 1953.
67 Leicester Webb, 'The Labour Party and the Future', *Australian Quarterly*, vol. 25, issue 1, 1953, pp. 122–123.
68 AW Stargardt, 'Preface', *Things Worth Fighting For*, pp. ix–x.
69 Nicholas Stargardt, 'Children and the Holocaust: An Interview with Nicholas Stargardt', *Limina Interview*, vol. 6, 2000, p. 2.
70 ibid. p. 3.
71 AW Stargardt, 'Preface', in *Things Worth Fighting For*, pp. ix–x.
72 Letter, Wolfgang S [Stargardt] to Professor Crawford, 8 March 1951, University of Melbourne Archives (hereafter UMA): Papers of RM Crawford, 91/113, Box 22, Series 7, Item 87, Correspondence with former students and members of staff, 1952–1953.
73 AW Stargardt, 'Introduction', in *Things Worth Fighting For*, p. 8.
74 Letter, Wolfgang S [Stargardt] to Professor Crawford, 8 March 1951, UMA.
75 Stargardt, 'Introduction', in *Things Worth Fighting For*, p. 9.
76 JB Chifley, 'This is a Country of Freedom of Expression', Address to the Annual Conference of the New South Wales' Branch of the ALP on 15 June 1947, in *Things Worth Fighting For*, p. 26.
77 *CPD*, HoR, 7 March 1951, pp. 83–84.
78 'Introduction', in *Things Worth Fighting For*, p. 9.
79 *CPD*, HoR, 20 March 1947, p. 1002.
80 ibid., p. 1003.
81 Akira Iriye, *Cultural Internationalism and World Order*, Johns Hopkins University Press, Baltimore, 1997, p. 3.
82 Roderic Pitty and Michael Leach, 'Australian Nationalism and Internationalism', in Paul Boreham, Geoffrey Stokes and Richard Hall (eds), *The Politics of Australian Society: Political Issues for the New Century*, 2nd edn, Pearson Longman, Frenchs Forrest, NSW, 2004, p. 99.

83 Glenda Sluga, *Internationalism in the Age of Nationalism*, University of Pennsylvania Press, Philadelphia, 2013, p. 2.
84 ibid., p. 9.
85 ibid., p. 79.
86 Iriye, *Cultural Internationalism and World Order*, pp. 3, 25.
87 Lee, *Search for Security*, p. 4.
88 ibid., p. 8. Lee notes that the exceptions are Gregory Pemberton in *All the Way: Australia's Way to Vietnam*, Allen & Unwin, Sydney, 1987, and Roger Bell, *Unequal Allies: Australian–American Relations and the Pacific War*, Melbourne University Press, Melbourne, 1977.
89 Lee, *Search for Security*, p. 3.
90 ibid., p. 5.
91 Waters, *Empire Fractures*, p. 21; Lowe, *Menzies and the 'Great World Struggle'*, p. 16.
92 Day, *Chifley*, p. 283. See also 'Macquarie Fight—Declaration of Poll', *National Advocate* (Bathurst, NSW), 9 January 1932, p. 2.
93 *CPD*, HoR, 20 March 1947, p. 1002.
94 ibid., pp. 1002–1003.
95 James Cotton, *The Australian School of International Relations*, Palgrave Macmillan, New York, 2013, p. 3.
96 ibid., p. 238.
97 ibid., p. 240.
98 ibid., p. 249.
99 ibid., p. 250.
100 ibid., p. 248.

Chapter Two
From Bathurst to Canberra

Ben Chifley was a member of the unfortunate generation that experienced the economic pain of two depressions and the horror of two world wars. He was greatly influenced by his experience of the 1890s depression, the economic crash of the Great Depression in the 1930s and the devastation caused by war. As a consequence, Chifley in government supported a rules-based internationalism that would establish a new post-war economic and political-strategic order. For Chifley, this was the only way to 'prevent the catastrophes that result from wars and financial and economic depressions'.[1] This chapter provides a brief biography of Chifley and a description of his achievements as treasurer and prime minister. It then explores how his rural upbringing, his commitment to the labour movement and the history he lived through—the impact of war and economic depression— influenced him. It examines the events and intellectual influences that generated Chifley's support for a rules-based internationalism. Chifley's speeches will be used extensively to demonstrate how his experiences and beliefs formed his view of the world in which he lived.

From a Limekilns Farm to Parliament House
Joseph Benedict Chifley was prime minister of Australia from 13 July 1945 to 19 December 1949. He was also treasurer retaining the

position he had held in the Labor government led by John Curtin from 1941 to 1945.[2] Chifley was born in the regional city of Bathurst in New South Wales on 22 September 1885.[3] His father, Patrick, was a blacksmith who worked at the agricultural firm, Fish and Sons, that supplied farms in the central west region of NSW.[4] His mother, Mary Anne Corrigan, who was born in Ireland, worked for a time as a domestic servant at St Benedict's convent in Queanbeyan. Patrick and Mary married in Bathurst in May 1884[5]. At the age of five, Chifley went to live with his grandfather on his farm at Limekilns,[6] approximately 26 kilometres to the north-east of Bathurst,[7] in a 'four room wattle-and-daub shack with earthen floor and white pipe-clayed walls'.[8] Mary had just had her third child, and Chifley's grandfather, when visiting his new grandson, suggested that Ben should return with him to his farm, to save him from the domestic chores, that, as the eldest child, he would be expected to carry out.[9] As David Day notes, Chifley's grandfather, whose third wife had died two years previously in 1888, ran the farm with his 21-year-old daughter, and obviously had need of the assistance that his grandson could provide.[10]

Life was hard on the farm. According to a school friend, Chifley 'never got much schooling ... he would always get the cows in to milk in the morning. His g. father would plough a lot of potatoes during the day. Ben on the way home would have to pick & bag them on his own, till almost too dark to pick'. As a young boy, Chifley spent most of his spare time reading. Even when he was 'waiting for the batting to come round' in a game of cricket, he would have 'some old reading matter'.[11] Chifley lived at Limekilns until his grandfather died in January 1899, when at the age of 13, he returned to his family in Bathurst.[12] Chifley said afterwards, 'I went for a holiday and came back nine years later'.[13]

In his biography of Chifley, LF Crisp explores the effect that his isolated childhood had on Chifley the man. Crisp attributes Chifley's later 'keen desire ... to belong to closely knit groups' and his 'drive towards becoming a loyal central member of the groups in which he lived his life thereafter' to the 'crisis of solidarity' that happened when he was separated from his family.[14] However, later oral history research suggests that Chifley was not as isolated as Crisp implies. He was very close to his two brothers, Patrick and Richard (Dick), and, according to his nephew John Chifley, the brothers regularly walked to the farm to see Ben: 'It was nothing for them to walk miles in those days'.[15]

After leaving school, Chifley went to work at a local store at the age of fifteen.[16] He left after several months because he and other juniors were exploited by their employer, a prosperous merchant and a pillar of the church, which left a 'deep and lasting impression' on the young worker.[17] In September 1903 he joined the New South Wales Railways as a shop-boy at the Bathurst railway yards and was subsequently promoted to labourer in January 1907.[18] He then worked his way up from cleaner and fireman to locomotive engine driver in July 1913.[19] Some time in 1907, he became involved in the union movement,[20] and he was later instrumental in the formation of the new federal union, the Australian Federated Union of Locomotive Enginemen (AFULE) in 1920.[21] Chifley was never a paid union official, but from 1917 to 1929, he was a member of the AFULE's state general committee, and during this period, he represented his union as a delegate at state and federal conferences.[22] An early demonstration of Chifley's internationalism was when he supported an AFULE motion at the 1921 union conference in support of locomotive enginemen thoughout the world working together 'with a view to prevention of wars'.[23] He proved to be a very effective advocate for his union in industrial tribunals,[24] appearing in front of the New South Wales Industrial Court as early as 1912.[25]

In 1914 he married Elizabeth McKenzie, whose father was a fellow locomotive engine driver. The McKenzies were as staunch Presbyterians as the Chifleys were Roman Catholics.[26] When contacted by a close family friend who wrote that there was great concern that he was marrying outside the Catholic church and 'what a deep wound he would inflict upon his family and close friends by doing this', Chifley replied in a lengthy letter that he:

> could not overcome his devotion to Elizabeth. He had tried to break away from it, but was powerless. As she would not be married by Catholic rites, he was going with her. Even if he had to lose his family & friends he must go on.[27]

Ben and Elizabeth would marry in a Presbyterian church in Glebe in Sydney, saving his family and friends in Bathurst the embarrassment of having to choose to attend the wedding or not.[28] By doing this, Chifley defied the 1908 papal decree, *Ne Temere*, under which Catholics were forbidden to marry outside the church. As a result, he was denied the sacraments.[29] After their marriage, they returned to Bathurst where Elizabeth was accepted by the Chifley family 'as their own' and 'life went on as usual, except for this shadow always in the background'.[30]

Chifley opposed conscription in World War I in 1916 and 1917. He also took part in the August–September 1917 railway strike, that started at the Randwick workshops in Sydney. It was called because of the introduction of the Card System—based on the Taylor Card System used at the Ford workshops in the United States— which recorded the work that an employee had to do on various jobs before he could 'obtain his maximum pay rate and escape being classed as a "slow worker" and paid accordingly'. These cards were kept secret and the workers were unable to access them, giving rise to fears of inaccuracies and bias. A railway town, Bathurst railwaymen went out on strike in solidarity with the workers at the Randwick workshops. Chifley was dismissed because of his support for the strike. He was later reinstated and downgraded to the rank of fireman. Chifley said later the strike had left 'a legacy of bitterness and a trail of hate'.[31] This experience meant that he was unconvinced of the effectiveness of a general strike and supported arbitration as a means of settling disputes. He 'believed that arbitration strengthened the social and industrial bonds that brought people together'.[32]

Chifley worked his way up in the Australian Labor Party (ALP) and stood unsuccessfully for preselection in 1922 and 1924 in the NSW elections.[33] In 1928, Chifley won the federal seat of Macquarie at the age of forty-three, winning a majority in the city of Bathurst.[34] After the election of the Labor government under James Scullin in 1929, Chifley became minister for Defence in March 1931, and for ten months he was assistant treasurer under EG Theodore,[35] with whom he developed a warm working relationship.[36] Prime Minister Scullin also placed him in charge of Australia's mandated territories.[37] With the onset of the Great Depression, ways and means to deal with it were fiercely contested and Chifley would reluctantly support the deflationary Premiers' Plan,[38] devised by economists DB Copland, LF Giblin, LG Melville and EOG Shann.[39]

One of the casualties of the landslide against the Labor government in the 1931 federal election, Chifley was caught up in a bitter factional war in the 1930s with former New South Wales premier JT Lang. In 1934 he became president of the federal Labor Party in New South Wales, where he worked hard to revive the party and to counter Lang's malevolent influence. Ultimately, unity was restored to the Labor Party, which would lead to a state election victory in New South Wales in 1941. During his time out of parliament, Chifley was active in local government and community groups. In 1933, he was elected to the Abercrombie Shire Council where he served until 1947. He was also a member of the Bathurst District Hospital committee and chair from 1937 to 1944 and continued as a director of the Bathurst daily newspaper, the *National Advocate*.[40] It was during this time when he was unemployed, having lost the federal seat of Macquarie, that it is said he 'quietly made a private trip on a cargo boat, around Indonesia and South East Asia, "just to see what was going on up in those parts"'.[41]

Chifley had very little formal education, something he would later say that he regretted deeply. He was largely self-educated and attended classes at the Workers' Educational Association and the Bathurst Technical School four nights a week over a period of fifteen years.[42] The Chifleys' modest house in Busby Street, Bathurst, was filled with books on economics, accountancy and public finance.[43] According to his close adviser, economist Dr HC 'Nugget' Coombs, Chifley had studied the latest in British political and economic thought for many years. He also had an understanding of Keynesian economics. His relationship with economist Professor RC Mills, from when they were both commissioners on the 1935–1937 Royal Commission into the Monetary and Banking Systems in Australia, also proved to be very rewarding.[44] Chifley's time as commissioner provided him with the opportunity for further education in economic theory and government financial policy through his association with 'thirteen of Australia's leading economists and an imposing array of the top men of Australian banking and commerce' who were witnesses at the commission's hearings.[45]

The War Years

In June 1940 Chifley was appointed director of labour supply in the Munitions Ministry on the recommendation of public servant JK Jensen,[46] with whom Chifley had worked when he was minister for Defence in the Scullin government.[47] A friendship formed between Chifley, Jensen and BHP's Essington Lewis, now director-general of Munitions—three men connected by 'dreams of a powerful, industrialized Australia'. Chifley, however, resigned from this position to contest the seat of Macquarie in the federal election. He was re-elected to parliament in September 1940.[48]

In 1941, when the Fadden conservative government fell and the Curtin Labor government took office on 7 October, Chifley was given the portfolio of treasurer, where he was responsible for financing the war effort and controlling inflation. He was also a member of the War Cabinet.[49] Chifley was a 'superb administrator with an unrivalled grasp of the complexities of international economic policy'.[50] As treasurer, he ensured that Australia was not weighed down by a huge war debt. He achieved this through 'increased taxation, loans from the Australian public, and central bank credit', which meant the nation was not saddled with the overseas debt that Australia had experienced after World War I.[51] The government introduced the National Welfare Fund in 1943, which would provide a comprehensive welfare scheme after the war. To offset public resentment at increased taxation to pay for the war effort, part of the additional tax was allocated to the fund. The National Welfare Fund also had the 'advantage of being an economic stabiliser', soaking up excess consumer income.[52] During the war years, the powers of the federal government were also increased in order to mobilise the war effort. In 1942 Chifley legislated a uniform income tax on a 'pay-as-you-earn basis', whereby the federal government was given sole responsibility for the collection of income tax.[53] The success of these war-time initiatives demonstrated the role that government could play in planning for the economic future of Australia.

Improved social services included making the Commonwealth the provider for widows' pensions (1942), maternity benefits for Indigenous mothers (1942), reciprocal old age and invalid pensions with New Zealand (1943), funeral benefits (1943), a second form of maternity benefit (1943) and unemployment and sickness benefits (1944).[54]

In May 1945, the government tabled a White Paper, *Full Employment in Australia*, which 'represented the authentic, forward-looking reformist tradition of the ALP'. This would be a central aim of the government's economic policy.[55] As treasurer and minister for Post-war Reconstruction from 1942 to 1945, Chifley's role was central to the government's plans for a full employment economy.

Planning for Australia's future in the years after the end of hostilities, the government introduced the Commonwealth Reconstruction Training Scheme (CRTS) in March 1944. Devised by the Department of Post-War Reconstruction, the CRTS was one of the most significant programs to facilitate social change in Australia. The scheme provided the training necessary for the almost one million ex-servicemen and women returning home, to re-establish themselves in suitable civilian occupations.[56] It delivered three categories of full-time training: 'professional training—at a university, technical college, teachers' college, agricultural college leading to a degree, diploma or equivalent; vocational training—for an established skilled adult vocation, trade or calling; and rural training—on approved farms or by short intensive courses in agricultural colleges'.[57] The scheme 'unlocked the talent of many who could not have gained a higher education without it'.[58]

Far-reaching legislative changes to Australia's monetary and banking system also occurred. In 1945 the Banking Act and the Commonwealth Bank Act were legislated, which meant that the Commonwealth Bank was recognised as Australia's central bank. This marked an important milestone in the evolution of central banking in Australia. The legislation was based on, as Chifley noted, the 'conviction that the Government must accept responsibility for the economic condition of the nation'. The Commonwealth Bank Act stated:

> It shall be the duty of the Commonwealth Bank, within the limits of its powers, to pursue a monetary and banking policy directed to the greatest advantage of the people of Australia.

The charter of goals outlined in the Commonwealth Bank Act—to ensure currency stability, full employment, and the economic prosperity and welfare of the Australian people—remains to this day.[59] The bills were introduced into parliament in March 1945, when Chifley was treasurer, and came into force by proclamation in August 1945, when Chifley was prime minister.

Chifley as Prime Minister

After the death of John Curtin on 5 July, Chifley became prime minister on 13 July 1945.[60] His government's achievements in domestic policy were many. The Commonwealth Hospital Benefits Act was passed in October 1945, in which the federal government subsidised the states, providing free public ward treatment for patients.[61] Since 1944, the Labor government had attempted to introduce a program for the free supply of prescribed medicines, with the chemists reimbursed by the Commonwealth—the Pharmaceutical Benefits Scheme (PBS). In doing so, it had faced intense opposition from the Australian branch of the British Medical Association (BMA). The Chifley government succeeded in legislating the Pharmaceutical Benefits Scheme in 1947.[62] A national tuberculosis screening and treatment program was implemented in 1945–1946.[63] In November 1947, vaccines prepared at the Commonwealth Serum Laboratories were provided by the government, free of charge, to immunise against diphtheria and whooping cough.[64] In 1948 bush nursing centres, inland missions and other comparable establishments, were granted hospital authority status under Section 12 of the Pharmaceutical Benefits Act 1947–1949 which meant that pharmaceutical benefits could be provided to people living in isolated regions.[65] Other legislation passed included the Wheat Stabilisation Act 1948—endorsed by wheat growers, it was designed to protect growers from unstable wheat prices; the Qantas Empire Airways Act 1948), under which the Commonwealth government finalised the purchase of Australia's overseas airline; and the Shipping Act, 1949, which established a Commonwealth shipping line.[66]

The National Health Service Act which sought to lay the foundations for a national health scheme, was introduced in November 1948. It was fiercely opposed by the Menzies Opposition and the British Medical Association, and poor drafting of the legislation meant that it had to be amended in 1949. The Act was gazetted just before the federal election was held in December 1949 and the

Chifley government lost office.⁶⁷ The Chifley government also embarked on a massive assisted immigration scheme.⁶⁸ The government established the Australian National University in Canberra in 1946.⁶⁹ It legislated for Commonwealth scholarships for university education in 1949. These scholarships were awarded on merit, under which students' fees and living expenses were paid. The scheme also provided a number of 'mature age' scholarships for those unable to afford further education because they had been forced to leave school at an early age.⁷⁰ The Commonwealth Office of Education, an advisory board to the government, was also established.⁷¹ In 1947 an Australian, WJ McKell, was appointed governor-general on the retirement of the Duke of Gloucester, who had served for just on two years. McKell, a former boilermaker and assistant secretary of the New South Wales Boilermakers' Union, took office on 11 March, after retiring as the Labor premier of New South Wales.⁷²

Other initiatives of the Chifley Labor government included the introduction in 1948 of a 'new category of Australian citizenship'. Previously, those who had citizenship rights in Australia were 'officially British rather than Australian citizens'.⁷³ Chifley personally sponsored Laurence Hartnett's plan for General Motors Holden to build an Australian-made motor car, establishing an Australian car industry in 1948.⁷⁴ The Snowy Mountains Hydro-Electric Power Act of 1949 established the Snowy Mountains Authority under which the waters of the Snowy River would be diverted to power stations to generate electricity, supplying New South Wales, Victoria, and the ACT. The water was then directed inland and utilised to 'serve agriculture and industry'.⁷⁵ The Australian Security Intelligence Organisation (ASIO) was formed in March 1949 in response to pressure from the United Kingdom to create an Australian counter intelligence agency.⁷⁶

The post-war Chifley government faced significant challenges to ensure Australia's future security and prosperity, one of which was how to reposition the Australian economy within the new world economic order. During the war and into the post-war period, there were many 'great international conferences concerned with the post-war reconstruction of the global economy and its institutions'.⁷⁷ In 1947, against fierce opposition from his own party, Chifley was able to achieve ratification of the Bretton Woods Agreement, through which Australia became part of the new international financial and economic system, which Chifley had long believed was essential.[78] The immediate post-war period was a time of momentous change in Australia, both domestically and internationally. Domestically, Australia had emerged from two world wars and a depression in which the unemployment rate reached 30 per cent in the June quarter of 1932.[79] And yet:

> By the end of the 1940s, when European countries were still trying to repair the destruction of war, and unemployment in the United States was rising again towards 10 per cent, Australia seemed to be about the most successful economy in the world.[80]

In the international arena, Chifley had a deep understanding of the radical changes occurring in post-war Asia and was a key architect of the Australian government's bold new approach to a decolonising Asia. The Chifley government supported the Indonesian nationalists in their struggle against the Netherlands' attempt to re-establish their pre-war colonial regime and, in 1947, backed independence for India. Chifley also played a significant role at the 1949 Commonwealth Prime Ministers' Conference held in London in developing the formula whereby a republican India was able to remain within the Commonwealth. As prime minister, Chifley travelled widely, attending important Commonwealth conferences. He established a close working relationship with Evatt, his minister for External Affairs, and made his mark on world affairs.

In 1947, Chifley sought to nationalise private banks, a move that was defeated, and some historians say led to his defeat by Robert Menzies and the Liberal–Country Party coalition, in the federal election on 10 December 1949.[81] Chifley attributed his government's loss to the successful campaign by the Menzies Opposition in 'linking up Communism with Socialism and Socialism with the Labor Party'.[82] As leader of the Opposition, Chifley suffered a major defeat from his own party when the federal executive directed the parliamentary Labor Party to allow the Communist Dissolution Bill 1950 through the Senate, without the civil liberties protections that Chifley had fought for.[83] Chifley led the Labor Party in the next federal election in April 1951, but was again defeated. He died of a heart attack on 13 June 1951.[84]

The Influence of Chifley's Rural Background

Chifley's rural background is highly significant in any attempt to appreciate how his beliefs and understanding of the world were shaped. Chifley's father, Patrick, was a blacksmith employed by an agricultural machinery manufacturer in Bathurst that supplied the farms of the central west of New South Wales.[85] His grandfather was a farmer who had selected land in Limekilns, north-east of Bathurst in April 1864, under the *New South Wales Land Act* (1861), which had sought to redistribute the vast pastoral leases of the squatters to promote intensive agricultural use of the land.[86] Chifley spent his childhood on his grandfather's farm in Limekilns until he returned to his parents' home in Bathurst.[87] Growing up in a rural city like Bathurst and its surrounding district meant that Chifley understood that Australia's economy was reliant on its exports of primary commodities. Every edition of the local newspaper, the *National Advocate*, contained reports on the price of wool and other rural commodities, evidence of Australia's interconnectedness with the world economy. Chifley's experience of the Great Depression, and its impact on rural Australia and the Australian economy in general, demonstrated to him how Australia's economic prosperity was dependent on world trading conditions.

Chifley's economic internationalist perspective carried through to his later support for the Atlantic Charter and for 'all international organizations', in order to prevent further wars and economic depressions.[88] Rural prosperity was dependent on: expansion of the world economy through full employment; freer trade; the economic advancement of poorer countries; and better nutrition throughout the world. All these 'aspirations' were embodied in the Atlantic Charter,[89] which was drawn up at a meeting of the US president and the British prime minister on the US ship *Augusta* in Newfoundland on 14 August 1941. In this Charter, President Franklin Delano Roosevelt and Prime Minister Winston Churchill adopted a 'rules-based approach to the international order.' The Charter committed the United States and Britain to 'a new order based on a few key principles': an end to territorial aggrandisement, or other changes;

respect for self-government and its restoration to those forcibly deprived of it; all States—'victor or vanquished'—should have access to trade and the raw materials necessary for their economic prosperity; collaboration between nations to secure 'improved labour standards, economic advancement and social security'; peace and 'freedom from fear and want'; high seas freedoms; and rejection of the use of force.[90]

A clear and comprehensive statement on the importance of international collaboration in promoting rural prosperity can be found in *A Rural Policy for Post-War Australia*, a declaration of Commonwealth policy in relation to Australia's primary industries, authorised by Chifley and released in 1946. In this statement, Chifley's understanding of how trade policy is, by its very nature, 'international' in essence,[91] is very clear:

> No country stands to gain more than Australia from an expansionist world policy. The Agricultural prosperity of Australia depends upon the widening of world trade. Our soil and climate enable us to produce a relatively few but important products for which world markets are needed. If these are denied us our special advantages are lost and our development retarded. It is for these reasons that Australia is vitally interested in an expansionist rather than isolationist world policy.[92]

A few years earlier, in a series of newspaper articles written when he was minister for Post-war Reconstruction in the Curtin government, Chifley had declared there were many countries in the Indian-Pacific region with large populations living at 'subsistence levels' whose 'economic productivity' was minimal. Unfortunately, these 'near neighbours' had traded very little with Australia in previous years. Chifley wrote:

> Any moves to increase the productivity of their economies and the living standards of the masses of their people, as well as being good in themselves, offer expanding markets for our foodstuffs and our manufactures. The ordinary people of these countries have not been able to afford even

our foodstuffs in the past. It follows that, if this and other countries combine to create the conditions necessary for greater world trade, Australia should also be prepared to take advantage of our trade opportunities.[93]

Chifley was aware of the need for an expansionist trade policy because of Australia's 'special advantages', and how important it was to pay attention to Australia's Asian neighbourhood. Australia was not only dependent on the world economy; it was part of a specific Indian-Pacific region. Any increase in the productivity of Australia's northern neighbours through international co-operation and the expansion of world trade would lead to improved living standards in the region. This would not only benefit these 'near neighbours', but Australia as well.

Member of the Labour Movement and the Australian Labor Party

For Chifley, the labour movement was an essential part of this fight for better living conditions. As he told the annual conference of the New South Wales branch of the Australian Labor Party on 12 June 1948, this was a fight to 'bring to the people of the world, not only of our own country, but to every worker throughout the world, a standard of living higher than the state of misery and degradation that workers have suffered in the past. We have seen what happened in the 1930s'. Chifley declared that the 'greatest glory in life' was to have served the labour movement. He likened it to 'a great army fighting for a great ideal'. As he said, 'Nothing is worth fighting for more in life'. And this was because, although Australian workers were 'only a segment of this thing called humanity', they not only achieved benefits for themselves, but the movement's achievements had 'repercussions in other parts of the world', so that others shared in these benefits.[94] Chifley had long regarded the labour movement as a religion. He viewed the movement and the Labor Party 'in the same light as the leaders of the great religious faiths regard their organizations'. Those who belonged were '*social* evangelists ... charged with a great responsibility'.[95]

Chifley believed the labour movement was greater than the sum of its individual members. This, perhaps, explains his reluctance, or indifference, to leaving traces and why he dismissed the idea, put to him by LF Crisp, that he should write a memoir. As he told the Bathurst branch of the federal Labor Party on 18 December 1933, 'In this great movement individuals do not count. It is not a matter of Scullin, Forgan Smith, Collier or Lang—it is the great movement'. He, himself, would 'step down' immediately if he thought he was preventing the party from presenting a unified policy to the people. He added:

> So far as individuals are concerned we are here to-day and gone to-morrow—we are like the shifting sands of the sea shore. The Labor movement should be more than a suicide club in which men do their best to cut each other's political throats. It is and should be a great and glorious movement—it is a religion.[96]

He thanked all those who had supported him 'at great personal sacrifice', for their 'kindness and assistance'. The only thing that mattered was 'the Labor movement', which needed to work together to 'find out what is best for this country, of which the workers form the major part'.[97] In a later speech he gave to the Bathurst Trades and Labour Council on May Day in 1939, he spoke of the movement he loved—the labour movement—and the party he loved—the Labor Party. Although Chifley condemned Jack Lang, who, as leader of the Labor Party in New South Wales, had 'spent some five years striding in seven league boots from one political blunder to another', he had no doubt that many Langites were sincere in their convictions, and, although he held different beliefs to some, he believed that all in the party saw

> that same 'light on the hill' and are trying to reach toward it. Our objective is that the great mass of the people may achieve some benefit from the efforts which he and I and you all are making. We may be taking different roads to reach it and are divided about the methods to be taken to achieve it. But I hope we will not lose sight of the fact that on humanitarian principles all our efforts must be directed to helping those who suffer most under the economic system in which we work.[98]

Chifley was devoted to the labour cause and to the Labor Party. But it was not the individual who mattered. As he said, ten years later, in June 1949, that although as prime minister he had attained a certain status in the labour movement, the movement's strength did not come from politicians such as himself. Instead, it came from the people who supported the movement. The 'great objective' was 'the light on the hill—which we aim to reach by working for the betterment of mankind not only here but everywhere we may give a helping hand'.[99]

Frederic Eggleston was an intellectual and a long-term adviser on international affairs for the Curtin and Chifley governments. He was a former independent liberal member of parliament in Victorian state politics from 1920 until 1927.[100] In his *Reflections of an Australian Liberal* (1953), Eggleston provides an incisive analysis of how the trade union movement and the Australian Labor Party were central institutions in Chifley's life, and the crucial role they played in the development and advancement of Chifley the politician.[101] Eggleston was not from 'Labor ranks',[102] but he was a great admirer of Chifley and Curtin, who, in his opinion, were 'great leaders and they died under the strain'.[103] He thought that the Labor government was 'more attuned to foreign policy problems' than the previous Menzies government, and he shared 'most of the [Labor] ideals of advanced policy'.[104] Eggleston's keen understanding of Australia's geopolitical situation led him to be an early advocate of 'Asian-Pacific regionalism';[105] his ideas would influence and reinforce Labor's foreign policy.

Eggleston wrote that the Labor Party, as well as being the largest party, was also the 'creative influence in Australian politics'. Labor government policy during the war gained popular approval from the Australian community. Its foreign policy was one of 'internationalism', while its domestic policies ensured that important social services were delivered to the people.[106] Writing about political leadership in Australia, Eggleston declared:

> Labour has had an unusual experience of real leadership in recent years. Curtin and Chifley were largely responsible for this in eight years of office. Curtin had everything but health—popular appeal, intellect, and culture and he was

a true representative of the people. Chifley was the most powerful personality ever seen in Federal politics, and he was able to impose himself on the party but, with all his intellect, he had not the educational background necessary to clarify his ideas.[107]

Eggleston also noted that Chifley had 'the most powerful mind in the politics of his day and he was able to learn more quickly than most parliamentarians, but it was one of his virtues that he was true to his mates and his class'.[108]

According to Eggleston, the Australian Labor Party was, from a 'political point of view ... a most efficient instrument ... and the most competent'. The trade union movement, although complicated in its organisation, functioned smoothly for the most part, and recruited many 'active workers'. It provided an exceptional training ground in politics, in which the Trades Hall Councils and their conferences, presented 'a unique forum' in which their members' abilities and competency could be tested. Eggleston wrote that he was 'amazed, coming from a sheltered life, at the terrific will-power or resistance' shown by the Labor parliamentarians he met. During his brief career as a Victorian politician, he never failed to be impressed by 'the superiority of the Labour Member as a parliamentarian. His command of tactics, his knowledge of the mentality of the people and his facility in their idiom were remarkable'. He noted that his side of politics—compared to Labor MPs, most of whom had not gone past primary school—'were like children'. Eggleston argued, however, that the weakness of the Labor Party was its 'lack of expert intellectual advice'.[109] Here he agrees with AW Stargardt's critique that, in a party not prone to engage in theory, it was not an exaggeration to say that there was very little 'independent Socialist thinking' in Australia during the period from the early 1920s to the latter part of the 1940s.[110] Eggleston wrote that, in fact, intellectuals were not supported: 'Most Labour men have not got over the idea that scholarship is weighted against them'. Intellectuals found it difficult to join the party, because the road to success was through the trade union movement.[111]

The Labor training ground proved to be a tough and testing one for Chifley. He had advocated for his union members in industrial tribunals,[112] and taken part in the 1917 railway strike, and, as a consequence, been sacked and reinstated in a lower rank.[113] He had waged a fierce battle against former New South Wales premier JT Lang and his supporters in union factional warfare;[114] and in 1931 he suffered the bitter ignominy of being expelled from the union he had helped to establish—the Australian Federated Union of Locomotive Enginemen. It was ten years before he was readmitted to the union in 1941.[115] He was also expelled from the Lang-controlled New South Wales Labor Party the day the Macquarie poll was declared in January 1932 in which he was defeated.[116] Chifley's education in Labor politics proved a difficult one:

> first faithfully sinking with the vacillating Scullin government and then slugging it out with the formidable Lang machine. He emerged from it with enormous prestige, with his independence and single-mindedness confirmed, with a masterly knowledge of ALP internal operations, and with the proven ability to dish it out with the best and to act just as ruthlessly as the situation demanded.[117]

Through all this, Chifley developed the capacity to 'impose' himself on his party and the union movement.[118] He eventually took up the highest office in the land, and fought to secure international cooperation to ensure peace and prosperity for Australia and the world.

And yet, although the labour movement worked to achieve better living conditions for all, Chifley's commitment to the movement worked against a total acceptance of internationalism, which, according to internationalist historian Akira Iriye, was 'open-ended' and 'inclusive', able to incorporate 'all nations and all peoples'. In contrast, 'racism by definition was exclusionary'.[119] It is difficult to reconcile Chifley's embrace of internationalism with his firm commitment to the White Australia policy. In May 1949, in one of his regular 'Report to the Nation' radio speeches, he spoke about Australia's immigration policy and how it applied to non-Europeans. He maintained it was a bi-partisan policy carried out since Federation:

> One of the earliest national ideals of Australia was the establishment of a nation of high living standards with

equal opportunity for all. Early Commonwealth legislators saw that the greatest possible threat to such an ideal was a pool of cheap labour. It was then, and still is, a fact that the most likely sources of cheap labour for those who wished to exploit it, were the Asian countries so near to Australia.[120]

Based on the labour movement's fear of competition for employment, it meant the 'protection of jobs and wages from the perceived threat of immigrants who may work for lower wages'.[121] Chifley argued that the reasons for Australia's immigration policy, were 'economic not racial' and 'the Australian nation did not and does not feel superior to nations of non-European people'.[122] But the commitment to a restrictive immigration policy remained. Historian Glenda Sluga, in her study of the relationship between twentieth century internationalism and nationalism, writes that 'the language of race and civilizational difference' gave nationalism in the twentieth century its deeply unedifying character.[123] Chifley was not immune from using this language. Although Chifley's interests were 'unusually wide' and in many cases progressive, there were some 'significant omissions' such as the White Australia policy. In this instance, Chifley revealed himself as a man of his time'.[124] While we might recoil at his support for the White Australia policy, in his personal and professional relations with Asian leaders, such as Nehru, Chifley demonstrated no racial prejudice. It was clear that he did understand that the old colonial order was ending in Asia and that Australia needed to adjust government policy to this new post-war, post-colonial world.

Impact of War and Economic Depression

Chifley had no actual experience of war as a combatant, and, as he said, he was not personally affected himself by the Great Depression of the 1930s.[125] And yet, as he said in the House of Representatives in November 1947, he could remember the depression of the 1890s, and the farmers living nearby who were 'desolated and grief-stricken at the closing of the banks'.[126] Similarly, the advent of the Great Depression, with its massive number of unemployed people and extreme poverty, had a huge impact on Chifley.[127] He could still remember, in his electorate, the '2000 men outside a factory in an attempt to secure the one job that was offering'.[128] He found it difficult to understand how in times of economic depression, with mass unemployment, money was tight, but in war-time, an enormous amount of wealth was used for destructive purposes. He said in parliament, in November 1941:

> for ten years, the working class, which is now expected to assist in the conduct of the war either on the battlefield or in the munitions factories, was treated worse than farm horses or pit ponies in the mines. They were thrown into the streets, where they were left to starve. Despite that treatment, they are now expected suddenly to develop intense feelings of patriotism.[129]

Historians such as David Stephens argue that the policies initiated by the Labor governments of the 1940s were driven by their memories of previous depressions and their fear of another world economic crash. This fear remained an overriding factor in Chifley's thinking on the economy: he feared it was inevitable that inflation would lead to another downturn. Although the post-war Australian economy was in a very healthy state, with 'record employment levels, good seasons, high export prices and healthy sterling balances', Chifley was apprehensive that this situation might end.[130] However, according to economist Selwyn Cornish, Chifley managed to keep inflation under control in the 'immediate' post-war period because of the 'continuation of wartime controls'.[131] This situation changed with the election of Robert Menzies in December 1949. Unlike Chifley, 'Menzies ... was not interested in economic policy-making and its detailed ramifications'.[132] In 1950/51 there was a 'sharp lift in the inflation rate. In the second quarter of 1950/51, it jumped to an annual 18 per cent and peaked at 28 per cent in the final quarter of the year. Over the four quarters the increase was 19.5 per cent, the highest in Australia's post-war history'.[133] The Menzies government had ignored advice from the Commonwealth Bank. It then introduced the 1951 'horror budget' and the era of 'stop-go' economic cycles began.[134] Stephens' argument is similar to David Lee's in *Search for Security* (1995)—the Chifley government's foreign policy was determined not so much by a fear of external threats to the nation, but a concern that Australia's future economic security was assured and that Australia had a part to play in the development of the post-war world economy.[135]

Although Chifley himself had no experience of serving in the military, he, like the rest of his generation, lived through the terrible times of two world wars and a host of other smaller conflicts. The legacies of those wars had a profound impact on his attitude towards the use of force by the state to settle international disputes and on his willingness as prime minister to commit Australian troops to battle. As he said, in October 1946, in off-the-record comments to journalists, as 'an old man he personally had nothing to fear from another war'. It was the younger generation of Australians who would have to serve on the battlefield if war broke out. It was therefore crucial that 'this long-term danger should be eliminated'.[136] In a fiery exchange in parliament on 2 September 1948, we can see the very different attitudes of Chifley and the Menzies Opposition to the possibility of another war. Opposition MP Percy Spender, charged the government and the minister for External Affairs with neglecting Australia's defence needs. Evatt had failed to tackle the issue of 'subversive activities of Communists'.[137] According to Spender, the 'language of force' was the only language understood by the Soviet Union.[138]

Chifley, in his response, denied Spender's suggestion that force could solve problems between states; the prospect of another war was 'something which ought to appal every human being'.[139] Any future war would be too terrible to contemplate with the 'new forms of warfare' available. He was scathing about those politicians who 'merely make speeches', and talked too much about sending young men to war when they themselves were not likely to fight on the battlefield.[140] Chifley's own personal experience of the devastation caused by war affected him profoundly. In a radio broadcast to the people of the Macquarie electorate after his return from London in July 1948, where he discussed certain economic issues with Prime Minister Clement Attlee and other members of the British government, Chifley spoke about his brief tour of Berlin, a city that

> presents a sad picture of the devastation of war. I have previously visited some of the worst war devastated cities, such as Hiroshima, Yokahama, Tokio, Manila and Rangoon.

> But, excepting Hiroshima, which was completely destroyed by the atomic bomb, I have not seen anything like the destruction in Berlin. Masses of bricks and rubble, gutted buildings, now mark this once beautiful city. It is a grim warning of the tragic consequences of war.[141]

He told his listeners that they were 'safe and secure' in their homes that night, surrounded by their families. They were able to find a job in a time of full employment, with unlimited opportunities ahead of them. In contrast, he had visited places and spoken to people 'in the grip of misery and hardship, indeed, with no future at all. Uneasy countries, worried peoples are to be found everywhere'. The 'devastating hand of war' had wreaked 'shocking havoc in people's minds'.[142]

This direct experience of war-time destruction reinforced Chifley's long-held views on the dreadful human and material cost of war. It led to his ongoing resistance to military intervention in conflicts in post-colonial Asia.[143] He refused to militarise Australia's response to the region. He believed the collective security provided by the United Nations, 'the world security organization', was the best way in which peace and security could be maintained.[144] Chifley and his policy advisers 'were firm believers in the principle of liberal internationalism': the way to avoid wars and economic instability was through 'international collaboration'.[145] Chifley's vision was a global one, in which, 'No one can live alone; we are all dependent on each other'.[146]

Intellectual Influences
To understand the development of Chifley's internationalism, we need to explore the intellectual environment within which he moved. Chifley gathered around himself some of the finest minds in the country, and this intellectual stimulus, combined with his own long-term self-education, gave him, as treasurer and prime minister, an education that no formal schooling could have matched. Yet he always regretted that missing dimension in his life and he was determined to create educational opportunities for others. As he said to his nephew, 'I'd rather have had Mr. Menzies' education than a million pounds'.[147] When elected to parliament, he showed an early interest in educational facilities in Canberra. On 21 March 1930 he

asked the minister for Home Affairs, Arthur Blakeley, if the proposed University College in Canberra would provide correspondence courses, such as those in the United States and elsewhere, to allow students in regional areas to take courses in arts, law, commerce and science.[148] Some years later, Chifley was instrumental in establishing the Commonwealth Reconstruction Training Scheme, which provided education and vocational training for returned servicemen and women.[149] In 1949, his government introduced legislation for a Commonwealth scholarship scheme.[150]

Chifley was also heavily involved in establishing the Australian National University, a 'new national research institute or post-graduate university'.[151] This was the first phase in a plan to improve the standard of university education across the nation. Canberra was to become an 'intellectual bell-wether'. The first step was to persuade eminent Australian scholars who had established distinguished careers overseas to return to Australia. In April 1946, during his visit to London to attend the first post-war Commonwealth Prime Ministers' Conference, Chifley spoke with Australian physicist Mark Oliphant in an effort to persuade him to take up a position at the new university. He arranged for the scientist to meet him at Hyde Park to walk and to talk. Oliphant recollected that they talked for nearly two hours about 'the problems of running Australia, and about human and world affairs generally'.

Oliphant said: 'The Prime Minister used pretty colourful language. Although he had never been to a university himself, he had a good idea of university requirements. He understood Australia's need to upgrade all its tertiary educational facilities. He also realized that modern industry depended increasingly on the output of university graduates'. Oliphant quoted a pledge to the prime minister that he thought summed up the mission of a university, which was to 'diligently ... seek the truth, and, having found it, to impart it to others'. According to Oliphant, the quotation appealed to Chifley. He added: 'For my part, I began to see that politics was not always just a power game: that there were people like Chifley who thought very deeply and sincerely about the problems of mankind. I suddenly knew I had met a politician with a profound feeling for humanity'.[152]

Chifley was an avid reader—in an interview with journalist James G Murtagh in March 1949, he said there were 'four great books he had read over and over again—The Bible, *The Myths of Greece and Rome*, *Plutarch's Lives* and Gibbon's *Decline and Fall of the Roman Empire*'. He admitted, after being pressed, that 'he had just finished reading The Bible for the tenth time'. Chifley added: 'No book had impressed me more than Bellamy', referring to Edward Bellamy's *Looking Backward, 2000–1887* (1888), a book that was very influential in the early labour movement. Murtagh wrote that Bellamy's novel told the story of

> the imaginary experience of a wealthy Bostonian … who in 1887 is put to sleep in a hypnotic trance in a subterranean room. In the year 2000 A.D., he is discovered and awakened and is amazed by the changes in the social life of the United States. The whole of industry is conducted by a single syndicate and carried on in the common interest for the common profit. There are neither rich nor poor, employment is handled by a guild system and crime is unknown.[153]

Bellamy's popular novel of a 'socialist utopia' sold more than a million copies when it was published.[154]

Journalist Alan Reid was a confidante of Chifley when he was treasurer and prime minister, and during his time as leader of the Opposition.[155] According to Reid, Chifley was an 'extraordinary man … one of the best read men' he had ever met. Robert Menzies told Reid that 'sitting on the Literary Board with Chifley was an experience' because Chifley would always know the precise details about the most obscure writers when others on the Board had never heard of them. Reid said that Chifley had 'a really fantastic memory'.[156] Chifley's official driver, Ray Tracy, provides a fascinating insight into Chifley's reading habits. According to Tracy, 'No Prime Minister … lived as simply as Ben Chifley'. He added, 'Unless it was raining heavily, I was never expected to call for him or to drive him home. He walked'. Tracey continued:

> And every second week, he relaxed completely. He would rise early, walk to church and go back to bed immediately he returned. There he would remain all day and all night.

> Those Sundays were curious days. The room would be stocked with a great collection of books ranging from involved reports on financial systems to the wildest 'whodunits'—and Ben would lie back, alternately reading and dozing, for the best part of 24 hours. He wouldn't be interrupted.[157]

Chifley said that the long rest 'refreshed him for another solid fortnight's work'. Tracy noted that if the 'amazing amount he could get through was any guide, his theory was correct'.[158] Chifley's reading ranged over many areas. He was not only interested in Australia: he looked at the global context, at human society, at high finance, at economics, how people interacted with each other. He had a sense of the emergent future, and this is shown by his interest in Bellamy's novel.

Chifley's methods of working—his insatiable interest in news sources, the information he received from personal contacts, and the material he read—were all ways by which he improved his own education in world affairs. According to Fin Crisp, with Chifley:

> The gears were always engaged, he was always giving something, or very frequently getting something and storing it away. I've never known a man to be such a jack-daw, picking up unconsidered trifles and storing them away and categorizing them and bringing them out again, in a telling way, later.[159]

In some of his speeches in parliament, Chifley would mock those on the Opposition benches. Percy Spender was often chosen as a target for Chifley's disdain. The prime minister would concede modestly that he was not as well informed as many in the Opposition. According to Chifley, Spender was 'the honourable member for Warringah' who spoke repeatedly about many aspects of international affairs. Chifley noted that, although he did not talk quite as much as Spender, many representatives from various governments gave him 'their impressions by letter, or otherwise, of all events happening in the world to-day, whether they be associated with either international politics or economic affairs'.[160] Harold Breen, who worked with Chifley in various positions in the public service, confirmed that Chifley was the recipient of a great deal of correspondence from around the globe. According to Breen, Chifley worked tirelessly, 'toiling from early morning until midnight and after'. Breen wrote:

> There was not an activity in Australia in those post-war years in which he was not interested or was not the driving force or the initiator; and often it was all three. Nor was his interest confined to Australia; it roamed over the world: Asia, Europe, America. He received from these places a steady stream of information—official and otherwise—which he absorbed and pondered upon and used.[161]

Chifley's interest in international politics and economic affairs was supported and sustained by many of the older advisers to government and also by the 'new wave' of university-educated economists and government advisers who played a major role in influencing the post-war policies of the Chifley government.[162] According to his press secretary, Don Rodgers, Chifley was 'a firm believer' in obtaining expert opinion on important issues, and he 'eagerly sought after the best possible advice'. A 'gregarious man, he liked nothing better than good company. He was always looking for brains and the products of good brains'. This was a part of what Rodgers called Chifley's 'brain-harvesting'. In addition, Rodgers said, 'he was the best listener I ever watched in Federal politics'. He was noted for his kindness to his staff.[163]

This was also very much a male world. According to Enid Lyons, who was elected member of parliament for the Tasmanian seat of Darwin on 21 August 1943, and was the wife of prime minister Joe Lyons, Chifley was 'what is often called a man's man'.[164] Eilean Giblin—a 'socialist and feminist',[165] whose husband Lyndhurst Giblin was an economist and adviser to the war-time government—met Chifley when he was treasurer at a dinner at Professor Douglas Copland's home. She wrote in her diary, 'a shrewd and honest man Mr. Chifley seemed to me—not used to talking to women.[166]

William Dunk, who was secretary of the Department of External Affairs from 1945 to 1947, had previously worked closely with Chifley when he was treasurer.¹⁶⁷ Dunk wrote that Chifley was a 'prodigious worker' in two very testing portfolios that 'hastened Chifley's death'. However, as a politician, he was 'by no means the simple, homespun type that he at times affected'. Indeed, 'he could be tough and direct'. He also had an exceptionally dry sense of humour. According to Dunk, it was Chifley's 'very human characteristics', which, together with 'an innate politeness', built up 'a firm line of respect and affection' between the prime minister and his official advisers. Dunk added: 'One can say without detracting from rugged male relationship that we loved him, and I have the warmest recollection of my friendship—it was indeed that—with Ben Chifley'.¹⁶⁸

Chifley gathered networks of bright, intelligent people around him to discuss ideas on policy. In a letter to Labor politician, John Dedman in December 1943, he wrote that it was vital that the Commonwealth public service should have the 'best young brains' available in the country. He went on to say:

> I have found in my own Department that, though youth may be difficult to understand at times it is the driving force of any organisation and it is essential that anything that is done should not prevent a strong leavening of capable young public servants who will assist to carry Australia through the difficult period that it will experience for perhaps the next two decades.¹⁶⁹

Chifley was part of this network; he was also its leader. This was especially so in Chifley's 'beloved' Treasury. This network formed a type of 'official family' led by

> a Treasurer (JB Chifley) who was at first a sort of Prime Minister for the economic home front and then, from 1945, the official Prime Minister, still retaining the Treasurership. The methods of economic co-ordination which were evolved in those days were largely built on the particular interests and temperament of the man who linked these two portfolios.¹⁷⁰

Treasury's influence in economic policy-making increased when it had treasurers who 'exercised both power and influence in cabinet'. This was especially so in the case of Chifley, who established the foundations for Treasury's future influence on government policy-making. According to historian and Liberal Party politician, Paul Hasluck, Chifley was a 'tower of strength ... receptive to his department, strong in the Cabinet, shrewdly practical and quiet moving'.[171] Hasluck wrote of 'the quiet and obdurate strength and sound sense of Chifley'.[172] He had 'an extraordinary grasp of detail', according to journalist Alan Reid. He was also 'one of the shrewdest men' in his understanding of finance that Reid had ever met. Reid said that public servants such as 'Freddy Wheeler and Roland Wilson, people like that who are very high in the treasury tell me that his grasp of detail was far superior to any politician they'd ever met. That he could match them in their own specialised areas'.[173]

Treasurers were always prominent in cabinet. Under Chifley, the Treasury became—mainly because of the abilities of the minister—'one of the creative forces in the Australian war effort'.[174] During his period as treasurer, and also as prime minister, Treasury's influence on policy through its recommendations and analysis was substantial, gaining a well-earned 'reputation for unsurpassed intellectual strength and expertise'.[175] In terms of decision-making, Chifley had a number of sayings that journalist Alan Reid thought were 'extremely sagacious', from both the administrative and the political point of view. One of these sayings was 'if you make a decision on moral grounds, the details usually fall into place'. Chifley also told Reid that, when dealing with public servants, don't ask them if you can carry out a certain action, because as experts, 'they'll provide you with a thousand to one reasons why you can't do it'. Instead, 'what you say to them is I'm going to do this. You tell me how to do it'. Then the public servant's 'real expertise comes out'. In approaching a problem, Chifley's advice was to 'cut away all the flesh of detail until you get down to the bone of principle. It then becomes simple to make a decision and the detail then builds up on that'.[176]

Chifley was proud of the team he had built in Treasury, and, when leader of the Opposition, he told treasurer Arthur Fadden:

> Although I do not expect the Treasurer to admit the fact publicly, I feel that he must realise the debt he owes to previous Labour Administrations for having assembled in the Treasury such a group of outstandingly able officers. When Labour was in office it always paid great attention to the selection of officers to fill important positions in the Public Service, and when I was Treasurer I did not pay regard to the personal convictions of prospective appointees but was concerned solely with their competence. I wanted the highest order of ability.[177]

Chifley was credited with being responsible for the appointment of some exceptional public servants, who would achieve under him, or later, the highest offices in the public service.[178] Dr Herbert Cole ('Nugget') Coombs was an outstanding recruit during the great wartime arrival of youthful economics graduates to the Australian Treasury. He had graduated with a doctorate from the London School of Economics, and, at the start of World War II was seconded to Treasury from the Commonwealth Bank. After working in Treasury as a senior economist, he became the director of rationing in 1942. He was later appointed director-general of the Department of Post-war Reconstruction.[179] Coombs often represented the Australian government at international conferences intent on creating a new post-war global economic order, where he played a significant and influential role. It was said of him, that, 'in his prime Coombs was able to charm birds out of trees'. Arthur Tange, an economist with the Department of Post-war Reconstruction, remembered him as 'one of the most persuasive men that I have ever met'.[180] On 23 November 1948, Chifley announced Coombs' appointment as governor of the Commonwealth Bank,[181] where he remained until July 1968.[182]

Coombs was described as 'immensely practical', with an 'unaffected, down-to-earth manner'. He gave the impression of 'great strength and vitality, despite his small stature'.[183] According to Coombs, Chifley was a 'remarkably tolerant man' given the fact that he had been a leader of the New South Wales federal Labor Party in the 1930s when it was riven with discord. Chifley would speculate about why people behaved the way they did, and why they thought in a certain way, in an attempt to understand what individuals were trying to achieve. He was 'a practising Catholic, but you would never know'. And, when he spoke about the zealots of the Catholic Social Movement, it seemed he 'understood where their prejudices were leading them and was sad about it, and sad about the divisions' this caused.[184] In Chifley's opinion, 'one of the most dangerous individuals you could have in public life was a religious fanatic'. Religious institutions were unlikely to sway him—the history of Europe and parts of the East showed that the churches were silent when people demanded improved living conditions, which did not reflect well on religious institutions. Chifley had always held the view that 'religious bodies should confine themselves to spiritual matters', and 'matters which affect the temporal welfare of the people' should be dealt with by the people at the ballot box.[185]

Chifley was also an exciting person to discuss ideas with. He worked with his officials, rather than his officials working for him. Coombs said, 'we tossed ideas around' and 'in that way I never felt as if I was just somebody producing things for him'. As a result, Coombs always felt that he was a 'participant ... in the process'. It was a creative meeting of minds, with Chifley and the economists who worked with him forming a lively group, interested in policy and its implementation. Chifley 'always read what you wrote'. He had the 'gift of picking the guts out of a document and concentrating on the issues'. He would never reject your work and dismiss it as not what was required. And 'he always welcomed disagreement'.[186] Coombs also had a 'reputation for frankness'; he was a confidante rather than a public servant in his relationship with Chifley. At times he gave Chifley 'blunt and unpalatable advice'. He was 'credited with having warned Chifley once that he was becoming arrogant and losing his sense of proportion because he was attaching too much credence to the adulation he received from sycophants'.[187]

Dr John Burton, secretary of the Department of External Affairs from 1947 to 1950, was, together with Coombs and others, part of the influx of university-educated economists. The son of a reformist Methodist missionary, Burton was educated at the University of Sydney and the London School of Economics. Burton brought to the Department of External Affairs the 'new reformist ideas and policies' that had emerged from the 'intellectual debate' over the Great Depression. An adherent of economist John Maynard Keynes, Burton argued that war was caused by social and economic factors. An advocate of liberal internationalism and an anti-imperialist, Burton played a key role in Australian post-war foreign policy-making.[188] His relationship with Chifley and Evatt was a meeting of minds, intellectually, politically, ideologically and temperamentally. Burton supported a re-orientation of Australian foreign policy away from Europe and the Middle East towards its own region.[189] He attended the New Delhi conference on the Indonesian–Dutch conflict in January 1949 and played an influential role there.[190] He urged the Chifley government to implement a program of educational assistance, technical training, diplomatic representation and promotion of trade in Southeast Asia. Burton believed—together with Chifley and Evatt—that the spread of communism could be prevented by eliminating poverty and supporting genuine nationalist movements in Asia.[191]

John Grenfell (Jack) Crawford was another of those brilliant and influential public servants who played a major role in Chifley's 'official family'. Crawford was director of research in the Department of Post-war Reconstruction in 1943, and in April 1946 he was appointed founding director of the Bureau of Agricultural Economics, where he remained until 1950.[192] Crawford was a pragmatist who understood that compromise was inevitable and believed it was unwise to overreach to achieve an ideal solution. He also had 'vision', aware of what might become important in the future.[193] In this, he was very similar to Chifley and his sense of the 'emergent future'. In fact, Crawford admired Chifley, 'whose vision of the country's future was an inspiration and reinforcement of his own'.[194] One of Crawford's main attributes in his personal relationships was 'loyalty'; he had a 'strong sense of loyalty to the ministers whom he admired' and Chifley was one of those he spoke about 'with affection'.[195] Crawford advocated a 'progressive and forward looking internationalism', emphasising the need to develop stronger trade ties with the Asia-Pacific region, in particular, with Japan.[196]

Chifley had always enjoyed and acknowledged the valuable work of the public service. When he was minister for Defence in the Scullin government in 1931, he found great satisfaction in ministerial administrative work and 'sometimes found himself working sixteen hours a day'.[197] His efforts were mentioned in the *Sydney Morning*

Herald, in June that year, in an article that stated, 'Mr Chifley ... in more ways than one seems to have blossomed into a most fruitful Minister'.[198] Chifley's work as minister in charge of Australia's mandated territories was also acknowledged. The *Pacific Islands Monthly* reported that:

> Mr. Chifley's strong and genial personality won for him many friends among the Islands Administrators and residents. Unlike some members of his party, he never allowed political prejudices to color his decisions—he was a just, fearless, far-seeing and hardworking Minister, who earned the respect of everyone with whom he came in contact. It is a great pity that political ties should sweep out of office a man who is so well qualified to give good service to his country.[199]

As his biographer Crisp noted, Chifley in his role as minister, 'liked to get to know all the senior staff at first hand and draw directly on their expertise'.[200] He also went out of his way to acknowledge the work of the Australian public service. Re-elected to Parliament in 1940, in June 1941 from Opposition, he paid tribute to public servants in general:

> Australia owes a deep debt of gratitude to hundreds of public servants who, without fee or reward, burn the midnight oil in connexion with the war effort. True, many of them are wrapped up in red tape, but there is no lack of sincerity, hard work or honesty of purpose in their endeavor.[201]

When the Labor Party came to power in October 1941 and Chifley became treasurer in the Curtin government, within two weeks he had consulted and received advice on various matters from Professor DB Copland, the economic consultant to the prime minister, and from Dr HC Coombs, economic adviser to the Treasury. Professor LG Melville, who was the Commonwealth Bank's economic adviser, was also consulted, together with Professor LF Giblin, chair of the Financial and Economic Advisory Committee, and AC Joyce from

Treasury, who advised him on budget matters.[202] Chifley worked productively with Treasury secretary SG ('Misery Mac') McFarlane, whose relationship with the treasurer, according to Coombs, was 'mutually cordial—indeed better than they were with Treasurers from the other side of the political fence'.[203]

Delivering his first budget in parliament, Chifley concluded his financial statement with a tribute to 'the zealous officers, particularly those in the Treasury and Taxation Departments, who have worked so strenuously and with great efficiency in its preparation'.[204] He also defended his public servants from media attacks. In his regular address to the nation on Sunday, 14 November 1948, Chifley paid tribute to the 'splendid work of public servants throughout the Commonwealth' and criticised the media for their constant and unreasonable attacks solely to 'score a mean political advantage'. Chifley concluded: 'The fact is that Australia can be as proud as any other country of its public service from any point of view—its training, its experience, its integrity, and its loyalty to every Government'.[205]

Conclusion

Chifley's rural upbringing, the intellectual and the working environment in which he moved, are all important factors in Chifley's development in his role as prime minister, and as treasurer. Chifley, the local man, the 'Ben Chifley of Bathurst', the trade unionist from regional New South Wales, who had experienced two world wars and two economic depressions, moved into politics and to the highest office in the land, where he gathered round him some of the best minds in the country. During this period, from 1941 and 1949, Chifley and the public servants he worked with played a major role in influencing international policy-making. Chifley, it seems, was in his element developing 'a close and confident working relationship with these advisers', who made up the Chifley 'official family'.[206] As 'Nugget' Coombs wrote: 'These were exciting times; dreams of rebuilding society can be a heady drink and we were all, ministers and officials, probably a little intoxicated'.[207] But before we consider how Chifley, in government from 1941 to 1949, supported a rules-based internationalism, we need first to look at the momentous events that influenced Chifley in his early career as a politician.

Notes

1. *CPD*, HoR, 20 March 1947, p. 1002.
2. Crisp, *Ben Chifley*, p. xii.
3. ibid., p. 2.
4. Day, *Chifley*, p. 14.
5. Crisp, *Ben Chifley*, p. 2.
6. Waterson, 'Chifley', p. 412.
7. Day, *Chifley*, p. 10.
8. Crisp, *Ben Chifley*, p. 3.
9. Day, *Chifley*, pp. 19–20.
10. ibid., p. 22.
11. Letter, Henry J O'Brien to Crisp, n.d. Papers of LF Crisp, NLA: MS 5243, Series 5, Folder 12.
12. Day, *Chifley*, p. 37.
13. Crisp, *Ben Chifley*, p. 3
14. ibid., p. 5.
15. Sam Malloy, (ed.), *Chifley Oral Project: A Collection of Oral History Interviews Focusing on the Lives of Ben and Elizabeth Chifley in Bathurst*, Funded by the National Council for the Centenary of Federation, 2002, pp. 34, 37.
16. Day, *Chifley*, pp. 53–54.
17. Crisp, *Ben Chifley*, p. 7.
18. Day, *Chifley*, p. 59; p. 64.
19. ibid., pp. 73–74; p. 88.
20. ibid., p. 71, fn. 50. According to Day, union records of the time are 'sketchy', but in 1925, Chifley said he had been involved in the union movement for eighteen years. See *National Advocate* (Bathurst, NSW), 21 November 1925, p. 2.
21. Day, *Chifley*, pp. 160–162.
22. Crisp, *Ben Chifley*, p. 13.
23. Day, *Chifley*, p. 170.
24. Waterson, 'Chifley', p. 413.
25. Crisp, *Ben Chifley*, p. 13.
26. McMullin, 'Joseph Benedict Chifley', p. 249.
27. Letter, Kate Clyne to Professor Crisp, 2 June 1952. Papers of LF Crisp, NLA: MS 5243, Series 5, Folder 12.
28. Day, *Chifley*, pp. 92–93.
29. Diane Langmore, *Prime Ministers' Wives: The Public and Private Lives of Ten Australian Women*, McPhee Gribble, Ringwood, Victoria, 1992, p. 153.
30. Letter, Kate Clyne to Professor Crisp, 2 June 1952.
31. Crisp, *Ben Chifley*, pp. 14–23.
32. Waterson, 'Chifley', pp. 413–414.
33. John Hawkins, 'Ben Chifley: The True Believer', *Economic Roundup*, Issue 3, 2011, p. 107.
34. Waterson, 'Chifley', p. 414; Crisp, *Ben Chifley*, p. 35.
35. Crisp, *Ben Chifley*, pp. xi, 57 and 154.

36   ibid., p. 63.
37   Crisp, *Ben Chifley*, p. 62; Day, *Chifley*, p. 258.
38   *CPD*, HoR, 25 June 1931, p. 3065.
39   Alex Millmow, 'The Power of Economic Ideas: Australian Economists in the Thirties', *History of Economics Review*, vol. 37, Winter, 2003, p. 84.
40   Waterson, 'Chifley', p. 414.
41   Peter Ryan, *Brief Lives*, Duffy and Snellgrove, Potts Point, NSW, 2004, p. 87.
42   Crisp, *Ben Chifley*, p. 6.
43   ibid., p. 86.
44   HC Coombs, *Trial Balance*, Macmillan, South Melbourne, 1981, p. 24.
45   Crisp, *Ben Chifley*, p. 168. See also Neville Cain, *Economists and the Monetary Commission of 1936: Ideals and Circumstances*, Working Paper No. 120, Department of Economic History, Research School of Social Sciences, ANU, Canberra, December 1988, p. 1.
46   Waterson, 'Chifley', p. 415.
47   Crisp, *Ben Chifley*, p. 64.
48   Waterson, 'Chifley', p. 415.
49   ibid.
50   Lee, *Search for Security*, p. 9.
51   Waterson, 'Chifley', p. 416.
52   Hawkins, 'Ben Chifley', p. 113.
53   ibid., p. 111.
54   Crisp, *Ben Chifley*, p. 190.
55   ibid., p. 194.
56   Darryl Dymock and Stephen Billett, 'Skilling Australians: Lessons from World War II National Workforce Development Programs', *Australian Journal of Adult Learning*, vol. 50, no. 3, 2010, p. 475.
57   ibid., p. 477.
58   Stuart Macintyre, *Australia's Boldest Experiment: War and Reconstruction in the 1940s*, Newsouth, Sydney, 2015, p. 327.
59   Selwyn Cornish, *The Evolution of Central Banking in Australia*, Reserve Bank of Australia, Sydney, 2010, pp. 20–21.
60   Waterson, 'Chifley', p. 416.
61   McMullin, 'Joseph Benedict Chifley', p. 259.
62   Clyde Sloan, *A History of the Pharmaceutical Benefits Scheme 1947–1992*, Commonwealth of Australia, Australian Government Printing Service, 1995, pp. 2–3.
63   Crisp, *Ben Chifley*, pp. 315–316.
64   Sloan, *A History of the Pharmaceutical Benefits Scheme 1947–1992*, p. 3.
65   ibid., p. 19.
66   Gavin Souter, *Acts of Parliament: A Narrative History of the Senate and House of Representatives Commonwealth of Australia*, Melbourne University Press, Carlton, Victoria, 1988, p. 393.
67   Macintyre, *Australia's Boldest Experiment*, p. 459.
68   Waterson, 'Chifley', pp. 417–418.
69   ibid., p. 417.
70   '3,000 Scholarships under New Federal Scheme', *Canberra Times*, 28 September 1949.

71 Waterson, 'Chifley', p. 417.
72 Souter, *Acts of Parliament*, pp. 382–383.
73 Pitty and Leach, 'Australian nationalism and internationalism', in Boreham, Stokes and Hall (eds), *The Politics of Australian Society*, 2nd edn, p. 96
74 Hawkins, 'Ben Chifley: The True Believer', p. 119.
75 Macintyre, *Australia's Boldest Experiment*, pp. 421–423.
76 Waterson, 'Chifley', p. 419.
77 Sean Turnell, 'Australia's "Employment Approach" to International Postwar Reconstruction: Calling the Bluff of Multilateralism', *History of Economics Review*, no. 36, Summer, 2002, p. 111.
78 Lee, *Search for Security*, pp. 21–22. See 'Macquarie Fight—Declaration of Poll', *National Advocate*, 9 January 1932, p. 2.
79 Tom Valentine, 'The Depression of the 1930s', in Rodney Maddock and Ian W McLean, (eds), *The Australian Economy in the Long Run*, Cambridge University Press, Melbourne, 1987, pp. 62–63.
80 David Meredith and Barrie Dyster, *Australia in the Global Economy: Continuity and Change*, Cambridge University Press, Cambridge, 1999, p. 168.
81 According to David Lee, the 'orthodox interpretation' for the defeat of Chifley's Labor government in the 1949 election was that it was due to issues such as the nationalisation of banking and a fear of communist influence in the party. Lee argues, instead, that it was because of Chifley's 'handling of the general economy' and 'two crises in 1949—the national coal strike and the dollar crisis'. See David Lee, 'The Federal Election: A Reinterpretation', *Australian Journal of Political Science*, vol. 29, 1994, p. 501.
82 Letter, Chifley to CR Brook, 23 November 1950. Papers of LF Crisp, NLA: MS 5243, Series 5, Folder 1.
83 Waterson, 'Chifley', p. 419.
84 ibid., p. 420.
85 Day, *Chifley*, p. 14.
86 ibid., pp. 10–11.
87 ibid., p. 20.
88 *CPD*, HoR, 20 March 1947, p. 1002.
89 AW Martin and Janet Penny, 'The Rural Reconstruction Commission 1943–47', *Australian Journal of Politics and History*, vol. 29, no. 2, 1983, p. 220.
90 Philippe Sands, *Lawless World: Making and Breaking Global Rules*, Penguin Books, UK, 2006, reissued 2016, pp. 8–9; Appendix 1: Atlantic Charter , 14 August 1941, pp. 284–285.
91 JG Crawford, *Australian Trade Policy 1942–1966*, Australian National University Press, Canberra, 1968, p. vii.
92 JB Chifley, *A Rural Policy for Post-War Australia*, Bureau of Agricultural Economics, Canberra, 1946, p. 20.
93 JB Chifley, 'Planning for Peace: 11. International Co-operation', *Sydney Morning Herald*, Thursday, 2 December 1943, p. 4.

94 JB Chifley, 'These Things are Really Worth Fighting For', speech to the annual conference of the NSW branch of the ALP, 12 June 1948, in *Things Worth Fighting For*, pp. 33–34.
95 Waterson, 'Chifley', p. 413.
96 'Labor Unity—The Movement—Not Individuals—Mr. Chifley's Views', *National Advocate* (Bathurst, NSW), 19 December 1933, p. 2.
97 ibid.
98 'National Advocate—Langites Attack—Spirited Reply By Mr Chifley', *National Advocate* (Bathurst, NSW), 1 May 1939, p. 3.
99 *Digest of Decisions and Announcements and Important Speeches by the Prime Minister (The Rt Hon JB Chifley)* (hereafter *DDA*), no. 145, 'Policy—Prime Minister's Speech, June 1949', 12 June 1949, p. 9. NAA: B5459, 145.
100 Warren Osmond, 'Eggleston, Sir Frederic William (1875–1954)', *Australian Dictionary of Biography*, National Centre of Biography, http://adb.anu.edu.au/biography/eggleston-sir-frederic-william-344/text10409 (accessed 20 January 2014).
101 FW Eggleston, *Reflections of an Australian Liberal*, FW Cheshire, Melbourne, 1953.
102 Christine de Matos, *Imposing Peace & Prosperity: Australia, Social Justice and Labour Reform in Occupied Japan*, Australian Scholarly Publishing, North Melbourne, 2008, p. 34.
103 Eggleston, *Reflections of an Australian Liberal*, p. 255.
104 Warren G Osmond, *Frederic Eggleston: An Intellectual in Australian Politics*, Allen & Unwin, North Sydney, 1985, pp. 204–205.
105 ibid., p. xii.
106 Eggleston, *Reflections of an Australian Liberal*, p. 46.
107 ibid., p. 13.
108 ibid., p. 82.
109 ibid., pp. 63–64.
110 AW Stargardt, 'Introduction', in *Things Worth Fighting For*, p. 7.
111 Eggleston, *Reflections of an Australian Liberal*, p. 64.
112 Crisp, *Ben Chifley*, p. 13.
113 ibid., pp. 14–23.
114 ibid., see chapters VI and VII.
115 ibid., pp. 81–82, fn. 7.
116 Day, *Chifley*, p. 284.
117 Sheridan, *Division of Labour*, p. 21.
118 Eggleston, *Reflections of an Australian Liberal*, p. 13.
119 Iriye, *Cultural Internationalism and World Order*, p. 41.
120 *DDA*, No. 144, 'Report to the Nation', 29 May 1949, p. 14, NAA: B5459, 144.
121 de Matos, *Imposing Peace and Prosperity*, p. 31.
122 *DDA*, No. 144, 'Report to the Nation', 29 May 1949, p. 14, NAA: B5459, 144.
123 Sluga, *Internationalism in the Age of Nationalism*, p. 3.
124 Barry Jones, *A Thinking Reed*, Allen & Unwin, Crows Nest, NSW, 2008, p. 143.
125 Chifley, 'These Things are Really Worth Fighting For', in *Things Worth Fighting For*, p. 33.

126 *CPD*, HoR, 11 November 1947, p. 1927.
127 Chifley, 'These Things Are Really Worth Fighting For', in *Things Worth Fighting For*, p. 33.
128 Waterson, 'Chifley', p. 416.
129 *CPD*, HoR, 13 November 1941, p. 427.
130 David Stephens, 'The Effect of the Great Depression on the Federal Labor Governments, 1941–49', *Australian Journal of Politics and History*, vol. XXII, no. 2, 1976, pp. 259–260.
131 Cornish, *The Evolution of Central Banking in Australia*, p. 53
132 Greg Whitwell, *The Treasury Line*, Allen & Unwin, North Sydney, 1986, p. 19.
133 Boris Schedvin, *In Reserve: Central Banking in Australia, 1945–75*, Allen & Unwin, St. Leonards, NSW, 1992, pp.172–174.
134 Selwyn Cornish, *The Evolution of Central Banking in Australia*, Reserve Bank of Australia, Sydney, 2010, p. 54.
135 Lee, *Search for Security*, p. 8.
136 Harold Cox Reports, 11 October 1946, NLA: MS 4554, Folder 2: 1945–1947.
137 *CPD*, HoR, 2 September 1948, p. 56.
138 ibid., p. 58.
139 ibid., p. 63.
140 ibid., p. 64.
141 *DDA*, No. 137, Radio broadcast, 25 July 1948, pp. 8–9. NAA: B5459, 137.
142 ibid.
143 Christopher Waters, 'War, Decolonisation and Postwar Security', p. 125.
144 Lee, *Search for Security*, p. 74.
145 ibid., pp. 73–74.
146 JB Chifley, 'They Think They Can Go Back to the Old Order: Well, They Cannot', speech to the ALP triennial federal conference, 30 September 1948, in *Things Worth Fighting For*, p. 38.
147 Crisp, *Ben Chifley*, p. 6.
148 *CPD*, HoR, 21 March 1930, p. 385.
149 Crisp, *Ben Chifley*, p. 195, fn. 7.
150 '3,000 Scholarships Under New Federal Scheme', *Canberra Times*, 28 September 1949, p. 4.
151 Stewart Cockburn and David Ellyard, *Oliphant: The Life and Times of Sir Mark Oliphant*, Axiom Books, Adelaide, 1981, p. 144.
152 ibid., pp. 145–146.
153 James G Murtagh, 'National Leader of Unstained Political Integrity', *Advocate*, (Melbourne, Vic.) 21 June 1951, p. 3, Papers of L.F. Crisp, NLA: MS 5243, Series 5, Folder 3.
154 ibid.
155 Alan Reid was born in 1914 and grew up in poverty in Liverpool, England. His family migrated to Australia in 1927 to live in Sydney, in Paddington. A member of the ALP until he was expelled in 1957, Reid was one of a select group close to both Curtin and Chifley. He was approached by members of the Labor Party to persuade Chifley to stand for prime minister after Curtin died. Chifley himself encouraged Reid to stand for

politics. Despite his later anti-Labor activities, Reid was close to Chifley, whom he admired tremendously. See Stephen Holt, 'Reid, Alan Douglas (1914–1987)', *Australian Dictionary of Biography*, National Centre of Biography, Australian National University, http://adb.anu.edu.au/biography/reid-alan-douglas-14435 (accessed 11 May 2014).

156 Alan Reid interviewed by Mel Pratt, 1972–1973. NLA: ORAL TRC 121/40, p. 79.
157 'I Drove the Great', Ray Tracy, *Herald*, (Melbourne, Vic.), 25 February, 1950, p. 13.
158 ibid.
159 John Thompson, *Five to Remember*, Lansdowne, Melbourne, 1964, p. 60.
160 *CPD*, HoR, 2 September 1948, p. 65.
161 Breen, 'JB Chifley', p. 239.
162 Waters, 'The Great Debates', p. 53.
163 Donald Kilgour Rodgers interviewed by Mel Pratt, 1971, NLA: ORAL TRC 121/14, pp. 22–24.
164 Dame Enid Lyons, *Among the Carrion Crows*, Rigby, Adelaide, 1972, p. 98.
165 Macintyre, *Australia's Boldest Experiment*, p. 115.
166 Diary of Eilean Giblin, 5 July 1942 in Papers of Lyndhurst F Giblin (1872–1951). NLA: MS 366, Series 6.
167 William Dunk, *They Also Serve*, privately published, Canberra, 1974, p. 13 and p. 117.
168 ibid., pp. 117–118.
169 Letter, JB Chifley to JJ Dedman, 15 December 1943. Papers of LF Crisp. NLA: MS 5243, Series 5, Folder 1.
170 ACT Regional Group, 'Commonwealth Policy Co-ordination', *Public Administration*, vol. 14, December, 1955, p. 198.
171 Whitwell, *The Treasury Line*, p. 22.
172 Paul Hasluck, *The Government and the People 1942–1945*, Australian War Memorial, Canberra, 1970, p. 245.
173 Alan Reid interviewed by Mal Pratt, 1972–1973, NLA: ORAL TRC 121/40, p. 78.
174 Hasluck, *The Government and the People 1942–1945*, p. 245.
175 Whitwell, *The Treasury Line*, p. 22.
176 Alan Reid interviewed by Mel Pratt, 1972–1973, pp. 78–79.
177 Whitwell, *The Treasury Line*, p. 22.
178 Don Whitington, *Twelfth Man?*, Jacaranda Press, Milton, Queensland, 1972, p. 111.
179 Whitwell, *The Treasury Line*, p. 10.
180 Stuart Macintyre, 'The Post-War Reconstruction Project', in Samuel Furphy (ed.), *The Seven Dwarfs and the Age of the Mandarins: Australian Government Administration in the Post-War Reconstruction Era*, Australian National University Press, Canberra, 2015, p. 48.
181 Tim Rowse, *Nugget Coombs: A Reforming Life*, Cambridge University Press, Cambridge, 2002, p. 160.
182 ibid., p. 290.
183 Don Whitington, *The Rulers: Fifteen Years of the Liberals*, rev. edn, Cheshire-Lansdowne, Melbourne, 1965, p. 154.

184 HC 'Nugget' Coombs, Interview by Robin Hughes, Tape 4, 23 January 1992, Film Australia's Australian Biography series, unpaginated. http://www.australianbiography.gov.au/subjects/coombs/ (accessed 12 March 2011); see Crisp, *Ben Chifley*, pp. 383–384, for more on the Catholic Social Movement.
185 Chifley to RW Hayter, 4 September 1950. Papers of LF Crisp, NLA: MS 5243, Series 5, Folder 1.
186 HC 'Nugget' Coombs, Interview by Hughes, Tape 4, 23 January 1992.
187 Whitington, *The Rulers*, p. 154.
188 Waters, 'The Great Debates', p. 53.
189 Christopher Waters, 'Creating a Tradition: The Foreign Policy of the Curtin and Chifley Governments' in David Lee and Christopher Waters (eds), *Evatt to Evans: The Labor Tradition in Australian Foreign Policy*, Allen & Unwin, St Leonards, NSW, 1997, pp. 43–44.
190 David Lee, 'Australia and the Security Council', in Cotton and Lee (eds), *Australia and the United Nations*, p. 72.
191 Waters, 'Creating a Tradition', pp. 44–45.
192 DB Williams, 'Contributions to Agricultural Economics', in LT Evans and JDB Miller (eds), *Policy and Practice; Essays in Honour of Sir John Crawford*, Australian National University Press, Sydney, 1987, pp. 24–25.
193 'Sir John Crawford: Profile of a public servant and economist', *History of Economics Review*. no. 32, Summer, 2000, Supplement, p. 27.
194 JDB Miller, 'The Man', in Evans & Miller, *Policy and Practice*, p. 197.
195 ibid., p. 200.
196 Pitty and Leach, 'Australian Nationalism and Internationalism', p. 99.
197 Crisp, *Ben Chifley*, p. 63.
198 'From the Gallery—Federal Notes—Prime Minister's Appeal, *Sydney Morning Herald*, 12 June 1931, p. 10.
199 'JB Chifley's Defeat—A Tribute from the Islands', *National Advocate* (Bathurst, NSW), 5 February 1932, p. 1.
200 Crisp, *Ben Chifley*, p. 64.
201 *CPD*, HoR, 18 June 1941, p. 118.
202 Crisp, *Ben Chifley*, pp. 147–148.
203 Coombs, *Trial Balance*, p. 6.
204 *CPD*, HoR, 29 October, 1941, p. 30.
205 'Chifley's Eloquent Tribute To Public Servants', *Australian Worker*, (Sydney, NSW) 17 November 1948, pp. 1, 12.
206 ACT Regional Group, 'Commonwealth Policy Co-ordination', pp. 199–200.
207 Letter, Nugget [Coombs] to Crisp, 9 April 1959. Papers of LF Crisp, NLA: MS 5243, Series 5, Folder 11.

Part II
Chifley and Economic Internationalism

Brendan Bell's photograph of the 'Chifley Home' at 10 Busby Street, Bathurst. Thank you to Brenda Bell for his kind permission to publish his photograph, courtesy National Library of Australia.

CHAPTER THREE
Chifley and the Great Depression

A 'drizzling rain fell intermittently' on federal election day in Bathurst on 12 October 1929. It did not, however, dampen the spirits of Ben Chifley's supporters who staffed the Labor pavilion at the front of the court house where voting took place. Their pavilion was a 'scene of bustle and cheery confidence', in contrast to the Nationalist pavilion, which 'wore a dispiriting air'.[1] Chifley's supporters' confidence was rewarded when he secured a record majority in his re-election as the member for Macquarie.[2] This was the greatest victory of his brief political career,[3] which had begun the previous year on 17 November 1928,[4] when he and John Curtin were among the new Labor members elected to federal parliament.[5]

The 1929 election was called after the conservative Bruce-Page Nationalist government was brought down when it had tried to force through its Maritime Industries Bill, under which the federal arbitration court would be abolished, and most of its powers transferred to the states.[6] In this election, Nationalist Prime Minister Stanley Bruce was defeated in his seat of Flinders, and Labor gained forty-six seats from a total of seventy-five in the House of Representatives. Chifley more than trebled his majority in Macquarie, from 3578 in 1928 to 12 078, in an election in which more than 96 per cent of those eligible to vote did so. Chifley even achieved a majority in Katoomba, where his Nationalist opponent CL Dash lived. The editor of the *National*

Advocate, Hilton West, wrote that the way in which 'the electors have rallied to his support indicates that the young politician has won such general confidence that his political defeat is indeed a long way off'.[7] Chifley was a candidate of the 'highest calibre and character,' and, with his youth and enthusiasm, he had already proven to be a 'worthy representative' of Macquarie.[8]

Unfortunately for the Scullin Labor government, it was elected in the month of the Wall Street crash in the United States. The financial and economic chaos that resulted in the wider world would have a devastating impact on the Australian economy. In addition, the Scullin government was hindered in its attempts to address the problems confronting it because of a number of factors. First, it did not control the Senate and it was unwilling to bring about a double dissolution of parliament; second, the deflationary policies favoured by the 'conservative and stiffly orthodox' Sir Robert Gibson, chair of the Commonwealth Bank Board, exacerbated the impact of the depression;[9] third, the Commonwealth Bank Board did not understand the problems confronting them;[10] and fourth, the government's own bitter internal divisions proved insurmountable. The Labor Party would discover it had achieved office, but did not have the power to implement its policies which included proposals for public works to create jobs for the unemployed.

Many of the beliefs and principles that would drive Chifley when he became treasurer and prime minister, were generated during the inter-war years. This is a crucial period in any study of his political life and the development of his ideas on economic and social policy. During this period, Chifley's ongoing interest in international affairs, and the global economic and monetary system can be traced in the speeches he delivered in parliament, to local Bathurst groups and at political meetings. In these speeches, we can see that Chifley's concerns during the inter-war years were neither parochial nor insular: his interests ranged over the global trading system, international finance, disarmament, and reparation and war debts. Chifley's speeches, or 'political rhetoric', reveal his thinking on the world and Australia's place in it during these years. These speeches will be used to trace the origins of Chifley's economic internationalism by examining how World War I and the Great Depression affected him and would influence his later policy decisions in relation to the international economy and its regulation. In this book, I argue that Chifley was an internationalist very early in his political career. Furthermore, he was an economic internationalist, who had believed, since his experience of the Great Depression, that there needed to be 'a very great change in the monetary and financial policy of the world'. A new rules-based economic order needed to be established.[11]

The World Economy in the Inter-war Years

The cost of World War I to Australia in terms of human lives was enormous. According to economic historian, Peter Yule, the number of Australians who served overseas with the AIF was 331 781. From a population of less than 5 million, the number of war dead was 59 342, and 152 171 were wounded. Yule estimates that 'about two-thirds of Australia's soldiers were killed or wounded'. He adds that the real casualty rate could be even higher.[12]

The severity of the war's impact on the Australian economy has not been widely recognised.[13] In 1918–19, Australian 'defence-related expenditure peaked ... at close to twenty per cent of GDP'.[14] The world's economic system was left devastated by the impact of the war. As a 'small and open economy, highly integrated into world labor, capital and commodity markets', Australia's prosperity was dependent on the 'health of the international economic system'. Australian exports at the time were limited by both the 'narrow' mix of commodities produced, and the restricted range of export markets available for its primary goods.[15] Agriculture made up about 90 per cent of Australia's exports, with wool making up more than 40 per cent of the total and wheat up to 20 per cent. Approximately two-thirds of Australia's exports were sold to Britain and to a small number of European countries.[16]

The end of the 1920s saw most countries experience a 'severe economic contraction' after the US stock market crash in October 1929. Primary commodity producing countries, such as Australia, were hit especially hard during this period.[17] With an economy reliant on 'exports and capital inflow', it was inevitable that Australia would be adversely affected by a downturn in the world economy.[18] In 1929, export prices in Australia plummeted by 30 per cent.[19] The huge price falls in Australia's most important agricultural exports, such as wool, together with Australia's unwillingness to abandon the gold standard led to a balance of payments crisis in Australia in the late 1920s.[20] Australia had suspended the gold standard during World War I, but after Britain reinstated it in April 1925, Australia followed suit. Central bankers favoured the return of the gold standard because of a 'long-standing mistrust of the capacity of a system of fiat money, not backed by gold, to deliver economic stability'.[21] Memories of hyperinflation in Germany in the early 1920s created something like 'a neurotic state in the minds of people' in their attitude 'towards inflation and credit expansion'. This had a 'profound effect' on the Commonwealth Bank and conservative parties in Australia.[22] Reinstatement of the gold standard made it very difficult, if not impossible, to introduce expansionary policies in response to the economic depression.[23]

Efforts to revive the post-war world economy were hindered by the fact that the international community was weighed down with war debts and reparation payments.[24] In Australia, the war had been financed by borrowing—both domestically and in London.[25] In addition, the Bruce–Page Nationalist government of 1923 to 1929 had borrowed 'extensively' in the 1920s.[26] This 'blind rush to development'[27] meant that Australia was faced with significant debt-servicing obligations.[28] As well as witnessing a fall in exports, London financial markets ceased to lend to Australia in April 1929,[29] which meant that the government could no longer borrow to honour its substantial interest payments as it had during most of the 1920s.[30] This end of credit was an important factor that 'constrained a more expansionary fiscal policy response' to the depression by governments. Thus, Australian monetary policy was 'tragically tight', as Australia moved further and further into economic depression.[31] The unemployment rate was one of the highest in the world, reaching 30 per cent in the June quarter of 1932[32] and Australians experienced extraordinary hardship during the depression.[33] These were the economic conditions in which the Scullin Labor government took office. The economic catastrophe of the 1930s depression was to scar many Australians, including Chifley.

The Scullin Government

The Scullin cabinet was sworn in on 22 October 1929, a week before the Wall Street crash on 29 October. Many have maintained that, in the history of Australia, no government has been confronted by more challenging economic conditions than the Scullin Labor administration.[34] David Lee, in his biography of the former Nationalist prime minister Stanley Melbourne Bruce, relates the story Bruce himself told, that his election defeat of 1929 was 'one of the most fortunate things that could have happened to us'.[35] Warren Denning, political journalist and confidante of many of the politicians he depicts in his story of the downfall of the Scullin government, described the dire economic situation confronting the newly elected federal government. He speculated that 'ministers might well have wondered whether the victory was worth the cost'. They would have been better off in Opposition, 'leaving their old friends, the enemy to carry that burden which, so they declared, the Nationalists had conceived in the womb of their own inconsequence'. The government had barely taken office when the 'threatening depression, deepened swiftly into menacing reality'. Wool prices plunged and dragged other primary commodities with them. 'Within a matter of months the depression which had been affecting the outside world made its impact felt in this country'.[36]

The Scullin government was not only facing an economic crisis, it also had to deal with a hostile Senate. Although Scullin had 'led Labor to what was then its greatest victory', the Senate was still controlled by the Opposition.[37] In May 1930 the Senate rejected treasurer EG Theodore's Central Reserve Bank Bill.[38] This bill would have established a Central Reserve Bank separate from the Commonwealth Bank, which would then be able to operate in competition with the private banks. The Central Reserve Bank would control the nation's currency, and hold the reserves of the private banks, which would be required to provide the Central Bank with reports on their operations.[39] It would also act as a clearing house. If passed by the Senate, the bill would have carried out the recommendations of the 1922 Genoa international financial conference that all nations should have a central bank for regulating the domestic economy and securing central bank cooperation at the international level. The Senate, however, acting on the advice of Sir Robert Gibson, chair of the Commonwealth Bank Board, rejected the bill.[40] The government's control over the country's financial system was thus rendered ineffective, because of resistance to its policies by the Commonwealth Bank Board and its chair, the 'resolutely conservative' Sir Robert Gibson.[41] According to economic historian, CB Schedvin, Australia's economic and financial policy during the depression was determined primarily by Gibson, who refused to listen to views that did not accord with his own 'narrow orthodoxy'. He was 'a man of exceptional administrative capacity and business acumen, but, with his limited economic and financial knowledge, it was a tragedy that he was able to influence policy to such an extent'.[42]

Leslie Melville, who in 1929 was inaugural professor of economics at the University of Adelaide, and, from 1931, economic adviser to the Commonwealth Bank, agreed.[43] Gibson 'certainly had little knowledge of central banking and certainly enjoyed his histrionic efforts. He liked the power that he had'.[44] According to Melville, the Commonwealth Bank Board had no understanding of the problems they would be facing,[45] indeed, apart from one of its members, the board had very little experience in banking.[46] Economist Douglas Copland was also highly critical of the board, which he described in 1932 as a 'thoroughly incompetent body that will not take advice from its own economic adviser [Melville]'. Furthermore, it was unduly influenced by a chair 'whose authority in the land will have to be upset if Australia is to avoid some very serious economic blunder'.[47]

The Labor government itself was deeply divided between the conservative forces of former Tasmanian premier, Joseph Lyons and his allies, and Jack Beasley and other supporters of the 'populist demagogue' JT (Jack) Lang.[48] Using Money Power rhetoric, Lang was re-elected as premier of New South Wales in October 1930.[49] Characterised by an isolationist mentality, the Money Power was a dominant force in the ideology of the labour movement. It was a theory of 'capitalist finance' in which prevailing 'ideas about nationalism and imperialism, monopoly and democracy, class and race, were woven into an elaborate conspiracy theory'.[50] Lang's xenophobia and 'virulent anti-Semitism' were essential aspects of his concept of the Money Power.[51] Chifley would wage a fierce battle with Jack Lang and proponents of the Money Power ideology throughout the 1930s and the 1940s.

The economic crisis worsened and dissension within the Labor Party increased with the election of Lang. The Scullin government was soon in 'disarray' with 'three mutually hostile camps'. In March 1931 Joseph Lyons and his allies crossed the floor and subsequently lined up with the conservative Opposition. Lyons was installed as leader of the Nationalists in April and, the following month, the party was renamed the United Australia Party.[52] The Lang faction would hive off most of the Labor members from New South Wales, which left Scullin and EG Theodore leading the moderates, which included Chifley.[53] While factional in-fighting prevailed in the Labor Party, economic policies that ranged from orthodox to extreme were developed to prevent further deterioration of the economy. These policies included the 'Lang plan of repudiation'; federal treasurer Ted Theodore's reflationist plan and the orthodox deflationist Premiers' Plan.[54]

Chifley and the Lang Plan

The Lang Plan proposed to repudiate interest owed to British bondholders. It was 'strongly populist with simplistic solutions'.[55] Chifley's attitude towards the Lang Plan reveals much about his early views on Australia's relationship with the world. He vehemently opposed the Lang plan. First, because as a member of the federal Labor caucus, he was bound to do so.[56] He also rejected it on the basis that it was economically irresponsible. According to Chifley: 'Mr Lang spent his time tickling the ears of the unfortunate sections of the people who were themselves so distracted by their position that they were prepared to chase any economic rainbow —and Mr Lang provided a number of those rainbows'.[57]

On 25 March 1931, Chifley argued in parliament that Australia was not alone in facing this, 'its greatest economic crisis'. This was a world-wide emergency[58] in which there was only one certainty—Australia was dependent on world trade. However, the international monetary and financial system was in need of far-reaching reform. According to Chifley, 'neither this nor any other country can get back to prosperity while the present system of monetary control prevails throughout the world'.[59] There was a note of resignation when he concluded his speech by declaring:

Nothing that the Government may do will bring about a return to complete prosperity; the most we can hope for is to pass measures that will tide the country over the present critical period, so that when the general economic position improves, Australia will be able to take advantage of it.[60]

Chifley's argument is supported by economic historian Ian W McLean, in his comprehensive historical study of Australia's economy. McLean argues that during the Great Depression, the Australian government was limited in its ability to 'offset' its 'negative impact ... by virtue of the structure of the economy and its poor state of health prior to the world economic downturn'. Economic recovery in Australia was therefore reliant on 'recovery elsewhere as only then would the external constraints on more rapid domestic growth be relaxed'.[61]

Chifley also opposed the Lang plan on moral grounds. On the night of Monday 17 August 1931, Chifley, as minister for Defence and the member for Macquarie, addressed supporters from the Bathurst branch of the federal Labor Party.[62] He declared: 'No man with any sense of public decency would have stood for such a plan, lowering, as it did, the whole moral tone of the nation'.[63] Chifley pointed out that Jack Lang had been forced to write to the federal government pleading for half a million pounds to pay public servants in New South Wales. Chifley declared that: 'The politician who stands on a public platform and tell[s] the people that anything you can do within your own country will bring complete prosperity back to Australia irrespective of world conditions is either a confidence man or ignorant of the real position'.[64]

This is a significant statement. In it, we can see Chifley's understanding of Australia's interconnectedness with the international economic system, and his recognition that Australia's prosperity was dependent on global trade conditions. Those who advocated a policy of economic isolationism, as Lang did, were either charlatans or ill-informed. Chifley also revealed the extent of his reading on economic issues, when he went on to say that financial experts, who had 'their fingers on the financial pulse of the world' a year ago, have been 'dumb-founded' by the state of the world today. The banks, 'which have been very conservative and even financially callous find that their estimates have simply fallen to the ground owing to the great change in world conditions'.[65] Economist Leslie Melville would later confirm Chifley's statement, declaring that the stock market collapse took most economists by surprise. Melville himself hadn't expected the Wall Street crash to impact so severely on Australia.[66] Until then, most people did not regard the depression as 'really serious'. However, events happened so fast, not only did the stock market crash, but companies also defaulted and the situation deteriorated rapidly.[67]

Theodore's Reflationist Plan

In his early life, Ted Theodore worked as a mine labourer and a prospector. He was an avid reader and founded the Amalgamated Workers' Association of North Queensland. He was its first secretary. When it became part of the Australian Workers' Union in 1913, Theodore was its state president from 1913 to 1916. At the age of 24, Theodore was elected to the Queensland Legislative Assembly as the member for Woothakata (which became Chillagoe in 1912). When TJ Ryan became premier in 1915, Theodore became his deputy and treasurer.[68] In 1927, he moved to New South Wales and won the federal seat of Dalley.[69]

Treasurer Ted Theodore's plan for a three-year strategy for financial stabilisation was presented at a premiers' conference in Canberra in February 1931.[70] The treasurer wanted a £20 million extension of credit[71] by issuing short-term Treasury bills using the Commonwealth Bank as the government's partner. This would allow an increase in public spending which would mean that prices would rise to the levels of 1928 as capital and labour would no longer be idle. Theodore called this 'reflation', an 'antidote to the downward spiral of deflation'.[72] The plan also emphasised the importance of financial prudence in government. However, Theodore's 'reflationary' plan was rejected by Sir Robert Gibson and the Commonwealth Bank Board. They 'refused to entertain any inflationary measure without "reductions in all wages, salaries and allowances, pensions, social service benefits of all kinds, interest and other factors which affect the cost of living"'.[73] A desperate Theodore then set about developing legislation to implement his policy of 'controlled inflation'.[74] This legislation was made up of three bills submitted to the House of Representatives in February 1931: a Bank Interest Bill; a Fiduciary Notes Bill; and a Commonwealth Bank Bill,[75] which would have made the 'Australian note issue legal tender without the backing of gold'.[76]

Theodore's Fiduciary Notes Bill was introduced to the House of Representatives on 17 March 1931. The bill provided for an amount of £18 million, without the backing of gold, to be added to the nation's money supply.[77] Of this amount, £12 million was to go towards 'providing employment on reproductive works', and £6 million would provide relief for wheat-growers.[78] Theodore argued that credit expansion was increasingly favoured by international economists and bankers.[79] In a 'virtuoso performance' in the House of Representatives on 17 March 1931,[80] Theodore quoted John Maynard Keynes and other international economists, such as JA Hobson and Gustav Cassel, together with Australian economists JB Brigden and CH Wickens, to support the Scullin government's policy.[81] He brandished a copy of Keynes' *A Treatise on Money* in the House and declared it would be 'accepted as a textbook that will stand for fifty years as a guide to the intellects of the nations on this subject'.[82] Theodore was the first in Australia to own a copy of the *Treatise*, which had been sent to him from London by the businessman and government adviser WS Robinson.[83] Theodore argued that the deflationary policy that the banks were determined to impose upon the Australian economy would only worsen economic hardship.[84]

The Senate, however, on the advice of Sir Robert Gibson, rejected Theodore's bills, because they 'breached the gold standard', which would lead to 'runaway inflation'.[85] As economic historian, Alex Millmow has noted, 'economists would later find— perhaps to their embarrassment—that some of Theodore's economic vision was ahead of their own'.[86] Leslie Melville argued later, that economically, the Theodore plan made quite good sense.[87] He thought that Theodore's accusation that Australia's monetary policy was mismanaged was 'justified' and agreed that the Commonwealth Bank was at fault. He was convinced that, after Labor's decisive defeat in the Parkes by-election on 31 January 1931, opponents of the Scullin government were confident of its future electoral demise. From then on, political opportunism dominated any consideration of

Theodore's economic policies.[88] In addition, the chair of the Commonwealth Bank Board, Sir Robert Gibson, 'refused to cash any more government cheques'.[89] On 2 April 1931 Gibson sent an ultimatum to Theodore that 'a point is being reached beyond which it would be impossible for the bank to provide further assistance for the Government in the future'.[90]

The Premiers' Plan

The Premiers' Plan was developed at a premiers' conference in May and June 1931.[91] It was devised by economists, DB Copland, dean of the Commerce Faculty at Melbourne University; his colleague LF Giblin; LG Melville, who would become economic adviser to the Commonwealth Bank; and EOG Shann from the University of Adelaide.[92] The plan, which was 'explicitly deflationary', included cuts to wages, salaries and pensions; a reduction in bond interest; and an increase in taxation.[93] Unable to get Commonwealth Bank Board approval for Theodore's plan, and faced with no further loans from the Commonwealth Bank, the Scullin government had the choice of defaulting, resigning or agreeing to the Premiers' Plan.[94] On 6 June 1931, Chifley and the rest of the cabinet, with one exception, reluctantly supported the Premiers' Plan put to them by the prime minister and the treasurer. Cabinet regretted that such extreme economic measures were needed, especially the cuts to pensions, but, after hearing the reasons for the plan, in light of the fact that the country would default the following month, they saw no other alternative.[95] The government then incorporated the Premiers' Plan within its Debt Conversion Agreement Bill.

In his speech to parliament on the second reading of the Debt Conversion Agreement Bill on 25 June 1931, Chifley stated that he agreed with the member for Fremantle, John Curtin, that there would be a 'revolutionary change in the world's monetary policy' within the next decade. That, however, did not solve the 'pressing needs of next month, and the month to follow'. Although he found it 'unpalatable and distasteful', he supported the Premiers' Plan, because if nothing was done, he believed 'national ruin' was unavoidable. Members of parliament, faced with their responsibility towards the nation, should set aside their own personal concerns. In reply to Edwin Yates, the Labor member for Adelaide, who 'airily' claimed he did not care what happened, Chifley replied: 'I do care. I do not want to lose my seat in Parliament. I appreciate the trust placed in me by my constituents, and regard it as an honour to represent them here. I am endeavouring to do the right thing'.[96] Although he risked 'political extinction' by supporting the bill, Chifley thought the plan embodied a solution that would prevent the nation from 'lapsing into chaos'.[97]

On the night of 17 August 1931, Chifley addressed members and supporters of the Bathurst federal ALP. He explained that although it went against their 'every inclination and against the interests of the people they represented', the Scullin government had been forced to adopt the Premiers' Plan. The situation was so dire, the federal government realised in July, there would be a shortage of funds to pay public servants' salaries and pensions. The Scullin cabinet was confronted with 'one of the most colossal tasks in the history of this country'. On taking office, the government had found itself in the position of being unable to borrow from overseas, whereas previous governments had 'lived for 30 years on foreign money'. In the year before the Scullin government came to office, Australia's exports had been totally outstripped by imports, which exceeded exports by £32 million, and national income had fallen from £650 million to £450 million since 1928. Chifley declared:

> All the ranting in the world could not set aside the fact that the national income had fallen to the extent of £200,000,000 a year, and the fact that loan money had been stopped; that our primary products sold in foreign markets had brought the country £60,000,000 a year less than before and that the value of our products, even if a larger quantity were exported would return only 54 per cent. of their former value. Until there was an upward trend in world prices for primary products we could not but hope to have a hard road on which to travel. Whatever might be said for any Plan, the basis of prosperity in this country had always rested on the sale of primary products in other countries.[98]

Chifley went on to say that the government had continued to meet its obligations, but unfortunately it became evident that a rapid increase in world prices was not likely. The Commonwealth Bank had indicated it would not finance the government by more than £25 million, an amount that had already been reached. The government was also faced with a short-term debt of £38,000,000 in London. The Premiers' Plan had been developed to meet the problems caused by these government deficits, which would no longer be supported further by the banks. Chifley added:

> Undoubtedly the Premiers' Plan struck a blow at some of the things which Labor held dear ... but the men who comprised the conference looked right down into the heart of Australia's troubles and evolved that plan as offering some solution, upon which they could all agree, to the problems facing this country.[99]

Chifley argued that, although the reasons for the present dire situation included World War I, which had cost £5,000 million together with the retention of the gold standard, this did not address the fact that the government was two weeks away from defaulting on its debts. He declared:

> It was not claimed ... that the Premiers' Plan would bring immediate prosperity and find work for everyone. It could not be said that it would put half the unemployed back into jobs, but it was hoped that such would be the case ... All we do know ... is that it will save the country from lapsing into complete chaos, when every principle of Labor and everything the people stand for would crash to the ground, when arbitration, pensions, and all social services would be lost. We hope that the plan will bring stability in its train ... whether we succeed or not we will know in our hearts that we have saved Australia from the degradation of having developed into a state of revolution and chaos as far as the mass of the people are concerned.[100]

In November 1931 the Scullin government fell, after the Langites, led by Jack Beasley, crossed the floor to vote with the United Australia Party.[101] In the federal election held in December 1931, the Labor government was 'routed', retaining a mere fourteen seats in the House of Representatives.[102]

Out of Office

In 1932 Chifley was out of office. Chifley had no parliamentary superannuation, but he did have his railway superannuation.[103] He had an income from his shares and his director's fees from the *National Advocate*. He administered his father-in-law's estate and earned commissions as an adviser and agent in business and property transactions.[104] Elizabeth's mother also came to live in the Chifley's house which meant that the McKenzie home could be rented out.[105] During the inter-war period, he maintained his interest in international affairs, and continued to observe the way in which the international economic and financial system interconnected with politics and society. His friendship with Theodore, who was, in Chifley's estimation, 'the best financial brain that this Parliament has ever known', continued,[106] and the former train driver and mine worker would meet for dinner and discussion throughout the years from 1932 to 1935.[107]

Chifley's Busby Street home in Bathurst was full of books on economics, accountancy and public finance,[108] including the latest in British political and economic thought.[109] In addition, he followed the various international conferences on disarmament, and economic and financial issues through reports in the *National Advocate*. Amidst racing results, local crime stories, gruesome murders and suicides brought on by the despair wrought by unemployment and homelessness during the depression, this Bathurst newspaper contained extensive coverage of international events, conferences and official reports. It included world news, such as the rise of fascism in Germany and Austria, and reports of German 'bonfires of protest' against the Treaty of Versailles, that 'blazed on every hilltop on Germany's eastern and western frontiers'.[110] It covered events in Asia, including the many outbreaks of civil war in China,[111] and the hostilities between China and Russia.[112] The campaign by Indian nationalists—led by activist Jawaharlal Nehru—to overthrow British imperialism was reported,[113] together with articles on Mahatma Gandhi's civil disobedience campaigns and his belief that the 'political salvation of India' could only come about through 'a creed of non-violence'.[114] There were extensive accounts of the Japanese invasion of Manchuria in September 1931.[115]

Editorials commented on overseas publications, such as the Macmillan Report into the economic situation in Britain.[116] The paper also reported the opinions of prominent economists on the 'chronic' state of the world economic system. In September 1931 the editorial noted that one of the world's 'great economists', John Maynard Keynes, had written about the Depression: 'We have managed to get into a hopeless muddle, having seriously erred in our manipulation [of a] sensitive piece of machinery, the working of which we do not understand'.[117]

Chifley also applied himself to consideration of this 'sensitive piece of machinery'. Throughout the inter-war years, a number of international conferences were held in attempts to revive the world economy and resolve the contentious issues of disarmament, war debts, and reparation payments. Many of these conferences were covered in the *National Advocate*. The paper was also an outlet through which Chifley's views on international affairs could be conveyed. As a former federal minister of Defence and assistant to the treasurer, he was a man of great influence in his community, considered to be an expert on international finance and world problems. Because of this, he was in great demand as a speaker by community groups in Bathurst. The *National Advocate* reported many of the speeches that Chifley gave to local community and political groups on the various international conferences held in the inter-war years. Chifley's ongoing interest in international affairs is very evident in his speeches to these groups. Not only was he interested in international efforts to revive the world economy, he was concerned with issues of arbitration, security and disarmament which had become the catchcry of the era throughout the inter–war years.[118]

World Disarmament Conference, February 1932

Attempts to implement disarmament policies in the inter-war years proved to be extraordinarily difficult. In 1931 Chifley was a signatory to a petition circulated by the Women's International League for Peace and Freedom, which was conducting a worldwide 'peace push' in which petitions calling for total and universal disarmament were circulated in at least forty countries and in eighteen languages. In Australia 112 000 signatures were collected. The federal treasurer, EG Theodore, and others from all sides of politics were some of the prominent citizens who lent their names to publicise the disarmament campaign. Other signatories included Sir John Monash; the Rev. JW Burton, president of the New South Wales Methodist conference; Sir Harrison Moore, professor of law at the University of Melbourne;[119] economist Professor Douglas Copland; and EC Dyason, president of the Economic Society of Australia and New Zealand.[120] The petition was presented at the opening of the League of Nations World Disarmament Conference in Geneva on 2 February 1932.[121] In an address to the Advance Bathurst League in October 1932, Chifley told his audience that it was unfortunate that the League of Nations World Disarmament Conference convened in Geneva had proven to be, at least for the present, a total failure. The world had not learnt a lesson from the last war, in which an enormous amount of wealth had been 'used up almost entirely for destructive purposes'. The world's nations were still spending £500 million a year on 'armaments and preparations for war'—more than was spent before the last war. Unfortunately, Chifley said, there was 'a martial spirit abroad in the world'.[122] The conference continued for two years, only to end in failure.[123]

Reparations Conference in Lausanne, June 1932

With the depression deepening, great hopes were held for a special conference to discuss Germany's reparations payments and war debts, which was convened in Lausanne in Switzerland in June 1932.[124] Chifley's speech at a Bathurst Rotarians luncheon on 19 July, on the 'influence on world economics' of the recent Lausanne conference, was given front-page coverage in the *National Advocate*. The newspaper introduced Chifley as a 'great student of humanity', whose 'wide knowledge of international affairs enabled him to speak with authority on present world problems, and he was listened to with intense interest'. In this speech, Chifley discussed both the Dawes and the Young Plans—previous attempts to solve the 'question of Germany's reparations payments'.[125] Although it was accepted at Lausanne that Germany was unable to pay reparations,[126] Chifley argued it would be a mistake to anticipate any instant benefits from the conference, but said it was a small step in the journey to 'a brighter and better world'. He warned, however, that the problem of war debts owed by Britain and European countries, such as France and Italy, had not been resolved at the Lausanne conference. This was the 'outstanding problem of Europe at the present time'. Chifley then spoke about the need for fundamental change to the world's economic system to end the present depression in which 36 million men in the world were unemployed. He declared he was a 'definite protagonist of a great change ... not by revolutionary methods', but 'in an orderly honest, common-sense way'.

Chifley also spoke about the British Imperial conference shortly to be held in Ottawa, Canada. He was hopeful that policy would be formulated there 'in regard to matters outside preferential tariffs which might ultimately bring to the world some definite benefits at a not too distant date'. He believed currency and exchange reform were essential, and hoped this would occur at Ottawa. He dismissed the possibility of Australia gaining benefits from further preferential trade—not even 10 per cent of Australian export trade would benefit, as commodities such as wool, wheat and metals had no chance of obtaining preferences at Ottawa. The existing policy framework needed to be adjusted in order to cope with the economic crisis. Chifley was hopeful that the empire would be able to take to the forthcoming world economic conference—convened by the United Kingdom and the United States—a cohesive and united proposal of the economic changes that were necessary for the welfare of the whole world.[127] However, Chifley was to be disappointed.

The Imperial Economic Conference, Ottawa, July 1932

Although most accounts of the Imperial Economic Conference, which met in Ottawa, Canada, from 21 July 1932 to 20 August 1932,[128] document a retreat into protectionism by the United Kingdom, it was 'about more than trade, it was also about money'. It was an opportunity for those countries in the sterling area to attempt to influence British monetary policy.[129] However, most accounts of Ottawa have focused on the agreement that came out of the conference, whereby preferential treatment was provided to those within the British imperial trade system by lowering tariffs.[130] As Chifley predicted, wool did not gain any benefit from the Ottawa agreement.[131] The leader of the

Australian delegation, former Australian prime minister Stanley Melbourne Bruce, sought concessions for a number of goods, but not for the major Australian commodities of wool and wheat. This was because the Empire produced more wool and wheat than it could consume.[132]

In his speech to the Advance Bathurst League later that year, on 18 October 1932, Chifley declared there had been hopes for monetary reform within the empire, but, 'in this most important matter the Conference had merely passed a few pious resolutions'.[133] This was also the opinion of economist Leslie Melville, adviser to Stanley Bruce at the conference. In a much later interview, Melville noted that the two main issues at Ottawa were imperial preference and monetary proposals.[134] There was a pressing need for an easing of monetary policy within the empire; the consequences of which would be an 'international revival of economic activity', through which Australia, as a trading nation, would benefit. According to Melville, the proposals regarding monetary policy were of much greater importance—the preferences issue was 'a bit of a side-show'. Australia, however, was unable to make any progress in persuading the British of the need for a relaxation of monetary policy to 'raise prices by making more credit available and on better terms'. Melville was extremely disappointed by Ottawa. 'We didn't get anything. We drew up something, but it didn't break any ice. Ottawa was quite a disappointment'.[135]

The League of Nations Gold Delegation's Report, 1932

During his time out of office, Chifley also kept abreast of reports from the League of Nations, the post-war international organisation that held the hopes of so many who had suffered through World War I and the economic chaos of the Great Depression. In his speech to the Advance Bathurst League in October 1932, Chifley declared that, in order to restore prosperity to the world, it was agreed there 'should be a determined co-operative effort by the nations of the world to restore price levels'. There was, however, a 'wide diversity of opinion' on the methods to be adopted. Chifley then cited the 'most authoritative verdict' on this question, the League of Nations Finance Committee, which had recently published both a majority and a minority report on this matter.[136] Three years previously, in June

1929, the committee had appointed a subcommittee to inquire into the reasons for the instability in the purchasing power of gold and its effect on the world's economies.[137] This decision reflected concerns about the ongoing viability of the international gold standard exchange system. The committee became known as the Gold Delegation.[138] Because of the enormous changes in the economic and financial situation of the world, the committee's terms of reference were extended to consider the circumstances that had led to the present world crisis.[139] The final report was published in June 1932.[140]

The Gold Delegation's majority report recommended that countries should remain on the gold standard, but that gold should be 'redistributed' throughout the world.[141] This very orthodox approach, according to historians of the period, Patricia Clavin and Jens-Wilhelm Wessels, was a passive acceptance that economic depressions were 'essentially unavoidable in the capitalist system' and a belief that the gold standard was indispensable.[142] Chifley's opinion, however, was that 'the gold standard was an illusion', intended to create a sense that the currency was sound. He noted that 'the leading economists of the world believed that the restoration of the gold standard in ten of the great countries of the world had been responsible for the depression to a larger extent than even the war itself'.[143]

The previous year, he had said in a speech to the Bathurst federal ALP branch, that he believed the gold standard as back-up for paper currency was a 'fetish' and it would be dispensed with at some stage.[144] According to Chifley, all those nations that abandoned the gold standard during the war had returned to it by 1926–1927, which led to 'economic paralysis' in the world's economies. Since then, the purchasing power of gold had grown, with the result that industries 'forced to meet commitments in terms of gold' were increasingly burdened, which was a major factor in the 'present world-wide depression'.[145]

The Gold Delegation's minority report, according to Chifley, was of a 'more radical character', which met 'entirely' with his 'own personal approval'. This report said that the solution involved 'the greater expansion of credit by means of central banks or some form of national control by all gold countries of the world'. According to the report, there was 'no reason to believe that such expansion of credit should get out of control'. Chifley declared: 'In these brief sentences is a world of wisdom'. This expansion of credit would provide a solution to the problem of the collapse in world prices, a way of building up to 1927–1928 price levels and the 'restoration of world prosperity'.[146] As reported in the *National Advocate*, Chifley told a reunion of the Bathurst branch of the Municipal and Shire Employees' Union two months later:

> The spirit of avarice and crass stupidity of the banks had been responsible for a policy of deflation which had crucified the world, and while he did not suggest wild inflation was the cure, it was apparent that the monetary system had advanced like a tortoise compared with the speed which other aspects of life had assumed'.[147]

Although the minority group's report had challenged the orthodoxy of the gold standard, the capacity to envision 'an international system of cooperation and control', such as that proposed in the later Bretton Woods Agreement, was 'beyond its imagination'.[148] In addition, the Gold Delegation's reports revealed the deep divide over monetary policy among the great powers, which 'made it impossible to effect international cooperation in the months and years to come'.[149] It is significant that the report and the data it had collected were widely circulated. The collection of data on gold supply and prices marked the first time that the 'system's global operations' had been mapped. This data was later used by the creators of the Bretton Woods system.[150] Patricia Clavin and Jens-Wilhelm Wessels argue that 'history has validated the view of the minority members', who had demonstrated that 'persistent deflation was incompatible with the changing nature of complex, modern national economies'.[151] Lessons learnt from the failure of the Gold Delegation, plus the enormous amount of economic data collected and published, played a significant role in 'the reconfiguration of international financial relations after 1940'.[152] Chifley was one of those politicians who later benefited from this vast array of information.

The World Monetary and Economic Conference, June 1933

The World Monetary and Economic Conference was the 'defining event in international economic and financial relations of the decade', according to League of Nations historian, Patricia Clavin.[153] The League had been called on to convene an international monetary and economic conference to consider global problems such as 'exchange-rate stability, deflation, tariffs and external debt'. In June 1933, in the midst of the depression, the leading industrial nations of the world attended the conference in London.[154] It was hoped that international economic collaboration could be achieved to solve these problems. Chifley had great expectations of the conference. In July 1932, in a speech to the Bathurst Rotarians, he had spoken of his hope that policies to establish the economic changes necessary for the welfare of the whole world would eventuate there.[155] Chifley—who favoured the cancellation of all war debts world-wide—hoped that the outcomes of the conference would include a 'scaling down' of war debts owed by the 'stricken nations of Europe ... unable to meet the commitments imposed upon them by previous agreements'.[156] However, Chifley and others who hoped for an international solution to the problems facing the world economy were once again disappointed. The 'momentous failure' of the conference led to 'even greater monetary instability, stagnant trade' and a deepening of the depression, all of which contributed to the rise of fascism in Germany and eventually led to war.[157] The World Monetary and Economic Conference was the last hope to find a multilateral solution to the world's economic problems before the outbreak of World War II.[158]

Chifley's speeches in parliament, to local groups and at political meetings provide a rich resource to trace the development of his views on economic policy and Australia's place in the world. In 1931 he had been somewhat equivocal in his support for Theodore's reflationary plan and had reluctantly accepted the deflationary Premiers' Plan. During his time out of office, he greatly extended his reading of finance and economics; he also followed the major international conferences and read the published reports of the League of Nations. He understood that great changes in the global economy were needed to ensure world prosperity. In 1932, he supported the League of Nations Gold Delegation's minority report, which had urged 'greater expansion of credit by means of central banks'.[159] He also observed how other leaders were addressing the economic chaos of the Great Depression.

In September 1933 Chifley addressed the Methodist Men's Brotherhood in Bathurst on 'The Roosevelt Plan and What it Aims to Achieve'. He was widely acknowledged as a 'student of economics', who had followed this issue 'closely' and could be 'relied upon to throw a great deal of light on the subject'.[160] In his address on what he called 'the American re-construction plan', Chifley provided a detailed description and analysis of Roosevelt's National Recovery and Farm Relief bills. His 'comprehensive grip of his subject and his able handling of its intricacies' impressed the audience greatly.[161] In response to many requests, a public forum was held in March the following year, in which Chifley again 'dealt exhaustively' with the Roosevelt plan. During this speech he noted that President Franklin Delano Roosevelt had provided new hope for the American people who were more supportive of him than when he was first elected in 1932. 'From a state of chaos they had at last seen the possibility of a new economic order in that country'. Chifley acknowledged that 'complete success had not been achieved', but Roosevelt had proven himself to be 'the most courageous statesman in the world to-day. Without any attempt at confiscation or repudiation he had set out to completely revolutionise the economic machine of America and had met with success in the face of insuperable obstacles from the vested interests of the country'.[162]

By August 1934 it seems that Chifley's views had evolved to a much greater acceptance of the need for credit expansion in a period of economic depression. As president of the New South Wales federal branch of the Australian Labor Party, he opened the party's federal election campaign that year. In this speech, broadcast on radio, he argued that the 'world's clearest thinkers' recognise that in an economic depression, 'wise' government spending on public works was the 'only true policy' to pursue in order to achieve economic recovery.[163] By the mid 1930s, Chifley's expertise in international finance and world affairs had developed to such an extent that he was widely respected as an expert in these matters. He was about to extend his education further, through the Royal Commission into the Monetary and Banking Systems in Australia.

Royal Commission into the Monetary and Banking Systems, 1935–1937

In 1935 Chifley was given the opportunity to contribute to banking and monetary reform in Australia with his appointment as a commissioner on the Royal Commission into the Monetary and Banking Systems in Operation in Australia (1935–1937).[164] As a member of the Scullin Labor government from 1929 to 1931, Chifley had seen its efforts to relieve unemployment and revive business activity thwarted by the Commonwealth Bank Board, its chair Sir Robert Gibson and the private trading banks.[165] During this period any legislative attempts to develop central bank functions for the Commonwealth Bank were blocked by the anti-Labor Senate. Chifley and the Labor Party were 'understandably bitter' about the 'economic and political roles' that the banks played in the ongoing 'catastrophe' of the depression and the impact this had on the Scullin government.[166]

In March 1933 Scullin was given approval by the Labor caucus to support a royal commission into banking in Australia, and he made this a campaign issue in the 1934 federal election. The Country Party, led by Earle Page, also campaigned for a royal commission. Nearing the end of the election campaign, Prime Minister Joe Lyons reluctantly agreed that the United Australia Party, if re-elected, would appoint a royal commission. After he was returned to office, Lyons was slow to honour his election promise,[167] and it was not until 15 November 1935 that the commissioners were appointed. The first public session was held in Melbourne on 15 January 1936, when the commission began hearing oral evidence. It held 105 sessions in Sydney, Melbourne, Brisbane, Adelaide, Perth, Hobart and Launceston, and heard evidence from 200 witnesses. The commission also received numerous written submissions from individuals and organisations.[168]

The commissioners appointed included the chair, Justice John Mellis Napier, a judge of the Supreme Court of South Australia; Joseph Palmer Abbott, a grazier from New England and later federal Country Party member for New England; Richard Charles Mills, professor of economics at the University of Sydney; Edwin Van-der-vord Nixon, a leading Melbourne accountant; Henry Arthur Pitt, Director of Finance in the Victorian Treasury,[169] who was president of the Victorian branch of the Economic Society; and Chifley.[170] The two volumes of evidence of the commission were published in 1936, and these volumes and the minority reports, including Chifley's, were presented to parliament in July 1937.[171]

Many in the labour movement were sceptical about the effectiveness of the royal commission. On 11 January 1935 the 'Langite' newspaper, *Labor Daily*, had written that the Lyons government would be able to control the commission by 'selective appointments', and its terms of reference would be limited. Federal politicians, Jack Beasley and Eddie Ward, members of Lang Labor, charged that any commission appointed by the United Australia Party and the Country Party government would ensure that its findings would not be detrimental to Australian or foreign banks.[172] Chifley, himself, observed in 1945 that some of his Labor colleagues suggested that he was appointed a commissioner because the Lyons government thought he would advocate a moderate Labor view.[173] Historian Peter Love argues, however: 'Whatever their original expectations, Chifley turned out to be a remarkably effective spokesman for his party'.[174] Enid Lyons, whose husband, Prime Minister Joe Lyons, appointed him commissioner, said: 'Both his knowledge of finance and the analytical habit of his mind fitted him admirably for such a task'.[175] Richard Casey, who was treasurer in the Lyons government at the time, later said, somewhat churlishly, that he had brought 'him [Chifley] off the street, not for the reason that he had any prior knowledge of banking, because I think that at that stage the right honourable gentleman did not know a bank from a public convenience'.[176]

In his study on the development of central banking in Australia, CB Schedvin wrote that the royal commission was the 'most competent economic investigation that had been conducted in Australia', and Chifley and the economist Professor Richard Charles Mills were the 'two most influential ordinary members'.[177] According to economist SJ Butlin, both Mills and Chifley were seen as 'safe' appointments to the commission. He notes, however, that 'neither lived up to such intentions. The Evidence, which has never had the attention its great value merits, shows them as quietly but pertinaciously pursuing the important questions'.[178]

The friendship that developed between the two men was very obvious.[179] An economist and historian, Mills was a man of 'quiet and studious demeanour, but warmly and generously concerned with social issues'.[180] In the 1930s he was a mentor to an exceptional group of intellectuals,[181] including HC Coombs and JG (Jock) Phillips.[182] While Mills prepared the commission's questionnaire that was sent to the trading banks, he and Chifley were responsible for drawing up the wide-ranging questionnaire that economists and the other banks were required to complete.[183] As economic historian, Alex Millmow notes in his study of the influential role that Australian economists played in government policy-making during the period 1929–1939, setting the questionnaires allowed Mills and Chifley to set the agenda for the commission. A complex set of questions that revealed an interest in domestic and international economic matters was developed by the two men. Although considered 'safe' appointments, Chifley and Mills and the commission's research assistant and economist, Jock Phillips, an economics graduate from the University of Sydney, favoured a strong and effective central bank to provide sound economic management. This view was not at first shared by the chair, Justice Napier, nor by Nixon and Abbott. Mills also drafted the final report,[184] and his influence is very evident throughout.[185] Chifley was also 'vitally important in the drafting process, and was a strong advocate of the recommendations for additional central bank powers', according to Phillips.[186]

During his time as commissioner, Chifley took every opportunity to further extend his knowledge of economics and finance. As Crisp recounts: 'At meals, in trains, in walks through the cities where evidence was taken, Chifley hammered Mills with questions and discussion'. During the early stages of the hearings, Chifley had been inclined to unsettle some of the commissioners. Mills is recorded as challenging Chifley saying: 'I know your tactics; you're out to scare us and then get us eating out of your hand'. However, by the end of the hearings, according to Mills, 'all the members were happy to claim they were friends of Chifley'.[187] Both men were familiar with Keynesian economics. In 1925, in Mills and FC Benham's *The Principles of Money, Banking, and Foreign Exchange, and their Application to Australia*, Keynes was acknowledged as a major influence. Mills' textbook *Money*, co-authored with E. Ronald Walker, was published in 1935; its enduring popularity was attributed to the fact that it was the first Australian publication putting forward Keynes' theories.[188] We have also seen that Chifley was well aware of Keynesian economic thought, through his association with Treasurer Ted Theodore, and the fact that the ideas of John Maynard Keynes had reached Bathurst as early as September 1931.

'Nugget' Coombs, who was assistant economist at the Commonwealth Bank under Leslie Melville, assisted in preparing the submission the bank put to the royal commission. During this period, he was also involved in discussions at the University of Sydney with Professor Mills and others, including Jock Phillips. According to Coombs, these discussions involved 'theoretical developments which were to influence both the content of the Commission's report and the thinking of JB Chifley' in his role as commissioner.[189] Coombs wrote that Chifley and Mills were 'firm friends' and 'Mills was the only person to whom Chifley's door was always open,whatever the pressures upon him.[190] Indeed, many have attributed Chifley's knowledge and understanding of economic theory and high finance solely to the influence of Mills during their time as commissioners on the royal commission. However, in a letter to Crisp, in response to his request for information about Chifley, Mills denied this.[191] Crisp was also informed that the chair of the commission, Justice Napier, when asked what sort of team he had, had replied, 'very good: the outstanding member is the labour man Chifley. He has a remarkable grip on high finance'.[192] Former commissioner HA Pitt wrote to Chifley in August 1945 to congratulate him when he became prime minister, writing:

> The happy association I enjoyed with you was founded not merely on personal friendship but largely on the knowledge that your qualifications for leadership must be recognised—that was agreed by all members of our Commission ... When a very prominent member of another party asked how I viewed your appointment [as Prime Minister], I told him it was the worst thing that could have happened to his party, and quickly convinced him that this was the case.[193]

It seems that Chifley's early knowledge of economics and finance and his leadership skills in this area have been greatly underestimated.

After a comprehensive and detailed inquiry, the royal commission presented a report which all members signed. There were some specific dissenting notes, but the report was in general accepted. The most contentious of the commission's proposals was that the federal parliament should be 'ultimately responsible for monetary policy' and the government in power at the time 'is the executive of the Parliament'.[194] The commission's report was a 'vindication' of the Scullin government's policies and a long overdue criticism of Sir Robert Gibson and the Commonwealth Bank Board.[195] The report then considered the appropriate policy for governments to follow in an economic depression—which was essentially a classic Keynesian response to a severe economic downturn. The report noted that governments should

> expand public works, refrain from increasing taxation, and avoid a general contraction of government expenditure, even although deficits are incurred. When conditions have improved as private enterprise revives and full employment is approached, the proper policy is to contract public works expenditure, maintain or increase taxation, budget for surpluses, and reduce the debt which has been incurred through the depression policy. We emphasize the view that the policy which we have outlined above is one requiring action in prosperous times, as well as in times of depression.[196]

The commission recommended that the best banking system for Australia was one in which private banks continued to function, but under greater control of a strong central bank.[197] The only significant dissenting report was from Chifley who, though he approved of most of the recommendations as 'interim measures', was 'convinced that a much more comprehensive control of banking must ultimately be necessary in the public interest'.[198] Chifley, in his minority report, stated: 'Contrary to what should be expected in an effective banking system the banks have been capable of creating boom conditions; and they have been ineffective in checking or minimizing a depression'.[199] In the years leading to a depression, banks encourage 'unhealthy economic conditions by unsound advancing of credit', but, while in the throes of depression, banks adopt 'a policy of contraction which intensifies the Evil'.[200] This statement resonates today in light of the recent global financial crisis, the worst since the Great Depression of the 1930s. In his report, Chifley presented a 'vigorous and cogent argument for bank nationalisation and other related reforms to the structure of the banking system'.[201] According to Chifley, banking was different to all other forms of business. The decisions made by banks affected every facet of the lives of Australians, therefore, a 'banking policy should have one aim—service for the general good of the community'.[202]

Chifley's opinion on the proceedings of the royal commission was widely sought by the Bathurst community. In October 1937 he agreed to give a series of lectures on the banking commission to the Bathurst Community Education Group.[203] On 30 November 1937, Chifley addressed the group, the first public occasion in Bathurst in which he spoke about the important work of the commission.[204] The next year, in February 1938, Chifley addressed the Bathurst Apex Club on the work of the royal commission. In his address, Chifley said that the purpose of the commission was to seek to understand if the Australian banking system had 'functioned in the best interests of the people' since the economic crisis of 1893. It was said that the banks had profited too much at the expense of the Australian community. Chifley argued:

> the principles of an economic system should aim to make the best possible uses of the nation's resources, and the banking system, as a part of the economic system, should have the same object. [205]

The commission had carried out an extensive inquiry into all aspects of the banking system and arrived at a number of recommendations and judgements. It found that 'undue profits were made prior to 1930'. Although the commission found that the 1930s depression was not caused by the banks, 'it was the Commission's opinion that the banks could have mitigated the hardships suffered by the people during the slump'. The commission found: 'In the event of depression, the Commonwealth Bank should expand credit. One way being to advance monies to Governments for public works'. In addition, the 'ideal system for the future according to the Commission, was that the Commonwealth Bank should be constituted a central bank owned by the Government which would control its policy, the trading banks carrying out whatever policy was formulated'.[206]

This was a position that Chifley had long held. In 1934, as leader of the federal New South Wales Labor Party, he had argued at a campaign meeting for a 'full and complete investigation and reform' of Australia's banking and financial system. The 'control of finance purely for profit has been the main evil in producing the appalling conditions' of the depression. He proposed that the Commonwealth Bank should be divided into two sections. A central reserve bank would control the note issue, exchange, treasury bills, and other matters not connected with the concerns of ordinary banking. The second section would compete in all areas to do with commercial banking business. All organisations and individuals receiving federal government loans or advances would be required to bank with the Commonwealth Bank. Against demands that there should be no change to Australia's 'economic life', Chifley told his large audience:

> Our economic laws must change with the changing needs of mankind—to stagnate is to perish. A suffering people, permeated with bitterness and despair, cry aloud for the things which are all around them, but which an obsolete economic system denies them.[207]

On 31 May 1938, Chifley addressed the Bathurst Rotary Club on the royal commission's majority report, from which he had dissented in a number of decisions. The commission found that the banking system had failed to 'avert the depression' and if, in 1929, at the start of the depression, proper measures had been taken—mainly by the Commonwealth Bank—to expand credit, the impact of the depression could have been lessened. Furthermore, in 1930, the banks had increased interest rates to check any further expansion—this was a 'mistaken policy'. With unemployment growing and 'depression creeping over the community', the Commonwealth Bank, together with the private banks, added 'more weight to the back' of those 'struggling' to make a living. Chifley was pleased that the present treasurer had said that the banking commission's report would be seen as a 'text-book on the banking system in Australia'. He himself thought that the report was 'very valuable'—it was a 'very thorough and conscientious investigation of the system'. At the end of his address, he was asked to give a lecture on his minority report to the Rotary Club at a later date, which he agreed to do.[208]

On 24 June 1938, the *National Advocate* reported that, in his speech to the Bathurst Rotary Club on his minority report, Chifley declared that the role the monetary banking system played in the community was much too important to be limited solely to profit-making. In this speech, Chifley emphasised the significance of the banking system to the economic life of the nation:

> So important is it in the economic functions of our system, that it represents to civilization what the heart represents to the human body ... The operation of the monetary system is reflected right throughout every section of the community. I hold that, as a thing influencing the lives of millions of people who do not understand what it does or how it does it, it is too important to be devoted to any other purpose than purely for the good of the whole of the community in which it operates. [209]

Chifley, like Theodore, viewed the problem inherent in the banking system as 'flowing not so much from conspiratorial manipulation by the banks, as from the profit imperative itself'.[210] The best banking system was one that did not include the profit motive, one which was 'under national control', in which the central bank controlled the volume of credit and currency.[211]

Labor did very well in the commission's report, which criticised the 'orthodox policy' of 1930–1932. The Scullin government's economic policy, which had been rejected by the Senate, was legitimised and given authority, because of the support of the royal commission, which had been appointed by Labor's ideological opponents. The Scullin government was also vindicated by the commission's recommendation that the federal government should have ultimate authority over any Commonwealth Bank board.[212] The Lyons government, however, treated the recommendations of the royal commission with 'benign neglect'. The government drafted certain bills proposing minimal changes to the monetary system, but these were scrapped when the private banks objected.[213] As Crisp notes, neither the Lyons nor the Menzies governments made any progress in implementing the commission's proposals in the period before war began in 1939. He attributes this to the influence of the private banks who fought a 'vigorous' campaign in opposition to any reforms to the banking system.[214] According to Peter Groenewegen and Bruce McFarlane, all of the major recommendations proposed in the royal commission's report were shelved until Chifley became treasurer in the Curtin government and the banking acts were legislated in 1945, in which some 'teeth' were added to the royal commission's original proposals.[215]

Conclusion

The inter-war years are crucial in understanding the development of Chifley's economic and social ideas. As he would later reflect, the depression constituted 'one of the saddest chapters in the economic history' of Australia. The 'misery, suffering and starvation' experienced in the depression could have been avoided if there had been 'a wise financial and economic administration', unconstrained by the deflationary policies favoured by an unelected Commonwealth Bank Board and chair, who refused to fund the elected government in its efforts to provide relief work for the unemployed and deliver assistance for farmers. And yet, some years later, as Chifley pointed out, 'hundreds of millions of pounds were found for the purposes of war'.[216] The effects of the depression seared itself into Chifley's soul, so much so, that at the time of his death, he still kept in his study a copy of EOG Shann and Douglas Copland's collection of original documents relating to economic policy in the depression, *The Battle of the Plans: Documents Relating to the Premiers' Conference, May 25th to June 11th 1931*.[217]

The human and material cost of World War I appalled Chifley. As he told the Advance Bathurst League in October 1932, lessons had not been learnt from the war, in which an enormous amount of wealth had been 'used up almost entirely for destructive purposes'.[218] He was horrified at the prospect of another war. In Chifley's fierce response to the Bruce–Page government's attempt to abolish the federal Arbitration Court, we can see his commitment to the principles of arbitration. This faith in the efficacy and fairness of arbitration in industrial relations in the domestic arena led to his belief in 'international arbitration', which would be achieved through the establishment of an international organisation committed to collective security and a rules-based international order.

In his concession speech outside the Bathurst court house in January 1932, after losing the seat of Macquarie in the 1931 election, Chifley said he had 'seen behind the wall'. He understood the difficult journey that Australia had to travel in order to return to prosperity. He acknowledged the mistakes that the Scullin government had made, but warned those who thought the newly elected conservative Lyons government would bring the 'promised land', that they were 'sadly deceiving themselves'. The problem was 'world-wide' and could not be fixed 'unless the majority of the nations act in concert'. There could be no economic recovery until, as he said, there was 'a very great change in the monetary and financial policy of the world'.[219] As treasurer and prime minister in the Labor governments of 1941 to 1949, Chifley, together with advisers such as 'Nugget' Coombs and John Crawford, would play a leading role in ensuring that Australia contributed to the creation of a new international monetary and financial system which would promote 'economic cooperation and collaboration' amongst the nations of the world.[220]

Notes
1. 'Bathurst's Remarkable Vote', *National Advocate* (Bathurst, NSW), 14 October 1929, p. 3.
2. 'The Federal Elections', *National Advocate* (Bathurst, NSW), 14 October 1929, p. 2.
3. 'Chifley's Remarkable Record Win', *National Advocate* (Bathurst, NSW), 14 October 1929, p. 3.
4. Crisp, *Ben Chifley*, p. 35.
5. Day, *Chifley*, p. 235.
6. Crisp, *Ben Chifley*, pp. 37–38.
7. Day, *Chifley*, pp. 246–248; Crisp, *Ben Chifley*, p. 39.
8. 'The Federal Elections', *National Advocate* (Bathurst, NSW), 14 October 1929, p. 2.
9. Crisp, *Ben Chifley*, p. 49.
10. Selwyn Cornish, *Sir Leslie Melville: An Interview*, Working Papers in Economic History, Working Paper No. 173, Australian National University, Canberra, June 1993, p. 8.

11 'Macquarie Fight—Declaration of Poll', *National Advocate* (Bathurst, NSW), 9 January 1932, p. 2.
12 Peter Yule, 'Part 1: Economy', in John Connor, Peter Stanley and Peter Yule, *The War At Home: The Centenary History of Australia and the Great War, Volume 4*, Oxford University Press, South Melbourne, 2015, p. 78.
13 Ian W McLean, *Why Australia Prospered: The Shifting Sources of Economic Growth*, Princeton University Press, Princeton, NJ, 2013, p. 147, fn 6. Fortunately, this gap is being remedied by the recent publication of the two impressive books cited: *Why Australia Prospered* and *The War At Home*.
14 McLean, *Why Australia Prospered*, p. 169, fn. 45.
15 ibid., p. 145.
16 David Gruen and Colin Clark, 'What Have We Learnt? The Great Depression in Australia from the Perspective of Today', *Economic Roundup*, issue 4, 2009, p. 36, fn 5; Alex Millmow, *The Power of Economic Ideas: The origins of Keynesian macroeconomic management in interwar Australia 1929–39*, ANU E Press, Canberra, 2010, p. 32.
17 Meredith and Dyster, *Australia in the Global Economy*, p. 77.
18 TJ Valentine, 'The Causes of the Depression in Australia', *Explorations in Economic History*, vol. 24, no. 1, 1987, p. 45.
19 Millmow, *The Power of Economic Ideas*, p. 33.
20 Gruen and Clark, 'What Have We Learnt?' pp. 35–36.
21 ibid., pp. 36–37.
22 Leslie Melville interviewed by Alan Hodgart, 1973, NLA: ORAL TRC 182, pp. 10–11.
23 Gruen and Clark, 'What Have We Learnt?' p. 37.
24 Meredith and Dyster, *Australia in the Global Economy*, p. 82.
25 McLean, *Why Australia Prospered*, p. 149.
26 Valentine, 'The Causes of the Depression in Australia', p. 47.
27 Alex Millmow, *The Power of Economic Ideas*, p. 33.
28 Valentine, 'The Causes of the Depression in Australia', p. 47.
29 Gruen and Clark, 'What Have We Learnt?' p. 40.
30 Valentine, 'The Causes of the Depression in Australia', p. 47.
31 Gruen and Clark, 'What Have We Learnt?' pp. 40–41.
32 Valentine, 'The Depression of the 1930s', in Maddock and McLean, (eds), *The Australian Economy in the Long Run*, pp. 62–63; Millmow, *The Power of Economic Ideas*, p. 35.
33 Gruen and Clark, 'What Have We Learnt?' p. 35.
34 Alex Millmow, *The Power of Economic Ideas*, p. 43.
35 David Lee, *Stanley Melbourne Bruce: Australian Internationalist*, Continuum, London, 2010, p. 95.
36 Warren Denning, *James Scullin*, Black Inc., Melbourne, 2000, p. 60.
37 John Hawkins, 'James Scullin: Depression Treasurer', *Economic Roundup*, Issue 2, 2010, p. 111.
38 Meredith and Dyster, *Australia in the Global Economy*, p. 133.
39 John Hawkins, 'Ted Theodore: The Proto-Keynesian', *Economic Roundup*, issue 1, 2010, p. 98.
40 Meredith and Dyster, *Australia in the Global Economy*, p. 133.

41 Peter Love, 'Frank Anstey and the Monetary Radicals', in RT Appleyard and CB Schedvin (eds), *Australian Financiers: Biographical Essays*, Macmillan, South Melbourne, 1988, p. 268.
42 CB Schedvin, *Australia and the Great Depression: A Study of Economic Development and Policy in the 1920s and 1930s*, Sydney University Press in association with Oxford University Press, Sydney, 1970, p. 85.
43 Cornish, *Sir Leslie Melville: An Interview*, p. 1.
44 Melville interviewed by Hodgart, 1973, p. 21.
45 Cornish, *Sir Leslie Melville: An Interview*, p. 8.
46 Schedvin, *Australia and the Great Depression*, p. 83.
47 Marjorie Harper, *Douglas Copland: Scholar, Economist, Diplomat*, Miegunyah Press, Carlton, Victoria, 2013, p. 210.
48 Day, *Chifley*, p. 261.
49 Love, 'Frank Anstey and the Monetary Radicals', p. 269.
50 Peter Love, *Labour and the Money Power: Australian Labour Populism 1890–1950*, Melbourne University Press, Carlton, Victoria, 1984, p. 1. This is the standard study of the Money Power ideology.
51 Barrie Dyster and David Meredith, *Australia in the International Economy in the Twentieth Century*, Cambridge University Press, Cambridge, UK, 1990, p. 143.
52 KH Kennedy, 'E.G. Theodore', in Appleyard and Schedvin (eds), *Australian Financiers*, p. 296; Anne Henderson, 'Joseph Aloysius Lyons', in Grattan (ed.), *Australian Prime Ministers*, p. 163; Day, *Chifley*, p. 258.
53 Love, 'Frank Anstey and the Monetary Radicals', p. 270.
54 Hawkins, 'Ted Theodore: The Proto-Keynesian', p. 101.
55 Day, *Chifley*, p. 255.
56 ibid., p. 256.
57 Crisp, *Ben Chifley*, p. 66.
58 *CPD*, HoR, 25 March 1931, p. 603.
59 ibid., p. 605.
60 ibid., p. 606.
61 McLean, *Why Australia Prospered* p. 165.
62 'Mr Chifley's Address', *National Advocate* (Bathurst, NSW), 18 August 1931, p. 2.
63 'No Gutter Tactics—Failure of the Lang Plan, *National Advocate* (Bathurst, NSW), 19 August 1931, 2nd edn., p. 3.
64 'No Chance—Lang Candidate in Macquarie—Mr Chifley's Lucid Address—Ding Dong Battle Promised—Why Labor Accepted Premiers' Plan', *National Advocate* (Bathurst, NSW), 19 August 1931, p. 2.
65 ibid.
66 Melville interviewed by Alan Hodgart, p. 16.
67 ibid., p. 19.
68 Hawkins, 'Ted Theodore: The Proto-Keynesian', p. 93.
69 ibid., p. 95.
70 Kennedy, 'EG Theodore', p. 295.
71 Love, 'Frank Anstey and the Monetary Radicals', p. 270.
72 Meredith and Dyster, *Australia in the Global Economy*, p. 131.

73 Kennedy, 'EG Theodore', p. 295.
74 ibid.
75 Millmow, *The Power of Economic Ideas*, p. 83.
76 Meredith and Dyster, *Australia in the Global Economy*, p. 133.
77 ibid.
78 *CPD*, HoR, 17 March 1931, p. 300; According to Millmow, 'reproductive' works were public works funded by governments, which had to yield 'within a reasonable period, revenue at least equal to the debt'. This was because of the 'waste of the 1920s'. See Millmow, *The Power of Economic Ideas*, p. 37.
79 Kennedy, 'EG Theodore', p. 296.
80 Millmow, *The Power of Economic Ideas*, p. 83.
81 *CPD*, HoR, 17 March 1931, pp. 305; 315; 316 and 317–318.
82 ibid., p. 318.
83 Melville interviewed by Hodgart, pp. 42–43.
84 Kennedy, 'EG Theodore', p. 296.
85 Meredith and Dyster, *Australia in the Global Economy*, p. 133.
86 Millmow, *The Power of Economic Ideas*, p. 81.
87 Melville interviewed by Hodgart, 1973, p. 44.
88 ibid., pp. 47–48.
89 Cornish, *Sir Leslie Melville: An Interview*, p. 11.
90 Letter from Gibson to Theodore, 2 April 1931, in EOG Shann and DB Copland (eds), *The Battle of the Plans: Documents Relating to the Premiers' Conference, May 25th to June 11th, 1931*, Angus and Robertson, Sydney, 1931, pp. 44–45.
91 Meredith and Dyster, *Australia in the Global Economy*, p. 133.
92 Alex Millmow, 'The Power of Economic Ideas: Australian Economists in the Thirties', *History of Economics Review*, vol. 37, Winter, 2003, p. 84.
93 Kennedy, 'E.G. Theodore', p. 297.
94 Hawkins, 'Ted Theodore', p. 105.
95 Cabinet Minutes, 6 June 1931, Scullin Ministry. Folders of Typed Copies of Cabinet Minutes, NAA: A3264, 1.
96 *CPD*, HoR, 25 June 1931, p. 3065.
97 ibid.
98 'No Gutter Tactics—Failure of the Lang Plan', *National Advocate* (Bathurst, NSW), 19 August 1931, 2nd edn, p. 3.
99 ibid.
100 'No Chance—Lang Candidate in Macquarie', *National Advocate* (Bathurst, NSW), 19 August 1931, p. 2.
101 Kennedy, 'E.G. Theodore', p. 298.
102 Lee, *Stanley Melbourne Bruce*, p. 98.
103 Day, *Chifley*, p. 284.
104 Crisp, *Ben Chifley*, p. 86.
105 Day, *Chifley*, p. 284.
106 Crisp, *Ben Chifley*, p. 42, fn. 1.
107 ibid., p. 86.
108 ibid.

109 Coombs, *Trial Balance*, p. 24.
110 'Against Versailles—Bonfires of Protest Throughout Germany', *National Advocate* (Bathurst, NSW), 1 July 1929, p. 2.
111 For example: 'In China—Reverse for Nationalist Forces', *National Advocate* (Bathurst, NSW), 26 September 1929, p. 1.
112 'Talk of War—Chinese Mobilising—Russia's Ultimatum—Japanese Watchful Waiting', *National Advocate* (Bathurst, NSW), 18 July 1929, p. 2.
113 'Indian Nationalists—Step to Overthrow Imperialism', *National Advocate* (Bathurst, NSW), 1 January 1930, p. 2.
114 'Indian Autonomy – Gandhi Sways Congress – Policy of Non-Violence', *National Advocate* (Bathurst, NSW), 2 January 1930, p. 2.
115 'China and Japan – Another Battle Looming', *National Advocate* (Bathurst, NSW), 22 September 1931, p. 3.
116 'John Bull Is Forced To Take Stock', *National Advocate* (Bathurst, NSW), 19 August 1931, p. 2.
117 Editorial, 'The Present System Must Go', *National Advocate* (Bathurst, NSW), 2 September, 1931, p. 2.
118 James Cotton, 'Australia in the League of Nations: Role, debates, presence', in Cotton and Lee (eds), *Australia and the United Nations*, p. 5.
119 Cotton, *The Australian School of International Relations*, p. 21.
120 'Working for Peace—International Declaration Disarmament Campaign', *Mercury*, (Hobart, Tasmania) Saturday 6 June 1931, p. 11.
121 Constance Browning, 'World Peace—A Struggle Renewed', *Canberra Times*, 25 October 1981, p. 4.
122 'World Problems', *National Advocate* (Bathurst, NSW), 19 October 1932, p. 2.
123 Constance Browning, 'World Peace—A Struggle Renewed', *Canberra Times*, 25 October 1981, p. 4.
124 BJC McKercher, *Transition of Power: Britain's Loss of Global Pre-eminence to the United States, 1930–1945*, Cambridge University Press, New York, 1999, pp. 140 and 143.
125 'Not Solved – War Reparations Problem', *National Advocate* (Bathurst NSW), 20 July 1932, p. 1.
126 McKercher, *Transition of Power*, p. 143.
127 'Not Solved—War Reparations Problem', *National Advocate* (Bathurst, NSW), 20 July 1932, p. 1.
128 Sean Turnell, Monetary Reformers, Amateur Idealists and Keynesian Crusaders: Australian Economists' International Advocacy, 1925–1950, PhD thesis, Macquarie University, 1999, p. 40.
129 ibid., p. 20.
130 Ann Capling, Mark Considine and Michael Crozier, *Australian Politics in the Global Era*, Longman, South Melbourne, 1998, pp. 27–28.
131 Meredith and Dyster, *Australia in the Global Economy*, p. 138.
132 Lee, *Stanley Melbourne Bruce*, pp. 100–101.
133 'World Problems', *National Advocate* (Bathurst, NSW), 19 October 1932, p. 2.
134 Cornish, *Sir Leslie Melville: An Interview*, p. 12.

135 ibid., p. 13.
136 'World Problems', *National Advocate* (Bathurst, NSW), 19 October 1932, p. 2.
137 'Gold and the Crisis—League of Nations Delegation', *Sydney Morning Herald*, 30 July 1932, p. 15.
138 Patricia Clavin and Jens-Wilhelm Wessels, 'Another Golden Idol? The League of Nations' Gold Delegation and the Great Depression, 1929–1932', *International History Review*, vol. 26, no. 4, 2004, p. 765.
139 'Gold and the Crisis', *Sydney Morning Herald*, 30 July 1932, p. 15.
140 Clavin and Wessels, 'Another Golden Idol?', p. 790.
141 'World Problems', *National Advocate* (Bathurst, NSW), 19 October 1932, p. 2.
142 Clavin and Wessels, 'Another Golden Idol?', pp. 790–791.
143 'World Problems', *National Advocate* (Bathurst, NSW), 19 October 1932, p. 2. Present-day economic historians such as Barry Eichengreen and Peter Temin also maintain 'there now exists agreement among most economists that the gold standard was a key element—if not the key element—in the collapse of the world economy' in the 1930s. See Barry Eichengreen and Peter Temin, 'The Gold Standard and the Great Depression', *Contemporary European History*, vol. 9, issue 2, 2000, pp. 184–185.
144 'No Chance—Lang Candidate in Macquarie', *National Advocate* (Bathurst, NSW), 19 August 1931, p. 2.
145 'World Problems', *National Advocate* (Bathurst, NSW), 19 October 1932, p. 2.
146 ibid.
147 'World Crucified—Evils of Deflation—Mr. JB Chifley on World Problems', *National Advocate* (Bathurst, NSW), 19 December 1932, p. 2.
148 Patricia Clavin, *Securing the World Economy: The Reinvention of the League of Nations, 1920–1946*, Oxford University Press, Oxford, 2013, p. 72.
149 Clavin and Wessells, 'Another Gold Idol?' pp. 794–795.
150 Clavin, *Securing the World Economy*, p. 72.
151 Clavin and Wessels, 'Another Golden Idol?', p. 793.
152 ibid., p. 795.
153 Clavin, *Securing the World Economy*, p. 72.
154 Barry Eichengreen and Marc Uzan, 'The 1933 World Economic Conference as an Instance of Failed International Cooperation', in Peter B Evans, Harold K Jacobson and Robert D Putnam (eds), *Double-Edged Diplomacy: International Bargaining and Domestic Politics*, University of California Press, Berkeley, 1993, pp. 175 and 171.
155 'Not Solved—War Reparations Problem', *National Advocate* (Bathurst, NSW), 20 July 1932, p. 1.
156 'Finance. May Be Issue for Election', *Sydney Morning Herald*, 3 March 1931, p. 9; 'World Problems', *National Advocate* (Bathurst, NSW), 19 October 1932, p. 2.
157 Andrew Moravcsik, 'Introduction: Integrating International and Domestic Theories of International Bargaining', in Evans, Jacobson and Putnam (eds), *Double-Edged Diplomacy*, p. 3.

158 Turnell, *Monetary Reformers*, p. 10.
159 'World Problems', *National Advocate* (Bathurst, NSW), 19 October 1932, p. 2.
160 'Methodist Church', *National Advocate* (Bathurst, NSW), 1 September 1933, p. 1; 'America's Plan', *National Advocate* (Bathurst, NSW), 2 September 1933, p. 2.
161 'Roosevelt's Plan—What it Aims to Achieve—Mr. JB Chifley's Address', *National Advocate* (Bathurst, NSW), 4 September 1933, p. 5.
162 'Mr. Chifley on the Roosevelt Plan', *National Advocate* (Bathurst, NSW), 15 March 1934, p. 2; 'The Roosevelt Plan Address by Mr. JB Chifley', *National Advocate* (Bathurst, NSW), 16 March 1934, p. 7.
163 'Federal Elections—Opens Campaign', *Sydney Morning Herald*, 10 August 1934, p. 8.
164 Commonwealth of Australia, *Royal Commission Appointed to Inquire into the Monetary and Banking Systems at Present in Operation in Australia* (hereafter *RCMB*), *Minutes of Evidence*, vols I and II, Commonwealth Government Printer, Canberra, 1936.
165 Stephens, 'The Effect of the Great Depression on the Federal Labor Governments, 1941–49', p. 263.
166 Crisp, *Ben Chifley*, p. 166.
167 Love, *Labour and the Money Power*, p. 141.
168 Commonwealth of Australia, *Report of the Royal Commission appointed to inquire into the Monetary and Banking Systems at present in operation in Australia* (hereafter *Report of the RCMB*), Commonwealth Government Printer, Canberra, 1937, p. 5.
169 *Report of the RCMB*, p. 4; Love, *Labour and the Money Power*, pp. 142–144.
170 Millmow, *The Power of Economic Ideas*, p. 201.
171 LF Giblin, *The Growth of a Central Bank: The Development of the Commonwealth Bank of Australia, 1924–1945*, Melbourne University Press, Carlton, Victoria, 1951, p. 213.
172 Love, *Labour and the Money Power*, p. 142.
173 Crisp, *Ben Chifley*, p. 167.
174 Love, *Labour and the Money Power*, p. 146.
175 Lyons, *Among the Carrion Crows*, pp. 97–98.
176 Hawkins, 'Ben Chifley', p. 108, fn. 39.
177 CB Schedvin, *In Reserve: Central Banking in Australia, 1945–75*, Allen & Unwin, St Leonards, NSW, 1992, p. 55.
178 SJ Butlin, 'Richards Charles Mills', *Economic Record*, vol. 29, November, 1953, p. 182.
179 ibid.
180 Coombs, *Trial Balance*, p. 219.
181 NG Butlin and RG Gregory, 'Trevor Winchester Swan 1918–1989', *Economic Record*, vol. 65, December, 1989, p. 370.
182 Coombs, *Trial Balance*, p. 108.
183 Kim Sutherlin, The Struggle for Central Banking in Australia: The Royal Commission of 1935–1937 on the Monetary and Banking Sectors, B. Ec. Hons. Thesis, ANU, 1980, p. 47.

184 Millmow, *The Power of Economic Ideas*, p. 201.
185 Robinson, *Economists and Politicians*, p. 87.
186 Sutherlin, The Struggle for Central Banking in Australia, p. 48.
187 Crisp, *Ben Chifley*, p. 168.
188 PD Groenewegen, 'Mills, Richard Charles (1886–1952)', *Australian Dictionary of Biography*, vol. 10, Melbourne University Press, Carlton, Victoria, 1986, pp. 517–519.
189 Coombs, *Trial Balance*, p. 108.
190 ibid., p. 219.
191 Letter, Professor RC Mills to Professor LF Crisp, 15 April 1952, Papers of LF Crisp, NLA: MS 5243 Series 5, Folder 2.
192 Letter, Geoffrey L Burgoyne to Crisp, 4 December [no year], Papers of LF Crisp, NLA: MS 5243, Series 5, Folder 4.
193 Crisp, *Ben Chifley*, p. 168.
194 *Report of the RCMB*, para. 530, p. 206.
195 Crisp, *Ben Chifley*, p. 171.
196 *Report of the RCMB*, para 541, pp. 209–210.
197 Love, *Labour and the Money Power*, pp. 146–147.
198 Giblin, *The Growth of a Central Bank*, p. 213.
199 'Dissent, Reservation and Addenda by Mr Chifley', in *Report of the RCMB*, para 7, p. 263.
200 ibid.
201 Robinson, Economists and Politicians, p. 130.
202 'Dissent by Mr Chifley', in *Report of the RCMB*, para 6, p. 263.
203 'Community Education Group', *National Advocate* (Bathurst, NSW), 5 October 1937, p. 2.
204 'Lecture on Banking Commission', *National Advocate*, 30 November, 1937, p. 2.
205 'The Banking Commission—Mr. Chifley's Address', *National Advocate* (Bathurst, NSW), 4 February 1938, p. 1.
206 ibid.
207 'Australian Labor—What It Stands For—The Martin Campaign Opened by Mr. JB Chifley', *National Advocate* (Bathurst, NSW), 30 June 1934, p. 1.
208 'Banking Commission—Address by Mr. JB Chifley', *National Advocate* (Bathurst, NSW), 2 June 1938, p. 3.
209 'Banking Commission—Mr. JB Chifley's Views', *National Advocate* (Bathurst, NSW), 24 June 1938, p. 3.
210 Robinson, Economists and Politicians, 1986, p. 141.
211 'Dissent by Mr Chifley' in *Report of the RCMB*, para 6, p. 263.
212 Love, *Labour and the Money Power*, p. 148.
213 ibid., p. 149.
214 Crisp, *Ben Chifley*, pp. 172–173.
215 Peter Groenewegen and Bruce McFarlane, *A History of Australian Economic Thought*, Routledge, London, 1990, p. 130.
216 JB Chifley, 'Big Business Always Hated the Commonwealth Bank', 28 March 1950, in *Things Worth Fighting For*, p. 319.
217 Hawkins, 'Ben Chifley', p. 105, fn. 19. This was EOG Shann and DB Copland (eds), *The Battle of the Plans: Documents Relating to the*

Premiers' Conference, May 25th to June 11th, 1931, Angus and Robertson, Sydney, 1931.
218 'World Problems', *National Advocate* (Bathurst, NSW), 19 October 1932, p. 2.
219 'Macquarie Fight—Declaration of Poll', *National Advocate* (Bathurst, NSW), 9 January 1932, p. 2.
220 Ann Capling, *Australia and the Global Trade System: From Havana to Seattle*, Cambridge University Press, UK, 2001, p. 2.

CHAPTER FOUR
Chifley and the World Economy, from 1941 to 1949

The immediate post-war period was a time of momentous change in both the domestic and international arenas. Australia had emerged from the damage caused by two world wars and a depression in which the unemployment rate reached 30 per cent.[1] According to James Cotton, historian of Australia's international relations, a significant feature of the 1940s was 'a strong expectation of the prospects for international organization' or 'international regimes'. This expectation 'marked a revival of the hopes held for international organization prior to 1936'.[2] Internationalism seemed for many, to be the only way to achieve a long-lasting peace. In the 1940s, those politicians, scholars, advisers, government officials and commentators who identified themselves as being 'internationally minded' saw this as the 'most realistic alternative to the perils of nationalism'.[3] Those who adhered to economic internationalism thought that the best way to prevent war caused by excessive nationalism was by 'encouraging economic activities across national boundaries', which they believed would weaken nationalism.[4] Their hopes were placed in the creation of international rules-based security and trading systems, such as the United Nations Organisation and the institutions created by the Bretton Woods Agreement.

These beliefs accorded with Chifley's own. During the Great Depression, he had repeatedly urged international cooperation to restore world prosperity. In October 1932 he had said that, in order to restore price levels, 'a determined co-operative effort by the nations of the world' was needed.[5] He had hoped that the 1933 World Monetary and Economic Conference would achieve the changes necessary for world peace and prosperity, but, as we have seen in the previous chapter, these hopes were dashed. The many international conferences held in the inter-war period, on disarmament, war debts, reparation payments and attempts to salvage the global economy from collapsing further into economic depression, failed to gain international cooperation.

Memories of these inter-war years were still very raw: there was a great deal of anxiety in Australia and within government that the post-war period would see a return of the economic conditions that had existed in the 1930s, with its high rates of unemployment and economic stagnation.[6] As Chifley said in July 1932, fundamental changes needed to be made to the world economic system to prevent future economic depressions and wars from erupting again.[7] The post-war Chifley government faced significant challenges to ensure Australia's future economic security and prosperity—namely, how to reposition the Australian economy within the new world economic order. In fact, planning for both the peace and post-war reconstruction began before the end of the war, with a succession of great international conferences concerned with global economic and strategic security. It was through the 'format of the international conference' that 'questions of the international economy were decided, thus giving them a significance unusual before or since'.[8]

In May 1944 members of the 'United Nations'—the name given to the Allies during World War II—received an invitation from US President Franklin Delano Roosevelt to attend a conference at Bretton Woods, New Hampshire, from 1 July.[9] The Australian government was one of the forty-four governments invited to 'discuss and formalize their plans for the coordination and management' of a new monetary and financial system to be created to assist trade between nations. This conference would establish important new international organisations to restore the world economy. The three organisations proposed were the International Monetary Fund (IMF), which would create the 'framework' for the international monetary system. The IMF would establish a 'stable and predictable' monetary regime in which national currencies could be converted, and it would provide 'technical and short-term financial assistance to member countries' to facilitate international trade and economic growth.[10] The International Bank for Reconstruction and Development (IBRD) would direct funds to European countries in need of post-war reconstruction, and the International Trade Organisation (ITO) would provide new rules for international trade to prevent a 'return to the malevolent forms of trade restrictions, bilateralism and trade diversion that had exacerbated the great depression'. The ITO was 'designed to create clear and comprehensive rules for the establishment of a new multilateral trade system',[11] eliminating trade discrimination and, in general, encouraging a reduction in trade barriers.[12]

The principle underlying the post-war rules-based Bretton Woods system created in the wake of the Great Depression was to 'liberalise international trade while regulating international capital movements'.[13] The Bretton Woods system is often acknowledged as playing a major role in setting up the 'relatively benign economic conditions' that existed in the 1950s and 1960s—an environment in which Australia prospered.[14] A major factor contributing to this prosperity was 'the emergence of a stable and well-functioning international economic system'. This was very different to expectations that the end of the war would see a return to the economic chaos and misery that had existed during the Great Depression of the 1930s.[15]

Chifley's Response to the Bretton Woods Agreement

The nature of Chifley's response to the Bretton Woods Agreement has been fiercely contested. In the late 1970s and early 1980s, a heated debate took place between historians CB Schedvin and Roger Bell, in which Bell claimed that the Labor government and its departmental officials saw US multilateralism as a subtle form of 'economic imperialism'.[16] Shedvin argued, however, that Chifley and Curtin believed that Australia had more to gain from an increase in international trade than in remaining within the imperial preference system.[17] Bell maintained that Labor's commitment to full employment was a ploy, in part, to counter US pressure to relinquish protectionism and commit to multilateralism.[18] According to Bell, multilateralism was seen by Australia as a 'threat to small power sovereignty'.[19] However, Bell's argument was undermined in an interview in 1993 with a major contributor to the Bretton Woods negotiations, economist Leslie Melville, head of the Australian delegation to the United Nations Monetary and Economic Conference at Bretton Woods in 1944. When asked about Chifley's attitude towards the organisations established by the agreement, Melville declared:

> Chifley was always going to join the IMF. No doubt he had some private discussions with his counterparts in England. It was quite clear that he saw it as an international institution, fundamentally of good will, that one should join. I think he saw it simply as that. He would have had advice along those lines from Stuart McFarlane and Fred Wheeler, who were advising him. I think Coombs, too, would have always been in favour of some international institution of this kind, even though he didn't altogether like the IMF. Still, he would have thought it was something Australia should join.[20]

A detailed study of Australian archival records supports Melville's statement and reveals Chifley's commitment to the establishment of a rules-based international economic system. In fact, he played a key role in ensuring that Australia became part of that system.

The Chifley government was concerned not so much with 'external threats', but with ensuring Australia's economic security in the post-war world. The government favoured multilateralism in the context of a policy of full employment and sought to 'shape' policy and to influence other countries in their policy-making. However, this 'crucial' aspect of Australian foreign policy in the years immediately after the war has barely been considered by Australian historians and political scientists.[21] Arthur Tange, an economist with the Department of Post-war Reconstruction, wrote some time later that the 'employment approach' has often been 'misunderstood' and 'derided'. But, according to Tange, it included ideas about the obligations of the major economic powers to other smaller powers that would endure.[22] Australia's employment approach advocated an international agreement in which countries would do everything 'in their power to maintain employment within their own territories', and in doing so, increase demand for international trade.[23] Australia would benefit from increased trade opportunities, but the 'full employment' policy also provided a clear and 'politically acceptable' justification for the internationalism of leaders such as Chifley.[24] The full employment policy had overtones of social justice that aligned with Labor beliefs, providing a bulwark against those in the party who were opposed to Australia's increased exposure to international financiers and 'Wall Street'. The Labor government also had a 'deeply felt obligation' to provide a better life for those returning to civilian life from war-time service.[25] The Chifley government hoped that the US version of multilateralism could be modified. Its advisers attempted to shape US policy into an international commitment to a program of full employment supported by the economic resources of the United States. This attempt failed.[26]

Economic historian Ann Capling makes the point, however, that Australia played a vital and influential role in the successful effort to re-establish a multilateral trade system after the unsuccessful attempts of the 1930s. The central argument of her book on Australia and the global trade system is that Australia exerted considerable influence in these multilateral trade organisations, much more so than its status in the global economy suggested. According to Capling, this has seen 'Australia play a pivotal role at key moments … in the establishment and maintenance of the system's rules and norms'. Capling also notes that, although this multilateral trading system is vital for Australia's economic security and Australia played a significant role in establishing and supporting it, this story has not received the recognition it deserves.[27] Chifley's campaign to gain the approval of his party to ratify the Bretton Woods Agreement is a crucial part of this story, and it, too, deserves much greater attention from historians.

The 'Tortuous Path' to Ratification of the Bretton Woods Agreement

In his study of cabinet government in Australia, political scientist Patrick Weller argues that Chifley's campaign to gain approval for Australia's ratification of the Bretton Woods Agreement is a demonstration of a 'political craftsman' in action. Chifley 'knew the Labor party well and understood how to use the various forums to best advantage':[28] he was a master of the Labor Party and its machinery. The party in general, and cabinet ministers such as Arthur Calwell, and Eddie Ward, were suspicious of international financiers: they assumed the IMF would be controlled by the big US banks and international financiers.[29] Fears of the 'Money Power'—a legacy of the depression years—were rampant. In May 1944 cabinet considered the invitation to attend the Bretton Woods conference, planned for 1 July to 22 July that year. Chifley's submission to cabinet sought to overcome ministers' resistance to the creation of the IMF. He thought there was a significant consideration that ought not be overlooked, which was

> the post-war position if there is no International Monetary Fund or co-operation. There are many people who view such a position with grave foreboding and prophesy competitive exchange depreciation and restrictions by countries in order to reap some temporary benefit. Such action would cut right across the aims of expanded trade and employment and might lead quickly to an era of economic nationalism rather than international co-operation. Australia is very interested in world trade. An International Monetary Fund on satisfactory lines which would increase world trade would help Australia directly and assistance to other countries by the Fund would bring further help to Australia indirectly.[30]

Chifley added that both the United Kingdom and the United States favoured the establishment of such a fund: it was 'an essential part of post-war plans'. If Australia declined membership or assumed an 'unfriendly attitude', there would need to be 'very strong grounds in principle'. Chifley concluded by recommending that Australia should accept the invitation to attend the Bretton Woods conference.[31]

In June 1944 cabinet decided that Australia should be represented at the conference by an official delegation of experts led by economist Professor Leslie Melville. The delegation included Treasury official Fred Wheeler and economist Arthur Tange from the

Department of Post-war Reconstruction.[32] Economist James (Jim) Brigden also attended in his role as financial counsellor to the Australian Legation to the United States.[33] Melville, Brigden and other senior economists had, from the time of the Premiers' Plan and the Bruce–Page government's inquiry into the Australian tariff system in 1929, 'hovered on the periphery of government'. Since the start of World War II, they had been involved in full-time public employment.[34] Many were members of the Financial and Economic Advisory Committee, which was established in December 1938 under the Defence Department and in September 1939, Treasury took charge. The committee included economists such as Lyndhurst Falkiner Giblin as chair, Leslie Melville, Douglas Copland, James Brigden, Richard Mills, Harry Brown, Daniel McVey, E. Ronald Walker and Roland Wilson.[35]

The World Monetary Economic Conference of 1933 had been the last forum where a world-wide solution to the Great Depression had been pursued before a world war intervened.[36] It had failed miserably, leaving in its wake disappointment and disillusionment that no global solution had been achieved. However, after lengthy negotiations, the agreement that came out of the Bretton Woods conference proposed to establish the International Monetary Fund, the International Bank for Reconstruction and Development, and the International Trade Organisation.[37] The ITO was later 'scuttled by the United States Congress, jealous to protect its autonomy and sovereignty to make trade policy as it saw fit'. It was replaced by the General Agreement on Tariffs and Trade (GATT) which was established to begin the process of trade liberalisation.[38] The GATT was implemented on 1 January 1948.

At the conclusion of the conference, the relief felt by James Brigden that it had succeeded when so many previous inter-war conferences had failed, is evident in his unofficial impressions of the conference.[39] In Brigden's notes, he quotes economist John Maynard Keynes' speech at the last session of the Bretton Woods conference. Keynes said he was 'greatly encouraged' by the 'critical, sceptical, and even carping spirit' that greeted the conference in the wider world. He added: 'How much better that our projects should begin in disillusion than that they should end in it'. Brigden wrote:

Even in the final scenes the ghosts of some 'inter-war' conferences were about. There was no undue rhetoric, but there was a general feeling that the conference had accomplished more than could reasonably have been expected at its beginning. Strains had been admirably controlled, and although the documents are bound to contain a few flaws, they seem to do what it was necessary to have done before the individual governments could consider the practical problems of action.[40]

The leader of the Australian delegation, Leslie Melville, reported back to cabinet in September 1944,[41] but cabinet had earlier deferred any definite decision on joining the agreement until it was known if both the US Congress and the UK Parliament would endorse the proposals.[42] In a later interview in 1992, with economist Selwyn Cornish, Melville said he doubted if Chifley had the numbers to force the issue. Melville also thought it was wise to delay a decision: it would be better to see what obligations Australia was committed to under the GATT, which would see a 'progressive liberalization of international commodity trade', before making a final commitment to the IMF.[43]

It was not until January 1946, by which time about thirty countries, including the United States and the United Kingdom, had joined together to establish the IMF, that Prime Minister Chifley brought the issue back to cabinet.[44] A motion that cabinet recommend 'to the Parliamentary Party that the Bretton Woods proposals be approved and that the necessary action be taken to obtain Parliamentary concurrence' was lost. According to political scientist Patrick Weller, this was the only time that cabinet records indicate that a motion was put to cabinet and lost.[45] John Dedman, minister for Post-war Reconstruction, later claimed it was fortunate that the vote was lost: caucus would 'undoubtedly have rejected the recommendation and the Party would have been *openly* disunited during the 1946 Federal Election campaign'.[46]

The possibility of exacerbating party disunity did not prevent the pugnacious member for East Sydney, Eddie Ward, from mounting a fierce attack against the agreement in March 1946. Ward stated in a radio broadcast that the 'very sovereignty of this Nation' was placed in jeopardy. The Bretton Woods Agreement would 'enthrone a World Dictatorship of private finance more complete and terrible than any hitlerite dream', in which small nations would be reduced to 'vassal states'. It would 'pervert and paganise our Christian ideals' and the government would be forced to 'open its doors to a flood of coloured labour'.[47] Despite Ward's public destabilisation of the party, the federal election was decided primarily on domestic matters, and on 28 September 1946 Chifley's Labor government achieved a resounding victory.[48]

It then took until 19 November 1946 for Chifley to once again bring ratification of the Bretton Woods Agreement to cabinet. Despite opposition from ministers such as Ward and Calwell, the motion was carried.[49] According to Dedman, it was not simply 'happenstance' that led to the eventual decision to ratify the Bretton Woods proposal. Instead, Chifley with 'infinite patience … masterminded a plan, whereby, under the rules of the ALP', he was able to achieve his goal.[50] On 27 November he moved a motion in caucus that the government should be given authority to ratify the Bretton Woods Agreement. After the debate, the meeting was adjourned until the following day.[51] Chifley had addressed the federal executive of the Labor Party on the Bretton Woods Agreement the previous evening. The next morning, the executive endorsed a motion that Australia should be a signatory to the Bretton Woods Agreement by seven votes to five.[52]

On 28 November Chifley conveyed the federal executive's resolution on the Bretton Woods proposal to caucus and read the federal executive rules which stated that the executive's decision was binding. A heated discussion followed until the meeting was adjourned.[53] At the next meeting, on 4 December 1946, caucus ignored the federal executive and cabinet's endorsement, and referred the Bretton Woods proposal to a special federal conference, by a vote of twenty-nine to twenty-six.[54] There were six ALP state executives, four of whom, under the rules of the ALP, had to make the request for a special conference. Chifley was able to convince three states to vote against the special conference, which meant that it could not be convened. The issue was referred back to cabinet yet again on 25 February 1947. At this meeting the prime minister again put forward a proposal that a recommendation be made to 'the Parliamentary Labor Party that Parliament be asked to ratify the

Bretton Woods Agreement on behalf of Australia'. Cabinet endorsed this recommendation.[55] At a meeting of caucus on 6 March 1947, Chifley put forward a motion that 'authority be given to introduce legislation to ratify Bretton Woods Agreement—entry being subject to Australia being allowed to join on conditions applied to original members'. After opposing amendments were defeated, Chifley's motion was carried by thirty-three votes to twenty-four.[56] According to Crisp, six ministers voted against the motion.[57]

Chifley had to work extraordinarily hard to persuade the Labor Party of the need to ratify the Bretton Woods Agreement; many in the party saw it as evil incarnate devised by Wall Street and the Money Power.[58] According to journalist Alan Reid, the Bretton Woods Agreement was a 'particularly difficult' issue for Chifley, because of fierce opposition within the party, led by Eddie Ward and Arthur Calwell, who were strident opponents of the Money Powers. Chifley had 'more of a global concept' of the Bretton Woods issue: he understood that 'Australia had been plagued by successions of external balance of payments problems and recognised that these problems were shared by other countries in the world'. He wanted to 'establish a world currency system that would obviate this and lessen the impact of sudden monetary movements around the world'.[59]

With such fierce opposition to the Bretton Woods proposal from his own side of politics, how did Chifley manage to get caucus support for the ratification of the agreement? International relations scholar JDB (Bruce) Miller gave an excellent and detailed contemporary account of the tortuous path to ratification of the Bretton Woods Agreement taken by the Labor government and how difficult it was for Chifley to achieve this goal.[60] Opposition to the agreement was based on a Labor tradition of 'isolationism and the belief that monetary policy is the most important element in politics'. These two strands of thought were combined in a mistrust of international financiers who were blamed for the 1930s depression. Isolationism had also been a recurring theme in Labor thinking since World War I. In the case of the Bretton Woods Agreement, the 'monetary aspect' reinforced this opposition.[61] According to Miller, 'monetary reformers' were a major influence in the party and were a dominant force until Labor gained power in war-time and came to understand that 'the problems of inflation in a Full-Employment economy could not be solved by interest-free loans from the Commonwealth bank'. Miller noted that it was very difficult for the government to counter the opposition to the Bretton Woods proposal: there was no Labor tradition it could call upon when attempting to gain support.[62]

Chifley was, however, able to give 'a clear and simple explanation of what Bretton Woods meant in relation to Australia' in a statement circulated to caucus members on 4 March 1947, two days before the decision was made to ratify the agreement by thirty-three votes to twenty-four.[63] Elwyn Spratt, biographer of Eddie Ward, also provides excellent coverage of Chifley's efforts to get his party's approval of the Bretton Woods Agreement. He describes Chifley's statement to caucus as the 'most closely reasoned analysis of the Agreement that members had heard or read'.[64] As a 'clear and simple' analysis of Chifley's views on Bretton Woods, the statement has not received the attention it deserves.[65] Apart from brief descriptions and acknowledgement of its existence by Miller and Spratt, Chifley's statement has not previously been scrutinised by historians.

Chifley's Plea to Caucus

In his 'strongly-worded' statement to the Labor caucus on 4 March 1947, Chifley stated that Bretton Woods was

> essentially a simple scheme with a straightforward purpose. Discussion of it, however, has become clouded with false interpretations, and the question whether Australia should accept membership has been surrounded with extravagant fears about the obligations entailed. I hope to dispel some of this confusion and allay some of these fears. In particular I want to give Bretton Woods its proper international setting and show how Australia's interest in it is linked inextricably with the part we have chosen to play in the framework of world security and the pursuit of the Four Freedoms.[66]

Here Chifley widens the concept of security to include economic security. Indeed, for Chifley, global 'politico-strategic security' was dependent upon achieving sound economic relations between nations.[67] Chifley makes a connection with Franklin Roosevelt's 1941

State of the Union address in which the US president had looked forward to a world founded on the 'four essential human freedoms' to which the people of the world were entitled: freedom of speech; freedom of worship; freedom from want; and freedom from fear.[68] In this speech, Roosevelt broke with the long tradition of isolationism that had shaped United States foreign policy since the end of World War I. No doubt Chifley hoped he might influence some of the isolationists in his own party.

Chifley's statement then put twelve questions to caucus that reflected criticism of the Bretton Woods Agreement by its opponents in the Labor Party. These questions were: What is Bretton Woods? What are the expected benefits? Who created Bretton Woods? Who controls Bretton Woods? What is the membership of Bretton Woods? What is the relative influence of various countries? What particular interest has Australia in Bretton Woods? Can Bretton Woods dictate home policy? What do the exchange obligations imply? Can Australia stay out of Bretton Woods? If we join Bretton Woods, can we withdraw? Are there advantages in delaying membership? He then addressed some fallacies circulated about the Bretton Woods Agreement.[69]

In his answers, Chifley emphasised the benefits that Australia would gain by becoming a member of the Bretton Woods international fund and bank. A newspaper account of Chifley's statement noted the care he took in his appeal to caucus, which 'reflected the economic importance' he attached to the agreement.[70] In answering the first question, 'What is Bretton Woods?', Chifley stated that the Bretton Woods Agreement was a 'branch of the machinery for world economic collaboration' that was being developed through the United Nations Organisation which was officially established on 24 October 1945. Other agencies included the Economic and Social Council; the Food and Agriculture Organisation and the International Labor Organisation. These organisations all played essential roles in achieving 'the one broad purpose of promoting throughout the world higher and more equal living standards, greater productivity, and a fuller and richer life for all peoples'. He noted that, specifically, the Bretton Woods Agreement comprised, first, the International Monetary Fund, which would promote international exchange stability and the ability to freely convert currencies; and second, the

World Bank for Reconstruction and Development, which would be responsible for providing loans to 'war-stricken' countries and industrially under-developed countries.[71]

In answering his second question on the expected benefits of joining Bretton Woods, Chifley argued that for countries such as Australia, which were dependent on world trade, stability of international exchange was essential in ensuring 'certainty as to returns' amongst trading nations.[72] Freely convertible currencies were also important. In a powerful statement in which the bitter memories of the depression years re-surfaced, Chifley declared:

> Once it was thought that international exchanges were self-regulating. The depression of 1930 killed that illusion. Then came the days of currency manipulation, the thirties—an epoch of chaos. Nations fought with the weapons of exchange depreciation, currency quotas, frozen currencies and the like in a fantastic economic warfare, that did incalculable harm to trade and went far to cause the armed conflict of 1939.[73]

In contrast, he said, the Bretton Woods Agreement was an example of international cooperation by the governments of the war-time allies, in an attempt to end this irrational economic warfare, to 'bring international exchange relationships under rational control'.[74]

Economic experts had gathered at the Bretton Woods conference in 1944 to frame plans for the fund and the bank, both of which would be established at the end of the war. According to the prime minister, Australia played a significant role in these discussions and 'influenced their outcome in material ways'.[75] Rejecting Eddie Ward's accusation that Bretton Woods would 'enthrone a World Dictatorship of private finance, more complete and terrible than any hitlerite dream',[76] Chifley declared that private financiers did not influence decisions made at Bretton Woods. Indeed, many had attempted to 'sabotage' the work carried out at the conference because they regarded it as a 'threat to their interests and power'.[77]

Economist Leslie Melville, leader of Australia's delegation to the Bretton Woods conference, would later support Chifley's statement. During the Bretton Woods discussions, Melville was told by a major

United States bank that there would be no IMF: it would be blocked. US banks thought the IMF would be 'too expansionary' and there was continual interference from both the US Congress and American banks in negotiations over the drafting of the IMF and the World Bank statutes.[78] In fact, the American Bankers' Association was intent on destroying the Bretton Woods Agreement and campaigned hard to convince the American public and Congress to reject it. Throughout the depression of the 1930s, private bankers had provided loans to 'stricken nations', and if the IMF, rather than private bankers, became the chief lender to countries confronted by economic crises, they believed American financiers would no longer benefit from such lending.[79]

In answering his fourth question, 'Who Controls Bretton Woods'? Chifley noted that it was an 'international organism, created by governments and controlled by governments in the interests of their countries and of the world community'. Forty-three countries had joined both the IMF and the World Bank, only Australia, New Zealand and Russia had not joined. These forty-three nations controlled in excess of 70 per cent of all world trade. In terms of the relative influence of the various countries, voting power was allocated according to quotas, which were determined by the amount of resources that each country contributed to the IMF and the World Bank. The US and the UK had the largest quotas. However, all countries had a say in formulating policy, which meant that the 'more countries that join, the less will be the relative influence of the big countries'. The power of the large countries could, therefore, be 'curbed and brought into line with world interest'. It was in the interests of the large countries that smaller countries developed, which meant higher standards of living and greater purchasing power.[80]

Chifley argued that Australia had a particular interest in the Bretton Woods Agreement because external trade made up one-fifth of the nation's national income. This meant that, for its size, Australia ranked 'among the largest trading nations of the world. Hence stable exchanges and free currencies mean a lot for us'. Of greater interest for Chifley was the 'United Nations scheme of economic collaboration' of which Bretton Woods was an 'integral and indispensable part'. Not only was it important to see 'full employment and rising living standards' in Australia, Chifley added that it was important to see these same conditions in other countries, 'both for our own sake and the sake of a peaceful and thriving world'. Chifley added: 'To that end Australia has worked strenuously and not ineffectually to improve these international agencies and we must keep on working to improve them. But we can only do that from within'.[81]

Chifley wanted to be 'completely clear' regarding Eddie Ward's charges that Australia's sovereignty would be endangered if these proposals were accepted.[82] There were certain limitations on Australia's international activities once it ratified an international agreement such as Bretton Woods. All member countries accepted these limitations. Chifley noted, however, that it was clear that the fund, for its part, is 'expressly forbidden to interfere with our domestic social and economic policies'.[83] Chifley asked if Australia could afford to stay out of the Bretton Woods Agreement. He answered his own question by stating that Australia would be regarded as 'a pariah among the nations', it could not seek to 'share the benefits, but escape the obligations of the scheme. We would get no addition to our reserves and have no right to aid in an emergency'.[84] Chifley added:

> And how much extra freedom would we retain? There should be [no] illusions on this point. If we stay out of Bretton Woods we will not be free to use exchange controls or manipulate our exchange at will, because other countries in whose trade we have vital interests could, and no doubt would, retaliate in ways that would nullify our actions and probably leave us worse off than before. They are expressly permitted to do this and we would have no redress against them. There is nothing, in brief, which could happen to us within Bretton Woods that could not happen to us in worse degree outside it.[85]

Chifley added that the Trade and Employment Organisation to be established by the United Nations would also be 'closely linked' to Bretton Woods. Rejection of the Bretton Woods Agreement would mean that Australia could not be a part of this trade organisation.

Australia would not benefit from tariff reductions made by other countries and could possibly incur discrimination when it attempted to sell to member countries. According to Chifley:

> Australia has a vital interest in expanding trade. Our primary industries can grow little further without new markets and some manufacture[r]s are reaching the stage where they must have outlets abroad. To share in the work of the Trade Organisation is an opportunity we cannot afford to miss.[86]

Chifley went on to answer the question of whether Australia could withdraw from Bretton Woods. He noted that Australia could withdraw at any time after giving notice and our subscription would also be returned. Some had advised that Australia should wait to see how the trade organisation panned out after it was established, arguing this would be 'shrewd tactics'. Chifley, however, thought they were 'very naïve and feeble tactics'. Australia could not hope to influence events by observing from afar, but needed to be an 'active' participant. Australia had been willing to 'mix it in world affairs' in the past and had been able to hold its own. Chifley argued that the Australian delegation attending the preparatory conference on trade and employment had done a 'magnificent job' and succeeded in altering the 'whole course of the negotiations'. Nations had at last pledged to maintain full employment, an objective that Australia had struggled to achieve for years. Australia needed to be a part of Bretton Woods, this new organisation, 'doing our utmost to influence its policies, rather than standing apart pretending to a detachment which is unreal and cannot be maintained'.[87]

Chifley then countered the fallacious arguments put forward by opponents of the Bretton Woods Agreement. He deplored the tendency of some in the party who extrapolated details from the agreement—out of context—and interpreted them as 'signs of a hidden plot to ensnare countries like ourselves into the bondage of the United States, or, alternatively, private international financiers'.[88] Chifley concluded by declaring, there were 'pitfalls enough in international affairs without inventing any out of our own imaginations'.

He argued that Bretton Woods should be considered in all its 'simple elements', and a 'sinister complexity' should not be read into it:

> I do not say that it is perfect as a piece of mechanism. Necessarily the scheme is experimental, and capable of improvements. But that to me is a most compelling reason why we should now be taking part in its activities. Of all the dangers that beset international relationships the greatest is the illusion that any country, least of all a small country, can stand apart in isolation.[89]

Chifley concluded his statement on the Bretton Woods Agreement by pointing out that this was not to say that Australia, as a small nation, would 'abandon' itself to the 'drift of events'—quite the opposite. History was 'full of instances of small nations asserting themselves successfully and beneficially in world affairs, and that has never been more true than of the last few years'.[90]

Through this very detailed and reasoned rebuttal of his opponents' arguments in his statement to his parliamentary colleagues, Chifley was able to convince caucus on 6 March 1947 to authorise Australia's ratification of the Bretton Woods Agreement. The next step in Chifley's long journey to ensure that Australia played a part in the reform of the international trade and monetary system was to introduce into parliament the bill that ratified Australia's accession to the Bretton Woods Agreement.

The International Monetary Agreements Bill 1947

On 13 March 1947, Chifley introduced the International Monetary Agreements Bill to the House of Representatives. Crisp notes that Chifley's speech was 'concise and rather formal'.[91] It was very detailed, providing technical information and the obligations involved in membership of the IMF and the International Bank for Reconstruction and Development (IBRD). The prime minister argued that these two institutions formed part of a new economic order—in which Australia had played a very active and energetic role—which was established to ensure 'peace, security and welfare in the post-war world'. The United Nations was at the very 'apex of this structure'.

Because it was now recognised that 'economic welfare' was essential to securing 'peace and security' in the future, special machinery had been developed within the United Nations system to facilitate 'world economic collaboration' to encourage 'expanded production, employment, trade and higher standards of living' throughout the world.[92] For Chifley, these Bretton Woods institutions, together with the United Nations, represented 'an attempt for the first time in history to grapple with world economic problems by concerted action on a world scale for the common good'. It was for this reason that his government wholeheartedly supported these organisations. Australia should participate and contribute to organisations such as the IMF, because 'political isolation in the world' would be an unrealistic policy for Australia to follow, and 'economic isolation would be disastrous'.[93]

On 20 March 1947, the second reading of the bill resumed in parliament. This time, Chifley's speech was more personal and passionate. The bill was supported by Opposition leader Robert Menzies, but Chifley's long-term enemy Jack Lang— who had been elected as an independent member of the House of Representatives in 1946— rose to declare the bill 'a betrayal of Australia and also of the Labour Party's platform'. It would deliver the nation into the hands of 'an international organization—an international financial cartel, a financial oligarchy'. Using similar Money Power concepts as Eddie Ward, Lang declared that Australia's sovereignty would be abandoned and the nation would become 'a vassal state'. He added that the Chifley government was 'so overpowered by internationalism', it would 'submit without a struggle' to any demands of the International Monetary Fund.[94] The ghosts of the past were evoked when he reminded parliament of the mission to Australia in 1930 by the Bank of England's representative, the very conservative Sir Otto Niemeyer, whose deflationary recommendations were opposed by many in Labor. This time round, the fund would control the nation. Lang concluded by stating that Australia should stay out of the Bretton Woods Agreement and demanded that parliament reject the bill.[95]

Chifley's reply in the House of Representatives late that night was not a 'point-for-point rebuttal of his critics', as was his statement to caucus on 4 March. It provided, in Crisp's words, 'a simple and moving declaration of the wider grounds' upon which he based his support for the Bretton Woods Agreement.[96] As Chifley said in his brief reply, he intended to consider 'the question of international organizations in a broader sense than material gain for some country'.[97] This is a crucial speech in understanding the nature of Chifley's internationalism and how his lived experience was the source of his support for a rules-based internationalism. In this speech, Chifley looked back over the past thirty years during which the world had 'experienced two major wars and a serious depression'. He hoped the 'misery and suffering of those years' would never be seen again. We can see how his experience of war and economic depression had impacted heavily on Chifley, the man and the politician. In the event of another war, scientific advances in warfare and weaponry would result in 'appalling devastation' and might even mean the end of civilisation.[98] Here he reflected the concerns of many Australian foreign affairs experts and public commentators, such as diplomat Frederic Eggleston, who feared that with modern technology, the weapons of war had become so destructive, that any use of them would be totally 'self-defeating'.[99]

Chifley argued that he had been 'an ardent advocate of all international organizations'. The Bretton Woods Agreement was a 'great human experiment', which was designed to 'prevent the catastrophes that result from wars and financial and economic depressions'. According to Chifley, such international organisations would not only contribute to a nation's prosperity, they would also lead to the 'preservation of peace', because 'many of the conflicts in our history have been due to economic causes'.[100] Many others in the prime minister's official circle held similar views. Economist and public servant, John Crawford had written some years previously, in an influential and percipient paper, that the causes of war were 'mostly economic'.[101] Chifley argued that it was not only Australia that would benefit, but the whole world, as well as future generations. He had no doubt that defects would be revealed in these international organisations and charters, but he rejected those who would instil fear in others by alleging that Australia would be adversely affected by signing up to such an agreement. Most organisations found that, after some time, they had to change certain details in their 'original arrangement'. It was, however, vital to establish a framework for this 'human experiment'.[102]

The prime minister then went on to consider the plight of postwar Britain. Chifley was a great believer in democracy, and Britain had been at the forefront in the defence of democracy against fascism, fighting the might of Nazi Germany. The British had 'poured out blood and treasure in the fight for human liberty and freedom'. Great Britain was now on its knees financially, and unless its economy could be restored to prosperity, the British people would have had a 'pyrrhic victory' and all their 'sufferings and sacrifices will have been in vain if, in the final analysis, they become economic serfs'. The creation of a new international monetary and financial system to assist trade between nations would contribute to the postwar reconstruction of Great Britain. Chifley's belief in democracy meant that he rejected the fears of those influenced by the Money Power ideology, that 'international financiers' would control the Bretton Woods scheme, thereby destroying the 'economic liberty of mankind'. Chifley thought it much better that, if a world monetary organisation was to exist, it should be controlled by democratic governments and their representatives.[103] This was preferable to the pre-war 'international economic order' which privileged the 'private interests of big banks and big business', answerable only to their own investors.[104] Furthermore, this was the first time in the world's history that the governments of so many countries had worked together in an attempt to 'create economic stability'.[105]

Chifley went on to explain that world peace was dependent on economic security. If economic stability could be achieved, the single factor that caused war would be solved, and enormous progress achieved. This would contribute to 'the welfare of not only Australia and its people, but also the people of the whole world, for generations to come'.[106] We can see here Chifley's belief in global interdependence and his conviction that world security was reliant on the creation of a stable international economic order, so that future generations could 'attain a reasonable and decent standard of living to which every human being, black or white, is entitled'. The advantages of such an international agreement should not be rejected by countries because of selfishness or fear, or 'because some ghosts of the past happen to walk'.[107] Here he echoes economist James Brigden's sentiments, when he wrote in 1944 that the Bretton Woods conference had succeeded, in spite of the fact that, 'in the final scenes the ghosts of some "inter-war" conferences were about'.[108] Chifley declared that memories of past economic depressions should not deter countries from joining the Bretton Woods Agreement. Although there were difficulties in establishing such international organisations, economic isolationism was not a course to follow. He pleaded:

> If we have any love for mankind and a desire to free future generations from the terrible happenings of the last 30 years, we must put our faith in these international organizations. Even the youngest member of this House has seen two world wars, and a world-wide financial and economic depression from which people are still suffering.[109]

Chifley also maintained that the world's nations should provide economic security not only for allies, but for 'the people of ex-enemy countries' as well. If this did not occur, Chifley declared that 'another fever spot' would be allowed 'to breed war in the future'.[110] This was a sentiment that Chifley had expressed many times. The economic recovery of ex-enemy countries was vital to ensure post-war peace and prosperity.

Chifley concluded his speech in support of the Bretton Woods Agreement by saying that all nations, 'great and small', must 'strive to build up safeguards through these world organizations'. Even the United States, the world's economic powerhouse, could not 'be blind to the possible disaster to civilization in the future'. Partisan politics should be avoided to prevent the return of the 'devastation, misery and sorrow which has visited the world, economically and militarily, during the last 30 years'.[111] Throughout this speech, Chifley uses words such as 'humanity', 'international', 'future generations' and 'civilization'. These are words he used many times in his political rhetoric. We see here the language of internationalism, which, in the words of historian, Akira Iriye, 'seeks to reformulate the nature of relations among nations through cross-national cooperation and interchange'.[112] As an economic internationalist, Chifley believed that economic interdependence would encourage and support peaceful relations between nations. Chifley hoped that, through the Bretton Woods Agreement, the changes necessary for world peace and prosperity would be achieved, and there would be no return to the 'economic warfare' of the inter-war years. In his emotion-charged reply that evening, Chifley exposed the 'shoddy provincial meanness of Lang's attack on the ratification Bill'. After a long and difficult journey in gaining his party's approval for the ratification of the Bretton Woods Agreement, Chifley did indeed achieve, as his biographer Crisp wrote, a 'triumph of really considerable proportions'.[113]

On 5 August 1947 Australia became an official member of both the International Monetary Fund and the International Bank for Reconstruction and Development. The draft agreement on tariffs and trade was accepted by Australia in October 1947, and the *International Trade Organisation Act* became operational in December 1948. Under this Act, Australia's decision to accept the General Agreement on Tariffs and Trade was approved. The Act also provided for Australia's 'conditional acceptance of the ITO'.[114] The GATT, of which Australia was one of the original twenty-seven countries to sign in 1947, survived the US Congress's rejection of the ITO.[115] The GATT was ratified by the US president under his executive powers, and it replaced the ITO, thereby beginning the process of trade liberalisation.[116] In joining these international organisations, the Australian government had also agreed to accept the 'obligations and privileges' that accompanied membership. These decisions produced extensive debate in parliament and fierce opposition within the Australian Labor Party. In confronting and defeating this opposition, Chifley scored a major achievement. As economist John Crawford wrote, these obligations 'amounted to a comprehensive undertaking to conduct the country's foreign economic policies under agreed rules amounting, for trade policy *per se*, to a code of fair trade ... a quite remarkable move forward in international co-operation compared with the situation prevailing between the two world wars'.[117]

In realising these dreams of rebuilding society through international collaboration, we can see that Chifley understood that, as Akira Iriye has observed, 'no nation is self-sufficient or self-isolating but is part of the international society that exists at a given moment in time'.[118] In his statement circulated to caucus in March 1947, detailing the reasons why Australia should ratify the Bretton Woods Agreement, Chifley had declared: 'Of all the dangers that beset international relationships the greatest is the illusion that any country, least of all a small country, can stand apart in isolation'.[119] Some years earlier, in the midst of the catastrophic economic depression of the 1930s, Chifley had said that any politician—and here he was referring to Jack Lang—who told 'the people that anything you can do within your own country will bring complete prosperity back to Australia irrespective of world conditions is either a confidence man or ignorant of the real position'.[120] Then, and in the post-war period, Chifley was opposed by Lang and others in his party. But Chifley had a much wider vision than many of his party colleagues and contemporaries. As early as 1932, in the depths of the depression, he had declared that until there was 'a very great change in the monetary and financial policy of the world', there could be no ongoing economic recovery—the problem was 'world-wide' and could not be solved 'unless the majority of the nations act in concert'.[121]

Conclusion

In the inter-war years, Chifley built up his expertise in international relations. He became a highly respected member of the Bathurst community with a 'wide knowledge of international affairs'.[122] He had followed international conferences, such as the Reparations Conference in Lausanne in 1932 and the World Monetary and Economic Conference in London in 1933, which had held such hopes for those who thought that international cooperation was the key to world peace and economic security. These hopes were dashed by the failure of these and other conferences and it was not until the post-war period that a new era of effective international institutions was established. Historians have consistently underestimated Chifley's interest and expertise in this area, but Chifley had a long-standing and consuming interest in international relations and the establishment of the various organisations that he hoped would ensure global stability in both the economic and security spheres. Chifley's early interest in foreign affairs carried through to his time as prime minister and into the period he spent as Opposition leader. It also led him to adopt innovative and radical policies towards the emergent nations of Asia in the immediate post-war years.

Notes
1. Valentine, 'The Depression of the 1930s', in Maddock and McLean, (eds), *The Australian Economy in the Long Run*, pp. 62–63; Millmow, *The Power of Economic Ideas*, p. 35.
2. Cotton, *Australian School*, pp. 246–247.
3. Sluga, *Internationalism in the Age of Nationalism*, p. 6.
4. Iriye, *Cultural Internationalism and World Order*, p. 25.
5. 'World Problems', *National Advocate* (Bathurst, NSW), 19 October 1932.
6. Coombs, *Trial Balance*, p. 46.
7. 'War Reparations Problem', *National Advocate* (Bathurst, NSW), 20 July 1932.
8. Turnell, Monetary Reformers, p. 103.
9. See Manu Bhagavan, 'A New Hope: India, the United Nations and the Making of the Universal Declaration of Human Rights', *Modern Asian Studies*, vol. 44, no. 2, 2010, p. 313; Turnell, Monetary Reformers, p. 157.
10. Capling, Considine and Crozier, *Australian Politics in the Global Era*, p. 38.
11. Meredith and Dyster, *Australia in the Global Economy*, p. 153; Capling, Considine and Crozier, *Australian Politics in the Global Era*, p. 39.
12. Meredith and Dyster, *Australia in the Global Economy*, p. 153.
13. Stewart Firth, *Australia in International Politics: An Introduction to Australian Foreign Policy*, Allen & Unwin, St Leonards, NSW, 1999, p. 277.
14. Ken Henry, Adam Kissack, Martin Parkinson, Alice Peterson and Karen Taylor, 'Australia and the International Finance Architecture—60 Years On', *Economic Roundup*, Spring, 2003, p. 72, http://archive.treasury.gov.au/documents/710/PDF/Australia_IFA.pdf (accessed December 2012).
15. McLean, *Why Australia Prospered*, p. 185.
16. Roger Bell, 'Testing the Open Door Thesis in Australia, 1941–1946', *Pacific Historical Review*, vol. 51, no. 3, 1982, p. 297.
17. CB Schedvin, 'Australia and Article VII-A Comment', *Australian Economic History Review*, vol. 18, no. 1, 1978, p. 76.
18. Bell, 'Testing the Open Door Thesis', p. 293.
19. ibid., p. 297.
20. Cornish, *Sir Leslie Melville: An Interview*, pp. 24–25.
21. Lee, *Search for Security*, pp. 8–9.
22. Arthur Tange, 'Plans for the World Economy: Hopes and Reality in Wartime Canberra. A Personal Memoir', *Australian Journal of International Affairs*, vol. 50, no. 3, 1996, p. 259.
23. Turnell, 'Australia's "Employment Approach" to International Postwar Reconstruction: Calling the Bluff of Multilateralism', p. 111.
24. Rowse, *Nugget Coombs*, p. 130.
25. Tange, 'Plans for the World Economy', p. 260.

26 Lee, *Search for Security*, p. 9.
27 Capling, *Australia and the Global Trade System*, p. 2.
28 Patrick Weller, *Cabinet Government in Australia, 1901–2006: Practice, Principles, Performance*, UNSW Press, Sydney, 2007, p. 80.
29 Cornish, *Sir Leslie Melville: An Interview*, p. 24.
30 Supplement by the Treasurer to Full Cabinet Agendum No. 669, 'International Conference on Post-War Monetary Organisation', JB Chifley, Treasurer, 30 May 1944, p. 1. NAA: A2700, 669.
31 ibid.
32 Memorandum from Secretary to Cabinet to J.B. Chifley, Treasurer, 13 June, 1944; p. 1 in ibid.
33 Roland Wilson, 'Brigden, James Bristock (Jim) (1887–1950), *Australian Dictionary of Biography*, vol. 7, Melbourne University Press, Carlton, Victoria, 1979, p. 414.
34 ACT Regional Group, 'Commonwealth Policy Co-ordination', p. 198.
35 Rowse, *Nugget Coombs*, p. 92.
36 Turnell, *Monetary Reformers*, p. 66.
37 AH Tange to Australian Legation, Washington DC, Supplementary Notes on the Monetary Conference, 1 August 1944, p. 1. NAA: M2271, 13.
38 Ann Capling, Mark Considine and Michael Crozier, *Australian Politics in the Global Era*, Longman, South Melbourne, 1998, pp. 38–39.
39 Letter, AH Tange to Colonel Hodgson, 1 August 1944, including notes by JB Brigden, 'The Bretton Woods Conference: Some Impressions, Not Wholly Without Prejudice', NAA: M2271, 13.
40 Letter, Tange to Hodgson, 1 August 1944, including notes by Brigden, p. 1. NAA: M2271, 13.
41 Weller, *Cabinet Government in Australia, 1901–2006*, p. 81.
42 'Agendum No. 669A of 28th August, 1944', in Cabinet Submission by Chifley, 'The Bretton Woods Agreements', 14 November 1946, in WJ Hudson and Wendy Way (eds), *Documents on Australian Foreign Policy* (hereafter *DAFP*), *Volume X: July–December 1946*, Australian Government Publishing Service (hereafter AGPS), Canberra, p. 359.
43 Cornish, *Sir Leslie Melville: An Interview*, p. 24; McLean, *Why Australia Prospered*, p. 185.
44 John J Dedman, 'The Practical Application of Collective Responsibility', *Politics*, vol. 3, no. 2, 1968, p. 157.
45 Weller, *Cabinet Government in Australia 1901–2006*, p. 81.
46 Dedman, 'The Practical Application of Collective Responsibility', p. 157.
47 'The Bretton Woods Financial Agreement', by the Hon. EJ Ward, MP, Minister for Transport & External Territories, Broadcast, 27 March 1946, pp. 1; 6–7, NAA: M448, 120.
48 Dedman, 'The Practical Application of Collective Responsibility', pp. 157–158.
49 Weller, *Cabinet Government in Australia, 1901–2006*, p. 81.
50 Dedman, 'The Practical Application of Collective Responsibility', pp. 158–159.
51 Patrick Weller (ed.), assisted by Beverley Lloyd, *Caucus Minutes 1901–1949: Minutes of the Meetings of the Federal Parliamentary Labor Party*,

Volume 3, 1932–1949, Melbourne University Press, Carlton, Victoria, 1975, pp. 404–405; Weller, *Cabinet Government in Australia, 1901–2006*, p. 81.

52   Patrick Weller (ed.), *Federal Executive Minutes 1915–1955: Minutes of the Meetings of the Federal Executive of the Australian Labor Party*, Melbourne University Press, Carlton, Victoria, 1978, pp. 330–331.
53   Weller (ed.), *Caucus Minutes 1901–1949*, p. 405.
54   ibid., pp. 405–406; Weller, *Cabinet Government in Australia, 1901–2006*, p. 82.
55   Crisp, *Ben Chifley*, p. 208; Minutes of meeting of full cabinet held at 11am on Tuesday, 25 February 1947 at Canberra', NAA: A2703, 151.
56   Weller, (ed.), *Caucus Minutes 1901–1949*, pp. 412–413.
57   Crisp, *Ben Chifley*, p. 209.
58   Lee, *Search for Security*, p. 21.
59   Alan Reid interviewed by Mel Pratt, 1972–1973, NLA: ORAL TRC 121/40, p. 75.
60   JBD Miller, 'Australian Public Opinion: The Bretton Woods Controversy', *Australian Outlook*, vol. 1, issue 3, 1947, p. 35.
61   ibid., pp. 37–38.
62   ibid., p. 39.
63   ibid., p. 35.
64   Elwyn Spratt, *Eddie Ward: Firebrand of East Sydney*, Rigby, Adelaide, 1965, pp. 156–157.
65   This statement can be found in the papers of Dr HC Coombs in the National Archives of Australia, M448, 120. These papers contain research material, drafts and papers directly associated with Dr Coombs' autobiography *Trial Balance* (1981) and other books. The document 'Bretton Woods: Issued by the Prime Minister (Mr Chifley)' is undated. There is, however, a report of Chifley's statement to the ALP caucus on 4 March 1947, in the daily newspaper *Morning Bulletin* (Rockhampton, Queensland, 1878–1954), on Wednesday, 5 March 1947. This article states that Chifley made a 'strongly-worded plea' to caucus to authorise Australia's ratification of the Bretton Woods Agreement. If Australia did not, Chifley declared that Australia would be 'a pariah among the nations'. The newspaper report notes that Chifley 'posed 12 questions which reflected criticism of the ratification by a large section of the Labour Party'. The archival document includes the twelve questions. The newspaper report quotes extensively from Chifley's statement circulated to caucus on 4 March. All of these quotes correspond to the document contained in the Coombs papers in the national archives. Crisp does not refer to the statement and, apart from mention of 'heated discussions' in caucus 'in March 1947', David Day does not mention it either.
66   'Bretton Woods', Issued by the Prime Minister (Mr Chifley), p. 1, n.d., NAA: M448, 120.
67   Lee, *Search for Security*, p. 4.
68   David M Kennedy, *Freedom From Fear: The American People in Depression and War, 1929–1945*, Oxford University Press, New York, 1999, p. 469.

69 'Bretton Woods', issued by the Prime Minister (Mr Chifley), pp. 1–8.
70 'Chifley's Strong Plea for Ratification of Bretton Woods Agreement', *Morning Bulletin*, (Rockhampton, Queensland), 5 March 1947, p. 1.
71 'Bretton Woods', issued by the Prime Minister (Mr Chifley), p. 1.
72 ibid.
73 ibid., p. 2.
74 ibid.
75 ibid.
76 'The Bretton Woods Financial Agreement', by Ward, p. 7.
77 'Bretton Woods', issued by the Prime Minister (Mr Chifley), p. 2.
78 Cornish, *Sir Leslie Melville: An Interview*, p. 23.
79 Ed Conway, *The Summit*, Abacus, London, 2014, pp. 290–291; 296–297.
80 'Bretton Woods', issued by the Prime Minister (Mr Chifley), pp. 3–4.
81 ibid., p. 4.
82 'The Bretton Woods Financial Agreement', by Ward, p. 1.
83 'Bretton Woods', issued by the Prime Minister (Mr Chifley), p. 4.
84 ibid., p. 5.
85 ibid., p. 6.
86 ibid.
87 ibid., pp. 6–7.
88 ibid., p. 7.
89 ibid., p. 8.
90 ibid.
91 Crisp, *Ben Chifley*, p. 209.
92 *CPD*, HoR, 13 March 1947, p. 590.
93 ibid., p. 593.
94 *CPD*, HoR, 20 March 1947, p. 936.
95 ibid., pp. 936–939.
96 ibid., pp. 1001–1004; Crisp, *Ben Chifley*, p. 210.
97 *CPD*, HoR, 20 March 1947, p. 1001.
98 ibid., p. 1002.
99 Cotton, *Australian School*, p. 66.
100 *CPD*, HoR, 20 March 1947, p. 1002.
101 JG Crawford, 'Australia as a Pacific Power', in WGK Duncan (ed.), *Australia's Foreign Policy*, Angus and Robertson, Sydney, 1938, p. 103.
102 *CPD*, HoR, 20 March 1947, p. 1002.
103 ibid.
104 Capling, Considine and Crozier, *Australian Politics in the Global Era*, p. 40.
105 *CPD*, HoR, 20 March 1947, p. 1002.
106 ibid.
107 ibid., p. 1003.
108 Letter, Tange to Hodgson, 1 August 1944, including notes by JB Brigden. 'The Bretton Woods Conference: Some Impressions Not Wholly Without Prejudice', p. 1. NAA: M2271, 13.
109 *CPD*, HoR, 20 March 1947, p. 1003.
110 ibid.

111 *CPD*, HoR, 20 March 1947, p. 1003.
112 Iriye, *Cultural Internationalism and World Order*, p. 3.
113 Crisp, *Ben Chifley*, p. 211.
114 Crawford, *Australian Trade Policy 1942–1966*, p. 30, fn. 1.
115 Capling, *Australia and the Global Trade System*, p. 2.
116 Lee, *Search for Security*, p. 25; Capling, Considine and Crozier, *Australian Politics in the Global Era*, p. 39.
117 Crawford, *Australian Trade Policy 1942–1966*, p. 30.
118 Akira Iriye, 'Environmental History and International History', *Diplomatic History*, vol. 32, no. 4, 2008, p. 643.
119 'Bretton Woods', issued by the Prime Minister (Mr Chifley), p. 8.
120 'No Chance—Lang Candidate in Macquarie', *National Advocate* (Bathurst, NSW), 19 August 1931, p. 2.
121 'Macquarie Fight—Declaration of Poll', *National Advocate* (Bathurst, NSW), 9 January 1932, p. 2.
122 'War Reparations Problem—Great Change Must Come: Mr JB Chifley's Address to Rotarians', *National Advocate* (Bathurst, NSW), 20 July 1932, p. 1.

Part III
Chifley and Australian Foreign Policy Towards Asia

India's First Prime Minister, Jawaharlal Nehru, 1947.

CHAPTER FIVE
Chifley and Post-colonial Asia

World War II unleashed anti-colonial forces in Asia demanding independence from the old colonial powers of Europe, with the result that 'Asia was transformed as nations struggled to break free from the British, French and Dutch empires'.[1] Kenneth H Bailey, professor of public law at the University of Melbourne and adviser to the government from January 1943 on foreign affairs and constitutional law,[2] wrote that some in the Curtin government were aware as early as 1942, that 'there could be no return to the colonial status quo in the Pacific area'. World War II had 'injected powerful new factors into colonial history all over the world'.[3] As Frederic Eggleston, Australia's first minister to China and foreign policy adviser to the Curtin and Chifley governments, wrote in 1942, 'vast new forces have been released in the Far East which will not subside quietly after the war'.[4] After Japan's surrender, however, the European colonial powers set out to restore their old regimes to 'preserve the privileged place' they had previously enjoyed. But their weakness had been exposed, and their retreat in the face of the Japanese assault played a major role in hastening the decolonisation of the European empires.[5]

On 17 August 1945, Indonesian nationalist leaders, Sukarno (1901–1970) and Mohammad Hatta (1902–1980), declared an independent Indonesian Republic. Sukarno became the Indonesian Republic's president, serving from 1945 to 1967 and Hatta its vice-president from 1945 to 1956.⁶ Hatta also served as Indonesia's prime minister. The Dutch refused to accept the loss of its colony, the Netherlands East Indies (NEI), and began a protracted campaign to re-establish their colonial regime. A fierce struggle ensued between the Indonesian nationalists and their former colonial rulers. In July 1947 and December 1948, the Dutch launched military offensives against the Republic.⁷ Vietnam also declared its independence, but had to fight a brutal war against the French. In 1946 the Philippines gained its freedom from the United States; and in 1947, after a long and bitter struggle, India and Pakistan achieved independence from the British Empire, as did Burma and Ceylon in 1948. Korea gained 'a troubled and divided independence from Japan', and nationalist movements emerged in Malaya, Singapore and elsewhere in Southeast and East Asia. Japan's own empire was ended by the war and any ambitions it had regarding China were abandoned.⁸ During this period of decolonisation, the Chifley government made policy decisions in support of its Asian neighbours that previous Australian prime ministers and governments would have found unimaginable.⁹ This chapter will consider those policy decisions and the principles that drove them. It will also address the issues of whether there is any evidence of Chifley's early interest in Asia; Chifley's response to Asian nationalism; the actions the Chifley government took in regard to Australian foreign policy towards Asia and whether Chifley's interest in Asia continued when he was in Opposition.

Did Chifley Have an Early Interest in Asia?

Chifley's interest in Asia, which ranged over several decades, has intrigued a number of historians and writers.¹⁰ In the course of writing his biographical sketch for the *Australian Dictionary of Biography*, historian Duncan Waterson discovered that Crisp's account of Chifley's life had left out significant information about a trip to Indonesia and India that Chifley made in the 1920s.¹¹ When Crisp was asked why he hadn't included this information in his biography, he said it had been too late for changes because his biography was almost ready for publication.¹² According to Waterson, Chifley's trip to Asia was confirmed in conversations he had with Sir Richard Kirby, who was close to Chifley, and by 'Nugget' Coombs, one of Australia's most outstanding and influential public servants, who was an adviser to Chifley in the 1940s.¹³ Kirby also confirmed Chifley's visit to Indonesia in interviews with historian Margaret George in 1972 and with Evatt's biographer Peter Crockett in 1985. In a briefing session with the prime minister on Kirby's appointment to the United Nations Good Offices Committee on the Indonesian Question, established after the first Dutch military offensive in 1947, Chifley gave his general views on the Dutch and the 'colonial question'. According to Kirby, these impressions were 'highly flavoured' by Chifley's own experience during his visit to Batavia, the capital city of NEI, later renamed Jakarta. Chifley said he 'strongly disapproved of the Dutch and their attitude to the natives'.¹⁴ He was appalled at the 'colonial attitude'.¹⁵ Chifley also intimated that the same situation would have occurred if the British had colonised Indonesia.¹⁶ This was the nature of colonialism.

Chifley's visit is often given as a reason for his early opposition to the Dutch actions in Indonesia and his support for the Indonesian republicans. At a workshop held in 1996 to examine Australian postwar foreign policy on Indonesia, political scientist and Indonesian scholar Professor Jamie Mackie suggested to Dr John Burton, a former secretary of the Department of External Affairs, that Chifley thought the Dutch were not giving the Indonesians a 'fair go'. According to Mackie, this 'relates to the fact, and it's not very widely known, that Chifley actually made a boat trip to Java somewhere in the early 1930s, when he was out of Parliament'. While he was there, he closely observed the 'trade union situation on the waterfront'.¹⁷ At this same workshop, Australian diplomat Tom Critchley, who had served on the United Nations Good Offices Committee, mentioned that he too had been told of Chifley's pre-war visit to the Netherlands East Indies, where he was unimpressed with Dutch colonialism.¹⁸

Historians and writers such as Geoffrey Bolton and Peter Ryan have also written about Chifley's trip to Asia. In *Brief Lives*, a collection of Ryan's memories of friends and acquaintances, he mentions that during an informal meeting with Chifley a few months after the 1949 December election loss, Chifley told him something not widely known and not mentioned in Crisp's biography. During the depression, after the defeat of the Scullin government when he was unemployed, having lost the seat of Macquarie, Chifley had:

quietly made a private trip on a cargo boat, around Indonesia and South East Asia, 'just to see what was going on in those parts'. He had been appalled at the near-slavery working conditions on the docks at Batavia. 'I said to myself then, that if ever a time came, I'd do all I could for those poor buggers'.[19]

Geoffrey Bolton, author of 'The Middle Way', volume five of *The Oxford History of Australia*, was also disappointed that Crisp did not include information about Chifley's Asian trip in his biography. This was because it revealed an interest in Asia that was very uncommon at the time, especially among trade unionists.[20] Apparently Crisp missed the significance of this information.[21] His decision to ignore this episode puzzled Bolton because, as he wrote, it 'would have enhanced Chifley's reputation for foresight and concern for social justice'.[22] Chifley's trip to Indonesia and India revealed an interest in Asia that was rare among politicians and trade unionists during this period. With the exception of Labor minister John Dedman, who spent some time in the Indian Army after being wounded in action in World War I, and the conservative MP Percy Spender, who travelled through Asia as a tourist between the years 1929 and 1937, very few politicians or trade unionists of Chifley's era could claim an interest in, or acquaintance with Asia.[23] This is a significant gap in our knowledge of Chifley and his interest in Southeast Asia and India. All the evidence indicates that Chifley did indeed visit the region in the inter-war years, and this experience inspired his deep interest in Asia, both before and during his prime ministership.

Chifley's Response to Indonesian Nationalism

One of the first post-war challenges confronting the Australian government in its region was how to respond to Indonesia's struggle for independence from the Netherlands. Historian Peter Dennis has argued that the Chifley government's policy towards Indonesia was determined solely by security concerns, and the government arrived at its position of supporting the Indonesian nationalists 'reluctantly'. According to Dennis, Chifley and Dr Evatt, as minister for External Affairs, initially thought that Australia's post-war security could be achieved through a 'readjustment but not abandonment of Dutch control over the NEI'. It was only when a breakdown in Dutch–Indonesian talks occurred, and the Dutch took military action against the Republic in July 1947, that the Australian government came out on the side of the nationalists.[24] Yet Chifley's interest and intervention in Australian foreign policy on Indonesia was evident much earlier than this.

On 25 September 1944 the Australian War Cabinet had indicated they would accept 'in principle', a request made in August by the Netherlands government to train, accommodate and maintain 30 000 Dutch troops in Australia.[25] These troops would undoubtedly have been used for future deployment to the Netherlands East Indies against the Indonesian nationalists. On 1 June 1945, however, Chifley as acting prime minister announced that Australia had only a limited capacity to 'accept additional commitments' to maintain other forces in Australia.[26] Later that month, the Advisory War Cabinet vetoed Australia's acceptance of the 30 000 Dutch troops and the dispatch of a further 5600 troops.[27] On 8 August Chifley, who was now prime minister, issued a press statement confirming the decision by the War Cabinet which, on the advice of the Advisory War Council, had rejected the Dutch government's request to base a Netherlands force in Australia. He also took exception to public criticism from the Dutch government over the Australian government's decision.[28]

On 10 August 1945 the Netherlands minister to Australia, Baron Van Aerssen, wrote a rather heavy-handed letter to Chifley in an attempt to pressure him to reconsider the 'completely unexpected change of attitude of the Commonwealth Government' regarding the basing and training of Dutch troops in Australia.[29] In his detailed and curt reply a month later, Prime Minister Chifley refused to budge, noting that the government's rejection of the proposal was 'unavoidable', as acceptance of Dutch troops in Australia would involve additional 'training, outfitting, feeding and maintenance', which would place an intolerable burden on an 'already overtaxed economy'. Furthermore, the September 1944 decision to consider the proposal to base 30 000 Dutch troops in Australia, was not a definite commitment.[30] Chifley's decision resulted in angry accusations against the new prime minister by the conservative Menzies Opposition, who hoped the Commonwealth would reconsider its decision, as there were many 'positive advantages' in training, accommodating and equipping these Dutch troops in Western Australia. According to Robert Menzies, these troops could be supplied with armaments by Australia in the Netherland's battle against the Indonesian nationalists. In addition, 'the warm reception of these troops would promote close mutual goodwill with the NEI which was of first importance'.[31] The media also accused the government of 'Cold Shouldering An Ally'.[32] The prime minister, however, withstood pressure from both the media and the Opposition and did not reverse his decision.

Chifley's early views on the situation in Indonesia and the possibility of conflict between the Dutch and the Indonesian nationalists were revealed in an off-the-record conversation with journalists in October 1945, when he accused the Dutch of 'opportunistic realism' in their campaign to regain their NEI colony following the end of World War II. He stated bluntly that their policy 'evidently was to allow' the allies 'to do the reconquest and then step in and resume possession'. Chifley told the journalists that information the Commonwealth had gained regarding Indonesia, 'indicated that the spirit of revolt against the Dutch was very deep seated and enthusiastic. It was a real independence movement but so far as he was aware there was no communist inspiration behind it'. He declared that, 'Australia would not send troops to participate in a civil war in the Indies'. Furthermore, 'public opinion would not be likely to tolerate such a project if it were mooted'.[33]

The next year, in August 1946, Chifley wrote to Evatt, who was overseas at the time, that the Dutch had recently sought Australia's assistance in their battle to maintain their hold on Indonesia. The Royal Netherlands Navy requested that Australia supply munitions and base facilities to support naval operations in the NEI. Chifley observed that, in essence, the government was being asked for permission for the Dutch to base a small fleet in Australia. Chifley wrote that cabinet denied the request, on the basis that 'the Dutch were not making a bone fide effort to negotiate a peaceful settlement and that if Australia facilitated the building up of Dutch military strength under these conditions we might well stir up lasting resentment amongst the Indonesians'.[34]

The tone of this letter makes it very clear that Chifley was in charge of Australian foreign policy on Indonesia. The previous month, on 3 July 1946, Chifley had written to British prime minister Clement Attlee, that every effort should be made to convince the Dutch that 'Nationalist aspirations in Indonesia are real and strong and that the Indonesians should be met more than half way'.[35] Chifley had outlined his government's attitude towards the situation in Indonesia in a cable to the British prime minister the previous year, in October 1945. Australia had a vital interest in ensuring that 'a satisfactory and enduring settlement guaranteeing political stability, social progress and our own military security' was achieved in Indonesia. He was unequivocal in his statement that 'the nationalist movement in Java is widespread' and Sukarno's administration was 'not simply a Japanese creation'. Until a negotiated settlement was reached, Dutch military forces should be banned from entering the region and Dutch authority should continue to be suspended.[36]

The argument that the Chifley government's policy on post-war Indonesia was determined solely by security concerns is based on a limited view of Chifley's concept of 'security', which needs to be understood in a much more complex context. World War II had 'shattered' the complacent belief that the British Empire could protect Australia in its region: it was obvious that Australia had to find new answers to the problem of its security.[37] Australia needed to 'make its own way in the world, and that included coming to terms with its own region'.[38] Moreover, security was not seen solely through a military prism. As Chifley stated to Attlee, security in the Pacific region was dependent on the adoption of policies that would 'ensure political, social and economic progress for the native inhabitants'—all three aspects being of equal importance. Chifley emphasised how critical it was that living standards improved and political and social progress was achieved.[39] War was not inevitable if economic and social deprivation could be prevented. For Chifley, 'short-term military solutions were no answer to the problems of poverty, and economic and social backwardness that prevailed throughout the region'.[40] There should also be some international responsibility for reform in the NEI, involving a degree of 'nationalist autonomy'.[41] Chifley's approach, as it was explained to Evatt in November 1945, by Dr John Burton,[42] was that the Australian government 'must avoid giving impression we are prepared to intervene in ways other than diplomatic. General approach we are following is to stress vital interests but to keep free of military obligations'.[43]

A Pressing Need for Intelligence on Indonesia

There was also a pressing need for intelligence about the situation in Indonesia and its nationalist leaders, which reflected an important principle that drove Chifley's foreign policy: his belief that policy should be based on expert knowledge of the situation on the ground, not on simplistic slogans. Political scientist, academic, author and journalist William Macmahon Ball had been a radio commentator with the Australian Broadcasting Commission since 1934.[44] He became a popular speaker on Asia and international relations, and Chifley was one of his 'keenest listeners'.[45] Ball had written earlier that, in order to develop a 'wise' Australian foreign policy, there was a desperate need in Australia for an informed public that was well-versed in world affairs. One of the essential conditions for the creation of a well-informed public was access to 'accurate information about other countries, so that we [Australians] may see the world in true perspective'.[46]

In November 1945 Ball made a major contribution to the provision of 'accurate information' about Australia's region when Chifley appointed him Australia's political representative to the Commander of the Allied Forces in the Netherlands East Indies, stationed in Batavia. In making the appointment, Chifley disregarded the advice of Esler Dening, political adviser to the British Supreme Commander in South East Asia, Lord Louis Mountbatten, that 'the future of the NEI was solely a matter for negotiation between the Dutch and the nationalists'. Chifley insisted that countries such as Australia, whose security was involved, should also have a say in any NEI settlement.[47] Ball's role was to gain first-hand intelligence on the situation in Indonesia and to exert some degree of influence on behalf of the Australian government over decolonisation policies in the NEI. He was to determine 'how far the Republic was a genuine nationalist movement and to assess the calibre of the Republican leaders'.[48] According to economist, JE Isaac, who accompanied Ball to Batavia as an assistant and observer, Australia had previously relied on the British Foreign Office to provide intelligence and guidance on policy. This was no longer acceptable to the Australian government.

Australia was 'no longer inhibited by quasi-colonial ties with the UK; indeed there was some disenchantment with the UK for the circumstances surrounding the fall of Malaya and Singapore'. Isaac noted that very little information had been gathered about the conditions in Indonesia during the Japanese occupation. It was essential to 'obtain an independent assessment of the situation'.[49]

Ball arrived in Batavia on 7 November 1945, where according to his diary, he was met with 'icy formality' by HJ Van Mook, the NEI lieutenant governor-general, and received a cool response from the British military and civil authorities.[50] In contrast, as he wrote to Burton, he was received 'most cordially' by Sukarno, vice-president Hatta, foreign minister Soebardjo, information minister Sjarifuddin, and other Indonesian cabinet members.[51] Ball concluded it was unlikely that a satisfactory settlement would be achieved between the Dutch and the Indonesian leaders. He doubted the accuracy of British intelligence, which was often 'generalised' and 'inaccurate', and conflicted with his own information, which was received directly from sources he had contacted. The British were totally reliant on the Dutch for their intelligence, but the Dutch were not only 'partisan', they had admitted misreading the situation in Java under the Japanese occupation. British policy was determined solely by their need to maintain friendly relations with the Netherlands in Europe.

Ball dismissed Dutch intelligence as propaganda. He emphasised that British 'apathy ignorance and misinformation' about the Indonesian nationalist movement made it essential that a third party, or indeed the United Nations, inquire into the situation.[52] Ball wrote in his report to Burton, that British and Dutch reports of Japanese complicity in the present troubles had been exaggerated, while the 'burning bitterness between Dutch and Indonesians' had been downplayed in official reports.[53] His belief was, that if the Dutch re-occupied Java under the protection of the British military, 'unlimited trouble' would result. Indonesian nationalist opposition to Dutch re-occupation was 'nearly, if not quite universal'.[54]

Ball's intelligence was in stark contrast to the views of the United States Department of State, which in June 1945 argued in a policy paper on post-war Asia and the Pacific, that in Indonesia, the 'great mass of the natives will welcome the expulsion of the Japanese and the return of the Dutch to control'.[55] This was a serious failure of intelligence by US policy-makers, who were more concerned with ensuring that their European allies—the United Kingdom, France and the Netherlands—regained their cohesion and strength to meet the Soviet threat in Europe.[56] Mountbatten would also later regret the lack of accurate information about the situation in post-war Indonesia. Neither the Americans nor Mountbatten's own staff had provided him with 'any idea of the strength of the nationalist movement'.[57]

In his report, Ball wrote that Indonesian leaders believed the British were biased towards the Dutch and had 'already prejudged the issue by its recognition of Dutch sovereignty'.[58] Most Dutch administrators and officers displayed 'a muddling ineptitude in almost every enterprise they undertake' and it seemed the only solution for the Dutch was the use of 'force, and still more force, to teach the "natives" a lesson'.[59] Ball noted that European technical and administrative support, and advice was needed, and Indonesian leaders agreed on this matter, though they emphasised that advisers and technical assistants were wanted, 'not rulers'. He wrote there was a 'deep emotional resentment' against the return of Dutch rule, which was 'nearly universal'.[60] The Dutch had exploited Indonesia for centuries and abandoned their colony to the Japanese, focusing on their own defence in Europe. In Ball's opinion, if no settlement was reached, 'nationalist resentment would grow in strength and we would be faced with the prospect of a long civil war in Java'.

While Ball appreciated the importance of the region to Australia, he could not see Australia being successful in taking up an independent role as mediator between the Nationalists and the Dutch. First, Australia would need to be accepted in this role by both parties, and it was doubtful the Dutch would agree; second, if Australia was accepted, there would be an obligation to back this 'political intervention with military force'. From his experience visiting Morotai and Borneo, any decision to transfer troops to Java would be met with resentment from the troops who were anxious to return home. A 'major domestic crisis' would eventuate. For this reason Ball recommended that if Australia was to play a part in the conflict in Java, 'we should do so, not as an independent nation, but as a member of the United Nations, which is specially concerned with an area of such strategic and political importance for our future'.[61] As James Cotton observes, Macmahon Ball, in his 'masterful' report on his mission to

Batavia emphasised, first, the uniqueness of Australia's interests in this region; second, the enormous scale of 'political and social change' occurring in Southeast Asia, and third, the 'lack of sympathy of European powers with either'.[62]

When Ball returned from his mission to Batavia in December 1945, Chifley requested an interview with him. The prime minister and the minister for External Affairs, Evatt, had earlier had a difference of opinion over how Australia should respond to the Indonesian Republic's struggle against the Netherlands' attempt to reinstate its colonial regime. In November 1945 Evatt had put forward a proposal that Australia send a military force to Java until an agreement was negotiated between Indonesian nationalists and the Dutch.[63] Chifley, however, had rejected Evatt's proposal. While Chifley believed that a settlement in Indonesia was essential before the situation deteriorated further, he ruled out any additional commitment of Australian forces. Instead, he thought it best to monitor the situation.[64] Chifley—according to his long-standing beliefs—thought that military engagement should be avoided at all cost.

During his meeting with Ball, Chifley was very keen to hear his views on Evatt's proposal that 'Australian military forces should relieve the Dutch forces in Indonesia'. Ball told Chifley that it would be a 'profound mistake' to take on this responsibility, and that an 'Australian military presence would inevitably mean political involvement, and almost certain conflict with the Dutch or the Indonesians or both'. Chifley's response was that he was pleased to hear Ball's opinion on this issue, 'because it made him surer he was right and the "Doc" wrong on this'.[65] Ball would recall later, that this meeting was the 'beginning of a long period of mutual trust between him and Chifley'.[66]

A Need for Intelligence on Asia

The Australian government also needed information about the wider situation in a decolonising Asia. One way of gaining this was by attending international gatherings. In 1947 the Chifley government provided financial and diplomatic support for private research organisations, the Australian Institute of International Affairs (AIIA) and the Australian Institute of Political Science (AIPS), who were invited by the Indian Council of World Affairs (ICWA), to send observers to attend the Asian Relations Conference in New Delhi which would be held from 23 March to 2 April 1947.[67] The observer chosen by the AIPS was John McCallum, a well-known commentator on international affairs. Gerald Packer, businessman, advisor to the government and vice-president of the AIIA was selected by this institute as their observer.[68] Convened by the ICWA, the conference was initiated by Jawaharlal Nehru who would become India's prime minister in August 1947. Nehru celebrated the conference as a landmark event in which 'Asia, after a long period of quiescence, has suddenly become important again in world affairs'.[69] Its main aim was to investigate the economic, social and cultural problems shared by all post-war Asian countries.[70] Of primary importance was to consider how to end foreign domination—both political and economic—of Asia.[71]

For the Australian government, it was an intelligence gathering exercise and an opportunity for the Australian observers to meet and observe influential Asian leaders. At the conference, highly qualified Asian experts compiled reports from various round table discussion groups on economic, social and cultural issues common to post-war Asian countries. These reports provided a representative selection of 'Asian informed opinion upon Asian problems'[72] providing the Australian government with a significant amount of information previously not available in Australia.[73] The reports indicated the 'direction that policy in Asia would take if the major nationalist Southeast Asian movements were to attain power'.[74] Political and economic imperialism was condemned at the conference, together with a demand for the 'complete withdrawal' from Asia of the European imperialists.[75] The Australian observers also identified an 'undercurrent of distrust of Soviet Russia'.[76] The observers noted that there was 'a frequently expressed desire to avoid the nascent Imperialisms; United States was mentioned but the Soviet was clearly in mind'.[77]

In addition, 'lines of cleavage' between Southeast Asian countries and India and China were also very apparent.[78] It was feared that India and China would replace the old European colonialists to become the new 'Imperialist powers exploiting Sout[h]east Asia'.[79] The great diversity in the 'political, social and economic development' of Asian countries was evident in the Australian observers' report on the 1947 conference.[80] The distrust of Soviet Russia so obvious at the conference, challenged the view propagated by the Menzies Opposition, that Russian influence and communist agitation were the driving forces behind Asian nationalist movements.[81] The information gained from the conference would undoubtedly have provided supporting evidence for Chifley in his determination to back the Indonesian nationalists against the Dutch.[82] It reveals the 'political and ideological divide' between the Chifley government and the Menzies Opposition and validates Chifley's stance on decolonisation and his support for Indian and Indonesian nationalist movements.[83]

Dutch Military Offensives Against the Indonesian Republic

In July 1947 the Netherlands launched their first military action against the Indonesian Republic. Australia, together with India, supported the republicans by referring the conflict to the United Nations Security Council. This was the start of a joint effort by Australia and India, two small to medium powers, to rally the United Nations in support of the 'beleaguered Indonesian Republic'. The Chifley government's actions were opposed by Britain and the United States, and criticised by Robert Menzies, the leader of the Opposition, as the 'very ecstasy of suicide', that Australia, 'a country isolated in the world, with a handful of people, a white man's country', should side against the Dutch, a former ally.[84] A truce was established when the Netherlands and the Indonesian Republic signed the Renville Agreement on 17–19 January 1948, an arrangement that was described by Justice Richard Kirby as 'unfair' to the Republic.[85]

Negotiations between the Dutch and the republican leaders continued, but broke down on 11 December 1948, when the Dutch delegation informed the UN Good Offices Committee that further talks would be pointless.[86] On 15 December 1948 Chifley wrote to the British Prime Minister, Clement Attlee, that he had been following the situation in Indonesia closely and was concerned that negotiations between the Republicans and the Dutch had broken down. He was greatly concerned that the Dutch were unwilling to negotiate with Indonesia's prime minister, Mohammad Hatta.[87] An 'intellectual' and 'a devout Muslim', Hatta was 'nonetheless committed to secular socialist political doctrines'.[88] According to DEA diplomat

Tom Critchley, Hatta was 'friendly and pleasant, small in stature but big in intellect'.[89] Chifley noted that Hatta was a 'moderate', who had shown he was capable of uniting the Indonesian nationalists and had suppressed a serious communist rebellion in Madiun.[90] The party he led, Masjumi, the 'main Islamic political party',[91] was opposed to the Indonesian Communist party, the PKI.[92] Chifley disagreed strongly with Attlee's argument that the republic needed to be persuaded to accept Dutch demands such as placing the republican army under Dutch command.[93]

In his cable to Attlee, Chifley wrote that Hatta had gone out of his way to accommodate the Netherlands. In fact, some of Hatta's supporters thought he had 'already gone too far'. The Dutch needed to include the Indonesian republic in a federal system in which it would be 'effectively represented and would take an effective part in administration'. Unless there was evidence that this had occurred, Australia would not attempt to persuade the republic to accept Dutch conditions. Chifley thought the repercussions would be very serious if Australia were to push the Indonesians to accept what he viewed as 'unreasonable demands'. This would 'widen the gulf between Eastern and Western countries in this area which throughout these negotiations we have persistently endeavoured to bridge'.[94]

Opposed to extremism in all its forms, both religious and political, Chifley was concerned that the Dutch were unable to recognise that Hatta was their best chance of reaching an acceptable and lasting resolution, and refused to assist Hatta in resolving the difficulties that confronted him with his own people, in having to make further concessions to the Dutch. Chifley argued it was 'impossible to discern much effort by the Dutch to meet Hatta half way, they had continued to stick rigidly to their main demands and the fact that the parties have come so far towards agreement is largely a measure of the lengths to which Hatta has been prepared to go'.[95] When the Dutch unleashed a second brutal military attack against the Indonesian Republic on 19 December 1948, Chifley acted promptly, issuing a press statement condemning the Dutch offensive.[96] At a meeting of the UN Security Council in Paris, on 23 December, Australia's representative accused the Netherlands of carrying out the first clear breach of the United Nations Charter, the consequence of which would be expulsion from the United Nations if the Security Council so ruled.[97]

The Security Council's response was half-hearted and ineffectual, calling for a cease-fire, rather than a withdrawal of Dutch troops.[98] This led the Indian prime minister, Jawaharlal Nehru, to propose a conference to be held in New Delhi in January 1949. Australia was invited to attend. The conference would 'provide regional support for the Indonesian Republic's cause and discuss the Indonesian-Dutch conflict'.[99] Australia's attendance was criticised by the Australian press and by a number of experts. Frederic Eggleston, government adviser on international affairs and an early supporter of Australia's engagement with the Asia-Pacific region, warned the government that although the 'Dutch action [is] totally unjustifiable', the risk of being associated with the 'extreme views of Asiatic people at the Conference' was significant. The 'dangers of acceptance ... outweigh the dangers of refusal'.[100] Public concern was fuelled further by Robert Menzies, who said that Australia's decision to attend the New Delhi conference when Great Britain was not invited was a 'great blunder'.[101] Australia should not take sides against a European colonial power such as the Netherlands, and, furthermore, Australia was represented by a delegation rather than observers, 'the only government outside Asia whose representatives attended the conference'.[102]

The New Delhi conference, however, proved to be highly successful. The 'unprecedented demonstration of Asian solidarity', and the extensive media coverage that the conference received,[103] forced the United States—which previously had been much more concerned 'about the political and economic stability of Western Europe and the retention of its solidarity in the cold war'—to reconsider its position. Because of popular support for the republicans, US policy became more supportive of the Indonesians.[104] Just over four years after the declaration of the republic, Indonesia would win its independence when a formal transference of sovereignty to the Republic of the United States of Indonesia (RUSI), occurred on 27 December 1949.[105]

Nationalism the Driving Force in Asia

In 1948, the Australian government had sent a goodwill mission to Southeast Asia and East Asia (May to July 1948), headed by William

Macmahon Ball.[106] Ball's report on the mission was invaluable, confirming a number of observations from the 1947 Asian Relations Conference. In his 1948 report, Ball wrote that he had witnessed a 'deep-rooted and passionate nationalism' that was 'the main driving force in every country he visited'. It was a resistance movement against political domination by the old colonial powers and against economic exploitation by European nations. Southeast Asian countries also resented economic encroachment by resident Chinese and Indian traders and financiers. He concluded that European colonialism was rapidly 'drawing to a close'.[107] Ball's report—according to John Burton, the secretary of the Department of External Affairs—was a comprehensive explanation of the Australian government's position regarding Southeast Asia. Moreover, the 'Prime Minister was particularly interested in the conclusions [Ball] reached, as they appeared to confirm his more casual observations when he passed through the area'. These conclusions were annotated as having been seen by the prime minister.[108]

The intelligence gathered by Macmahon Ball on his mission to Batavia in 1945, his 1948 goodwill mission to Southeast Asia, together with the Asian expert opinion contained within the report by the observers from the Australian Institute of International Affairs and the Australian Institute of Political Science on the 1947 Asian Relations Conference in New Delhi was extensive. It informed and lent weight to the views Chifley expressed in the House of Representatives on 2 September 1948. In this speech, Chifley declared:

> The disturbances which are taking place in the world go a good deal deeper than just the issue of communism ... It is quite true that wherever there is a fire the Communists put on their uniforms and go to the fire to pour oil on a blaze that is already burning. I have no illusions about that, but the great upsurge of nationalism that is occurring now throughout the East has roots that go deeper than communism. This upsurge may not have any clear objectives. It is a rebellion, sometimes an economic rebellion, against conditions under which the people have been living.[109]

This speech is a clear account of Chifley's response to the rise of Asian nationalism and reveals his understanding of the radical changes taking place in Asia.[110] According to Chifley, communism was not the source of unrest in Asia: instead, communists took advantage of the desperate 'economic conditions' which provided 'a fertile bed in which communism can take root and flourish'.[111] A few months later, in a report to the nation, the prime minister said that international cooperation to improve economic conditions in Asia was necessary to resolve and to prevent further conflict from occurring.[112] He would say later that to imagine that all the problems in the East could be attributed to communism was 'utter delusion'.[113]

During the post-war period, tension increased between the two super powers—the United States and the Soviet Union—and 'the world divided into two armed camps'. With the intensification of the Cold War in the latter part of the 1940s, there was increased speculation about the likelihood of another war. The United States initiated a 'policy of containment' towards the Soviet Union, while the British government endeavoured to establish a Western Union, consolidating Western Europe as an anti-Russian bloc. Australia, however, rejected the direction that the United States and Britain's foreign and defence policies had taken. Instead, the Chifley government continued to place its faith in collective security, preferring to work through the United Nations to settle international conflicts in order to avert war.[114]

As the Cold War intensified, it was played out in proxy sites in post-war Asia, which increasingly became, as Chifley later described South Korea, 'the battlefield of two world ideologies'.[115] Chifley opposed military intervention in 'conflicts arising out of the revolutions in East Asia', refusing to militarise Australia's response to the region, believing that another war was to be avoided at all cost. As a 'fiscally conservative Treasurer', he would not agree to open-ended military commitments.[116] In 1948 and 1949, the United Kingdom asked the Chifley government four times to send Australian troops to Malaya and Hong Kong, when communists challenged British colonial authority. Four times Chifley said no.[117] The Chifley government also rejected Britain's strategic plan for the Commonwealth in which Australian troops would be sent to the Middle East in the event of war.[118] As historian David Lowe notes, one of the most distinctive aspects of the latter part of the 1940s was that the Chifley government, at home and abroad, refused to accept the American and British Cold War 'framework for understanding change' and sought to escape the constraints of the emerging Cold War that divided the world into two polarised camps.[119] Unlike the Menzies Opposition, Chifley and his government refused to conflate the rise of nationalist movements throughout Asia with communist insurrection.

There was an intractable and unyielding divide between the Chifley government and the Menzies Opposition in their understanding of the changes happening in the post-war Asia-Pacific. This is revealed in a heated exchange between the prime minister and Percy Spender, the Opposition's foreign affairs spokesperson on 2 September 1948.[120] In this debate, Chifley's belief that the emergent nationalism in Asia was real and deep seated and not the result of communist agitation is evident. Chifley also reveals his wide-ranging knowledge of Asia. Spender accused the government of neglecting, first, international affairs; second, the defence of Australia; and third, the threat that communists posed in Australia. Curiously, Spender accused Evatt, the minister for External Affairs, of neglecting Australia's interest in international affairs by spending too much time abroad, adding 'he could be better engaged in this country!'

Spender spoke of the 'shadows of war lengthening on the horizon' and 'the mounting fires of hostility throughout the world'. He censured the government for a lack of guidance in this area and accused it of ignoring the issue of communism—'the monster that is seeking to destroy it'. Spender charged the Chifley government with 'a complete lack of reality' in Australia's foreign policy and a failure to 'grapple realistically' with the issue of communist subversion.[121] According to Spender, Australia was becoming 'more and more isolated from the world. We are a handful of white people in a coloured sea, and all the nations of the East—Burma, Malaya, Indonesia, Indo-China—are becoming more and more under the domination of the Communist ideology ... activated or aided from one place, namely, Moscow'.[122] Spender accused the Chifley government of appeasing Russia, of being oblivious to the fact that Russia's ultimate intention was world domination[123] and ignoring the dangers posed by the communist insurgency in Malaya by delaying aid.

Australia should have volunteered assistance, rather than waiting to be asked. Instead, 'we have done nothing except to send to Malaya a few miserable rifles and sten guns'. The insurgency was 'not only a direct threat to our own country, but was also a threat to British interests throughout the world'.[124]

In a scathing response to Spender's speech, Chifley noted: 'One of the most amusing things about the honorable member for Warringah is his conceit', in that he professed to be a 'world authority on international affairs'.[125] He then addressed Spender's suggestion that Australia should rush troops and warships to Malaya to assist Britain in putting down the communist insurgency there. Chifley argued that the situation in Malaya was a 'difficult problem'. While he acknowledged he was not as 'fully informed as the honourable member for Warringah about so many aspects of world affairs', and he was certainly not as garrulous as the honourable member, a number of government representatives from many countries provided him with information on international politics and economic affairs.[126] In this speech, Chifley revealed that he was well informed about Malaya and its 'complex ethnic' mix, providing facts and figures about the Malay, Chinese, Indian and European populations living there. He also revealed his opinion of European colonialism. Of the Europeans he said, 'it is a fact that a great many of those 17 000 Europeans went to Malaya, not for love of the country, but for what profit they could make from it'—a comment greeted with outrage from the Menzies Opposition.[127]

Chifley accepted that Asian nationalist aspirations were based on a desire for independence from European colonial rule and improved living standards. These were ambitions that 'could not be ignored'. Military intervention in nationalist conflicts was therefore rejected in favour of diplomatic initiatives.[128] This had been a continuous theme in Chifley's thinking. The destruction caused by war, together with the massive expenditure incurred by nations to support a war industry, was of great concern to him. Chifley had been appalled at the human and material cost of World War I; he was dismayed that lessons had not been learnt from the war, in which an enormous amount of wealth had been 'used up almost entirely for destructive purposes'.[129] He believed military intervention was not a solution to conflict and argued there should be a limit to how much was spent on defence needs, otherwise a country would become laden with debt.[130] We can see here the ongoing impact that the tragic waste of war had on Chifley's thinking. It meant that he would oppose military intervention in conflicts in Asia, unless it was under the direction of the United Nations.

Chifley in Opposition

Chifley's interest in Asia continued and intensified when he was leader of the Opposition after his government's defeat in the 1949 election on 10 December. According to his biographer Crisp, Chifley was 'very interested in the development of the new nation states of Asia, particularly on the economic side'.[131] Although no longer in government, with all the resources available to a prime minister, it is obvious that Chifley was well informed, receiving advice from various well-known international figures and experts.[132] Chifley looked in detail at the various countries and kept up-to-date with reports on the economic and political situation in a number of countries in Asia. As the Cold War polarised the world into competing ideological and strategic alliances, Chifley opposed the West's policy of aligning itself with undemocratic and corrupt Asian regimes in its crusade against communism. Chifley's views converged with those of Jawaharlal Nehru, whom he often quoted in his speeches in parliament when he was leader of the Labor Opposition.

The United Nations decision to support South Korea, after the invasion by North Korea on 25 June 1950, was given bipartisan support in the Australian parliament.[133] In a speech in the House of Representatives in September 1950, Chifley expressed surprise at the Menzies government's support for the United Nations. Especially since members of the government, 'only a few years ago, used to sneer and scoff at the United Nations'—an institution the labour movement had always supported.[134] In fact, 'the Menzies government was not a "latter-day" convert to the cause of the UN'.[135] As Menzies declared to cabinet on 25 August 1950: 'We are pretending that Korea is a UN operation. But we would not be in it unless US were in, and we are in it because they are in it … on a political basis we have been pretending that everything is based on the UN'.[136]

Chifley then provided his views on the role of the United Nations. Its main value was that it delivered a form of 'international arbitration'.¹³⁷ It was a forum in which grievances could be discussed and vexatious matters could be 'brought out into the open'. For Chifley, the United Nations provided the opportunity for 'mediation and conciliation in the settlement of disputes'. While understanding the constraints confronting the United Nations, and somewhat doubtful that it was capable of enforcing its decisions, Chifley saw its 'very great value as a forum for the expression of views, for the adjustment of grievances, and for the exercise of conciliation among the nations'. The Labor Party and others had supported this international organisation because it was the only way to avoid another world war. He noted, however, that the use of the word 'peace' was not very 'fashionable' nowadays: indeed, the word 'peace' was an 'anathema' to some. He deplored the fact that those who advocated peace were accused of being sympathetic to communism.¹³⁸

Chifley emphasised that the labour movement was fully alert to the dangers of the 'pernicious doctrines that have been promulgated in the ideology of communism'. He condemned Russian imperialism and the Soviet Union's failure to show any commitment to the attainment of peace through the United Nations.¹³⁹ However, Chifley was troubled by the fact that if the term communist was applied to revolutionary movements or movements of dissent in Asia, and people were denied what would eventually be given them, then Western countries would find themselves in a difficult position.¹⁴⁰ The West was making a tragic mistake in supporting corrupt regimes to counter communism. If the West persisted in involving itself in various nationalist struggles in support of 'outmoded, reactionary and feudal forms of government' in its crusade against communism, this would invite the ongoing 'hatred and hostility of the Eastern peoples'.¹⁴¹ The Syngman Rhee regime in South Korea was one of those governments.

Chifley was in no doubt that North Korea was a police state: it had shown 'wanton and brutal aggression' in its 'premeditated' attack on South Korea. But, although Labor supported the United Nations intervention in Korea, this did not mean that the party supported a government such as the 'completely corrupt' South Korean government led by Syngman Rhee. Chifley then referred to a United Nations report on Korea which stated:

> [I]n 1949, under the national security provisions of the Rhee government, 118,000 people were arrested and thrown in gaol, that the Constitution of the country was violated, that the arrests were, in many instances, made brutally, and that some of the arrested persons were subjected to torture. That is an indication of the kind of government that was in power in South Korea prior to the outbreak of the present fighting.[142]

Chifley repeated that, although the Labor Party accepted that North Korean aggression should be resisted, it would not support corrupt regimes.[143] When in government, he had been fully briefed on the nature of the South Korean administration. Respected diplomat Patrick Shaw, head of the Australian Mission in Japan, informed the Department of External Affairs in November 1947, that he had endeavoured to gain information about South Korea from people in Tokyo who had recently visited the country. Shaw reported that Australian journalist Denis Warner, local manager of news agencies Reuters and AAP, provided the Australian mission in Japan with valuable accounts of conditions in South Korea. Warner described the situation there as 'extremely difficult'. Shaw wrote that the local South Korean government was generally described as 'inefficient and riddled with nepotism and corruption'. In addition, there was no Korean leader with any aptitude for leadership. Dr Syngman Rhee, who was sponsored by the United States,[144] was a 'self-seeking' and 'aged rightist leader with [a] strong following'.[145] In his seventies, he was a 'strong anti-Communist', who had spent twenty-six years in exile in the United States.[146] Described as a 'would-be dictator', Rhee had put together a formidable political machine and became the leader of the extreme right in South Korea.[147] Shaw reported that real authority and power lay in the hands of the 'ruthless' South Korean police force which was controlled by Syngman Rhee and the G-2 section of the US Headquarters in Korea. The United States was intent on suppressing the left and did not look too closely at the methods used. Shaw wrote that 'torture and murder' were common, and 'Korean prisons are now fuller of political prisoners than under Japanese rule'.[148]

According to Shaw, the situation in Korea was very similar to that in China, where the United States was committed to supporting an 'inefficient and corrupt' Nationalist government, led by Chiang Kai-shek, whose main concern was to maintain its own 'privileged position' and to forcibly suppress all political opposition. In both instances, the US was committing itself to supporting an unstable 'narrow reactionary group'. Shaw wrote that in both Korea and China, US interest was 'strategic', in that the United States intended to establish a bulwark against the Soviet Union. The region was seen to be important strategically because the Americans in Tokyo considered it a possible 'starting point' for what they saw as the inevitable conflict between the United States and the Soviet Union.[149] Receiving all this information from trusted advisers such as Patrick Shaw, during his time as prime minister, meant that Chifley was fully informed about the corrupt nature of the Syngman Rhee government and the devastating impact that the war would have on the civilians of South Korea.

For some time Chifley had also been concerned about the considerable evidence of corruption in the Chinese Nationalist administration.[150] In August 1946 Douglas Copland had reported after his appointment as the Australian Minister to China, that the Nationalists were 'inept and incapable of pulling the country together'; furthermore, he thought it was inevitable that a communist regime would supplant the Nationalists.[151] Chifley had also been informed that aid provided to China by the United Nations Relief and Rehabilitation Administration (UNRRA) had been 'squandered' and diverted to the black market.[152] Chifley declared that the Nationalist administration was so corrupt that it 'was prepared to sell, give away or surrender large quantities of goods which America was providing to assist the Allies against Japan'.[153] At the time, the Chifley government was forced to be guarded in its comments in public: it did not wish to publicise the issue because it could put at risk the whole UNRRA aid program.[154]

The Nationalist government was defeated by the communists led by Mao Zedong and the People's Republic of China was established in October 1949.[155] In September 1950 Chifley argued in parliament that the United States had made a 'grave diplomatic mistake' in refusing to allow China admission to the United Nations.

He said that if Western countries wished to resist aggression and create a buffer against Russian ideology and imperialism, then it must also be acknowledged that 'there is an upsurge of nationalism in the East'. Furthermore, Chifley's reading of Chinese history led him to believe that China would never become a 'satellite' of another country. He condemned the Australian government for voting with the United States. In response to Menzies' claim that his government was pursuing a 'realist' position, Chifley suggested instead, that the Menzies government's policy was to deny the reality of the situation in China. A country with a population of about 460 million people could not be ignored. He argued that it was 'diplomatic foolishness' to deny recognition of China because of a disagreement with that country's political system. Britain's recognition of the People's Republic of China was contrasted with the policy followed by Australia and the United States. What was needed was 'cold logic' when considering these issues. Any attempt by the Western democracies to suppress 'nationalist movements for self-determination' would be disastrous.[156]

When accused by Spender of not recognising the People's Republic of China when his government was in power, Chifley replied that with a general election imminent, a controversial decision such as this should be decided by the incoming government. But, if returned to office, Chifley declared that his government would have backed China's admission to the United Nations. This was not because of support for communism but 'simply because we prefer to be realists'.[157] Labor minister John Dedman, who was close to Chifley, later recollected that in cabinet, prior to the 1949 election, the prime minister had made a 'forceful exposition of the ethical argument' that it would be 'ethically wrong' for his government to make such an important decision to recognise communist China, thereby binding the incoming government.[158] There is little doubt, also, that domestic political considerations played a large part in the Chifley government's decision to delay the recognition of the People's Republic of China, with the prime minister unwilling to add more ammunition to the Opposition's anti-communist campaign against the government. But if Chifley had won the 1949 election, there is no doubt that his government would have provided diplomatic recognition.

Chifley was greatly concerned about the Menzies government's proposal that men who joined the permanent army should no longer enlist for service in Australia only, but agree to serve anywhere, a decision agreed to by cabinet on 13 September 1950.[159] This meant that Australian soldiers would be sent to Europe and to 'certain places in the Orient'. Chifley argued against further expansion of Australia's military program: there was 'a certain point in the allocation of men, materials and money beyond which Australia should not go', otherwise the country would become weighed down with debt. Instead, Australia's future security was dependent on increasing its population and developing its resources.[160] Chifley rejected the notion that Australian troops should be sent to 'any fight that springs up anywhere in the world'. He argued that it was because of this policy that the Menzies government was losing the support of India.[161] Both Chifley and India's prime minister, Nehru, were united in their opposition to Cold War politics believing that war should be avoided at all cost.[162]

Chifley was also troubled by the situation in Indochina. The Vietnamese had fought a long battle against French conquest and control of their country since the 1800s. During World War II, a number of nationalist groups emerged, the strongest of which was the Viet Minh (the League for the Independence of Vietnam), which was made up of groups of democrats, socialists and communists.[163] The Viet Minh fought both the Japanese and the pro-German Vichy French administration for an Allies' victory and for the independence of Vietnam.[164] At the end of the war, on 2 September 1945, the leader of the Viet Minh, Ho Chi Minh, declared Vietnam's independence, quoting from the 1776 Declaration of Independence of the United States of America.[165]

In February 1950 one of the first acts of the newly elected Menzies government was to recognise the regime of the emperor Bao Dai, which was backed by the French and supported by the US government,[166] despite the fact that by the end of 1949, the Viet Minh controlled most of post-war Vietnam.[167] Bao Dai had been the emperor of Annam—a French protectorate in central Vietnam—for twenty years, and for a brief period under the Japanese, when Japan's forces overthrew the French administration in Vietnam in a coup in

March 1945.[168] After the Japanese were defeated in August 1945, Bao Dai abdicated and briefly became Supreme Political Advisor to the newly independent Vietnamese state headed by Ho Chi Minh.[169] In 1949 Bao Dai returned from 'self-imposed exile' in France to be head of the French-backed government of Vietnam.[170] On 7 February 1950 the United States and Great Britain recognised the Bao Dai government and the Menzies government followed soon after.[171] Bao Dai was a ruler who was widely considered in Asia to be a 'Western puppet'.[172] Consequently, both India and Indonesia refused to recognise his regime as the legitimate government of the Vietnamese people.[173]

By the end of 1949, 150 000 soldiers—more that a quarter of the French army—were fighting in Indochina and more than half of France's military budget was being spent there. Most of the country was held by Ho Chi Minh's forces.[174] France, according to Chifley, was 'bleeding itself white' because of its military expenditure in Indochina. The 'new-old regime' did not inspire confidence and Chifley noted that 'Pandit Nehru has stated that he regards the set-up in Indo-China as hopeless'.[175] In November 1950 Chifley also wrote, in a letter to William Sydney Robinson, businessman, former financial journalist and adviser to Australian governments, that the situation in France was dire because of its military and financial commitments to maintain its colony. He wrote:

> Nehru told me some time ago that to enable the French to carry on the war in Indo-China, America had to find about £300m. sterling, and in my talk with Schumann [Robert Schuman, French Foreign Minister from 1948 to 1952] last year he made it clear that France could not afford to maintain 150 000 members of the regular army in Indo-China and that they were now involved in liability in that area to the equivalent of £100m. at per annum.[176]

It is clear that Chifley's deep interest in Asia continued into his years as Opposition leader. He refused to fall into simplistic Cold War explanations for the crises that bedevilled the region. He condemned European colonialists who were 'anxious to make big profits' and had 'grossly exploited' workers in India, China and Malaya. According to

Chifley, the independence gained by India, Pakistan, Ceylon and Burma was brought about not as a result of communist agitation, but because of the 'upsurge of nationalism' in these countries.[177] He later wrote that the 'popular thing to say appears to be that all the discontent in Asia is arising as a result of Communist activities'. This view was 'so far from the truth that it would be ludicrous if it was not tragic'. If Russia 'dropped off the world tomorrow the discontent and the desire for self-government and self-determination, which is generally called nationalism, would continue to assert itself'. Of course, the 'fanatical Communist minority' would always seek to appropriate an organisation with popular support, such as the nationalist movement, but what concerned him most, was 'the fact that in the Western nations' crusade against Communism, they appear to be prepared to give their support to regimes or governments which are entirely corrupt or feudalistic'.[178] Chifley's sentiments were similar to those of Macmahon Ball who wrote:

> Propaganda which seeks to equate liberty with the rule of Chiang Kai-shek, or Bao Dai, or Syngman Rhee does immeasurable damage to the Western cause, for it makes the peoples of East Asia doubt our basic integrity. It makes them suspect that we only use words like democracy and liberty to conceal our intention to use them as pawns in our own struggle with the Soviet Union.[179]

In March 1951 Chifley told the federal conference of the Labor Party in Canberra that the West had to confront the fact that 'the people of Asia no longer want white government'.[180] As he said in Launceston, during the 1951 election campaign: 'In the East, millions of people are still economic serfs. Is it any wonder they are dis-contented? They are tired of being under white domination'.[181]

Conclusion
Chifley's insight into and knowledge of events in Asia in this era of decolonisation was extensive, but his intellectual and practical contribution to Australian foreign–policy making has been greatly underestimated. There has, however, been a slow recognition, but no detailed exploration, of the significant role that Chifley played—one

much greater than was at first supposed. In her study of the historiography of Australian foreign policy and diplomacy, historian Joan Beaumont wrote that Prime Minister Ben Chifley's contribution to the Labor government's foreign policy is 'now recognised to have been significant'.[182] Historian Peter Edwards has suggested: 'Chifley had more knowledge of and interest in foreign affairs than he chose to make public' during his prime ministership, and the minister for External Affairs, Herbert Vere Evatt, was not the 'one-man band' generally supposed. He notes that in the case of the Australian government's policy towards the Indonesian revolution, former diplomat Alan Renouf had 'conceded that Chifley deserves the credit that was generally given to Evatt'.[183] Historian David Fettling has also recently demonstrated Chifley's 'centrality in the crafting of Australia's policy to back the Indonesian nationalist movement'.[184] There has been a growing awareness of the importance of Chifley's contribution to his government's foreign policy.

As prime minister, Chifley understood that momentous change was occurring in Asia. In Opposition, he revealed his sense of 'the emergent future'[185] when he reflected on the reasons his government had supported the Indonesian nationalists in their battle to win freedom from the Dutch. As he said in parliament, 'in the long view—looking 40 or 50 years ahead', it was 'essential' that friendly relations were developed between the peoples of Australia and Indonesia. For that reason, Australia had referred the Indonesian–Dutch conflict to the United Nations. As a result, Indonesia was now experiencing a 'degree of harmony'.[186] Australia's engagement with the Indonesian nationalists' campaign for independence also reveals the Chifley government's commitment to the United Nations as an international organisation facilitating peace and security in the post-war world. As David Lee notes, in his account of Australia's contribution to the United Nations Security Council, the 'involvement of the Security Council in Indonesian independence, involvement that was instigated and strongly supported by Australia, led to one of its earliest and most emphatic successes'. Thus, instead of 'prolonged military conflict, as occurred in France's colonies in Indochina', the Security Council's involvement in negotiations in this conflict resulted in the 'birth of an independent Indonesian state'.[187]

In his study of Australia's Asian policies published in 1977, Stargardt wrote that the Indonesian nationalists' fight for independence against the Dutch presented a major challenge for the Chifley government in the post-war period. The government was 'faced with the alternatives of supporting the restoration of the colonial power, or of giving the Indonesians a chance'. He argued that the Chifley government's 'far-sighted decisions' and 'independent Asian policy … reflected historical foresight and moral courage of a high order', enabling them to forge bonds with their Asian neighbours, especially with India and Indonesia.[188] Both William Macmahon Ball and distinguished diplomat Tom Critchley agreed that if a Dutch–Indonesian settlement had not been reached, a protracted civil war would have occurred.[189] Critchley said in an interview in November 1993, in words that echoed Stargardt's sentiments, that if there had been no settlement, the Indonesian nationalists would have continued their guerilla campaign against the Dutch. He believed that the Indonesians would have defeated the Dutch in the end, but the subsequent struggle would have meant a great loss of life. 'The struggle in Indonesia could well have developed along lines similar to what happened in Indochina with heavy loss of human life and much suffering'.[190]

Because of the lessons learnt from Australia's involvement in, and support for Indonesia's struggle against the Dutch, Chifley said it was 'a grave mistake' to say that the disturbances caused by Asian peoples' efforts to free themselves from colonial rule were due to communism. He quoted Nehru who had stated: 'If anybody thinks he can stop the spread of radicalism in Asia by guns, soldiers and ships, he makes the greatest possible mistake'. Chifley agreed with Nehru when he said, what was needed to counter the challenge of communism was economic advancement and improved standards of living. Until this was achieved, 'nothing could happen except, perhaps, a worse state of affairs than existed in the first place'.[191] In Nehru, Chifley had found a world leader whose world-view corresponded to his own.

A number of principles drove Chifley and his government's engagement with Asia. First, Chifley understood that the days of European imperialism were rapidly drawing to a close—the old colonial order was ending. Second, Chifley believed in the value of basing policy on local knowledge. Third, he believed that nationalism, not communism, was the driving force of events in Asia, reflecting a desire for independence from colonial rule and better living and working conditions. Fourth, he emphasised the economic over other dimensions in understanding and dealing with international relations. Fifth, he believed in a rules-based internationalism, not an anarchic international society. And finally, Chifley thought that war had to be avoided at all cost and that conflict should be resolved through diplomacy and negotiations at the United Nations. In following these principles in support of Indonesia and India, the Chifley government made a number of radical policy decisions, opposed by the Menzies Opposition and most of the Australian media.

The minister for External Affairs, Dr Herbert Vere Evatt has often been seen as the driver of these decisions. This radicalism has also been attributed to Dr John Burton, secretary of the Department of External Affairs. While both men were important, Chifley deserves to join Evatt and Burton as a key architect of his government's policy towards Asia. The greatest foreign policy issue that confronted post-war Australia was 'the upsurge of Asian demands for self-government'.[192] While acknowledging the radical nature of the Labor government's response to Asian nationalism, the argument by some historians that it was from 1947, after the appointment of Dr John Burton as secretary of the Department of External Affairs, that Australia's foreign policy 'shifted towards the more radical posture of support for immediate Asian self-determination'[193] has been refuted by Burton himself.

According to Burton, it was Chifley's personal decision to refer the Indonesian dispute to the United Nations Security Council in 1947. It was also Chifley's decision to send an Australian delegation to the 1949 New Delhi conference, despite fierce condemnation from the press and from the Menzies Opposition. As Burton noted: 'These were amongst the most dramatic and important decisions of the time'—decisions driven by Prime Minister Ben Chifley, who played a major role in Australian foreign policy–making towards post–war Asia during this period of decolonisation.[194] Moreover, at the 1949 Commonwealth Prime Ministers' Conference, Chifley would find in

Jawaharlal Nehru, Prime Minister of India, a source of inspiration and 'confirmation of many of his own conclusions about Asian affairs'.[195]

Notes

1. Lee, 'Indonesia's Independence', in Goldsworthy (ed.), *Facing North*, p. 134.
2. Jack E Richardson, 'Bailey, Sir Kenneth Hamilton (1898–1972)', *Australian Dictionary of Biography*, vol. 13, Melbourne University Press, Carlton, Victoria, 1993, p. 89.
3. KH Bailey, 'Dependent Areas of the Pacific: An Australian View', *Foreign Affairs*, vol. 24, no. 3, 1946, p. 494.
4. Cotton, *The Australian School*, p. 63; Eggleston to Evatt, Chungking, 30 June 1942, p. 7. NAA: A4144, 608/1943.
5. John Darwin, 'Decolonisation and World Politics', in Lowe (ed.), *Australia and the End of Empires*, pp. 17–18.
6. MC Ricklefs, *A History of Modern Indonesia Since c.1300*, 2nd edn, Macmillan, Houndmills, UK, 1993, pp. 210–213.
7. Lee, 'Indonesia's Independence', in *Facing North*, pp. 154; 164.
8. Waters, 'War, Decolonisation and Postwar Security', in Goldsworthy (ed.), *Facing North*, p. 122.
9. Christopher Waters, 'Conflict with Britain in the 1940s', in Lowe (ed.), *Australia and the End of Empires*, p. 78.
10. For example, in Labor circles, it is widely thought that Chifley had a long-standing interest in Japanese history. See Bob Ellis and Robin McLachlan, *A Local Man: A Play about Ben Chifley*, Currency Press, Sydney, 2005, p. 20. According to Ellis and McLachlan, Chifley studied 'economics, medieval social history, Japanese history, world literature' at classes at the local Workers' Educational Association in Bathurst.
11. Bolton, 'Duncan Waterson: A Lapidary Historian', p. 15. Other sources, such as Peter Ryan, say the trip occurred after Chifley lost the seat of Macquarie in the 1931 election. See Ryan, *Brief Lives*, p. 87.
12. Email from Professor Geoffrey Bolton to author, 24 December 2009.
13. Letter from Professor Duncan Waterson to author, 10 February 2010.
14. Richard Kirby, interviewed by Margaret George, 1972, NLA: ORAL TRC 202, p. 1/12.
15. Richard Kirby, interviewed by Peter Crockett, 7 June 1985, Papers of PW Crockett Relating to the Life of HV Evatt, Box 30, Manuscripts Library, State Library of Victoria (hereafter SLV), MS 13347, Box 30, p. 32, cited in Fettling, 'JB Chifley and the Indonesian Revolution', p. 518.
16. Kirby, interviewed by George, p. 1/14.
17. Burton, 'Indonesia: Unfinished Diplomacy', in John Legge (ed.), *New Directions in Australian Foreign Policy: Australia and Indonesia 1945–50*, Monash Asia Institute, Clayton, Victoria, 1997, pp. 33–51. Jamie Mackie mentions this trip in his interview with John Burton in the Appendix to this paper, pp. 45–46.

18 TK Critchley, 'View from the Good Offices Committee', in Legge (ed.), *New Directions in Australian Foreign Policy*, p. 53.
19 Ryan, *Brief Lives*, p. 87.
20 Bolton, 'Duncan Waterson: A Lapidary Historian', p. 15; See Geoffrey Bolton, *The Oxford History of Australia, Volume 5: The Middle Way 1942–1995*, 2nd edn, Oxford University Press, Oxford, 1996, p. 5.
21 Bolton, 'Duncan Waterson: A Lapidary Historian', p. 15.
22 Bolton, 'The Art of Australian Political Biography', p. 4.
23 Andrew Spaull, 'Dedman, John Johnstone (1896–1973)', *Australian Dictionary of Biography*, vol. 13, Melbourne University Press, Carlton, Victoria, 1993, p. 606; David Lowe, 'Brave New Liberal: Percy Spender', *Australian Journal of Politics and History*, vol. 51, no. 3, 2005, p. 393.
24 Dennis, 'Australia and Indonesia: The Early Years', in Lowe (ed.), *Australia and the End of Empires*, p. 51.
25 Contained within 'Notes of a Deputation Consisting of Representatives of the Netherlands Government Which Waited on the Acting Prime Minister on 2 July 1945', NAA: A5954, 562/3; Lee, 'Indonesia's Independence', in Goldsworthy (ed.), *Facing North*, p. 145.
26 *CPD*, HoR, 1 June 1945, p. 2427.
27 Memorandum for DEA, 3 July 1945, War Cabinet Minute No. 4293, 28 June 1945, NAA: A1838, 401/4/3/1.
28 'Basing of Netherlands Forces on Australia', Statement by Prime Minister, 8 August 1945. NAA: A5954, 562/3.
29 Letter, Van Aerssen to Chifley, 10 August 1945, in ibid.
30 Letter, Chifley to Van Aerssen, 11 September 1945, NAA: A1838, 401/4/3/1.
31 'Many Advantages if Dutch Troops Came: Mr Menzies', *Herald*, (Melbourne, Vic.) 4 August 1945, NAA: A5954, 562/3.
32 'Cold Shouldering An Ally', *Herald*, (Melbourne, Vic.), 8 August 1945, in ibid.
33 Harold Cox Reports, 12 October 1945, NLA: MS 4554, Folder 2: 1945–1947.
34 Cablegram P146, Chifley to Evatt, 'Indonesia', 12 August 1946, in Hudson and Way (eds), *DAFP, Volume X: July – December 1946*, pp. 114–115.
35 Cablegram 263, Chifley to Attlee, 3 July 1946, in ibid., pp. 20–21.
36 Cablegram 374, Chifley to Attlee, 31 October 1945, WJ Hudson and Wendy Way (eds), *DAFP, Volume VIII: 1945*, AGPS, Canberra, 1989, pp. 552–553.
37 Waters, 'War, Decolonisation and Postwar Security', p. 97.
38 ibid., p. 107.
39 Cablegram 374, Chifley to Attlee, 31 October 1945, Hudson and Way (eds), *DAFP, Volume VIII: 1945*, pp. 552–553.
40 Waters, *Empire Fractures*, p. 176
41 Cablegram 374, Chifley to Attlee, 31 October 1945, Hudson and Way (eds), *DAFP, Volume VIII: 1945*, pp. 552–553.
42 Dr John Burton was officer-in-charge with the Economic Relations Division in the Department of External Affairs, and from 1 October to 15 November 1945, he was acting secretary. From 15 November he was first secretary in the Economic Relations Division. See Hudson and Way (eds), *DAFP, Volume VIII: 1945*, p. 805.

43 Cablegram 1620, Burton to Evatt, 2 November 1945, Hudson and Way (eds), *DAFP, Volume VIII: 1945*, p. 558.
44 Ai Kobayashi, *W. Macmahon Ball: Politics for the People*, Australian Scholarly Publishing, North Melbourne, Victoria, 2013, p. 46.
45 'Chifley's Worried Look—In Canberra Today', *Cairns Post*, (Cairns, QLD) 31 May 1948, p. 5.
46 W Macmahon Ball, 'Preface', in WGK Duncan (ed.), *Australia's Foreign Policy*, Angus and Robertson, Sydney, 1938, p. vii.
47 Lee, 'Indonesia's Independence', in Goldsworthy (ed.), *Facing North*, pp. 138 and 146.
48 Philip Dorling (ed.), *Diplomasi: Australia and Indonesia's Independence, Documents 1947*, AGPS, Canberra, 1994, p. xiii.
49 JE Isaac, 'The Macmahon Ball Mission November 1945', in Legge (ed.), *New Directions in Australian Foreign Policy*, p. 21.
50 Alan Rix (ed.), *Intermittent Diplomat: The Japan and Batavia Diaries of W Macmahon Ball*, Melbourne University Press, Carlton, Victoria, 1988, pp. 235–237.
51 Cablegram 4, Ball to Burton, 10 November 1945, Hudson and Way (eds), *DAFP, Volume VIII: 1945*, p. 587.
52 Cablegram 12, Ball to Burton, 17 November 1945, in ibid., p. 620.
53 Memorandum, Ball to Burton, 22 November 1945, in ibid., pp. 626–627.
54 ibid., pp. 628–629.
55 Joseph C Grew (Acting Secretary of State) to Stimson (Secretary of War), Washington, June 28, 1945, 'Policy Paper Prepared in the Department of State', 22 June 1945, in United States Department of State, *Foreign Relations of the United States: Diplomatic Papers 1945. The British Commonwealth, the Far East* (hereafter *FRUS*), vol. VI, United States Government Printing Office, Washington, 1945, p. 573.
56 ibid., pp. 557–558.
57 Frank C Bennett Jr, *The Return of the Exiles: Australia's Repatriation of the Indonesians, 1945–47*, Monash Asia Institute, Monash University Press, Clayton, Victoria, 2003, p. 164.
58 Memorandum, Ball to Dunk, 'Report on NEI', 17 December 1945, Hudson and Way (eds), *DAFP, Volume VIII: 1945*, p. 717.
59 ibid., p. 719.
60 ibid., p. 720.
61 ibid., pp. 721–722.
62 Cotton, *The Australian School*, p. 185.
63 Cablegrams E47 and E48, Evatt to Makin and Chifley, 'Indonesia', 23 November 1945, Hudson and Way (eds), *DAFP, Volume VIII: 1945*, pp. 633–638.
64 Cablegram 1802, Chifley to Evatt, 26 November 1945, in ibid., p. 641.
65 Letter from Macmahon Ball to Kylie Tennant. Cited in Kylie Tennant, *Evatt: Politics and Justice*, Angus and Robertson, Sydney, 1970, p. 200.
66 Kobayashi, *W. Macmahon Ball*, p. 77.
67 DEA, For the Minister, 2 January 1947, NAA: A1068, M47/9/6/15 Part 1.
68 Julie Suares, 'Engaging with Asia: the Chifley Government and the New

Delhi Conferences of 1947 and 1949', *Australian Journal of Politics and History*, vol. 57, no. 4, 2011, pp. 499–500.
69   *Asian Relations: being Report of the Proceedings and Documentation of the First Asian Relations Conference, New Delhi, March–April, 1947*, Asian Relations Organization, New Delhi, 1948, p. 21.
70   ibid., p. 3.
71   ibid., p. 1.
72   Gerald Packer, 'The Asian Relations Conference: The Group Discussions', *Australian Outlook*, vol. 1, no. 2, p. 4.
73   Suares, 'Engaging with Asia', pp. 501–502.
74   ibid., p. 509.
75   G Packer and JA McCallum, 'Australian Observers' Report on Asian Relations Conference, New Delhi, March 1947', p.17, NAA: A1068, M47/9/6/15 Part 3.
76   ibid., p. 26.
77   ibid., p. 11.
78   Cablegram 138. Australian High Commissioner New Delhi (Letter incomplete, probably to Min and DEA), 'Asian Relations Conference', 26 March 1947, NAA: A1068, M47/9/6/15 Part 1.
79   Packer and McCallum, 'Australian Observers' Report', p. 17, NAA: A1068, M47/9/6/15 Part 3.
80   ibid., pp. 25–26.
81   Suares, 'Engaging with Asia', p. 502.
82   ibid., p. 509.
83   ibid., p. 508.
84   Lee, 'Indonesia's Independence', in Goldsworthy (ed.), *Facing North*, pp. 154–155; *CPD*, HoR, 24 September 1947, p. 179.
85   Philip Dorling and David Lee (eds), *DAFP 1937–49, Australia and Indonesia's Independence: The Renville Agreement, Documents 1948*, AGPS, Canberra, 1996, p. xvi.
86   ibid., p. xxi.
87   Cablegram 321, Chifley to Attlee, 15 December 1948, Canberra, in ibid., pp. 421–422.
88   MC Ricklefs, *A History of Modern Indonesia since c.1300*, 2nd edn, Macmillan, Basingstoke, Hampshire, UK, 1993, p. 189.
89   Mavis Rose, *Indonesia Free: A Political Biography of Mohammad Hatta*, Cornell Modern Indonesia Project, Cornell University, Ithaca, NY, 1987, p. 154.
90   Cablegram 321, Chifley to Attlee, 15 December 1948, Canberra, Dorling and Lee (eds), *DAFP 1937–49, Australia and Indonesia's Independence*, p. 422.
91   Ricklefs, *A History of Modern Indonesia since c.1300*, p. 221.
92   ibid., p. 229.
93   Cablegram 309, Attlee to Chifley, 14 December 1948, London. Dorling and Lee (eds), *DAFP 1937–49, Australia and Indonesia's Independence*, pp. 417–419.
94   Cablegram 321, Chifley to Attlee, 15 December 1948, Canberra, Dorling

and Lee (eds), *DAFP 1937–49, Australia and Indonesia's Independence*, pp. 421–422.
95   ibid., p. 422.
96   Press Statement by Chifley, 21 December 1948, in ibid., p. 461.
97   Cablegram 281, Hodgson to DEA, 23 December 1948, in ibid., pp. 495–496.
98   Lee, 'Indonesia's Independence', p. 164.
99   Cablegram 1, Australian High Commissioner in New Delhi to DEA, 1 January 1949, NAA: A1838, 383/1/2/5.
100 Letter, Eggleston to Burton and Memorandum to Evatt, 5 January 1949, in ibid.
101 '"Blunder" to Attend Asia Conference—Menzies Critical', *Daily Telegraph*, (Sydney, NSW), 10 January 1949, NAA: A1838, 383/1/2/5.
102 *CPD*, HoR, 15 February 1949, pp. 269, 271–272; see also Gordon Greenwood (ed.), with the assistance of Pamela Bray, *Approaches to Asia: Australian Postwar Policies and Attitudes*, McGraw-Hill, Sydney, 1974, pp. 22–23.
103 Lee, 'Indonesia's Independence', in Goldsworthy (ed.), *Facing North*, p. 166.
104 Critchley, 'View from the Good Offices Committee', in Legge (ed.), *New Directions in Australian Foreign Policy*, p. 71.
105 Lee, 'Indonesia's Independence', in Goldsworthy (ed.), *Facing North*, p. 169.
106 Garry Woodard, 'Macmahon Ball's Goodwill Mission to Asia 1948', *Australian Journal of International Affairs*, vol. 49, no. 1, May 1995, p. 129.
107 W Macmahon Ball, 'Report on a Mission to East Asia: May 27–July 6, 1948', 27 July 1948, p. 1, NAA: A1838, 381/1/3/1.
108 Letter, Burton to Ball, 9 August 1948, in ibid.
109 *CPD*, HoR, 2 September 1948, p. 66.
110 Waters, 'War, Decolonisation and Postwar Security', p. 124.
111 *CPD*, HoR, 2 September 1948, p. 66.
112 Report to the Nation, No. 11. Broadcast by the Prime Minister (Mr Chifley): 'Asia and the Far East', 21 November 1948, NAA: A1838, 380/1/9.
113 *CPD*, HoR, 7 March 1951, p. 82.
114 Lee, *Search for Security*, pp. 105–106.
115 *CPD*, HoR, 7 March, 1951, p. 83.
116 Waters, 'War, Decolonisation and Postwar Security', p. 125; Waters, *The Empire Fractures*, p. 179.
117 Christopher Waters, 'Review of Wayne Reynolds, *Australia's Bid for the Atomic Bomb* (2000)', in *Australian Journal of International Affairs*, vol. 56, no. 1, 2002, p. 165.
118 David Lee, 'Britain and Australia's Defence Policy, 1945–1949', *War and Society*, vol. 13, no. 1, 1995, pp. 61–80.
119 Lowe, *Menzies and the 'Great World Struggle'*, p. 14.
120 *CPD*, HoR, 2 September 1948, pp. 56–67.
121 ibid., p. 56.
122 ibid., p. 58.

123 ibid., p. 57.
124 ibid., p. 59.
125 ibid., p. 62.
126 ibid., p. 65.
127 Edwards, with Pemberton, *Crises and Commitment*, pp. 46–47; *CPD*, HoR, 2 September 1948, p. 65.
128 Waters, *The Empire Fractures*, p. 169.
129 'World Problems', *National Advocate* (Bathurst, NSW), 19 October 1932, p. 2.
130 *CPD*, HoR, 27 September 1950, p. 26.
131 Letter, LF Crisp to Myron M. Cowen, 8 February 1952, Papers of LF Crisp, NLA: MS 5243, Series 5, Folder 2.
132 Breen, 'JB Chifley', p. 239.
133 Peter Gifford, 'The Cold War across Asia', in Goldsworthy (ed.), *Facing North*, p. 182.
134 *CPD*, HoR, 27 September 1950, p. 22.
135 Jodie Boyd, Conservative Discourse at the Time of the Korean War, 1950–52, PhD Thesis, Deakin University, 2005, p. 101.
136 Cabinet Notebook 1/1, notes on meeting on 25 August 1950, [transcript pp. 3–4]. NAA: A11099, 1/1.
137 Lowe, *Menzies and the 'Great World Struggle'*, p. 20.
138 *CPD*, HoR, 27 September 1950, p. 22.
139 ibid., pp. 22–23.
140 ibid., p. 24.
141 ibid., pp. 23–24.
142 ibid., p. 23.
143 ibid.
144 Departmental Despatch No. 29, Patrick Shaw, Head of Australian Mission in Japan, to DEA, 'Korea', 11 November 1947, p. 1, NAA: A1838, 3127/2/1 Part 3.
145 Dept 485, Jackson, Australian Mission Tokyo, to Dr Evatt, 20 December 1947, NAA: A1838, 3123/4/5 Part 1.
146 'Korea Elects President', *Melbourne Herald*, 20 July 1948, NAA: A1838, 3127/2/1 Part 3.
147 Hugh Deane, 'Dollars and Force Required For US Hold On Korea', *China Weekly Review*, 18 October 1947, in ibid.
148 Departmental Despatch No. 29, Shaw to DEA, 'Korea', 11 November 1947, p. 2, in ibid.
149 ibid., pp. 3–4.
150 *CPD*, HoR, 23 March 1950, p. 1174.
151 Henry S Albinski, *Australian Policies and Attitudes Toward China*, Princeton University Press, Princeton, NJ, 1965, p. 12.
152 ibid., p. 7.
153 *CPD*, HoR, 23 March 1950, p. 1174.
154 Albinski, *Australian Policies and Attitudes Toward China*, p. 8.
155 Peter Gifford, 'The Cold War across Asia', in Goldsworthy (ed.), *Facing North*, p. 190.

156 *CPD*, HoR, 27 September 1950, pp. 24–25.
157 *CPD*, HoR, 7 March 1951, p. 85.
158 David Stephens, 'Three Labor Veterans Look Back', *Australian Quarterly*, vol. 46, no. 3, 1974, pp. 87–88.
159 *CPD*, HoR, 27 September 1950, p. 26; Cabinet Notebooks, 13 September 1950, NAA: A11099, 1/5, p. 20.
160 ibid., p. 26.
161 ibid., p. 28.
162 Sahni, 'Vision, Honesty and Courage Personified'.
163 Marvin E. Gettleman, (ed.), *Vietnam: History, Documents, and Opinions on a Major World Crisis*, Penguin Books, Ringwood, Victoria, 1965, pp. 45–46.
164 *Vietnam and Australia: History Documents Interpretations*, University Study Group on Vietnam, Gladesville, NSW, 1966, p. 18.
165 Gettleman, (ed.) *Vietnam: History, Documents, and Opinions on a Major World Crisis*, pp. 64–66.
166 *CPD*, HoR, 23 February 1950, p. 55; *CPD*, HoR, 27 September 1950, pp. 26–27.
167 Cotton, *The Australian School*, p. 182.
168 Gettleman, Marvin E (ed.), *Vietnam*, pp. 46–47.
169 W Macmahon Ball, *Nationalism and Communism in East Asia*, Melbourne University Press, Carlton, 1952, p. 82.
170 Gettleman (ed.), *Vietnam*, p. 80.
171 Ball, *Nationalism and Communism in East Asia*, p. 83.
172 ibid., p. 63.
173 Gettleman (ed.), *Vietnam*, p. 87.
174 ibid., p. 81.
175 *CPD*, HoR, 23 March 1950, p. 1175.
176 Letter, Chifley to WS Robinson, 15 November 1950, Papers of LF Crisp, NLA: MS 5243, Series 5, Folder 1; Robert Schuman was the French Foreign Minister from 1948 to 1952.
177 *CPD*, HoR, 23 March 1950, p. 1175.
178 Letter, Chifley to Ian Lasry, 8 August 1950, Papers of LF Crisp, NLA: MS 5243, Series 5, Folder 1.
179 Ball, *Nationalism and Communism in East Asia*, p. 203.
180 JB Chifley, 'Clear Cut Decisions', address to the federal ALP conference, Canberra, 2 March 1951, in *Things Worth Fighting For*, p. 369.
181 JB Chifley, 'Election Round-up—"Inflation will Go On"—Chifley', *Argus*, (Melbourne, Vic), Friday, 20 April 1951, p. 20.
182 Joan Beaumont, 'Making Australian Foreign Policy 1941–69', in Joan Beaumont, Christopher Waters, David Lowe, with Garry Woodard, (eds), *Ministers, Mandarins and Diplomats*, p. 6.
183 PG Edwards, 'On Assessing HV Evatt', *Historical Studies*, vol. 21, no. 83, 1984, pp. 262–263.
184 Fettling, 'JB Chifley and the Indonesian Revolution, 1945–1949', p. 519.
185 Stargardt, 'Introduction', in *Things Worth Fighting For*, p. 9.
186 *CPD*, HoR, 23 March 1950, p. 1176.

187 Lee, 'Australia and the Security Council', in Cotton and Lee (eds), *Australia and the United Nations*, p. 72.
188 AW Stargardt. *Australia's Asian Policies: The History of a Debate 1839–1972*, The Institute of Asian Affairs in Hamburg, Otto Harrassowitz, Wiesbaden, 1977, pp. 212–213.
189 Memorandum, Ball to Dunk, 'Report on NEI', 17 December 1945, *DAFP, Volume VIII: 1945*, p. 721.
190 TK Critchley, Interviewed by Michael Wilson for the Australian diplomacy 1950–1990 oral history project, 25 November 1993, NLA: TRC 2981/7, p. 16.
191 *CPD*, HoR, 23 March 1950, p. 1177.
192 Gregory Pemberton, 'An Imperial Imagination: Explaining the Post-1945 Foreign Policy of Robert Gordon Menzies', in Frank Cain (ed.) *Menzies in Peace and War*, Allen & Unwin, Sydney 1997, p. 164.
193 For example, Pemberton in Cain (ed.) *Menzies in Peace and War*, p. 164.
194 Burton, 'Review of Ben Chifley: A Biography by LF Crisp', p. 96.
195 Crisp, *Ben Chifley*, p. 277.

CHAPTER SIX
Chifley and Nehru—Fellow Internationalists

There was a growing awareness of the potential for closer diplomatic, economic and strategic ties between Australia and India in the period during and after World War II. An Australian High Commission—Australia's first diplomatic mission in Asia—had been established in Delhi in 1944, under the hard-working and enthusiastic Lieutenant-General Sir Iven Mackay.[1] A senior army officer who served in both world wars, Mackay was a former school-teacher and lecturer in physics at the University of Sydney.[2] He was appointed Australia's first high commissioner to India in 1944, where he remained until 1948.[3] In 1945 India set up a High Commission in Canberra.[4] By 1946 Britain no longer had the resolve or the means to maintain its empire in India, and an interim Indian government was established in September that year, with Jawaharlal Nehru as its leader.[5] India would gain its independence on 15 August 1947; adopt a democratic constitution in November 1949 and the country would become a republic on 26 January 1950.[6]

The Chifley government responded to the announcement of India's impending independence by asking Mackay to convey to Nehru 'a special message of friendly greeting and to wish him and his new government success in their task of building up a National Government'. Australia would assist the new government in whatever ways it could. In addition, the Australian government hoped that, while India would become an independent nation, it would choose to remain a member of the British Commonwealth.[7] Nehru asked Mackay to thank Evatt for this 'message of good will'; India would welcome Australia being a part of future discussions 'concerning the peoples of Asia and the Indian Ocean'.[8]

The Australian government was also looking at the advantages of increased trade between Australia and Asia. A few years before becoming prime minister, Chifley, as minister for Post-War Reconstruction, had written about the benefits of developing economic links with Australia's near neighbours in the Indo-Pacific region. He argued that the 'development of hitherto under-developed countries', which had previously had far too little trade with Australia, would have a very beneficial impact.[9] In his 1946 election speech, Chifley saw the emergence of the new post-colonial states, such as India, as an opportunity to expand Australia's trade in the region.[10] In February 1947, Dr HC Coombs wrote a highly significant memorandum to the prime minister on the international situation that would confront Australia in the future, and the economic issues that would impact on the government's policy-making.[11] The memo stated that the 'tide of nationalism was running strongly in India' and other Asian countries. Apart from being a political force, this nationalism was aimed at improving living standards and Australia should, therefore, 'make a conscious attempt to identify herself with these developments'. India was the country that was expected to advance rapidly and Australia had already made a good start in establishing trade relations there.[12]

The Chifley government had also shown a willingness to send representatives, both unofficial and official, to attend conferences in India. The 1947 Asian Relations Conference held in New Delhi provided a valuable opportunity for the government to gain a better understanding of India and its region. As noted in the previous chapter, the conference presented the government with significant intelligence on political, economic and cultural issues in Asia.[13] In January 1949 Chifley had decided, against fierce criticism from the Menzies Opposition and the Australian press, to send an official delegation to the New Delhi Conference, convened by Nehru, to discuss the Indonesian–Dutch conflict. The conference proved to be highly successful and very productive, with participants working constructively together. The relationships formed there augured well for future co-operation between Australia and India.

John Burton, the leader of the Australian delegation, wrote that the 'good common sense and honest purpose' shown by the 'middle and small powers' was most impressive.[14] Nehru also declared in his closing speech that it was often difficult for international conferences to come to 'satisfactory conclusions', with all the different voices and opinions expressed. However, the New Delhi Conference, within a very short period of time, had reached agreement on a difficult issue that affected not only Indonesia, but also the prospect of peace in Asia and the world. Nehru declared: 'it may be said that the most significant feature of this Conference has been the friendly and cooperative approach of all those who attended it as delegates or as observers'.[15] In fact, he thought it could well 'serve as a model to others'.[16] He hoped it signified a 'period of close cooperation' between the countries who had attended.[17] Burton wrote that, in the future, Australia could count on the support of Nehru, with whom 'unreserved and friendly relations' had been established. He added that Nehru had shown himself 'determined to maintain the peaceful conditions in Asia and to avoid racial arguments or disputes'.[18]

Consequently, by the time the 1949 Commonwealth Prime Ministers' Conference convened to consider a republican India's future status in the Commonwealth, Prime Minister Chifley had developed a sophisticated understanding of the changes occurring in Asia and in India. There were hopes for a much better and broader relationship between Australia and India than in the past, and the Australian government was well placed to take advantage of its situation in the region. As noted by international relations scholar Meg Gurry, who has written extensively on the history of the India–Australia relationship, Chifley viewed India as the 'lynchpin of Asia'. He believed that India would be 'an extremely important country in the postwar international community'.[19] He looked forward to India remaining a member of the Commonwealth, an institution whose foreign policy was based on 'enthusiastic and sustained support of the United Nations'.[20] Both Chifley and Nehru were staunch supporters of the new global organisation that they believed would deliver international peace and security. Chifley's attendance at the 1949 Commonwealth Prime Ministers' Conference provides an opportunity to consider, first, his views on India's desire to remain a member of the Commonwealth as a republic; and second, evidence of the remarkable convergence of world-views of two fellow internationalists, Chifley and Nehru.

Proposal for Meeting of Commonwealth Prime Ministers

On 19 March 1949 Nehru announced that a meeting of the Dominion Prime Ministers had been proposed by British Prime Minister Clement Attlee, to be held in late April. One of the subjects to be discussed at the conference would be India's status in the Commonwealth, after it became a republic. It was hoped that a formula could be worked out, so that 'India's continued membership of the Commonwealth will not be inconsistent with her status as a Republic'.[21] Nehru, however, was reluctant to attend the conference, he thought it would prove to be 'rather inconclusive'.[22] Nevertheless, he could not refuse to attend—there were very good reasons for India to remain within the Commonwealth. Membership would ensure that India would be able to secure 'economic, technical and other assistance from the Commonwealth countries and from the United States'. Importantly, membership of the Commonwealth would also mean that India would be able to influence British and US policies towards Southeast Asia. Over the past year, India had pressured the United Kingdom and the United States to adopt 'a more liberal policy towards subject countries in South East Asia'. Other than remaining a member of the Commonwealth, there were two options available for India: abandon the non-aligned position in foreign affairs by becoming part of the United Kingdom–United States power bloc, or leave the Commonwealth. India would then be categorised as a 'foreign' country and would relinquish all those benefits that a member of the Commonwealth received. Taking everything into consideration, Nehru argued it was far better for India to remain within the Commonwealth.[23]

The problem, however, was the nature of India's association with the Commonwealth and the Crown and how to resolve this issue. For Nehru, the question of India remaining within the Commonwealth as a republic was essentially a political rather than a technical or legal issue. The political aspect had to be considered first. It had to be dealt with on the basis of establishing a 'new relationship between an independent Republic and the Commonwealth containing a King'. He noted that some in the British press understood the issue much better than the 'legal luminaries'.[24] For example, an article in *The Times* argued that popular political opinion in India maintained that India must 'assert its newly found nationhood by repudiating allegiance to the British Crown and substituting for it some other legal link which would preserve existing close relations with the Commonwealth'.[25]

Attlee had earlier written to Nehru to inform him that India's initial proposal for an ongoing association with the Commonwealth minus any connection to the Crown, was not satisfactory. He hoped that India would modify its position to align more with the views of the United Kingdom, Canada, Australia and New Zealand. Commonwealth members would be informed of the situation and a personal emissary would be sent out to assist in preliminary discussions on this issue.[26] On 20 March 1949 Attlee again wrote to Nehru in an attempt to persuade him that India should retain the link with the Commonwealth through the Crown, as it had delivered stability for such a long period of time. Attlee wrote that the Commonwealth's real ties were provided by the king and the royal family; these links were 'something universal … transcending creeds and races'. He argued that the connection with the monarchy would appeal to Indians because of tradition, as it did to other dominions. In contrast, the head of a republic was only temporary, and would not possess the same appeal throughout India. Attlee therefore urged India to retain the king in its constitution.[27]

Australia's External Affairs minister, Dr HV Evatt, had also written to Nehru, urging him to take into account public opinion in India, where the king was regarded as the 'symbol' of the Commonwealth relationship.[28] On 26 March Nehru wrote to Vallabhbhai Patel, his deputy prime minister, that Attlee's letter was a 'surprisingly naïve document'. He despaired at the British prime minister's attitude and could not imagine what issues would be discussed at the conference. He added that the 'other approach, that of Dr Evatt, is in its own way, simple and childlike'.[29] With these competing and conflicting views on India's future relationship with the monarchy, the negotiations to accommodate India's desire to remain a member of the Commonwealth as a republic, promised to be 'a complex legal problem for all members'.[30]

Before the Conference

In March 1949 Attlee's emissary, the British minister of state for Colonial Affairs, Lord Listowel, visited Australia to discuss a number of issues, including the future of India in the Commonwealth.[31] When Chifley was informed of Listowel's forthcoming mission to Australia, the United Kingdom's high commissioner in Canberra wrote that Chifley, 'spoke most strongly about [the] need for political and strategic reasons to keep India within [the] Commonwealth by hook or by crook and felt confident it would be possible to devise some solution to achieve this object'.[32] During his meeting with Listowel, Chifley told him that while every effort should be made to persuade India to retain the link with the crown, if this was not possible, then 'he would welcome India as a "Sovereign Republic"'.[33]

At the next day's meeting, Chifley told Listowel that India was a 'bulwark against Communism in Asia' and a 'member whose loss would weaken the Commonwealth structure'.[34] According to Chifley, both the Indian and the Australian governments opposed colonialism. He emphasised that the Indian government's foreign policy was favourable to Commonwealth interests. The fact that India would become a republic was not the paramount issue here, so long as confidence in the Commonwealth was maintained and lines of communication and consultation were kept open. He noted, however, that it was inevitable that his government's position on the importance of keeping a republican India within the Commonwealth would be attacked by Menzies, leader of the Opposition. Nevertheless, the prime minister was emphatic that the risk had to be taken, because 'political considerations' outweighed all other factors in this issue. Although he agreed with Canada and South Africa in their rejection of reciprocal Commonwealth citizenship rights with India, Chifley declared that he valued Australia's relationship with India more than links with others in the Commonwealth.[35] Chifley was supported by the minister for Defence, John Dedman, who told Listowel that it was essential that Australia had a 'powerful friend in Asia' and 'the only country which could fill this role was India'.³⁶

In correspondence with the Canadian prime minister, Louis Stephen St Laurent, Chifley put forward his own position on the issue:

> I feel the question to be decided is of very great importance and I think that we should do all that is possible to retain India as a friendly power. Although I recognise there would be very great difficulties in retaining India within the Commonwealth should it become a republic, I am not so much concerned with formalities as with the need to maintain friendly relations. I feel that India must certainly be the leader of the Asian peoples and provide a bulwark against any onward rush of Communism through that area.³⁷

Chifley's pragmatism is obvious here—in contrast to the legalistic approach that his External Affairs minister, Evatt, took to accommodating India's desire to remain a member of the Commonwealth. Before leaving for the 1949 Commonwealth Prime Ministers' Conference, Chifley raised the issue of India's future relationship with the Commonwealth in a submission to cabinet on 7 April 1949. It stated that Prime Minister Nehru and his government 'clearly' wished to 'maintain existing relations' between a republican India and the British Commonwealth. There were a number of problems associated with this, namely, how it could be achieved. At present, the legal test of membership of the Commonwealth was one of 'common allegiance to the Crown', but this was not acceptable to India. A concept of 'common citizenship' had been suggested, but if it did not include reciprocal citizenship rights that applied throughout the Commonwealth, then such a proposal would be regarded as inadequate by India. Furthermore, there was the possibility that this could be used against Australia's immigration policy. Australia was unlikely to accept any 'radical constitutional change' relating to India's relationship with the Crown. While admitting this, Chifley's submission was emphatic in its statement that 'India is more important to Australia, economically and strategically, than some members of the British Commonwealth who are prepared to accept the present constitutional framework' (such as South Africa and Canada). It would therefore be unwise to take an 'inflexible attitude', intended to protect Australia's relationships with South Africa and Canada, at the 'expense of close relations with India'.[38]

After canvassing some possible proposals, the memorandum stated that the issue was primarily 'political and practical rather than legal and academic', and there seemed no reason why the Commonwealth could not accommodate India's requirements. There did not appear to be any reason to formalise India's position through 'any attempted definitions'. Furthermore, any media announcements should be brief, emphasising 'historical and evolutionary factors rather than legal concepts'.[39] Chifley had committed his government to a position of doing everything possible to keep India in the Commonwealth. This cabinet submission reflected the pragmatism of Chifley, who once described the monarchy as a 'handy constitutional fiction'.[40] As historian Frank Bongiorno argues in his account of Australian policy on Indian membership of the Commonwealth, the prime minister was determined that, 'for political and strategic reasons', India should remain in the Commonwealth.[41] Evatt's failure to understand India's position in wanting to remain within the Commonwealth, while refusing to recognise the king's authority in its constitution, reflected his 'historicism and legalism'.[42] It reveals the limitations of Evatt's 'mental framework' when dealing with an emerging Asian nation such as India.[43]

Nehru was also dismissive of the 'lawyers and jurists' who were not able to make up their minds regarding this issue. He had written in December 1948 that he did not know what form India's future relationship with the Commonwealth would take, but India had shown how keen it was to remain a member.[44] At the time, Nehru was 'thoroughly dissatisfied' with how Attlee and the British government had treated the issue of India and the Commonwealth. He was also displeased with the United Kingdom's actions regarding Indonesia and Kashmir. He thought the United Kingdom showed an 'anti-Indian bias' in relation to the dispute between India and Pakistan over Kashmir after the partition of India in 1947. In addition, Nehru was scathing in his assessment of British policy towards the

Indonesian–Dutch conflict and the reluctance of the British to condemn Dutch military action against the Indonesian Republic. He argued that: 'the British attitude is so completely wrong that I am just amazed at their effrontery. They put themselves wholly in the wrong certainly in Asia and possibly elsewhere, and it will take them a mighty long time to get over the discredit that now attaches to them'.[45]

Nehru also had to manage domestic opposition to India remaining a member of the Commonwealth.[46] This was a 'politically sensitive' issue because of the ongoing 'psychological resentment against a relationship with the former rulers', especially from the left in India's political parties, who saw 'it as a guise for retaining British domination'.[47] Nehru argued, however, that the Commonwealth relationship was an 'informal' one. If India retained this relationship with the Commonwealth, it would be 'on the basis of complete equality' in which India would be free to shape its own foreign and domestic policy.[48] Chifley would also face hostility at home from the Menzies Opposition, which opposed the Australian government's support for a republican India remaining a member of the Commonwealth.

The Commonwealth Prime Ministers' Conference, 22–27 April 1949

In London, on 22 April, Chifley's sole engagement before the opening of the Commonwealth Prime Ministers' Conference was a two-hour meeting with Nehru over breakfast at Claridge's Hotel, the first time they had met since arriving in London. The previous day, he had met with Sir Stafford Cripps, the British Chancellor of the Exchequer; Peter Fraser, the New Zealand prime minister; Lester Pearson, Secretary of State for External Affairs, who attended the conference in place of the Canadian prime minister Louis Stephen St Laurent; and Philip John Noel-Baker, Secretary of State for Commonwealth Relations.[49]

The conference was attended by all the dominion representatives,[50] which included the United Kingdom, Canada, Australia, India, New Zealand, South Africa, Pakistan and Ceylon.[51] After Attlee made an introductory speech on the problem facing the Commonwealth governments, which was 'whether it was possible to reconcile India's desire to remain in the Commonwealth, which all would welcome, with her desire to become a Republic',[52] Nehru explained India's position, and the rest of the dominions put forward their own opinions. According to Nehru:

> Australia and New Zealand while expressing desire for our continuing membership of Commonwealth were emphatic that any adjustment of India's continuing membership of Commonwealth to her impending status of Republic must in no way change or weaken nexus of allegiance to King for those member nations which desire to keep it. They made it clear that any other solution would be entirely unacceptable to their people and would create grave political difficulties for them.[53]

The Australian and New Zealand governments were concerned about the 'political difficulties' of any overall change in their countries' link with the Crown. This concern reveals the domestic political constraints under which politicians operate—a factor often ignored or glossed over by historians. Both prime ministers were apprehensive about the ramifications in Australia and New Zealand of any change in their relationship with the Crown. In Australia, public opinion had been roused because of the Opposition's criticism of the Labor government's 'unconcern with the continuance of the British Commonwealth of Nations'.[54] Because of these concerns, Nehru acceded to the use of 'British' in the first paragraph of the proposed declaration, which merely stated the present statutory position. However, India would not agree to the use of the term 'British Commonwealth' elsewhere in the draft.[55]

In other areas covered during the conference, Chifley proved to be much more amenable. In his study of the Australian government's contribution to the question of India's post-war relationship with the Commonwealth, Frank Bongiorno argues that Chifley's significance in facilitating a satisfactory solution and 'wresting control of this issue from Evatt should ... not be underestimated'. The fact that he attended the conference attests to the significance he placed on this issue.[56] Furthermore, it was only when Prime Minister Chifley 'took control of Australia's policy in this field, and adopted a more flexible and less legalistic approach, that a resolution of the difficulty began to emerge'.[57] Chifley's support for Nehru showed he was quite willing to exert his authority and take control in an area historians have often considered was 'dominated by Evatt'.[58] It is obvious that Chifley had progressed beyond Evatt in his commitment to internationalism; his position here is consistent with the general framework that he brought to international affairs. In fact, as Bongiorno notes, the 'failure of Evatt's postcolonial imagination' meant that his influence on the emergent new Commonwealth would be less than that of his 'more astute Prime Minister JB Chifley', who was somewhat 'less intellectually gifted'.[59] The New Zealand government's approach to the changing post-colonial situation differed significantly from that of the Chifley government.[60] As Bongiorno observes, it is 'misleading to lump the antipodean dominions together, as most historians have done'. New Zealand's prime minister, Peter Fraser, preferred to align New Zealand foreign policy with British policy in Asia and the Pacific.[61]

On the night of 26 April 1949, at the fifth meeting of the prime ministers, a draft declaration on India's membership of the Commonwealth was considered and approved.[62] A formula clarifying India's membership of the Commonwealth was finally devised that was acceptable to all attending and one that would satisfy a republican India's constitutional requirements. It became known as the London Declaration. The words that ensured the conference was a success stated that the Indian government had 'declared and affirmed ... her acceptance of The King as the symbol of the free association of its independent member nations and as such the Head of the Commonwealth'.[63] Nehru was convinced that the agreement was much better than expected, and entirely to India's advantage, in that it was 'clear that the King is a symbol only and has no functions at all as such'. India gained certain advantages whilst maintaining autonomy in its domestic and foreign policy.[64] As Nehru told his sister Vijayalakshmi Pandit: 'An India which was isolated completely from the Commonwealth would inevitably have had to slope in some direction,' and 'that sloping could only have been in the direction of the US'. He added that America wanted India to align itself with US foreign policy, but this would have been 'dangerous', making it very hard for India to 'play the role of a friendly neutral to any of the parties concerned'.[65]

Some time later, Nehru would write that Chifley played a significant role at the 1949 Commonwealth Prime Ministers' Conference in 'evolving the Commonwealth formula which enabled India, while a Republic, to remain in the Commonwealth'. With his 'broad outlook' Chifley was very influential at the meetings.[66] Chifley was also congratulated by the Canadian minister for External Affairs, Lester Pearson, on 'his great contribution' to the success of the conference. Pearson added: 'it was a great relief and pleasure to participate in a gathering where the spirit was so good and the friendly feeling so obvious'.[67] According to Nehru's biographer, Judith M Brown, India's continuing membership of the Commonwealth after becoming a republic 'broke the old mould' of the 'tight group of old Dominions' of the 1940s.[68] Chifley saw this as part of the evolutionary nature of the Commonwealth. An evolution that he had noted in his address to the nation the previous year, on 7 November 1948, when he spoke about the 'long-term significance' of the attendance for the very first time, with 'full membership and representation', of India, Pakistan and Ceylon at the 1948 meeting of British Commonwealth prime ministers.

In his address to the nation, Chifley emphasised that these new dominions were, after New Zealand, Australia's closest Commonwealth neighbours. It was easy to understand their 'aspirations for self-government'—it was not long since Australia's own 'campaign for democratic self-government' was achieved. It was just on fifty years ago that Australia had attained 'national unity'. The British Commonwealth had evolved over many years and Australia had advocated many times for 'changes in Imperial relations'. It was therefore no surprise that the new dominions might agitate for changes in the 'forms and working of the British Commonwealth'. This 'progressive development' should not cause undue concern. Chifley emphasised that the 'important thing is not this or that form but the reality of practical co-operation in the pursuit and defence of certain ideals of freedom, human decency, economic collaboration and peace'.[69]

Opposition to the London Declaration

There was, however, no bipartisan support in Australia for India's desire to remain within the Commonwealth as a republic. The leader of the Liberal Party Opposition, Robert Menzies, had earlier opposed the granting of independence to India. His speech in March 1947 on India's impending independence can only be described as an 'ungracious' response—an indication of the future dysfunctional relationship between India and the conservative government that Menzies would lead.[70] In this speech, Menzies argued that India was a country which 'quite obviously, has not yet reached the stage at which the majority of its people are, by education, outlook and training, fit for self government'.[71]

Menzies—who had previously questioned the whole notion of dominion independence—opposed the London Declaration. He could not understand how a republic could remain a member of the Commonwealth.[72] According to Menzies, the London Declaration 'damaged considerably the family relationship under the Crown', and was 'indicative of a process of retreat and disintegration and was disturbing to millions of British people'.[73] In attempting to find a formula to accommodate India, Menzies argued: 'we have abandoned the substance of a unity and power which the world needs very greatly today'.[74] However, the point was surely, as Frank Bongiorno has observed, that the conference had revealed that the 'substance of a unity' existing within the Commonwealth no longer existed. King George VI himself had acknowledged the need for change. He told Lester Pearson that he had 'little patience with Menzies' speech' and was 'somewhat sad that Smuts should have taken the same line'. As Bongiorno notes, the fact that Menzies had such a negative response to the London Declaration boded ill for Australia's relationship with India in the coming years. 'The man who ultimately became Australia's longest-serving Prime Minister was never really reconciled to the changes in the Commonwealth brought about by the events of 1949'.[75]

Menzies reflected later, when he delivered the first Smuts Memorial Lecture at Cambridge University, on 16 May 1960, that his views on the London Declaration were very similar to those of Smuts, the former prime minister of South Africa, who was 'dismayed' at this 'historic decision'. Menzies went on to say:

At the time when the declaration was announced by Mr. Chifley at Canberra, my own views as Leader of the Opposition were not dissimilar [to Smuts's views]. I prepared what I thought to be a powerful and pungent speech. Chifley, who, to use the homely phrase 'didn't come down in the last shower', guessed at my intentions, and with studied calm, left the item at the bottom of the Notice Paper.[76]

Menzies had spent considerable time in the preparation of this speech, in which he argued that if India was not prepared to sign up to the existing Commonwealth as it was, then they should stay out.[77] After some months, acknowledging defeat, he tore up his 'undelivered speech'.[78] However, his 'British Empire-centred world view' continued, and he maintained his antipathy towards a republican India remaining a member of the Commonwealth.[79]

Chifley, on the other hand, saw these changes as part of an ongoing evolutionary process that demonstrated the flexible and collaborative nature of the Commonwealth;[80] he also believed it was imperative to keep India within the Commonwealth. He thought that India would play a pivotal role in ensuring the economic and political security of the region. Similarly, Nehru thought that India was central to the security of 'Asia and Indian Ocean, more especially of the Middle East and South-East Asia'.[81] On a personal level, Chifley greatly admired Nehru and quoted him many times in his speeches. He regarded Nehru as 'the most powerful figure in Asian politics, and, indeed, in the Asian world'.[82] As demonstrated at the 1949 Commonwealth Prime Ministers' Conference, Chifley and Nehru were in remarkable agreement on many issues that challenged their two nations in the post-war period.

Convergence of World Views
On 27 April 1949 the sixth meeting of the prime ministers' conference focused on the Commonwealth's future policy response to the political unrest and changes happening in Asia. The discussion at this meeting is highly significant, because it reveals the convergence of world views of India's Prime Minister Nehru and Australia's Prime Minister Chifley. In the years 1948 to 1949, political unrest had

increased in Southeast Asia and South Asia. In April 1948 the Burmese Communist Party staged a revolt against the Thakin Nu government.[83] In Malaya a state of emergency had been declared in June, and the Malayan Communist Party had been banned.[84] There were communist uprisings in the Philippines in August,[85] and in the Javanese city of Madiun in September 1948.[86] In India, communists were in 'open conflict with the Government'.[87] The success of the Chinese communists led to British concern about how this would impact Hong Kong, as well as Malaya and Singapore, countries with significant Chinese populations. In addition, the long drawn-out French war against the Democratic Republic of Vietnam had begun in 1946.[88]

In the context of this unrest in the region, New Zealand's Prime Minister Peter Fraser called for the conference to confirm the new Commonwealth's unity of purpose in foreign policy, trade and defence—that its members should assist each other 'whether in peace or in war'. In this he was supported by Pakistan's Prime Minister Liaquat Ali Khan. Nehru objected. While agreeing that Commonwealth members should consult and cooperate with each other on 'all matters of common concern',[89] he did not regard the Commonwealth as a 'pact with military implications'.[90] Instead, Nehru argued that the situation in Asia, for example, was a very complex one. It would be an enormous blunder if the Commonwealth governments viewed it through the prism of 'defence against aggression'. He gave as an example the present conflict in China, which had 'deep-seated' historical causes. Although communists were influencing and exploiting this unrest, it

> was due fundamentally to a widespread sense of dissatisfaction with the existing regime. It must be seen in this wider context. And policy must be so directed as to appeal to the great masses of people throughout Asia who were not committed to any particular ideology but were in a state of unrest due to dissatisfaction with their conditions of life. The problem was to capture the minds and imagination of these peoples. It was not in essence a military problem.[91]

The first objective of any policy, according to Nehru, should be to 'prevent war'. It was evident from the last two world wars that war only intensified 'the very conditions which created that social dissatisfaction and unrest on which communism flourished'. Nehru deplored the fact that world problems were viewed 'in terms of Power *blocs*'. Instead, there needed to be a 'positive policy for preventing war', which meant removing the desperate economic conditions that encouraged the spread of communism. Political developments in Asia were also adding to the existing unrest. The aggressive military operations undertaken by the Dutch in Indonesia had exacerbated the situation there, creating an adverse effect on public opinion in Asia. Furthermore, the policies pursued by the French in Indochina would only incite those forces planning the 'violent overthrow of Colonial domination in Asia'. If these 'irritants to public opinion in Asia' were removed, international security would benefit much more than any military intervention.[92] At this point—as RJ Moore notes in his study of the new Commonwealth—after 'a long and ... "impressive dialectical statement" he [Nehru] won Chifley's ready assent'.[93] Chifley declared that he agreed with Nehru. The Dutch government's policy in Indonesia was 'a serious threat to the peace of the Pacific'.[94]

The opinions voiced by Nehru at the Commonwealth Prime Ministers' meeting were views that Chifley had also held for some time. He had consistently argued that to counter the spread of communism in Asia, political reform and improved living standards, rather than a military response, were required. As he had stated in the House of Representatives in September the previous year, the 'great upsurge of nationalism that is occurring now throughout the East has roots that go deeper than communism'. In most cases, it was 'an economic rebellion, against conditions under which the people have been living'.[95] Furthermore, the possibility of another war was something that should 'appal every human being'—any future war would be too terrible to contemplate with the 'new forms of warfare' available.[96] Nehru also abhorred war and feared that the deployment of power politics by the great powers would lead to an even more destructive war.[97] Both leaders were united in their belief that a military response to nationalist uprisings demanding self-government would be counter-productive.

Nehru told the meeting that 'free democracy' was 'infinitely preferable' to the communist regime established by the Soviet government. In founding its own political institutions, India had drawn on the 'democratic ideals' and institutions established in the United Kingdom. However, democracy was in danger from both communist encroachment and by 'unfavourable economic conditions'. Nehru believed that, if the second danger could be addressed, communism would be deprived of the conditions that enabled it to flourish. He reminded the meeting that Western colonialism was still mistrusted in Asia, and the Commonwealth needed to keep this in mind. The Soviet government's 'expansionist' policies had to be resisted, but it was the 'political encroachment of communism' that must be challenged. This could 'only be done by persuading peoples who were exposed to Communist encroachment that the democratic way of life had better things to offer'.[98] Chifley agreed with Nehru:

> The primary object of Commonwealth policy should be to create, in countries exposed to Communist influence, social conditions in which it would be impossible for communism to flourish. It was by these methods that the advance of communism must be checked. In Asia certainly, and possibly in other countries also, military strength was not an effective weapon against Communist encroachment.[99]

Both Nehru and Chifley argued that the conditions that inevitably led to war involved economic grievances. Both leaders believed that desperate economic conditions encouraged the spread of communism. Nehru was concerned, however, that 'America was allying with reactionary regimes, and this in turn would play into Communist hands: moreover America seemed to be using the same strategies of world power as the Communist bloc, particularly the acquisition of bases for defence and aggression'. The critical factor in preventing the spread of communism was to improve living standards and ensure economic development in Asia.[100] As Nehru would state later, 'political democracy' was not enough, there needed to be 'economic democracy' as well.[101]

Chifley echoed Nehru's sentiments expressed at the Commonwealth Prime Ministers' Conference, when, two weeks later, he addressed the federal executive of the Australian Labor Party on 11 May 1949. Chifley declared that if Western democracies were to succeed against communism, they needed to demonstrate in the material world that they could deliver better living conditions for their people. The 'only way to win the support of the East for the democracies is to improve the economic welfare of the Asian peoples, to win their spirit and so defeat any spread of Communism'. He agreed with Nehru—who had 'very great influence' in the East—that communism could not be defeated with military might. Improvement in living standards would show that 'democracy, liberty and freedom doesn't just mean freedom to starve'.[102] But, as he wrote later, instead of addressing the appalling living conditions in which many people existed: 'What troubles me most of all is the fact that in the Western nations' crusade against Communism they appear to be prepared to give their support to regimes or governments which are completely corrupt or feudalistic'.[103]

Chifley's biographer, Crisp, made an intriguing observation when he wrote that, in meeting Nehru at the 1949 Commonwealth Prime Ministers' Conference, Chifley 'seems to have received both stimulus and at the same time confirmation of many of his own conclusions about Asian affairs'.[104] Nehru's influence on Chifley was also noted by the *Sydney Morning Herald*'s Canberra correspondent, who wrote, after Chifley's death:

> One man who exercised a deep influence upon him [Chifley] was the Prime Minister of India, Pandit Nehru. The views which Nehru expressed to him during the Prime Minister's conference of 1949 in London were very largely the basis of his recent and frequently expressed opinions on Far Eastern affairs.[105]

Engagement with Nehru on a personal level at the Commonwealth Prime Ministers' Conference would certainly have validated Chifley's own views on Asian affairs in the post-war period. Together with the intelligence gathered previously from the 1947 Asian Relations Conference and the William Macmahon Ball missions to Indonesia in

1945 and to Southeast Asia in 1948, Nehru's views informed and provided supporting evidence for the direction that the Chifley government's foreign policy took in its support for nationalist movements in India and Indonesia.

The 1949 conference provides evidence of the extraordinary convergence of world-views of these two leaders. This convergence can be seen in their views on the need to adjust to a changing world; their internationalism; their support for the United Nations; their rejection of the United States and the United Kingdom's Cold War framework through which the post-war world was viewed; and their opposition to Western colonialism. In September 1946, Nehru had declared that India's attitude towards the world organisation was one of 'wholehearted cooperation and unreserved adherence' to the United Nations Charter. In particular, India would campaign for 'the independence of all colonial and dependent people and their full right to self determination'.[106] In a speech delivered in India's Constituent Assembly in May 1949, Nehru stated that no country could live in 'isolation, because the world as constituted today is progressively becoming an organic whole'.[107] The old world was changing, and in this new era of the Cold War, isolationism was risky. Both Nehru and Chifley regarded membership of the United Nations and the Commonwealth as vital elements contributing to their countries' economic and strategic security. Nehru had been disappointed that the League of Nations had failed to '[revolutionize] the fabric of human affairs';[108] the newly established United Nations was therefore 'the new hope, the great salvation for humankind'.[109]

However, historian Manu Bhagavan, in his study of India and the United Nations, expresses surprise at Nehru's whole-hearted endorsement of the United Nations' Charter, considering the failure of the Charter to 'adopt the straightforward anti-colonial language of its Atlantic predecessor'.[110] In addition, a notable feature of the conference held to establish the United Nations was 'its exclusion of colonized people'. But, although it has been claimed that the United Nations, even at its founding, was 'an instrument of Western imperial power', many saw great potential in this new international organisation because of the hopes raised by the Atlantic Charter[111] which was adopted by US President Franklin Delano Roosevelt and the British Prime Minister Winston Churchill, when they met aboard the US flagship *Augusta* in Ship Harbour, Newfoundland on 14 August, 1941. The charter proclaimed 'certain common principles' which would establish a rules-based approach to the international order. They committed the United States and the the United Kingdom to:

> a new order based on a few key principles: an end to territorial aggrandizement or territorial changes; respect for self-government; social security; peace and freedom from fear or want; high seas freedoms; and restraints on the use of force.[112]

Bhagavan argues that India's presence as the 'physical manifestation' of a post-colonial state,[113] or an 'about-to-be-independent-India' as Nehru termed it,[114] 'imbued the UN Charter with the anti-imperial ambitions of the original Atlantic Charter'.[115] Nehru believed that although there were weaknesses in the United Nations, it was, after all, the idea on which it was based that counted: only a great idea could bring peace. Although the United Nations might make mistakes, the basic principles on which it was based were just principles. He argued that the United Nations needed to be made strong, because 'if it collapses what will happen after it?' There was no alternative.[116]

Chifley also provided 'complete and absolute support' for the United Nations, although, as Crisp notes, 'his views about the relationship of power and law in international affairs were perhaps more wary and realistic than those of his juristically-minded colleague', HV Evatt.[117] Chifley thought the United Nations' main virtue was as an international forum for 'the adjustment of grievances, and for the exercise of conciliation among the nations'. The labour movement in Australia had, therefore, always supported this great international organisation. 'Indeed, the United Nations must have the full support of every man and woman who believes that we should do everything we can to avoid another world conflict'.[118] Although there was provision under its charter to mobilise a force in the event of another world war breaking out, Chifley did have doubts as to the United Nations' capacity to carry out its decisions. Nevertheless, despite its limitations, he strongly believed in the value of the United Nations. As Crisp notes, for Chifley, the United Nations with its 'potentialities and limitations' in the area of international law, reflected the same opportunities and constraints experienced by governments, courts and conciliation commissioners in the domestic area of industrial relations.[119]

Both leaders' attitudes toward the United Nations were reflections of their own personal experiences. Chifley's views on the potential benefits of the United Nations and its subsidiary organisations were formed by his long experience as a union delegate and advocate—Chifley was a firm believer in arbitration.[120] This faith in the efficacy and fairness of arbitration in industrial relations in the domestic arena led to his belief in 'international arbitration' and collective action through the United Nations. As David Lowe has noted, the United Nations represented a new form of 'international arbitration' that was embraced by both Chifley and Evatt.[121] For Nehru, the United Nations was an organisation that was closely aligned with India's optimism for the nation and hopes for humanity's future. According to Bhagavan, it bought out in him 'an astounding idealism tempered by a steady wariness of falling short of expectations'. In this era of decolonisation, the new international institution presented an opportunity for 'radical social restructuring'. An example of this was India's contribution to the drafting of the Declaration of Human Rights.[122]

There was a distinct convergence in foreign policy between the Australian and Indian governments during this period.[123] One of the most distinctive aspects of the early post-war period was the Chifley government's opposition to the Cold War polarisation of the world in which East and West were 'implacably opposed to each other'.[124] As Meg Gurry has stated, Chifley appreciated India's non-aligned position in its approach to international relations—a policy that later Australian leaders were either unable or refused to comprehend.[125] Although both leaders were staunch opponents of communism, they refused to conflate Asian nationalism with communist agitation. Nehru argued that the old Western colonial powers did not understand that Southeast Asia was in 'turmoil' because radical political and economic change was critical.[126] He had fought a long battle against colonialism and spent more than a decade in jail 'over nine separate terms, (one of three continuous years) between 1921 and 1945'. Nehru's personal experience of the 'exploitation and brutality' of colonialism were major influences in his attitude towards the post-war world.[127]

Chifley also opposed those who put forward the suggestion that there was a world-wide monolithic communist force at work. Many people attributed all the conflict in the world to communism. This was a 'fallacy'. The 'situation in Asia' which had 'been developing for hundreds of years' was 'aggravated by the rapid growth of populations in which the percentage of poverty and misery' was increasing rapidly.[128] Chifley paid tribute to Nehru's long struggle for India's independence, when he said in parliament: 'Pandit Nehru was a member of a minority movement and he spent over ten years in gaol because of his ideas. Today, he is an honoured guest of kings and presidents and notables throughout the world'.[129] Chifley's own experience of British colonialism in India did not impress him. Travelling through Calcutta, on his way to an earlier prime ministers' conference in London in 1946, Chifley declared that he was appalled at the poverty and 'the untold millions of wealth which have flowed out of this country to Europe'.[130]

There was, however, one area of divergence which was a major impediment to the Chifley government's efforts to establish closer ties with its Asian neighbour—that was the bipartisan, exclusionary White Australia policy. The Australian government had been warned repeatedly by its diplomats and officials from the Department of External Affairs of the 'resentment and hostility caused by the government's policy'.[131] Iven Mackay, Australia's high commissioner in New Delhi, wrote that while officially it was stated that the White Australia policy was based on 'economic and social, and not on racial grounds', it had to be acknowledged that it was indeed, 'racial'. Mackay urged a review of the policy in which regulations governing the number of Indians arriving in Australia would be modified. This would be, he suggested, 'a gesture of goodwill to India as she enters upon her new national status'.[132] Colin Moodie, an officer in the Department of External Affairs, who accompanied John Burton to the 1949 New Delhi conference,[133] wrote that in order to ensure long-lasting cordial relations with India and Pakistan, the White Australia policy had to be modified by not referring to it by that name and by making it more flexible.[134] He urged the government to educate the Australian people that 'discrimination or prejudice against Asiatics is wrong and completely against our best interests'.[135]

However, the Chifley government continued with its 'stubborn commitment' to the White Australia policy,[136] a policy of which India's 'political elite was aware and resentful of its presence'.[137] Yet, for all his opposition to racial discrimination, Nehru did not raise this issue during Commonwealth conferences, because, as he stated in an interview in London in December 1952, he saw these forums as 'an occasion and a body for seeking agreement and friendship rather than pressing on differences'.[138] The countries of the Commonwealth, it was hoped, would enjoy friendly relations and would 'deal with each other as independent countries'. It was, therefore, not appropriate to bring to the Commonwealth, disputes between members. The Commonwealth was not to be a tribunal.[139] Instead, these issues were raised in the United Nations, which Nehru saw as the appropriate forum in which to condemn other nations for their discriminatory racial policies.[140]

According to Crisp, Chifley met two men at the Commonwealth prime ministers' conferences that he had 'a very special admiration' for—Nehru and the British Chancellor of the Exchequer Sir Stafford Cripps.[141] He regarded both men as friends.[142] They were 'the two keenest Ministerial minds' he had met since Edward Granville Theodore, treasurer in the Scullin government. Chifley did not see much of Cripps until 1948, and at the conference in 1949[143] when he made a great impression on the chancellor.[144] Chifley met Nehru at the prime ministers' conference in London in 1949,[145] where they were able to establish a warm relationship, both at the 'official and the personal level'.[146] Chifley 'warmed to the charm and the swift, shrewd wit of the man'. As Crisp relates, one of Chifley's favourite stories about Nehru concerned

> an occasion when Nehru displayed singular mastery in making a blunt, direct statement of his viewpoint on one of the more troublesome issues under discussion. Cripps remarked: 'Pandit Nehru, you have an extraordinary grasp of this subject'. Instantly the amiable answer came: 'Yes, Sir Stafford, I had over ten years in British gaols to think it through'.[147]

In a letter to Crisp, in March 1952, Nehru wrote that he greatly appreciated the role that Chifley had played at the 1949 Commonwealth Prime Ministers' Conference. He wrote that Chifley had

> a most vivid memory of our meeting on several occasions in London, and, in particular, of his coming to breakfast with me in my hotel. Mr Chifley struck me as an outstanding personality and I was greatly attracted to him. He was somewhat unlike the average run of politicians and disliked the pomp and circumstance that sometimes surrounded us in London. Simple and straightforward in his behaviour, he had a broad outlook. Whatever he said in the Prime Ministers' Conference made an impression. He was very helpful in that Conference in evolving the Commonwealth formula which enabled India, while a Republic, to remain in the Commonwealth. I was deeply distressed to learn of his passing away.[148]

Sir Norman Mighell, who was Australia's deputy high commissioner in London from 1946 to 1949,[149] was a 'tremendous admirer' of Chifley 'for his ability, but perhaps above all—for his humanity and his personal kindness'.[150] Mighell wrote that Chifley played an important role in the negotiations at the conference.[151] Australia's high commissioner to India in the 1950s, Walter Crocker, 'confirmed the great respect Nehru held for Chifley. They "got on very well", he reported'.[152]

Conclusion

The 1949 Commonwealth Prime Ministers' Conference provides invaluable evidence of Chifley's commitment to a new approach to Asia and to internationalism. Despite a lack of bipartisan support—and, indeed, very vocal criticism from the Australian press and the Menzies Opposition—Chifley was prepared to go out on a limb to push for India to remain in the Commonwealth. The conference also reveals a convergence of views between two internationalists—Chifley and Nehru—who both saw the need for international cooperation to ensure global prosperity and security. There was every possibility that a productive and ongoing relationship at both the official and the personal level would develop between India and

Australia. During this early post-war period, as Meg Gurry has observed, Australian views of Asia in the 1940s were not 'marked by the ambivalence which characterised so much of the later contact'. Gurry noted that:

> In policy formulation, the Cold War had not yet assumed the commanding position of later years and, in ideological terms, India was seen as an ally and a friend, not a 'suspicious' neutral. Importantly as well, it was seen as a neighbour and, also unlike in later years, India was definitely included *within* the boundaries of Australia's regional interests and concerns.[153]

Similarly, Australia was seen by Nehru as belonging to the Southeast Asia region and as a partner in advocating for the 'freedom of the countries of South East Asia'.[154]

Notes

1. Ivan Chapman, *Iven G Mackay Citizen and Soldier*, Melway Publishing, Melbourne, 1975, pp. 293–302.
2. ibid., pp. 1–2; p. 8.
3. ibid., pp. 281–282; p. 301.
4. Gurry, *India: Australia's Neglected Neighbour? 1947–1996*, pp. 2–3.
5. Manu Bhagavan,'A New Hope: India, the United Nations and the Making of the Universal Declaration of Human Rights', *Modern Asian Studies*, vol. 44, issue 2, 2010, p. 317.
6. Ramachandra Guha, (ed.), *Makers of Modern India*, Belknap Press of Harvard University Press, Cambridge, MA, 2011, p. 284.
7. 'Note by Mackay of Conversation with Evatt', 26 August 1946, Karachi, in Hudson and Way (eds), *DAFP, Volume X: 1946, July–December*, pp. 146–147.
8. Mackay to Evatt, 2 September 1946, New Delhi, in ibid., p. 178.
9. JB Chifley, 'Planning for Peace: 11. International Co-operation', *Sydney Morning Herald*, 2 December 1943, p. 4.
10. 'Prime Minister Announces Labour Policy', *Sydney Morning Herald*, 3 September 1946, p. 5
11. Turnell, Monetary Reformers, p. 185.
12. Coombs to Chifley, 'International Economic Policy', 11 February 1947, NAA: A1068, ER47/70/7. The Australian government had established a trade commission headed by H Roy Gollan in India in December 1939. See Boris Schedvin, *Emissaries of Trade: A History of the Australian Trade Commissioner Service*, Department of Foreign Affairs and Trade, Barton, ACT, 2008, p. 65.

13 Gerald Packer, 'The Asian Relations Conference: The Group Discussions', *Australian Outlook*, vol. 1, no. 2, June 1947, p. 4.
14 Cablegram 68, Burton to Evatt, 21 January 1949, NAA: A1838 383/1/2/5.
15 'An Era of Closer Asian Cooperation', 23 January 1949, in *Selected Works of Jawaharlal Nehru*, Second Series, vol. 9, S Gopal (ed.), Jawaharlal Nehru Memorial Fund, New Delhi, 1990, p. 170 (hereafter cited as *SWJN(2)*).
16 ibid., p. 171.
17 ibid., p. 172.
18 Burton to Evatt, 'Asian Conference on Indonesia', 26 January 1949, p. 5. NAA: A1838 383/1/2/5.
19 Gurry, *India: Australia's Neglected Neighbour?*, p. 4.
20 *CPD*, HoR, 19 June 1946, p. 1558.
21 'India's Relationship with the Commonwealth', Remarks at a Meeting of the Legislature for the Ministry of External Affairs and Commonwealth Relations, 19 March 1949, in *SWJN(2)*, vol. 10, Jawaharlal Nehru Memorial Fund, New Delhi, 1990, p. 146.
22 Nehru to VK Krishna Menon, 14 March 1949, in ibid., p. 145.
23 'India's Relationship with the Commonwealth', 19 March 1949, in ibid., pp. 146–147.
24 Jawaharlal Nehru to V.K. Krishna Menon, 12 January 1948, *SWJN(2)*, vol. 9, pp. 189–190.
25 Jawaharlal Nehru to V.K. Krishna Menon, 12 January 1948, in ibid., p. 190, fn. 8.
26 Nehru to VK Krishna Menon, 25 February 1949; 28 February 1949, in *SWJN(2)*, vol. 10, p. 143.
27 Nehru to Vallabhbhai Patel, 26 March 1949, in ibid., p. 151, fn. 2.
28 ibid., p. 151, fn. 3.
29 ibid., p. 151.
30 Pamela Andre (ed.), *DAFP, Volume XIV: The Commonwealth, Asia and the Pacific 1948–49*, DFAT, Canberra, 1998, p. x.
31 'Pacific Regional Defence Pact Likely: Lord Listowel to Meet Cabinet', *Argus* (Melbourne), 15 March 1949, p. 3.
32 UK High Commissioner to CRO, 27 February 1949, National Archives United Kingdom: (hereafter NAUK) CAB 21/1820, cited in RJ Moore, *Making the New Commonwealth*, Claremont Press, Oxford, 1987, p. 174.
33 Listowel to CRO, 15 March 1949, NAUK: CAB 21/1820, cited in ibid., p. 176.
34 Listowel to CRO, 16 March 1949, NAUK: CAB 21/1820, cited in ibid., p. 176.
35 Moore, *Making the New Commonwealth*, p. 177.
36 Listowel to CRO, 16 March 1949, cited in ibid.
37 Crisp, *Ben Chifley*, pp. 284–285.
38 Andre (ed.), *DAFP, Volume XIV: The Commonwealth, Asia and the Pacific 1948–49*, pp. 116–117.
39 ibid., p. 118.
40 Frank Bongiorno, 'Commonwealthmen and Republicans: Dr HV Evatt, the Monarchy and India', *Australian Journal of Politics and History*,

vol. 46, no. 1, 2000, p. 42. Chifley made this statement to the Irish Minister in Australia.
41 ibid., p. 46.
42 ibid., p. 48.
43 ibid., pp. 47–48.
44 Nehru to Rob Lockhart, 29 December 1948, in *SWJN(2)*, vol. 9, p. 185.
45 Nehru to VK Krishna Menon, 30 December 1948, in ibid., pp. 186–187.
46 Editorial note, in *SWJN(2)*, vol. 10, unpaginated.
47 Nihal Randolph Henry Kuruppu, An Indian Perspective of the Relationship Between India and Australia, 1947 to 1975: Personalities and Policies, Peaks and Troughs, PhD Thesis, Victoria University of Technology, 2000, pp. 135–136.
48 'No Secret Pact with Britain', 26 January 1949, in *SWJN(2)*, vol. 9, p. 445.
49 Letter, Norman R Mighell to Crisp, 7 December 1954, Papers of LF Crisp, NLA: MS 5243, Series 5, Folder 2; 'Chifley's Talk with Nehru', *Western Australian*, 23 April 1949, p. 3.
50 Nehru to Vallabhbhai Patel, 22 April 1949, in *SWJN(2)*, vol. 10, pp. 170–171.
51 Minutes of the 1st Meeting of the Commonwealth Prime Ministers, London, 22 April 1949, p. 1, NAA: A5954, 1685/3.
52 ibid., p. 2.
53 Nehru to Patel, 22 April 1949, in *SWJN(2)*, vol. 10, p. 171.
54 Moore, *Making the New Commonwealth*, p. 175.
55 Nehru to Patel, 26 April 1949, in *SWJN(2)*, vol. 10, p. 173.
56 Bongiorno, '"British to the Bootstraps?" HV Evatt, JB Chifley and Australian Policy on Indian Membership of the Commonwealth, 1947–49', *Australian Historical Studies*, vol. 37, issue 125, 2005, p. 37.
57 ibid., p. 18.
58 ibid., p. 37.
59 ibid., p. 21.
60 Suares, 'Engaging with Asia', p. 506.
61 Bongiorno, 'British to the Bootstraps?', p. 36.
62 Minutes of the 5th Meeting of the Commonwealth Prime Ministers, London, 26 April 1949, p. 2, NAA: A5954, 1685/3.
63 'Meeting of Prime Ministers', Memoranda, 'Approved Text of Final Communique', PMM (49) 6, 26 April 1949, in ibid.
64 'Note on the Commonwealth Prime Ministers Conference', 7 May 1949, *SWJN(2)*, Volume 11, pp. 300–301.
65 Nehru to Vijayalakshmi Pandit, 8 June 1949, in ibid., p. 356.
66 Letter, Nehru to LF Crisp, 6 March 1952, Papers of LF Crisp, NLA: MS 5243, Series 5, Folder 2
67 Crisp, *Ben Chifley*, p. 286.
68 Judith M Brown, *Nehru: A Political Life*, Yale University Press, New Haven, CN, 2003, p. 251.
69 'Report to the Nation', 7 November 1948, pp. 16–17, *DDA*, No. 140, 12 Oct 1948–21 Nov 1948, NAA: B5459, 140.
70 Kuruppu, An Indian Perspective, p. 193.
71 *CPD*, HoR, 19 March 1947, p. 855.

72 EM Andrews, *A History of Australian Foreign Policy*, 2nd edn, Longman Cheshire, Melbourne, 1988, p. 60; Bongiorno, 'British to the Bootstraps?', p. 38.
73 Kuruppu, An Indian Perspective, p. 132.
74 *Manchester Guardian*, 29 April 1949. Cited in Bongiorno, 'British to the Bootstraps?', p. 38.
75 Bongiorno, 'British to the Bootstraps?', p. 38.
76 The Rt Hon RG Menzies, 'The First Smuts Memorial Lecture', at the University of Cambridge, 16 May 1960, p. 5. http://pmtranscripts.dpmc.gov.au/browse.php?did=183 (accessed 21 June 2014).
77 Harold Cox, confidential report to Keith Murdoch, 22 May 1949, Reports of Harold Cox, NLA: MS 4554.
78 Menzies, 'The First Smuts Memorial Lecture', p. 5.
79 Kuruppu, An Indian Perspective, p. 156.
80 'Report to the Nation', 7 November 1948, p. 17.
81 Srinath Raghavan, *India's War: The Making of Modern South Asia 1939–1945*, Penguin Books, London, UK, 2017, p. 455.
82 *CPD*, HoR, 23 March 1950, p. 1174.
83 'Basic Principles—Guidelines for the Coming Session of the United Nations General Assembly', 12 September 1948, in *SWJN(2)*, vol. 7, Jawaharlal Nehru Memorial Fund, New Delhi, 1988, p. 611, fn. 3.
84 Andre (ed.), *DAFP, Volume XIV: The Commonwealth, Asia and the Pacific 1948–49*, p. xii.
85 Moore, *Making the New Commonwealth*, p. 141.
86 Critchley, 'View from the Good Offices Committee', in Legge (ed.), *New Directions in Australian Foreign Policy*, p. 66.
87 'Basic Principles: Guidelines for the Coming Session of the United Nations General Assembly', 12 September 1948, in *SWJN(2)*, vol. 7, p. 611, fn. 3.
88 Moore, *Making the New Commonwealth*, p. 141.
89 Minutes of the 6th Meeting of the Commonwealth Prime Ministers, London, 27 April 1949, p. 3, NAA: A5954, 1685/3.
90 Hector Mackenzie, 'An Old Dominion and the New Commonwealth: Canadian Policy on the Question of India's Membership, 1947–49', *Journal of Imperial and Commonwealth History*, vol. 27, no. 3, 1999, p. 88.
91 Minutes of the 6th Meeting of the Commonwealth Prime Ministers, London, 27 April 1949, p. 3. NAA: A5954, 1685/3.
92 ibid., pp. 3–4. NAA: A5954, 1685/3.
93 Moore, *Making the New Commonwealth*, p. 191.
94 Minutes of the 6th Meeting of the Commonwealth Prime Ministers, London, 27 April 1949, p. 4. NAA: A5954, 1685/3.
95 *CPD*, HoR, 2 September 1948, p. 66.
96 ibid., pp. 63–64.
97 Srinath Raghavan, *War and Peace in Modern India*, Palgrave Macmillan, Basingstoke, UK, 2010, p. 20.
98 Minutes of the 6th Meeting of the Commonwealth Prime Ministers, London, 27 April 1949, p. 4. NAA: A5954, 1685/3.

99   ibid., p. 5.
100 Brown, *Nehru: A Political Life*, p. 255.
101 Ramachandra Guha, (ed.), *Makers of Modern India*, Belknap Press of Harvard University Press, Cambridge, MA., 2011, p. 323.
102 Address by the Prime Minister (Mr Chifley) to the Federal Executive of the Australian Labor Party, Canberra, 11 May 1949, in Weller (ed.), *Federal Executive Minutes 1915–1955*, p. 392.
103 Letter, Chifley to Ian Lasry, LLB, 8 September 1950, Papers of LF Crisp, NLA: MS 5243 Series 5, Folder 1.
104 Crisp, *Ben Chifley*, p. 277.
105 'Leadership of Mr Chifley: Strong Influence on Party', *Sydney Morning Herald*, 14 June 1951, p. 2.
106 Kuruppu, An Indian Perspective, p. 354.
107 'Continuance in the Commonwealth', speech in the Constituent Assembly, 16 May 1949, in *SWJN(2)*, vol. 11, p. 332.
108 Bhagavan, 'A New Hope: India, the United Nations and the Making of the Universal Declaration of Human Rights', p. 320.
109 ibid., p. 321.
110 ibid.
111 ibid., p. 314.
112 Philippe Sands, *Lawless World: Making and Breaking Global Rules*, Penguin Books, London, UK, 2006, pp. 8–9.
113 Bhagavan, 'A New Hope', p. 322.
114 ibid., p. 317.
115 ibid., p. 322.
116 'Mahatma Gandhi', Speech delivered by Nehru at a public meeting in Delhi on Mahatma Gandhi's birthday, 2 October 1948, in *SWJN(2)*, vol. 7, p. 149.
117 Crisp, *Ben Chifley*, p. 287.
118 *CPD*, HoR, 27 September 1950, p. 22.
119 Crisp, *Ben Chifley*, p. 288.
120 ibid., p. 22.
121 Lowe, *Menzies and the 'Great World Struggle'*, p. 20.
122 Bhagavan, 'A New Hope', p. 312.
123 Kuruppu, An Indian Perspective, p. 78.
124 Lowe, *Menzies and the 'Great World Struggle'*, p. 16.
125 Gurry, *India: Australia's Neglected Neighbour?*, p. 4.
126 Letters to the Premiers of Provinces, VI, 1 September 1948, in *SWJN(2)*, vol. 7, pp. 360–361.
127 Kuruppu, An Indian Perspective, p. 155, fn. 1.
128 *CPD*, HoR, 7 March 1951, p. 82.
129 *CPD*, HoR, 9 May 1950, p. 2268.
130 Coombs, *Trial Balance*, p. 77.
131 Suares, 'Engaging with Asia', p. 510.
132 Mackay to Evatt, 22 December 1946, in Hudson and Way (eds), *DAFP, Volume X: 1946, July–December*, pp. 534–535.
133 Suares, 'Engaging with Asia', p. 504.

134 Minute, Moodie to Deschamps, 11 February 1948, in Andre (ed.), *DAFP, Volume XIV: The Commonwealth, Asia and the Pacific, 1948–49*, p. 282.
135 Minute, Moodie to Burton, 29 December 1948, in ibid., p. 285.
136 Suares, 'Engaging with Asia', p. 510.
137 Kuruppu, An Indian Perspective, p. 105.
138 'Commonwealth Relations: The Commonwealth Conference', *The Round Table: The Commonwealth Journal of International Affairs*, vol. 43, 1952, p. 363.
139 'Note on the Commonwealth Prime Ministers' Conference', 7 May 1949, in *SWJN(2)*, vol. 11, p. 301.
140 'Commonwealth Relations: The Commonwealth Conference', *The Round Table*, p. 363.
141 Crisp, *Ben Chifley*, p. 277.
142 Letter, Crisp to JA Ferguson, 11 March 1952, Papers of LF Crisp, NLA: MS 5243, series 5, Folder 2.
143 Crisp, *Ben Chifley*, p. 277.
144 Letter, Norman R Mighell to Crisp, 7 December 1954, Papers of LF Crisp, NLA: MS 5243, Series 5, Folder 2.
145 Crisp, *Ben Chifley*, p. 277.
146 Kuruppu, An Indian Perspective, p. 91.
147 Crisp, *Ben Chifley*, pp. 277–278.
148 Letter, Nehru to LF Crisp, 6 March 1952, Papers of LF Crisp, NLA: MS 5243, Series 5, Folder 2.
149 Richard Kingsland, 'Mighell, Sir Norman Rupert (1894–1955)', *Australian Dictionary of Biography*, vol. 15, Melbourne University Press, Carlton, Victoria, 2000, pp. 366–367.
150 Letter, Mighell to Crisp, 2 September 1953, Papers of LF Crisp. NLA: MS 5243, Series 5, Folder 2.
151 Letter, Mighell to Crisp, 7 December 1954, Papers of LF Crisp. NLA: MS 5243, Series 5, Folder 2.
152 Gurry, *India: Australia's Neglected Neighbour?*, p. 4.
153 ibid., p. 1.
154 'Basic Principles', 12 September 1948, in *SWJN(2)*, vol. 7, p. 610.

Part IV
Chifley and the Establishment of a New Collective Political–Strategic Order

Chifley, Evatt and Attlee at Dominion and British Leaders Conference, London 1946.

CHAPTER SEVEN
The Japanese Peace Settlement

The Allied Occupation of Japan continued from 1945 until 1952.[1] It took more than three months after the signing of the surrender document on board the USS *Missouri*, on 2nd September 1945, for the Occupation's control mechanisms—which would decide the terms of the post-war peace settlement—to be created at a meeting of the Council of Foreign Ministers in Moscow in December 1945.[2] The council, the Occupation's principal negotiating organisation, was established at a great power conference in Potsdam held in late July and early August 1945.[3] Australia took part in the Occupation in both a military and a civilian role. Australia, together with Britain and New Zealand, provided military forces to participate as part of the British Commonwealth Occupation Forces in the Hiroshima district. In addition, an Australian led the Forces, with Lieutenant-General John Northcott serving as the first commander, and later, Lieutenant-General HCH Robertson. US General Douglas MacArthur was the Supreme Commander for the Allied Powers under whom the Australians operated.[4]

The Allied Council for Japan (ACJ), situated in Tokyo, was part of the Occupation's civilian machinery. The British Commonwealth was represented on the council by an Australian, William Macmahon Ball, who served from 1946 to 1947; Patrick Shaw was the next Australian representative serving from 1947 to 1949 and William R

Hodgson from 1949 to 1952. This four power advisory organisation included the United States, the British Commonwealth, the Soviet Union and Nationalist China.[5] The Supreme Commander, General MacArthur, maintained control over the ACJ through his executive power.[6] In Washington DC an organisation known as the Far Eastern Commission was formed, whose function was to develop policies for the Occupation. It was made up of eleven nations that had fought Japan in World War II: the United States, Britain, the Soviet Union, China, France, Australia, New Zealand, India, the Philippines, the Netherlands and Canada.[7] The Soviet Union boycotted the meetings in protest against the advisory nature of the Commission.[8]

The fundamental question confronting the Chifley government at the end of the war was how to achieve peace and prosperity both within Australia's region and globally.[9] Pre-war certainties that Australia's safety was assured because of the protection of the British Empire had been 'destroyed'.[10] In the immediate post-war period, the Chifley government's main aim was to ensure that Japan would not be a threat to Pacific security in the future. To do this, the government believed it needed to be a participant in the peace process on the basis of equal representation.[11] The Chifley government argued that Australia's contribution to the war effort entitled it to be included as a party principal in negotiations over the terms of the Japanese peace settlement.[12] At the Potsdam conference, however, Australia was excluded by the great powers from participating in the Council of Foreign Ministers—the key post-war negotiating organisation—which was made up of the United States, the United Kingdom, the Soviet Union, plus France and China. In addition, the Australian government was not informed of the armistice terms that the Allies would offer to Japan until after those terms were made available to the public. It was obvious that the peace settlement negotiations would be dominated by the great powers, in particular, the United States. This meant that small to medium powers such as Australia would have little influence in determining the post-war peace settlement.[13]

With the change in government in Britain from conservative to Labour, which occurred during the Potsdam conference in July 1945, the Australian government had hoped that a Labour Attlee government would be more sympathetic to Australia's desire to be a participant in the peace negotiations.[14] However, it became increasingly obvious that Britain's dire economic circumstances and its dependence on aid from the United States meant that Australia could not rely on Britain's support.[15] In any divergence in policy where British interests were involved, the British government would support the United States.[16] The Australian government found it very difficult to be heard in the negotiations over the peace settlement.

The Chifley government believed that Japan's economic recovery was vital to ensure post-war peace and prosperity in Australia's region. To achieve these aims, radical changes were needed in 'Japan's social political and economic pattern', in order to eliminate 'Japanese militarism and its constant threat to Pacific security'.[17] The Chifley government and the United States differed substantially in their attitude towards post-war Japan. In August 1945, the Chifley government had condemned US policy on Japan—as embodied in the Potsdam Declaration—for its lack of plans for economic, political and social reform in Japan.[18] In addition, the Chifley government regarded agrarian reform as part of these radical changes. This chapter will explore Chifley's views on the Japanese peace settlement. It provides a further example of his deep involvement in his government's foreign policy and investigates whether he applied his internationalist principles to the security dimension of this policy.

Chifley's Attitude towards the Japanese Peace Settlement

In 1940 Ben Chifley was re-elected to parliament as the member for the regional seat of Macquarie in John Curtin's Labor Opposition. In June 1941 Chifley addressed the New South Wales regional group of the Institute of Public Administration.[19] His biographer David Day, described it as a 'landmark' speech, in which Chifley argued the need for a 'wider national outlook' and strengthened federal control over matters impacting on Australia as a nation.[20] In this wide-ranging speech, Chifley also declared that developments since World War I had shown the tragic consequences of the mistakes made in settling economic problems through a punitive peace settlement. Chifley argued that arrangements should have been made after World War I to ensure that countries who could not supply raw materials for 'their own civilian requirements' would be guaranteed a sufficient supply from those countries that had such resources. Instead, the victors focused on the importance of indemnities. According to Chifley, the 'desire of any nation shut off from necessary raw materials to expand its territory was not difficult to understand'. For Chifley, economic recovery was essential for post-war peace and prosperity. In his words, the 'outstanding need of reconstruction was to remove from the minds of the people the fear of want and insecurity'.[21] In his biography, David Day only briefly mentions this aspect of Chifley's speech, preferring to focus on how Chifley would achieve domestic peacetime reconstruction in Australia.[22] In this speech, Chifley was clearly advocating a non-punitive approach to peace settlement negotiations and the need for economic reconstruction to ensure a country's security and well-being, including former enemy countries.

Chifley maintained this non-punitive approach to peace settlement after World War II as well, although it would have been a radical position, not widely held in the years immediately after World War II, especially since so many Australians had fought and suffered in the Pacific War. At the time, most Australians favoured a policy of retribution against former wartime enemies, particularly the Japanese. As an American scholar, Roger Dingman, has written: 'By the time the Pacific War drew to a close, the passions it [the war] had stirred ran high. Like a rain-swollen river they might sweep away the political leader who did not protect himself with a life jacket of anti-Japanese rhetoric'.[23]

Chifley believed that unless Japan was assisted back to economic prosperity, there would be another war in a generation's time. He regretted, however, that feelings were so strong on this issue that, 'this is something I cannot discuss even with my colleagues'.[24] Chifley's non-punitive approach to former war-time foes was a position he had held for many years. There were earlier occasions when Chifley had spoken about the need to ensure the economic recovery of ex-enemy countries. In addition, during the inter-war years Chifley had argued many times for the 'scaling down' of war debts which were a burden upon the 'stricken nations of Europe ... unable to meet the commitments imposed upon them by previous agreements'.[25] He expressed similar opinions after World War II.

In 1946 Chifley undertook an official visit to attend the Commonwealth Prime Ministers' conference in London. At the conference, Chifley declared that the main objective of the Australian government in attending this meeting was to ensure the future defence of the Pacific. He noted the very precarious position Australia had been in during 1942–1943, adding that his government wanted to ensure this situation did not occur again and to prevent any possibility of future aggression from Japan. He was 'anxious, therefore, that properly coordinated arrangements should be made in advance for defence against aggression in the Pacific, so that the future security of Australia and New Zealand could be assured'.[26]

Chifley also restated his belief that economic recovery was vital to post-war peace and prosperity, which meant a policy of revenge would be counter-productive. In this instance, referring to Germany after World War II, he expressed concern at the way in which Allied policy was developing and declared that, 'he would find great difficulty in subscribing to some of the decisions reached at the Berlin [or Potsdam] Conference about Germany's economic future'. Chifley agreed that Germany's heavy industries should be controlled to prevent any potential threat to Europe, but he thought 'it would be a short-sighted policy to try to prevent the renascence of German militarism either by seeking to reduce Germany to economic serfdom' by removing its main industrial areas such as the Ruhr and the Rhineland or by separating Germany into a number of states as the French desired. According to Chifley, it was important that the German people accept 'full responsibility for the havoc they had caused in Europe', but a policy of retribution was not the way to reconstruct the European economy. If this path was chosen, it was inevitable that further conflicts would arise in the future.[27]

After the Prime Ministers' Conference, Chifley, together with 'Nugget' Coombs, then director-general of the Department of Post-War Reconstruction, travelled across the Atlantic to Washington, and from there to Tokyo, where they witnessed the destruction that had been inflicted upon Japan during the war. Coombs wrote that in Tokyo: 'American dominance was so absolute that they had been able to select areas which should be spared—the Imperial Palace, the streets of foreign embassies, and the large hotels which were to accommodate the generals and their staff when the occupation began. But the rest of the city, industrial and residential, was laid waste with a completeness that filled me with horror'. Further south, they saw the 'ultimate destructiveness' of Hiroshima. Together, Chifley and Coombs walked over—in Coombs's words—'soil fused to a kind of glass among the tattered fragments of a city once thronged with people'. This experience made an indelible impression on the two men.[28]

According to Coombs, Chifley's attitude towards the Japanese peace settlement process differed markedly from British Commonwealth representatives in Tokyo, who took a 'punitive' approach to negotiations and sought to 'dismantle what remained of Japanese industry and to strip Japan economically as well as militarily'. Chifley, however, was more concerned about the possibility of a 'recrudescence of militarism' if the Japanese economy did not recover. While acknowledging that it would not be easy politically, the prime minister maintained: 'Australia must help the Japanese find an economic place for themselves in the world'. To Coombs, who had been influenced by John Maynard Keynes's *Economic Consequences of the Peace*, a damning indictment of the Versailles settlement after World War I, this was sensible advice. He was impressed with Chifley's 'wisdom'.[29]

Coombs's story again demonstrates how important the 'economic dimension' in international relations was for Chifley: economic recovery was vital to ensure post-war peace and prosperity in the world. A policy of revenge against former enemies Japan and Germany would be counter-productive and result in further international instability—a return to the disastrous period after World War I when world trade collapsed, resulting in the economic devastation of the Great Depression. This was a sentiment that Chifley expressed many times. As he said in parliament, when speaking about the need for economic reconstruction of former enemy states such as Germany:

> I know the deep feelings of revenge and of sorrow that come to all of those who lost sons and husbands in the fight to quell the Nazis. It is therefore very difficult to advocate—although I have always advocated it myself—that the victorious nations should immediately commence the task of building up the economic strength of Germany so

that it can make its due contribution to the economic strength of the other nations of Europe.[30]

Attitudes Towards Japan

In arguing in his June 1941 speech that those countries who could not supply raw materials for 'their own civilian requirements' should be guaranteed a sufficient supply from those countries that did have these resources,[31] Chifley foreshadowed the sentiments of the Atlantic Charter, signed by US President Franklin Delano Roosevelt and British Prime Minister Winston Churchill and announced on 14 August 1941. The fourth clause of the charter guaranteed all states 'great and small, *victorious or vanquished*, of access on equal terms to trade and to the raw materials of the world which are needed for their economic prosperity'.[32] Chifley's observation that it was not difficult to understand the desire of a nation cut off from access to essential raw materials to expand its territory was a radical view, not held by most of the general Australian public. However, it was a position held by a number of intellectuals and advisers to the Australian government. Understanding the intellectual environment in which Chifley moved is important in tracing the influences on him as prime minister and treasurer. As his press secretary, Don Rodgers, stated, Chifley was 'always looking for brains and the products of good brains'.[33] What can a study of this milieu tell us about Chifley's attitude towards the Japanese peace settlement? Is there evidence of a shared intellectual perspective amongst politicians, bureaucrats and intellectuals on, first, the reasons Japan entered the war and, second, the need for a non-punitive approach to the Japanese peace settlement?

In May 1937, a group of influential Australians sent a manifesto to the Australian government led by Prime Minister Joseph Lyons, leader of the conservative United Australia Party, calling for an end to restrictive trade policies, and a commitment to meet the complaints from those who had suffered trade discrimination, such as Japan. The previous May in 1936, the Lyons government had introduced a disastrous trade diversion policy into parliament. Under this policy, the Australian government imposed discriminatory trade restrictions on goods from Japan and the United States in favour of goods from

Great Britain.³⁴ Signatories to this manifesto against restrictive trade policies included a number of academics from the University of Melbourne: Raymond Maxwell Crawford, professor of history; Lyndhurst Falkiner Giblin, Ritchie professor of economics; Douglas Copland, dean of the faculty of commerce; William Macmahon Ball, senior lecturer in political philosophy; Herbert Burton, senior lecturer in economic history and W Brian Reddaway, research fellow in economics.³⁵ Many of these academics would later be advisers to the Curtin and Chifley Labor governments. Economists denounced the trade diversion policy because it impeded the revival of world trade after the Great Depression, on which Australia, as an exporting nation, depended so much. The Lyons government abandoned the policy in 1937, but it had an adverse effect on the Australian economy.³⁶ The United States cancelled wool contracts as a punishment; Japan, which was Australia's best customer for wool, turned to other competitors,³⁷ and to the domestic synthetic fibre industry which expanded tremendously.³⁸

Other advisers to the Curtin and Chifley governments also advocated the easing of international economic tensions as the most viable way of achieving political security. Frederic Eggleston, politician, scholar and commentator, visited Japan in 1929, a visit that affected him 'profoundly'. He developed a great affection for Japan, although he regretted Japanese militarism.³⁹ According to Eggleston, the Japanese economic system was such that Japan was forced to be an aggressor because of the lack of markets for its products. What was needed, Eggleston believed, was to 'improve the economic and social position' of the agricultural and industrial populations, and to raise the standard of living in Japan by encouraging trade unions and other social movements.⁴⁰ Economist John Grenfell Crawford, was another member of a group of influential academics and intellectuals, who was a valued and important senior adviser to the Chifley government. In the 1930s he was one of a number of prominent intellectuals who contributed to debates on foreign policy embracing a 'progressive and forward looking internationalism, stressing the need to reorient Australia's external relations towards Asia'.⁴¹

In a prescient and quite radical paper, 'Australia as a Pacific Power', delivered at a summer school organised by the Australian

Institute of Political Science in 1938, Crawford considered Australia's relationship with Japan and the Pacific region.[42] At the time, Crawford was twenty-eight years old, and lectured in rural economics at the University of Sydney.[43] In this paper, Crawford emphasised that 'economic relations are fundamental in our political understandings and misunderstandings'.[44] He then went on to argue that Australia's 'political security and economic appeasement in the Pacific go together'. A term of disparagement now, 'appeasement' in the economic sense then meant the easing or alleviation of international economic grievances. Crawford stated that the only way to ensure security for Australia was to embark on the path of easing these grievances, which also needed to be linked to 'collective agreements in the interests of political security'.[45] In his article, Crawford described two different ways of approaching Australia's relations with other states: power politics or collective security.[46] Unfortunately, the inter-war years had seen a 'relapse to power politics', which was innately 'expensive and uncertain'.[47] The most important objective to ensure Australia's security in the future was 'to rebuild the collective system in the Pacific'.[48] Crawford predicted that Australia would develop closer trade ties in the region;[49] he also noted that the expansion of Australian trade in the Pacific was dependent on industrialisation in East Asia.[50]

As the director of research in the Department of Post-war Reconstruction in 1943 and as the founding director of the federal Bureau of Agricultural Economics in 1946, Crawford worked closely with Chifley.[51] He admired Chifley, whose vision of Australia's future was 'an inspiration'.[52] Chifley, together with this group of intellectuals, advisers and public servants, had a vision in which a rules-based international system would be established through which economic stability and collective security could be attained. All understood that, in Crawford's words, 'economic relations are fundamental in our political understandings and misunderstandings'.[53] With Chifley as prime minister, Australian foreign policy went a long way towards achieving these internationalist goals by working through the newly established international organisations of the United Nations.

A Harsh Peace?

Historians have often characterised Australia's policy towards the post-war Japanese peace settlement negotiations as a punitive one. American scholar Roger Dingman wrote that historians have tended to assign Australia the role of the 'villain' in the Japanese peace settlement, saying they desired a 'harsh peace'.[54] Australian historian Christopher Waters argues that the harsh treatment of Australian prisoners of war and Japanese war-time atrocities meant that many in Australia wanted 'retribution'. As a result, the government pushed for a 'punitive peace settlement':[55] its main aim in early post-war policy towards East Asia was to ensure that Australia would never be threatened by Japan again.[56] However, Waters notes that the government's policy was not totally 'negative', it also pushed for radical reform and the democratisation of the Japanese political system, which included education and land reform.[57]

Christine de Matos, historian of Australia's role in the Allied Occupation of Japan, also questions the 'simplistic notion that the Australian government's policies towards Japan during the occupation were solely "harsh" or vengeful', based exclusively on retribution.[58] In her investigation into Australian social justice and labour reform proposals for occupied Japan, de Matos examines the conflict between the Chifley government and its allies, the United States and Great Britain, over reform policy in Japan. The conflict was engendered within the context of the developing Cold War. De Matos argues that, while the Chifley government's democratisation aims can be regarded as 'paternalistic and a desire to impose the victor's ideology upon the vanquished', they were part of a general 'socio-politico-economic' restructuring of Japanese society that would benefit the people of Japan, who were seen as victims of the autocratic political system that had led their country to war. For de Matos, the important point here is that Australian policy towards the Japanese peace settlement was 'a more complex mosaic than heretofore appreciated, and a term such as "hard-line policy" is an inadequate and, at times, misleading label'.[59]

As a result of the historical focus on the 'harsh peace' objectives of the government, de Matos argues that Australian policy towards occupied Japan has not been fully understood. According to de Matos, it was American political scientist Richard N Rosecrance whose ground-breaking work on Australia's occupation of Japan first revealed the 'complexities in Australian policy that have since been oversimplified and personified'.[60] In his study of this period, Rosecrance argues against a simplistic reading of Australian policy as a reflection of the 'old isolationism and fear' of Japan.[61] Instead, Australia's approach to Japan was more complex and ambivalent than it seems.[62] Robin Gerster, in his social history of Australia and the occupation of Japan, agrees that the principal aim of Australian government policy towards Japan was to ensure Australia's security in the region by seeking to prevent Japan from ever being a military threat in the future. He adds, however, that there was also 'a constructive, even visionary' quality to the Chifley government's proposals for Japan.[63] Most importantly, it was Chifley who was one of the chief architects of this constructive Australian approach to the reconstruction of Japan. In developing such an approach, Chifley drew on his well-developed internationalist principles, which have been laid out in earlier chapters of this book.

The Chifley Government's Policy Towards Post-war Japan

Much of the 'constructive' aspect of the Chifley government's policy towards post-war Japan related to its proposals for land reform. As de Matos suggests, a great deal of the government's antagonistic discourse directed at Japan was designed for 'public consumption'.[64] Although the government sought to ensure that Japan would never threaten Australia again, its principal objective was to 'attack the social and economic discontent' that generated 'nationalist aggression' in Japan.[65] In view of this, how then did the 'economic dimension', so important to Chifley, influence his government's policies on the Japanese peace settlement negotiations? A cable sent by the Chifley government to the Dominions Office in London on 11 August 1945, is crucial to our understanding of this question.[66] Chifley announced in a speech to parliament that, just before the Japanese government accepted the Allies' terms of surrender on 14 August 1945, his government had sent a cable providing 'a general statement of our views on the treatment of Japan' to London. Chifley went on to say, 'Particularly we considered that the Emperor and the whole imperial and militarist system and the economic dictatorship of a few great concerns must be discredited, and a complete transformation of Japan's internal structure brought about'.[67]

In the cable sent on 11 August, the Chifley government provided a detailed statement of the 'overall framework of Australian policy' towards post-war Japan.[68] The government's main objective in the Pacific was to ensure that Japan would not be a threat to Australia in the future. Chifley wanted to achieve this by, first, participating in the Japanese peace settlement on a basis of equality with the major powers; and second, by bringing about 'radical' social, political and economic changes in Japan to ensure that Japanese militarism did not re-emerge as a threat to the security of the Pacific.[69] These radical changes would involve the removal of the emperor; the dismantling of the Zaibatsu, the industrial and financial monopolies at the heart of imperial Japan;[70] improving the economic and social circumstances of the agricultural population; encouraging the growth of trade unions in order to improve living standards;[71] the 'elimination of Japanese militarism'[72] and encouraging the development of 'democratic tendencies'.[73] Chifley's cable stated: 'The roots of Japanese militarism are embedded in the totalitarian political economic and social system built up over the past 70 years by Japan's ruling groups'.[74]

Agricultural policy was specifically mentioned in this cable, which includes a detailed and sophisticated analysis of how poverty in the agricultural sector in Japan ensured a supply of 'cheap industrial labour' and 'large supplies of military manpower' for the Japanese armed forces. The cable said: 'Economic policies, we feel, should be guided by the general aim of fostering a Japanese society capable of living in peace'. However, Japanese industry was characterised by the 'intense pressure for exports' due to the 'depressed conditions of the agricultural population and industrial workers, with consequent low consumption standards and limited domestic demand'. These conditions led to the desire for external markets, which was a significant element in Japan's territorial expansionism.

All these factors contributed to a 'distortion of the Japanese economy', with an 'over-emphasis on heavy industries as war potential'. Because of this, the Chifley government thought it was imperative that policies ensuring an improvement in the economic and social conditions of agricultural workers should be implemented. Encouragement and support for trade unions and other movements that would raise living standards in Japan were also essential in fostering the conditions necessary for the development of a peaceful Japan. There was also a need for greater participation by the Japanese themselves. The government's statement emphasised: 'The success of any controls will in our view depend on the extent to which Japanese participation is secured'.[75]

Chifley and Land Reform

In this overall framework of economic, social and political reform, outlined in the Chifley government's cable, we can see the 'constructive, even visionary' quality of the Chifley government's policy towards post-war Japan.[76] A significant part of this economic restructuring lay in land reform. As economic historian Ian W Mclean argues in his study of the reasons for Australia's prosperity over the past two centuries, an important factor in the development of a functioning democracy and its economic growth is the removal of entrenched property rights through land reform.[77] Chifley's rural background played a major role in the development of his ideas on the need for land reform, which he saw as one of the essential elements needed to establish a prosperous, peaceful and equitable society. His father had been a blacksmith employed by a manufacturer of agricultural machinery supplying farms in the central west of New South Wales.[78] His grandfather, Patrick, had been a farmer who had initially selected 40 acres (about 16 hectares) of land at Limekilns in April 1864 under the *New South Wales Land Act* (1861), which sought to redistribute to farmers the extensive pastoral leases held by the early squatters.[79] Other Irish-Australian families, like Chifley's grandfather, took the opportunity to become farmers in the region: 'all intensely proud of their status as landowners, as only men from a land-hungry agricultural country like Ireland could be'.[80] Crisp notes that during the period Chifley spent at his grandfather's farm at Limekiln: 'Labour had more or less appropriated the established cry of the landless rural workers and struggling small farmers', like Chifley's grandfather. There were heated discussions at the farm about banking reform, the nationalisation of land and the eradication of freehold tenure when friends and neighbours visited.[81] Chifley grew up in a 'politically-charged atmosphere', and, as a result, he showed a 'precocious' interest in politics during this period, expressing a desire to be a 'Member of Parliament' when he became an adult.[82]

Chifley's interest in land reform in an international context is very evident in his speeches in parliament. He had long argued that land reform was vital to ensure that 'landless farmers' and the poor attained justice. In September 1948 he said he was greatly concerned that in European countries such as Italy, 'unless the problem of the landless farmer and the unemployed can be solved', the poverty that existed there would provide 'a fertile bed in which communism can take root and flourish'. Chifley declared: 'I cannot help thinking that in Europe for hundreds of years past the seeds have been sown of which to-day we are reaping the harvest, namely, the growth of communism or rebellion of some kind against … the established order of things'.[83]

Chifley's concern about the need for western Europe to implement land reform continued when he was no longer in government and became leader of the Labor Opposition. In 1950 he argued that the only way that Europe could remain safe from communism was by providing for their people. However, in 'many European countries, such as Italy, Hungary and Poland, more than two-thirds of the land was held by wealthy absentee landholders'. In contrast, Chifley noted that in central Europe, many of the large estates had been 'broken up' by communist governments. The institution, however, that had the most sway in Europe, the Christian church, had done 'little if anything to ensure that justice was done to landless farmers and to the poor sections of the community'. This inaction had given rise to the spread of communism in Italy, France and elsewhere in central European countries.[84] Unless the people in certain parts of Europe were offered a better way of life, then communism would succeed. The reason that communism had spread in Italy, for example, was because:

> Thirty million peasants—70 per cent of the population—are working under Italy's inefficient land system. Some of them earn only 1s a day and lie at night in windowless stone huts with their cattle. That is happening while noble

families own vast tracts of Italy's best land, on which miserably paid, illiterate peasants slave from dawn to dusk. And so there is a wave of communism in the world today.[85]

Chifley's interest in this issue extended to Asia. In China, the new communist government was engaged in a redistribution of the great estates among the peasants.[86] He asked what had been offered to the people in Calcutta and Bombay by the Western democracies in 'days long gone', where tens of millions of people live in 'incredible misery and poverty'.[87] Chifley's interest in land reform spanned many years and many countries.

Land Reform in Japan

It was extremely difficult for the Australian government to exert any influence on Allied policy concerning the Japanese peace settlement negotiations. It was successful, however, in achieving agrarian reform. Eric E Ward, from the Department of External Affairs—later appointed First Secretary, Economic Relations Section of the DEA in 1948— acted as economic adviser to William Macmahon Ball, the Australian representative on the Allied Council for Japan. Ward provides a first hand account of the council's role in land reform in Japan.[88] According to Ward, Prime Minister Ben Chifley asked William Macmahon Ball to take up the position as the Australian representative for the Commonwealth on the Council in 1946. Chifley persisted in his choice of nominee, despite British hostility to the appointment because it was alleged that Ball had insufficient diplomatic experience. Ward noted that, in November 1945, Ball had led an official mission from Australia to Indonesia, where his assessment of rising nationalism in Asia differed markedly from that of the British stationed there.[89] Ball also said that it was Chifley who contacted him, because the prime minister thought he had done well in this mission to Indonesia.[90]

Writer Peter Ryan, a friend of Ball, who met Chifley for the first time a few months after his 1949 election defeat, commented that Chifley's 'tactful influence bore on an important appointment which greatly lifted international perceptions of Australia's new and independent status in foreign relations'. When Australia was invited to appoint the British Commonwealth's representative on the Council, Ryan noted that, 'Distinguished—even titled—names were at first canvassed with Chif, and later pressed upon him. To the chagrin of the British, Chifley insisted on Macmahon ('Mac') Ball, from the Political Science Department at Melbourne University'.[91] Ryan added that Chifley knew of his friendship with Ball, and, during this meeting sensed Ryan's desire to hear more. 'But all he would say, with a little grin, was, "I always thought that Mister Ball was an honest man; I liked the cut of his jib".'[92]

Despite the difficulties the Australian government experienced in influencing Allied policy on the Japanese peace settlement, historian Alan Rix has stated that the government's land reform proposals did make a difference. In his detailed study of the history of Australia's trade relations with Japan from 1945 to 1957, Rix argues that the most important contribution to policy by the ACJ were proposals for land reform put forward in June 1946 by Macmahon Ball and his economic adviser, Eric Ward.[93] These proposals were eventually accepted by the Supreme Commander, General MacArthur.

In his account of the development of the Council's proposals for land reform, Eric Ward wrote that the program implemented in October 1946—in which more than three million tenants were able to buy the land they farmed—was one of 'the most successful and enduring of the occupation reforms'.[94] Although querying if the reforms would lead to increased productivity, a contemporary historian, Norman D Harper, wrote at the time that Japan's Rural Land Reform Act of 1946 was intended to establish peasant ownership of land as a foundation for 'agrarian democracy'.[95] According to Japanese agriculturalist Dr Takekazu Ogura, the program generated 'profound changes in Japanese rural life'.[96] Macmahon Ball's biographer, Ai Kobayashi, wrote:

> Land reform was a significant part of Japan's economic democratisation and it had a lasting impact on Japan's social and economic structure, enabling Japan's stable development in the post-war era. It was the chief success of the ACJ [Allied Council for Japan], and one of the most important post-war reforms.[97]

Alan Rix argues that the land reform policy was not the outcome of official representation by the Australian government or the Commonwealth: instead, it was the result of Ball's own personal concern about the Japanese agricultural system.[98] Rix, however, ignores the statement by the Chifley government in which agricultural policy reform was specifically mentioned.[99] It seems that this cable sent on 11 August 1945, has not received the attention it deserves as a detailed exposition of the Chifley government's policy towards post-war Japan.

It is significant that during this period, when the land reform proposals were formulated, Chifley was kept closely informed of developments. John Crawford, who at the time was director of the federal Bureau of Agricultural Economics,[100] was advised of the progress of Ball's land reform proposals, which Chifley referred to him for comments.[101] This policy had also been influenced by economist Major James Plimsoll, who wrote a comprehensive report on the economic situation in Japan, after a three-week visit there in January 1946, as an Australian representative on the Far Eastern Commission. According to Rix, Plimsoll's report encouraged Australian government interest in the future benefits to be gained from trade with Japan.[102] In his report, Plimsoll argued that 'economic reform must be accompanied by basic social reform'.[103] He also wrote that land reform, 'covering ownership, rents, credit, and prices', was essential.[104] Plimsoll's background as an economist meant that he could see that those 'policies which advocated dismantling of the Japanese industry for reparations were nonsense'.[105] Rix agreed with Coombs's statement that 'Chifley ... was impressed' with the report: it had a 'significant influence on his attitude and on subsequent Australian policies'.[106] Chifley's astute view of Japan's future owed much to Plimsoll's 1946 report.[107]

While working on the land reform proposals, Macmahon Ball had written to the Supreme Commander for the Allied Powers, General Douglas MacArthur, in June 1946, advising that the Japanese government's rural reform plans were 'evasive and unsatisfactory and calculated to defeat the main purpose of rural reform'. The government's plan would make less than 20 per cent of land currently farmed by tenants available for purchase by them. Instead, Ball advised that all land in excess of two and a half acres should be available for purchase by tenants. As a result, up to 70 per cent of land worked by tenants would be available to them to buy and would thus provide the basis for meaningful land reform in Japan. Ball added that discussion with agricultural advisers to the supreme commander revealed grave doubts about the Japanese government's land reform program and 'substantial agreement' with Ball's proposals.[108] He then put forward certain principles that should be followed in any land reform program:

> I do not suggest that these proposals of ours do provide in themselves for the complete economic security of the Japanese farmer because that is a question that is bound with all sorts of economic and financial issues that do not properly come within the scope of this particular directive. What we have attempted, however, is to ensure that these land reforms would not merely mean the transfer of a nominal title from a landowner to a tenant but that the tenant the new owner would be assured of some kind of stability, some kind of security, in the conduct of his new plot of land.[109]

After careful consideration of Macmahon Ball's proposals at a special meeting held specifically for discussion on land reform, Ball wrote that the Japanese government's rural reform bill that would be introduced to the National Diet incorporated:

> in a most exact and detailed way the 10 points programme I submitted to the Allied Council. It represents almost complete reversal of the Japanese Government's Plan of 15th March and will, if passed, mark an economic and social revolution in the Rural life.[110]

According to Eric Ward, the land reform policy was one area in which MacArthur took the advice of the Allied Council for Japan. It was 'one of the success stories of the occupation'.[111] While MacArthur was hostile to the council, he was pragmatic enough to use it when it suited him.[112] In his report to the prime minister on his mission as the

Commonwealth representative on the Council, Ball noted MacArthur's warm reception of his land reform program and the fact that the Japanese land reform act included most of his plan's 'substance and much of its detail'.[113] As he wrote later, 'Land reform was the only question ... on which [MacArthur] consulted the Council'.[114] Ward also made the point that post-war Japan was 'ready for land reform. It was not a new idea introduced and imposed by the occupation'.[115] Chifley and his government had, therefore, made a significant contribution to this aspect of the reconstruction of the Japanese economy and society. It fitted neatly with Chifley's experience of the global economy over the previous decades and his general approach to international economic policy. The emergence of the Cold War, however, did much to hinder the efforts of internationalists such as Chifley.

Cold War Fears

In 1947 the Chifley government became increasingly concerned about US policy in Japan. Eric Ward attended all Allied Council for Japan meetings from April 1946 through to November 1947. He witnessed how the 'emerging cold war' meant that the council was 'frozen out of any useful role in the occupation, with the notable exception of land reform'.[116] In his account, Ward notes that British and Australian interests differed in the region—they did not always have the same objectives. Britain wanted to resume its 'political and economic position in the region', which meant 'business as usual', whereas Australia was concerned about security in the region, and the prevention of any 'resurgence of Japanese militarism'. Ward wrote that the Australian government was also aware of the 'need to live with the nationalist independence movements which had been released by the war'.[117]

According to Ward, MacArthur thought that the 'USSR had designs on Japan'. He observed that MacArthur's views were 'shared and probably urged on by the inner military circle' around him. He related a conversation in April 1946, with Brigadier General Bonner Fellers—a confidante of MacArthur—after Ward arrived in Tokyo:

> In an unguarded moment, given the well known differences between MacArthur and Roosevelt over geographic priorities, I expressed my regrets at the death of President

Roosevelt at such a critical time just before the Potsdam meeting and was met with a vehement denunciation of Roosevelt and all his works that nearly left me speechless. Roosevelt had led America into war and against the wrong enemy. The real enemy had now to be faced. This was more than a dispute about strategic priorities. With such preconceptions the Allied Council was not a place to seek advice but a place in which to wage the cold war.[118]

There were also alarming reports from DEA diplomat, Patrick Shaw, who replaced Macmahon Ball as the British Commonwealth representative on the Allied Council for Japan from 1947 to 1949. He was also head of the Australian Mission in Japan.[119] Shaw reported information about the United States' animosity towards the Soviet Union. According to Shaw, the US generals thought that all the dangers and unrest in today's world derived from the Soviet Union and that the 'only way to deal with Communists was to exterminate them and that the USA should do this by using atomic weapons against the USSR'. It was for this reason that the US bomber air force was being built up in Europe and the Far East. Shaw wrote that he was struck by how far advanced their planning was.[120] The general opinion of the US army officers he spoke to was that Japan would be useful in the future, both as a base and as an ally in the fight against the Soviet Union. He noted, however, there was some scepticism among the Japanese, who were somewhat doubtful of the advantage of being an 'anchored air-craft carrier in a new global war'.[121] It was also assumed that Australian forces would play a role in any future operations.[122] The United States Occupation forces thought war between the United States and the Soviet Union was not only imminent, but inevitable.

These reports were so disturbing that Chifley referred the correspondence to the minister for External Affairs, Evatt, commenting that the issue was so 'serious' he needed to learn if the sentiments expressed were a 'reflection of official US policy'. If correct, then consideration must be given to the immediate withdrawal of Australian forces from Japan. He added:

> I have watched with interest New York reports and the growing tension, not only in New York, but in Europe. At the moment, attention is focused away from the Japanese area, but this might finally be the critical area. Looking ahead, we must be careful not to be placed in a position in which we have no free choice, but are led by a series of circumstances into political disputes which have a relatively indirect bearing upon Australia and perhaps even the British Commonwealth of Nations.[123]

Chifley then asked Evatt to consult with political and military leaders in the United States and inform him of their general thinking on these issues. Chifley also requested that Evatt seek further intelligence in the United Kingdom.[124]

Shaw's opinions were confirmed in November 1947 by Australian economist Douglas Copland. In his report to John Burton, the secretary of the Department of External Affairs, after what was, as he acknowledged, a brief stay in Japan, Copland's most significant observation was that the 'early enthusiasm' of the Americans for 'political and economic reform in Japan' had changed to an increased concern with 'strategic problems in the North Pacific area'. This shift had occurred early in the Occupation, but it had become increasingly apparent. The Americans were mainly concerned about the possibility of war, and how to curtail the Soviet Union's influence and counter the spread of communism. The US saw its relationship with Japan exclusively in terms of gaining an ally and using Japan as a base to launch an attack against the Soviet Union. Copland commented that the Americans had a very different attitude towards what constitutes a democratic system to the Australians and the British. He wrote that the Americans were 'too prone to believe the adoption of a constitution is a guarantee of democracy'.[125]

Conclusion

From 1947, the Cold War impacted on efforts to reach a peace settlement in Japan, which was now regarded by the United States and Britain as a future 'bulwark against Soviet expansionism in Northeast Asia'. The Australian government, on the other hand, regarded this 'reverse course' as a huge mistake. Japan, rather than the Soviet Union, was the main danger to peace in East Asia and the Pacific.[126] But there was no longer any US desire for further reform in Japan. As a result, the United States

> progressively modified the economic and industrial controls that had been imposed, eased restrictions on the level of Japanese trade, halted the abolition of the *zaibatsu*, reduced its purge of militarists and right-wing supporters from politics, limited its reform of the labour laws and cracked down on left-wing political groups.[127]

It became evident by mid-1949 that the United States would defer a Japanese peace settlement, which for them had become an intrinsic part of the Cold War framework through which the United States and the United Kingdom viewed a changing world. For the United States, it was vital to prevent the spread of communism in Japan, which would become a strategic buffer against the Soviet Union in Asia. As relations between the United States and the Soviet Union deteriorated, further negotiations regarding the Japanese peace settlement came to a standstill and did not resume until 1950.[128]

For Australia, it was important that economic and democratic reforms eliminated Japanese militarism so that Japan would never re-emerge as a threat in the region. The Chifley government was firm in its belief that the Japanese peace settlement should not be held hostage to relations between the West and the Soviet Union, which meant that peace in Asia and the Pacific was dependent on a 'thawing of the Cold War' in Europe.[129] However, US policy-makers 'turned away from a program of reform in Japan to a policy of re-building Japan' as an 'ally of the west against the Soviet Union'.[130] In contrast, the Chifley government's perspective was driven by the need both to ensure Japan's economic recovery and to put in place effective democratic reforms. Significantly, Chifley and his government rejected the Cold War view of the world that determined US and British foreign policy on Japan.

Notes

1. de Matos, *Imposing Peace and Prosperity*, p. 11.
2. ibid., p. 2.
3. Waters, 'War, Decolonisation and Postwar Security', in Goldsworthy (ed.), *Facing North*, p. 113.
4. de Matos, *Imposing Peace and Prosperity*, pp. 2–3.
5. ibid., p. 3.
6. Waters, 'War, Decolonisation and Postwar Security', p. 115.
7. de Matos, *Imposing Peace and Prosperity*, p. 13.
8. ibid., p. 71.
9. Waters, 'War, Decolonisation and Postwar Security', p. 108.
10. ibid., p. 97.
11. Waters, *Empire Fractures*, p. 30.
12. Waters, 'War, Decolonisation and Postwar Security', p. 112.
13. ibid., pp. 112–113.
14. Waters, *Empire Fractures*, p. 33.
15. Capling, *Australia and the Global Trade System*, p. 20.
16. Waters, *Empire Fractures*, p. 30.
17. Cable 225, Australian Government to the Dominion Office, London, 11 August 1945, p. 1. NAA: A3317, 102/1945.
18. de Matos, *Imposing Peace and Prosperity*, p. 45.
19. JB Chifley, 'Reconstruction After The War', *Public Administration*, vol. III, no. 3, 1941, pp. 103–108.
20. Day, *Chifley*, pp. 360–362.
21. Chifley, 'Reconstruction After the War', p. 103.
22. Day, *Chifley*, pp. 360–362.
23. Roger Dingman, 'The View from Down Under: Australia and Japan, 1945–1952', in Thomas W Burkman (ed.), *The Occupation of Japan: The International Context*, MacArthur Memorial Foundation, Norfolk, VA, 1984, p. 102.
24. Waterson, 'Chifley', p. 417.
25. 'World Problems', *National Advocate* (Bathurst, NSW), 19 October 1932.
26. Minutes of Meetings of Dominion Prime Ministers, London 1946, 1st Meeting, 23 April 1946, p. 3, NAA: A5954, 258/2.
27. Minutes of Meetings of Dominion Prime Ministers, London 1946, 9th Meeting, 1 May 1946, p. 3, in ibid.
28. Coombs, *Trial Balance*, p. 88.
29. ibid., p. 89.
30. *CPD*, HoR, 2 September 1948, p. 63.
31. Chifley, 'Reconstruction After the War', p. 103.
32. Julius Stone, 'Peace Planning and the Atlantic Charter', *Australian Quarterly*, vol. 14, no. 2, 1942, p. 15.
33. Donald Kilgour Rodgers interviewed by Mel Pratt, 1971, NLA: ORAL TRC 121/14, p. 23.
34. Shannon L Smith, 'Towards Diplomatic Representation', in Goldsworthy (ed.), *Facing North*, pp. 81–85.
35. 'Advice From University: For Mr Lyons', *Age*, 17 April 1937.

36 Smith, 'Towards Diplomatic Representation', p. 84.
37 Capling, Considine and Crozier, *Australian Politics in the Global Era*, p. 28.
38 Smith, 'Towards Diplomatic Representation', p. 84.
39 Cotton, *Australian School*, p. 48.
40 Memorandum, Australian Legation, Washington to Balfour, Charge d'Affaires, British Embassy, Washington, 'Future of Japan—Views of the Government of the Commonwealth of Australia', 13 August 1945, pp. 2–3, NAA: A3300, 290.
41 Pitty and Leach, 'Australian Nationalism and Internationalism', in Boreham, Stokes and Hall (eds), *The Politics of Australian Society*, 2nd edn, p. 99.
42 Crawford, 'Australia as a Pacific Power', in Duncan (ed.), *Australia's Foreign Policy*, pp. 69–121.
43 Peter Drysdale, 'The Relationship with Japan: Despite the Vicissitudes', in Evans and Miller (eds), *Policy and Practice*, p. 67.
44 Crawford, 'Australia as a Pacific Power', p. 71.
45 ibid., p. 72.
46 ibid., p. 90.
47 ibid., pp. 111–112.
48 ibid., p. 101.
49 ibid., p. 77.
50 ibid., p. 111.
51 Williams, 'Contributions to Agricultural Economics', in Evans and Miller (eds), *Policy and Practice*, pp. 24–25.
52 JDB Miller, 'The Man', in ibid., p. 197.
53 Crawford, 'Australia as a Pacific Power', p. 71.
54 Dingman, 'The View from Down Under: Australia and Japan, 1945–1952', p. 100.
55 Waters, 'War, Decolonisation and Postwar Security', p. 97.
56 ibid., p. 112.
57 ibid., pp. 97–98.
58 de Matos, *Imposing Peace and Prosperity*, p. 4.
59 Christine de Matos, 'Diplomacy Interrupted?: Macmahon Ball, Evatt and Labor's Policies in Occupied Japan', *Australian Journal of Politics and History*, vol. 52, no. 2, 2006, p. 193.
60 ibid., p. 194.
61 RN Rosecrance, *Australian Diplomacy and Japan, 1945–1951*, Melbourne University Press, Parkville, Victoria, 1962, p. 7.
62 ibid., pp. 8–9.
63 Robin Gerster, *Travels in Atomic Sunshine; Australia and the Occupation of Japan*, Scribe, Carlton North, Victoria, 2008, p. 42.
64 Christine de Matos, 'Encouraging "Democracy" in a Cold War Climate: The Dual-Platform Approach of Evatt and Labor Toward the Allied Occupation of Japan 1945–1949', *Pacific Economic Papers*, no. 313, 2001, p. 2.
65 Gerster, *Travels in Atomic Sunshine*, p. 43.

66 Cable 225, Australian Government to Dominions Office, London, 11 August, 1945, NAA: A3317, 102/1945.
67 *DDA*, No. 106, Speech in Parliament, 29 August 1945, p. 12, NAA: B5459, 106.
68 Waters, 'War, Decolonisation and Postwar Security', p. 113.
69 Cable 225, Australian Government to Dominions Office, London, 11 August, 1945, p. 1, NAA: A3317, 102/1945.
70 ibid., pp. 2–3.
71 ibid., p. 2.
72 ibid., p. 1.
73 ibid., p. 3.
74 ibid., p. 1
75 ibid., p. 2.
76 Gerster, *Travels in Atomic Sunshine*, p. 42.
77 McLean, *Why Australia Prospered*, pp. 96–97.
78 Day, *Chifley*, p. 14.
79 ibid., pp. 10–11.
80 Crisp, *Ben Chifley*, p. 3.
81 ibid., p. 4.
82 ibid., p. 5.
83 *CPD*, HoR, 2 September 1948, p. 66.
84 *CPD*, HoR, 23 March 1950, p. 1172.
85 *CPD*, HoR, 7 March 1951, p. 86.
86 *CPD*, HoR, 23 March 1950, p. 1172.
87 *CPD*, HoR, 7 March 1951, p. 86.
88 EE Ward, *Land Reform in Japan 1946–1950, the Allied Role*, Nobunkyo, Tokyo, 1990, p. I.
89 ibid., p. 10.
90 Ai Kobayashi, *W Macmahon Ball: Politics For The People*, Australian Scholarly Publishing, North Melbourne, Vic., 2013, p. 79.
91 Ryan, *Brief Lives*, pp. 87 88.
92 ibid., p. 88.
93 Alan Rix, *Coming to Terms: The Politics of Australia's Trade with Japan 1945–57*, Allen & Unwin, Sydney, 1986, p. 39.
94 Ward, *Land Reform in Japan 1946–1950*, p. 1.
95 ND Harper, 'Australian Policy Towards Japan', *Australian Outlook*, vol. 1, no. 4, 1947, p. 19.
96 Ward, *Land Reform in Japan*, p. I
97 Kobayashi, *W. Macmahon Ball*, p. 87.
98 Alan Rix, 'W Macmahon Ball and the Allied Council for Japan: The Limits of an Australian Diplomacy under Evatt', *Australian Outlook*, vol. 42, no. 1, 1988, p. 24.
99 Cablegram 225, Australian Government to Dominions Office, 11 August, NAA: A3317, 102/1945.
100 Evans and Miller (eds), *Policy and Practice*, p. 204.
101 See note referring Memorandum to Director, Bureau of Agricultural Economics, Department of Commerce & Agriculture, 'Agricultural

Reform Policy in Japan, 25 September 1946, NAA: A1067, ER46/13/27.
102 Rix, *Coming to Terms*, p. 41.
103 'Report on Visit to Japan with the Far Eastern Advisory Commission', January 1946, by Major J. Plimsoll, forwarded by Dunk, 12 April 1946, NAA: A606, R40/1/22, para 12, p. 5.
104 ibid., para 19, p. 9.
105 Rix, *Coming to Terms*, p. 42.
106 Coombs, *Trial Balance*, p. 89.
107 Rix, *Coming to Terms*, p. 218.
108 Cablegram, Macmahon Ball, British Commonwealth Member Allied Council for Japan to Minister and Acting Minister External Affairs and DEA, 8 June, 1946, NAA: A1067, ER46/13/27.
109 Cablegram, Ball, British Commonwealth Member, Allied Council, Tokyo, ACJ17, 'Report of meeting on 12 June 1946', 14th June 1946, p. 1, in ibid.
110 Cablegram, Ball, British Commonwealth Member, Allied Council for Japan, to the Minister No. 9, A/G Minister and Dept External Affairs, 8th July 1946, in ibid.
111 Ward, *Land Reform in Japan 1946–1950*, p. 12.
112 ibid., p. 1.
113 Macmahon Ball, 'Report to the Prime Minister on a Mission to Japan', 30 August 1947, p. 3, NAA: M1455, 204.
114 W Macmahon Ball, *Japan: Enemy or Ally?*, Cassell, Melbourne, 1948, p. 30.
115 Ward, *Land Reform in Japan 1946–1950*, p. 111.
116 ibid., p. i.
117 ibid., p. 10.
118 ibid., p. 11.
119 de Matos, *Imposing Peace and Prosperity*, p. 176.
120 Top Secret, Ministerial Dispatch 3/47, Patrick Shaw, Head of Australian Mission in Japan to JB Chifley, Acting Minister for External Affairs, 30 September 1947, p. 1, NAA: A1068, DL47/5/8C.
121 ibid., p. 2.
122 ibid., p. 3.
123 Letter, Chifley to Evatt, 24 October 1947, NAA: A1068, DL47/5/8C.
124 ibid.
125 DB Copland, 'Notes on the Situation in Japan', 19th November 1947, DB Copland (in Manila) to Dr John W Burton, Secretary DEA, 24 November 1947, pp. 1–2, NAA: A1838, 476/1/1/3 Part 2.
126 Waters, 'War, Decolonisation and Postwar Security', p. 115.
127 ibid., p. 116.
128 ibid., p. 117.
129 Lee, *Search for Security*, p. 102.
130 Waters, *Empire Fractures*, p. 96.

Chapter Eight
Chifley and the Cold War

The United States entered the post-war period as the most powerful nation in the world. It emerged from World War II 'richer and stronger than it had ever been before'. The strength of its economy, and its technological innovation and expertise ensured an 'American preponderance' of power, both economically and in terms of military power.[1] The United States had almost doubled its gross national product during the war,[2] and it was now three times the size of the Soviet Union and over five times that of Great Britain.[3] 'By 1945, it accounted for around half of the world's manufacturing capacity, most of its food surpluses, and almost all of its financial reserves'. In contrast, Britain was on its knees after six years of warfare, having lost one-quarter of its national wealth and facing a restive empire.[4] Similarly, the Soviet Union emerged from the war 'an exhausted, devastated nation'.[5] At least 25 million people from the Soviet Union had died in the hellfire that was World War II; thirty per cent of Soviet pre-war capital stock was lost; 6 million buildings had been destroyed; and 25 million people had been left homeless.[6]

Although allies in fighting World War II, the 'tenuous wartime "Grand Alliance"' between the United States, Great Britain and the Soviet Union collapsed in the post-war period.[7] A number of events contributed to the emergence of the Cold War, which saw a polarisation of the world into two power blocs: the United States and its

Western allies, and the Soviet Union and the eastern European states under its control. The USSR's increasing influence in Europe led to Winston Churchill's 'iron curtain' speech, which he delivered on 5 March 1946 at Westminster College, in the Missouri town of Fulton. In this speech, Churchill announced that an 'iron curtain' had fallen across Europe.[8] According to Churchill, communist fifth columns, directed by Moscow, had been established in many countries throughout the world. The previous month, George F Kennan, the acting head of the US embassy in Moscow, sent his 'Long Telegram', in which he argued that the Soviet Union would retreat when faced with 'strong resistance'. According to Kennan, war with the Soviet Union could only be avoided by strong, vigorous opposition by the West. In this statement, Kennan articulated what is now known as 'the strategy of containment'.[9]

In an effort to counteract Soviet influence, Democrat president Harry Truman announced a 'major shift' in US foreign policy in March 1947. Truman had succeeded Franklin Delano Roosevelt, who died on 12 April 1945 after four terms in office during which Roosevelt steered the United States through the Great Depression and most of World War II. The Truman doctrine stated that the United States would 'support free people who are resisting attempted subjugation by armed minorities or by outside pressures'.[10] The inference in this statement was that democracies would be supported by the United States in their fight against communism. It was assumed by the West that 'Soviet imperialism' was behind all communist movements in Europe. In June 1947, George C Marshall, the US secretary of state from 1947 to 1949, proposed a massive European aid program, known as the Marshall Plan. Eastern European countries, however, were banned from participating by the leader of the Soviet Union, Joseph Stalin. In September 1947 the Soviet Union reacted by establishing the Cominform (Communist Information Bureau), an official forum of the international communist movement, in what seemed to be a revival of the 'pre-war coordination of communist parties under the Comintern' which advocated world communism.[11]

In December 1947, the acrimonius breakdown of the Council of Foreign Ministers over the failure to reach agreement on the terms of the German peace settlement, meant the end of any further great power cooperation in the post-war period.[12] It also meant that the

British Labour government's foreign secretary, Ernest Bevin, was free to advance his anti-Soviet policy.[13] The British government saw the Soviet Union's goal as one of 'world domination', in which the 'norms of international relations' did not hold.[14] In such a situation, Bevin believed the United Nations was quite ineffectual in preventing Soviet expansionism.[15] Bevin was intent on consolidating western Europe and obtaining the support of the Commonwealth: his ultimate aim was to achieve a confrontation with the Soviet Union, in which the expectation was that the Soviets would retreat. This policy required the support of the United States. Bevin's hand was strengthened after a communist coup in Czechoslovakia in late February 1948, which rallied official support for Bevin's policy in Britain, the United States and western Europe.[16] The Berlin blockade was also a contributing factor.

Post-war Germany was divided into four occupied zones: the British in the north; the Americans in the south; the Soviets in the east and the French in the west.[17] Berlin, located within the Soviet zone, was also occupied by Britain, the United States, France and the Soviet Union.[18] On 24 June 1948, the Soviet Union imposed a total blockade on those areas of Berlin under Western control—blocking rail, road, and river access.[19] The blockade was imposed to prevent the West from establishing a German state aligned to the West and because the Soviet Union needed to consolidate its own authority over eastern Germany. It was meant to compel the West to withdraw from Berlin without inciting war.[20] In response, an airlift was carried out by Britain, the United States and the Commonwealth, delivering food and supplies to the people of West Berlin.[21] It took until 12 May 1949, for the blockade to be lifted.[22] The blockade provided a further incentive for negotiations on the North Atlantic Treaty (NATO) between the United States, Canada and ten European states, excluding Germany. The treaty was signed on 4 April 1949 and officially endorsed in July.[23] It committed the United States to a long-term military commitment to defend western Europe.[24]

With the post-war balance of power so emphatically in favour of the United States, why was the US so preoccupied with future threats from the Soviet Union? It seems that US perceptions of a Soviet threat were based, not on Soviet might, but rather on concerns that communist 'exploitation of postwar economic dislocation and social and political unrest' would threaten US economic and strategic interests in Europe and Asia.[25] By contrast, the Cold War division of Europe into 'two armed camps', in which the Soviet Union, a member of the United Nations, was depicted as a belligerent force in Europe, was regarded by Chifley and the minister for External Affairs, Evatt, as 'undermining the system of global collective security' that had been established through the United Nations Organisation.[26] This meant a return to a crude form of power politics that portrayed the world as one of inevitable conflict in which a state's success in pursuing its interests depended upon the power it could utilise.[27]

This chapter provides a detailed analysis of the ideas and assumptions underlying Chifley's speeches in order to reveal his thinking about the Cold War and to explain his government's subsequent policies and actions in foreign affairs. How did Chifley's internationalism shape his views on the emerging Cold War? How did his concern for economic and social security influence his attitude toward the Cold War debate? The chapter focuses on Chifley's response to the Attlee government's request for support for a Western Union alliance against a perceived threat from the Soviet Union. This was the British foreign secretary, Ernest Bevin's 'anti-Soviet strategy' for western Europe, a consolidation of western countries in opposition to Moscow.[28] The Australian government viewed the Western Union policy as one of dividing Europe, a return to power politics and a rejection of the new 'era of international relations when all countries would adhere to the principles of the United Nations Charter'. It was a strategy that prioritised Europe and neglected the Pacific.[29] Chifley's world-view meant that he refused to accept the British and US Cold War 'framework for understanding change'[30] and sought to escape the constraints that divided the world into two polarised camps. Chifley rejected the 'central proposition of the Cold War'—that war with the Soviet Union was inevitable.[31] All these strands are evident in a speech that Chifley delivered to the federal executive of the Australian Labor Party, the morning of Wednesday, 11 May 1949.

Chifley's Attitude Towards the Cold War

Chifley's speech sums up much of what was at the heart of his position on the Cold War—it is a fundamental statement of his views. Various issues of great concern to Chifley were touched on, including the possibility of a third world war; the decolonisation of Asia; the state of the world's economy; the dire economic conditions that Britain was experiencing; the possiblity of an economic recession in the United States and the security situation in Europe. Chifley believed that the Soviet Union was incapable of waging war against the United States. He reminded his audience that twelve months ago he had said that he did not think that 'war was inevitable'. In 1949 he felt that the likelihood of war had, in fact, 'receded'. In a strongly worded statement, Chifley said: 'Russia does not want war with the US now. Russia is 30 years behind the US in industrial capacity and it's of no use any country talking about war without that capacity'.[32]

Chifley understood that the Soviet Union was operating from a position of economic and military weakness when compared to the might of the United States, with its technological and military innovation. In 1946, Chifley and his advisers, including 'Nugget' Coombs, had attended the Commonwealth Prime Ministers' Conference in London, where the 'vision of the American cornucopia overflowing with productive technology derived from the spin-off from military invention' had dominated these talks.[33] Chifley and Coombs then travelled on to Washington; they came away from their visit overwhelmed by the United States' technological advances. In February 1948, Chifley noted that 'American production to-day is enormous; it amounts … to 55 per cent. of the total secondary production of the world'.[34] Some months later, he again declared that the 'United States is the greatest nation today—the greatest nation the world has known and will remain so for some time to come'.[35] Although Chifley did not believe that the Soviet Union wanted war, he thought that in order to gain 'territorial or economic' advantage or to extend its ideological reach, it would 'push its policy as far as it possibly can without producing war'.[36] However, if the Soviet Union did advance through Europe, it would eventually have to confront the 'enormous resources, man-power and industrial potential of the United States of America':[37] a war it could neither afford, nor win. Furthermore, the devastation caused by a future war would be up to fifty to one hundred times as great as the last war because of technological advances and the new forms of warfare, a prospect that should 'appal' all humanity.[38]

In Chifley's May 1949 speech to the federal executive of the Australian Labor Party, we can see his rejection of vague abstractions such as 'liberty' and 'freedom'. Chifley noted that Nehru had 'very great influence' in Asia. He agreed with Nehru that communism could not be defeated with military might. The 'only way to win the support of the East for the democracies is to improve the economic welfare of the Asian peoples'. What was needed was to demonstrate in the material world that better living conditions could be delivered. Improvement in living standards in Asia would show that 'democracy, liberty and freedom doesn't just mean freedom to starve'.[39] As historian Sean Scalmer notes in his study of Labor discourse, Chifley spurned 'abstract principles': instead, he argued that he was 'concerned with the lives of ordinary people'.[40] He thought talking in abstractions such as 'liberty' and 'freedom' was 'sheer, utter hypocrisy'. He had witnessed the 'freedom to starve' in the depression, when thousands of workers had lined up outside a factory in his electorate to secure the one job that was on offer. He had also seen, at the start of the war, the same workers expected to protect the very people who had 'lived in luxury while they starved' during the depression.[41] Instead of talking in abstract terms, Chifley believed it was necessary to tackle the 'real needs' of people.[42]

While his opponents would talk up the dangers of communism, Chifley told the executive that, in Australia, the 'only bulwark between the people and economic chaos, or Communism … is the Labor Party'. The Labor government was concerned about 'the economic welfare of the whole community'. He concluded with a rallying call for the forthcoming federal election by saying: 'Ours is a great party. We have solidarity. The party's spirit is high. I don't think the electors will overlook these things'.[43] This speech is highly significant because of the debate over whether Chifley, after visiting London in June 1948, moderated his opposition towards British foreign policy, so that his position aligned more with the Attlee government's attempt to establish a Western Union of European countries to counter what the British saw as the threat from the Soviet Union.

The Western Union Proposal

Because of the rift in relations between the Western allies and the Soviet Union in December 1947, British foreign secretary Ernest

Bevin accepted the US suggestion that western Europe should form a political and economic alliance in return for Marshall aid from the United States. The United Kingdom would initiate a 'defensive alliance' to challenge the Soviet Union.[44] Prime Minister Attlee then wrote to the dominions seeking their support for Britain's Western Union policy.

On 14 January 1948 Chifley received a cable from Attlee that provided information about the British government's proposal. Attlee wrote that Britain was determined to provide a 'moral lead' to western European countries and to take a more active stance against communism. Attlee saw the struggle against communism as a moral crusade—an apocalyptic struggle—in which the 'ethical and spiritual forces' of the West were organised to defend Western civilisation from Soviet encroachment. The Soviet government now controlled the area from the Baltic through to the Black Sea and threatened western European countries such as France, Germany, Greece, Trieste and Italy. Improving economic conditions in these countries would not be enough, even if the Marshall Plan was successful. Attlee declared that 'economic progress alone will not suffice' and western Europe was 'seeking some assurance of salvation'. Britain, therefore, proposed to set up a 'Western Democratic system' made up of 'France, the Low Countries and Scandinavia, Portugal, Italy and Greece'. Spain and Germany would join later. The British government expected fierce opposition from the Soviet government to the formation of this alliance, but it was the only way to mobilise the 'moral and material force' needed to encourage confidence in western Europe and to prevent the Soviet Union's western advance. Strong 'political and moral leadership' was required from Britain in order to offset the attraction of communism. To do this, Britain needed the support of the countries of the British Commonwealth and the United States. Attlee welcomed any comments on this 'Western System'.[45]

Chifley's Response to the Western Union Proposal

After referring Attlee's message to Evatt for his comments and making corrections to the reply drafted by John Burton, secretary of the Department of External Affairs, Chifley responded to Attlee in a cable on 22 January 1948. His response summed up the Labor government's philosophy on foreign policy. In fact, it was central to Chifley's internationalist ideas. In his reply, Chifley stated that he fully understood the difficulties that the United Kingdom was experiencing with the Soviet Union, adding that Australia was also concerned about the 'world situation'. He stressed, however, that Australia would not support policies put forward without 'the fullest prior consultation and agreement by us at every stage of consideration of that policy'. The Australian government had not been consulted and neither had it been informed of recent policy decisions made by the United Kingdom and the United States—an ongoing irritant in the relationship between Australia and its former allies in post-war negotiations. Chifley reiterated the Australian people's opposition to all extremist ideologies—communist and fascist. He questioned the wisdom of forming a Western alliance directed against the Soviet Union, especially one that would include such undemocratic states as Greece and Spain which since 1939 had been ruled by the fascist military dictator General Franco.[46] He also emphasised the importance of providing 'stability and the necessities of life' for those living in western Europe. According to Chifley, 'spiritual forces' were not only sapped by 'Communist infiltration' but equally by poverty.[47] In addition, Chifley argued that Attlee was being overly optimistic in his reliance on the United States; he feared that the United Kingdom would be forced to carry out policies that the United States was unable 'for constitutional reasons' to implement itself.[48]

Chifley then went on to explain his government's foreign policy. It favoured a 'more positive' approach, based on 'justice' rather than 'strategy'. For instance, it was essential to recognise the 'undemocratic' nature of the Greek government.[49] The Chifley and the Attlee governments had very different views on the conflict occurring in Greece which received extensive coverage in the Australian media.[50] During World War II the Greek Communist Party had led the struggle against the Germans. After the liberation of Greece in October 1944, the British installed an anti-Communist right-wing government in Athens. The military arm of the Communist Party (ELAS), the National People's Liberation Army, was commanded by the prime minister to lay down their arms and disband. Conflict then broke out between the anti-Communist troops supported by the British, and ELAS, in which the communist forces soon capitulated. Elections—boycotted by the Communist Party—were held in March 1946, which resulted in a win by the Populist People's Party, a 'conservative' royalist group.[51] Civil war then ensued between guerrilla groups which included communists, and the right-wing government backed by Britain.[52]

The Attlee government argued that the existing Greek government was as democratic as the current conditions allowed. It was alleged by Britain that the Soviet Union was using Greece's northern neighbours, Albania, Yugoslavia and Bulgaria to subvert the Greek government. The Australian government, however, perceived the crisis as a civil war. The 'undemocratic and fascist nature' of the Greek government, together with the 'repressive and reactionary' policies it carried out, were key elements leading to the conflict.[53] In addition to the government's 'excessive internal repression', the appalling economic and social conditions exacerbated the situation.[54] Chifley noted that he and Evatt had indicated, when in London: 'we prefer not to allow considerations of strategy to influence our considerations of disputes which can only be settled permanently on a basis of justice'. Chifley then elaborated: 'we consider foreign policy, if it is a policy based on strategy and not permanent settlement of disputes, tends to become a policy of despair bringing about just those situations it should be designed to avoid'.[55] Unfortunately, the mutual suspicion that existed pre-war between the Western powers and the Soviet Union had not been alleviated by their cooperation during the war and could well lead to further conflict. Setting up a Western alliance directed against the Soviets would only confirm their fears and justify their post-war policies.[56]

For these reasons, Chifley went on to say, the Australian government could not support Attlee's proposals. Instead, the government would take a very different and positive approach to international emergencies by supporting the United Nations and advocating 'principles of justice rather than policies of strategy and expedience'. This approach would acknowledge the 'undemocratic nature' of the Greek regime and push for reform and early elections there. Chifley also rejected the use of power politics, arguing that 'secret alliances' should be avoided. The Australian government would not countenance support for those fascist states that survived the war. Furthermore, policies in which economic aid and power was used to 'determine forms of government' should be ended.[57] Instead, 'when justice demanded … the strongest action should be taken through the United Nations against the Soviet or any other power in order to uphold the United Nations Charter'. Chifley cited the Australian government's Indonesian policy as a successful demonstration of 'the value of standing by principle despite seemingly strategic or other doubtful interests'.[58]

Chifley then mentioned the Australian government's policy of refusing to export the 'munitions of war'. If the United States and the Soviet Union were asked to pursue such a policy, their real intentions would be revealed by their response. If the munitions trade could be halted, then the threat to peace posed by conflicts in Greece, the Middle East and China would no longer exist. He noted that the United States benefited from this situation and therefore had not discouraged the arms trade. However, the struggle in Europe was increasingly one of ideology and the Western democracies were losing 'moral support' in this struggle, because of their support for the export of weapons, especially to small European nations. Chifley then reaffirmed Australia's commitment to the Pacific region, emphasising that, if a European war broke out, Australia might well need to commit solely to the defence of its own region. He noted the instability of governments in the Southeast Asian and Pacific regions; these governments could adopt hostile policies towards Australia if persuaded by powers fighting in a European war.[59]

Finally, Chifley believed that Australia could play a role as 'mediator in the broader dispute which already exists between western powers and the Soviet'.[60] For this reason, the Australian government did not wish their position to be compromised by 'association direct or indirect with any anti-Soviet alliance'. Otherwise, future opportunities to safeguard peace might be endangered. Because of this, if any statement was released by the British government along the lines of Attlee's message of 14 January, the Australian government might find it necessary to indicate it had not been consulted in the development of the Western Union policy.[61]

Historian Neville Meaney argues that Chifley's rejection of Attlee's request for support for the British government's Western

Union policy was a resentful expression of 'panic-stricken fear'—an expression of vulnerability revealing a concern about Australia's 'national security' if war was to break out in Europe. Meaney adds that, although it was 'poorly expressed, poorly composed, and poorly argued', it was nevertheless 'one of the most remarkable documents in the history of Australian foreign policy'.[62] Chifley's cable was, indeed, a most significant document. As historian Christopher Waters notes, this was the 'first time in peace' that the Australian government had 'rejected not only the major foreign policy of the United Kingdom, but questioned the very assumptions upon which it was based'.[63] It was a very clear expression of opposition to the turn that British foreign policy was taking, but it was certainly not an expression of 'panic-stricken fear'.

In an earlier study of Australia and the great powers in the context of the Cold War, Meaney noted that, in refuting the key premise of the Cold War—that war with the Soviet Union was inevitable—the Chifley government's 'perception of Soviet policy' was 'subsequently justified by historical scholarship'. But he goes on to say it was not because of 'a superior knowledge of Russian motivation, a more profound study of Russian behaviour or a more sophisticated assessment of the meaning of great power rivalry. Rather it was, like Australia's liberal internationalist view of the great powers, a by-product of its search for security in the Pacific'. According to Meaney, the Australian government's 'unhappy experience' of 'seeking British and American cooperation in the Pacific' led to its opposition to the Cold War view of the post-war world, making it apprehensive that Britain and the United States would become fixated on Europe to the detriment of the Pacific region. Australia, like the United States and Britain, required a Soviet Union that would 'serve its ends'—this meant 'a non-threatening Russia'. Meaney argues that the Chifley government clung to the hope that the United Nations would function as an international mediator and arbiter, and that the disputes between the great powers would be solved. The government had therefore 'constructed its Soviet Union accordingly'.[64]

Meaney is mistaken here. While the Chifley government was concerned that policies such as the Western Union were Europe-centred—at the expense of the Pacific—Chifley's view that the Soviet Union was a much weaker power when compared with the military might of the United States, and consequently no threat to the United States, must be given credence. Chifley's was a considered opinion. As he said later, 'cold logic' should be used when considering matters of importance in foreign policy.[65] As prime minister, he received an enormous amount of information from his departments and from overseas, which he 'absorbed and pondered upon and used'.[66] He understood that the Soviet Union was weak—both economically and in a military sense—when compared with the might of the United States, an analysis formed by a leader widely known and credited for his astuteness and economic expertise. Chifley's views on US military and industrial might were also based on empirical evidence. During his visit to Washington in 1946, Chifley had been greatly impressed by the technological advances made in the United States. Chifley's main concern, however, was that if the Soviet Union was targeted as the enemy of the West, constructive dialogue and negotiations through the United Nations would be impossible. Chifley's concept of the United Nations as having a function 'analogous to an arbitration Court in relation to international situations and disputes' would no longer be achievable.[67] The United Nations would be side-lined.

Attlee's Response

The British government devoted a considerable amount of time and attention to drafting a reply to Chifley. On 5 February 1948, Edward J Williams, the British high commissioner in Canberra, met Chifley personally to deliver Attlee's response directly to him.[68] Williams told him that the British government was 'rather upset' about his reply to Attlee's Western Union proposal. According to Williams, the discussion that followed was 'somewhat discursive and inconsecutive'. Chifley reiterated his opinion that Greece was not a democratic country and spoke of the surprise he felt during meetings with the British chiefs of staff in London some two years previously, when he realised that even though the war had just ended, 'plans were in hand which assumed Russia was [the] next enemy when she had just proved to be a good ally'. Chifley noted that many Americans visiting Australia had said that, 'United States opinion was definite about war in [the] short time'. He did note shrewdly that a 'feeling of fear would help in getting [the] Marshall Plan accepted by Congress and keeping [the] United States in Europe and meeting her commitments'.[69]

Williams informed the Commonwealth Relations Office that Chifley was apprehensive about how the Western Union would impact on Australia's economic and financial interests; he was also concerned that a political decision of great significance had been taken without the necessary details having been worked out yet. The discussion with Chifley was 'most friendly and he did not indicate opposition to the substance' of Attlee's response. Chifley told Williams that he had read *Speaking Frankly* (1947) written by James F Byrnes, the US secretary of state from 1945 to 1947, a book that showed the expansionist nature of the Soviet Union. The high commissioner noted that, like most Australian Labor Party politicians, Chifley was 'bitterly anti-communist'. Williams wrote, somewhat patronisingly, that if he was provided with 'reasoned arguments from the United Kingdom' which he could take straight to the prime minister, 'this kind of talk, if repeated in small but regular doses', might make him realise that 'his reliance on Evatt should not be overtaxed'.[70]

In his reply, Attlee thanked Chifley for his 'frank comments', but expressed surprise at Chifley's criticism of the British government's proposals. Attlee assured him there was no expectation on the part of the British government that Australia would play a role without the 'fullest prior consultation'. He apologised for the lack of consultation prior to the foreign secretary's speech[71] delivered to the House of Commons on 22 January 1948,[72] in which Bevin condemned the Soviet Union's political expansionism and called for the unification of western Europe. But extra time was needed to allow cabinet to discuss these proposals prior to consulting with the Australian government. Attlee denied that Britain was urging military action against the Soviet Union. Instead:

> Our object is primarily to consolidate the ethical and spiritual forces inherent in Western civilization, thereby building up for the countries of Western Europe a counter-attraction to the baleful tenets of communism within their borders and recreating a healthy society wherever it has been shaken or shattered by war.[73]

According to Attlee, the Soviet Union had established a communist bloc, forming alliances with states within eastern Europe and was now intent on extending their sphere of influence to France, Italy, Trieste and Greece. The West needed to 'mobilise a moral and material force' that would engender 'confidence and energy in the West and inspire respect elsewhere'.[74]

Attlee argued that the Western world needed to 'make a stand against Soviet expansionism' from a 'position of strength', and it needed to impress upon the Soviets that it would not be pressured further. He explained the inclusion of Spain, in this 'Western democratic system', by emphasising that it would occur when circumstances permitted. At present, Britain agreed that, 'circumstances in Spain do not permit'. He also denied that the Greek government was 'undemocratic'. The United Kingdom had criticised certain actions of the Greek government; however, it was 'freely elected', notwithstanding the fact that the 'extreme Left' boycotted the elections.[75] Attlee refused to countenance Australia's policy on banning the arms trade, which would only advantage the Soviet Union as it sought to extend its reach into Western Europe and the Mediterranean. According to Attlee, the West needed to 'face the facts'. Communism was gradually extending its influence westwards after succeeding in eastern Europe. It appealed to poor countries and those who had suffered through a disastrous war.[76] The Western Union policy was therefore needed to counter this appeal. 'If the present fatal drift is to be arrested and the tide turned in our favour we shall need—and need badly—the wholehearted backing of the Americas and of the Commonwealth'. Attlee acknowledged that Australia's interests were focused on the Pacific region, but concluded by arguing that, 'when all is said and done the key to the situation lies in Europe.[77]

Chifley's Reply to Attlee

Chifley replied to Attlee's message in a cable sent on 10 February 1948. According to historian Peter Edwards, his reply was 'very different in tone' to the cable sent on 22 January,[78] which was 'more like a political manifesto than a diplomatic communication between friendly governments',[79] inferring that it reflected the radical influence of John Burton, secretary of the Department of External Affairs.

However, the tone of Chifley's reply might have been different, but the message was the same—and it was a very blunt message. Historian Christopher Waters also rejects the possibility that Burton influenced Chifley in his response and argues that Chifley did not 'repudiate his first message'; instead, his position was that they would 'agree to disagree'. Waters adds that, in view of Chifley's long-standing 'interest and deep involvement in foreign affairs' and the bold directions taken in foreign policy by his government, 'it cannot be believed that Chifley had been tricked into rejecting Bevin's policy'.[80]

Chifley, in his reply, stated candidly and forthrightly, that it was important that Australia and the United Kingdom engage in a frank discussion on 'matters of peace and war', especially when the 'drift to war' was noticeable. He painstakingly pointed out: 'Even though we cannot agree, we at least, by these means, know each other's point of view, and developments in our foreign policies will then come with less surprise'. Chifley wrote that he could not 'emphasise too much or too often', the necessity for 'the fullest prior consultation' with the Australian government before any decisions were made by the Attlee government that involved Australia. While understanding Britain's need for the 'sympathy and support' of the United States, this 'support should not be obtained on the basis that war with the Soviet is inevitable'—a view fostered by certain financial and commercial interest groups in the United States according to 'private advice' received by Chifley and his government. He acknowledged the economic and political difficulties confronting the United Kingdom; however, he argued that although the Australian government's problems were much less, they were 'still problems which we have to face locally'. Chifley concluded by assuring Attlee of his 'friendship and sympathy' in these difficult times, even though it was necessary to be 'frank in our opinions to you'.[81] In his reply, Chifley again emphasised the need for open and comprehensive consultation between Australia and the United Kingdom, but it was a mistake to assume that the two countries' interests necessarily converged. Australia had its own regional issues to address.

What does this correspondence between prime ministers Chifley and Attlee reveal about Chifley's general world view, his influence on Australian foreign policy and his thinking on the Cold War?

Although Peter Edwards notes that many historians assumed that Australian foreign policy from 1945 to 1949 was created by Evatt, a 'one-man band', he argues that it is clear that this 'greatly underestimates the respective roles of Chifley and Burton'.[82] However, Burton is credited with undue influence over Chifley, in regard to the cable sent to Attlee in response to his request for support for a Western Union.[83] A letter from Patrick Duff, the United Kingdom's high commissioner in New Zealand, to Sir Eric Machtig, under-secretary of state at the Commonwealth Relations Office, is cited. Duff referred to the fact that Alister McIntosh, secretary of the New Zealand Department of External Affairs, had just returned from Canberra.

> I had a long talk with him yesterday ... (McIntosh had learned in Canberra, by the way, that Mr Chifley's telegram of January 22nd to Mr Attlee was drafted by Mr Burton. Burton got Dr Evatt to agree to it though the latter said 'We shall never get this past Chif'. Burton, however, said, 'Leave it to me': and, sure enough, after about an hour's conversation he <u>did</u> 'get it past Chif'. When, however, Mr Attlee's dignified and cogent response (repeated to me in your telegram No. 39 of February 2nd) reached Mr Chifley, he realised that he had been led astray and drafted the next reply—(described by Mr Fraser when he saw it as 'Chifley at his best')—himself ...)[84]

This seems to be a quite remarkable underestimation of Chifley's skill as a politician and an administrator. There are innumerable accounts of Chifley's ability and the extent of his interest in foreign policy as prime minister. Harold Breen was a long-term public servant who had worked closely with Chifley and had therefore, seen him 'in action at very close quarters over a number of years'. In his article on Chifley, Breen mentions certain characteristics that made working with him a 'pleasure'. He had an 'excellent memory', and he was able to make firm decisions that he upheld. Breen added:

> It often happens that, in a discussion across a table, an understanding is reached which is, in effect, a decision by the Minister. But it is often difficult to get it confirmed in

writing on an official document, especially if it is the Prime Minister who made the decision, because so many things and so many people crowd his every day. By the time the necessary paper work has been done and the document has reached him, his memory is hazy or he has had second thoughts, perhaps at the prompting of someone else. It is a necessary rule never to act on an oral decision until you see it confirmed in writing. But, so far as my experience is concerned, there were no worries on that score with Chifley, provided you had tabled all the facts at the meeting or interview. His clear head and good memory enabled him to look at the document, recognize it for what it was, recall what was said and, if all tallied, write his approval on it.[85]

Thus, according to Breen, the prime minister was meticulous in his signing of documents. William Dunk, secretary of the Department of External Affairs from 1945 to 1947,[86] had worked closely with Chifley when he was treasurer. Dunk also attested to the fact that he was a 'prodigious worker' with a 'first rate administrative sense'. Chifley 'appreciated what had to happen to translate decision into practical action—the follow through which is the essence of sound management'.[87] Chifley was also described as the 'co-ordinator' of government policy. His advisers knew him well and played their role by gathering, organising and presenting the information upon which the prime minister's decisions would be made. Chifley's 'faculty for prompt, firm and generally consistent decision' then enabled policy to be coordinated and implemented successfully.[88]

If Chifley as the Australian prime minister signed off on an official cable, then it has to be assumed that this was his considered decision after receiving advice from his advisers. It would be difficult to argue otherwise. As to undue influence from the secretary of the Department of External Affairs, Burton himself stated that it was Chifley who decided some of the 'most dramatic and important decisions of the time', including the referral of the Indonesian dispute to the United Nations Security Council and the decision to send Australian delegates to the 1949 New Delhi Conference.[89] The relationship between Chifley and Burton seems more to be a meeting of minds. As Burton said later, Chifley was 'an amazing person ... [he]

had very, very little education. But his intuitive insights were just amazing … He could be firm. He could make up his mind very quickly. It was a pleasure to work with him as a Minister, and, of course, as Prime Minister'.[90]

In addition, Chifley and Evatt were not alone in their doubts about the Western Union proposal. The United Kingdom's high commissioner in New Zealand, Patrick Duff, reported that Peter Fraser's Labour government had serious doubts about Bevin's Western Union policy and where it would lead Britain. There was also concern in the government about Britain's closeness to the United States. Duff wrote that the New Zealand government was generally nervous about US intentions world-wide. Fraser believed that US policy was 'guided by perfectly irresponsible businessmen with an outlook anything but altruistic and with the dominating idea that he who pays the piper is entitled to call the tune'.[91]

Chifley, Evatt and Bevin

A further complication for Chifley in his government's dealings with the Attlee government was the acrimonious relationship that had developed between Evatt, as minister for External Affairs, and the British government. Chifley was aware of the difficult relationship between Evatt and Ernest Bevin, the British foreign secretary, and attempted to ease the situation.[92] In April 1948 John (Jack) Beasley, the Australian high commissioner in London, informed Bevin of the difficulties he was having with his own government, in particular, with Evatt. He was involved in a 'very bitter correspondence with Evatt', who ignored his advice and belittled his work as ambassador, saying Beasley had no influence with the Attlee government. Beasley had also contacted Chifley about these difficulties. Bevin replied that he wished to maintain talks on 'frank and open terms' and to conduct negotiations on foreign affairs with the Australian government on that basis. Bevin added that Chifley did know of 'certain difficulties which had handicapped the Secretary of State in this respect, but the Secretary of State was doing his best to get these difficulties removed, and he hoped he would be able to speak frankly and openly to Mr Beasley, with whom he wished to work closely'.[93]

Further evidence of this strained relationship is provided in a series of talks between Chifley and Esler Dening, Bevin's chief adviser on the Far East.⁹⁴ Dening had been sent to Australia and New Zealand because of the supposed failure of the Australian government, and, to a lesser degree, the New Zealand government, to understand the Attlee government's policies on Europe and Asia.⁹⁵ On his first night in Canberra, Dening met with the United Kingdom's high commissioner, Edward J Williams, who informed him that, in meetings, Evatt was quite a changed person when in the company of Chifley, rather than on his own. This was borne out in his first meeting with Chifley and Evatt, during which Dening put forward Bevin's assessment of the crisis situation in Europe. Dening noted that Evatt was 'subdued and said little'. Chifley had an excellent understanding of what was happening in Europe and of the international situation in general. He had 'no illusions about Soviet aims'.

On 7 May 1948, in Chifley's next meeting with Dening, whom he had specifically asked to meet alone, Chifley enquired if there was a 'special message' for him from Attlee or Bevin. He was aware there were certain difficulties between Evatt and Bevin and that some of the cables that Evatt had sent were not welcome. Chifley then said he appreciated the difficult situation facing Attlee and Bevin. He also raised the 'perennial question of consultation'. Dening then told Chifley that Bevin hoped he would be able to visit London and the prime minister replied that he would be glad to visit. Dening wrote that he came away from a long interview, in which Chifley did most of the talking, feeling that 'Chifley was not unaware of what was going on, and while not prepared to discuss the matter in detail, was anxious to smooth things over'. Dening concluded by saying that if Chifley were running foreign policy, the United Kingdom should 'expect no difficulty'; however, he was sure that the difficult relationship between Australia and the United Kingdom would persist under Evatt and Burton.⁹⁶ Like most members of the Attlee government, Dening blamed his government's difficulties with the Chifley government on the influence of Evatt and Burton.

The Great Divide

One of the few British ministers to understand the 'geo-political' basis for the great divide in the two countries' international policies⁹⁷ was Hector McNeil, a junior minister in the Foreign Office,⁹⁸ who was asked by Bevin to report on Dening's correspondence from Australia.

McNeil expressed concern that an 'essential point' in Australia's foreign policy was neglected. According to McNeil, Britain's 'reasonable suspicion' of Evatt had caused this matter to be overlooked. McNeil wrote: 'It is undoubtedly true that the general run of Australian politicians ... are more concerned with the danger of Japanese aggression than with Soviet aggression. Geographically this is easy to understand'. McNeil believed that the psychological trauma caused by the 'threat' of a Japanese invasion continued: it was an ongoing problem, a source of conflict between Australia and the Americans that would not disappear.[99]

There was little understanding from members of the Attlee government of the divide in the two governments' approach to foreign affairs. The British government embraced power politics, whereas the Australian government used liberal internationalism as a way of ensuring it had a say in foreign affairs.[100] Also, post-war Britain was in dire financial straits. A review of Soviet policy carried out by the UK Foreign Office argued that the political and social unrest in Asia, which was seen as communist-inspired, was endangering Britain's 'long-standing commercial and financial interests in Asia'. The review stated that the lack of return on Britain's 'substantial investments in that continent is an important factor contributing to our present financial difficulties'.[101]

Chifley and his government believed that the unrest in post-war Asia was driven by a legitimate nationalist desire for independence from European colonial rule and improved living conditions. But the British government continued to conflate nationalist agitation for self-government in Asia with communist attempts to 'turn Asiatic races against the Western democracies and to pose as the champion of oppressed colonial peoples'.[102] The review into Soviet policy claimed it was the Communist Party that was the driving force behind unrest in Britain's colonial possessions, such as Malaya, Hong Kong, and Borneo. Furthermore, it was argued, a similar technique of inciting 'local nationalist sentiment' against colonial rule was used by communists in the Netherlands East Indies and in French Indochina.[103]

The review, however, agreed with Chifley's view that it was doubtful that the Soviet Union intended to start a war with Britain or the United States. The Soviets recognised that their chances of winning were not good and 'mutual destruction' would be the result. Confirming Chifley's assessment of the 'American preponderance of power', the report stated that the Soviet Union was also still 'backward' technologically when compared with the United States and Great Britain and had suffered much greater losses during the war.[104] Although in this instance the views of Chifley and the British Foreign Office coincided, there was a radical divide in the Australian and British government's understanding of the causes of unrest in Asia. As the Cold War heated up, the Chifley government was greatly concerned that it was increasingly played out in post-colonial proxy sites in Asia.

Chifley's Visit to London in 1948

Chifley had the opportunity to discuss a number of his concerns with the Attlee government when he visited London in July 1948. The prime minister left Sydney for London on the night of 3 July 1948—a visit undertaken on his own initiative to discuss certain economic issues with Prime Minister Clement Attlee and other members of the British government. These included the dollar problem in the sterling region; increased trade possibilities for Australia; and the government's access to Australia's sterling reserves. Domestic security issues were also added to the agenda.[105] The Australian prime minister's health had not been good, as he had just recovered from a bout of influenza, but he had brought along a 'batch of his favourite detective fiction', hoping to relax during the three-day trip to London. According to Chifley, his mission was about 'hard realities and no dreams'; once he arrived he would be occupied almost every minute with formal engagements with the British Labour prime minister, Clement Attlee, foreign secretary Ernest Bevin and chancellor of the exchequer Sir Stafford Cripps. He would also have discussions with secretary of state for Commonwealth Relations, Philip John Noel-Baker, to explore the possibility of mass migration to Australia.[106]

A great deal of preparation had gone into Chifley's visit to London: Attlee had even cancelled his visit to Germany to be in London when Chifley was there.[107] At the first meeting he attended, Chifley explained that he had arranged this visit to consult with UK ministers on urgent issues affecting Australia. He was concerned that the need for 'rigorous control of dollar expenditure' was a difficult concept for the Australian people to understand.[108] Australia was a member of the sterling bloc, which was made up of countries from the British Empire—excepting countries such as Canada who were part of the dollar group—and those countries whose economies were dependent on the United Kingdom.[109] The sterling bloc pooled their gold and dollar reserves in exchange for sterling which expedited trade with the Commonwealth, but imports were strictly controlled, especially from the United States.[110] This meant that Australia was 'dependent on the sterling area pool of dollars to finance its imports from the United States'[111] and Chifley was keen to draw down US dollars from the pool.[112]

The chancellor of the exchequer suggested that the dollar expenditure problem could be resolved by drawing from the International Monetary Fund. Chifley replied that Australian public opinion was innately distrustful of the IMF and it had been very difficult for him to persuade his own colleagues to join the fund. He had 'achieved this only by assuring them that the Fund would be employed solely for maintaining economic equilibrium under internal conditions'.[113] Chifley also took the opportunity to discuss the development of Australian food production.[114] During these meetings, Chifley revealed his mastery of economic matters, together with his aptitude and expertise in Australia's foreign and defence policies.

Chifley's main concern in his meetings with members of the Attlee government involved economic matters. But he also had discussions with Ernest Bevin on foreign affairs and consulted the UK Minister for Defence, Albert Victor Alexander, about defence and security issues.[115] In June 1948 the United States had placed an embargo on the free exchange of classified information between the United States and Australia because of domestic security concerns.[116] According to historian Christopher Waters, this embargo was more likely to be because of US alarm over the Australian government's policies, rather than security concerns. Australia was seen by the United States as a 'fellow traveller government'.[117] Waters notes that confirmation of this viewpoint was demonstrated when Dean Rusk from the State Department confided to a British official that the United States was concerned about Evatt's presidency of the United Nations General Assembly, where he 'vigorously pursued his even-handed policy of conciliation between the western and Soviet blocs at the United Nations'.[118]

Chifley wanted this embargo lifted. He later sent Frederick Shedden, secretary of the Australian Defence Department, to Washington and London in April and May of 1949, in an attempt to get the embargo revoked.[119] Chifley and his formidable and conservative secretary of Defence shared a mutual anger that Australia, which had a record of substantial contribution to the war effort, was treated in this way. Shedden wrote to Chifley that he had told London that the Australian government would 'be satisfied with nothing less than a total settlement of the whole question' of the embargo on classified information. We were 'not importunate bankrupts' who would settle for a pittance. Australia's 'past record of defence co-operation in war and peace ... and the measures taken for the protection of defence information' entitled the government to a total repeal of this embargo.[120] Shedden asked that Chifley provide him with his views on the opinions expressed by him. On 15 July, Chifley replied that he was in full agreement with Shedden. If the parties concerned would not settle the issue, then Shedden could 'tell them to go to Hades, repeat Hades, and let us know the date of their going'.[121]

In addition, 'leakages' of security information had occurred in the United States and Shedden had also been informed that Australian security measures were now in advance of the United States.[122] Shedden wrote that the embargo was politically motivated and the US intended to wait until the result of the next election in the expectation that the Chifley government would be defeated.[123] He did not succeed in his mission, however, and it was not until 6 January 1950, after the election of the conservative Menzies government in December 1949, that the United States partially lifted its embargo.[124]

During his time in London, Chifley had a private meeting with Bevin on 10 July 1948, in which he said 'he wanted to talk frankly about Dr Evatt'. Chifley asked Bevin's views on Evatt, as he felt that the relationship between the secretary of state and Evatt could be improved—it was 'not as good' as it should be. According to Bevin, Evatt was 'a brilliant man and very ambitious', but the UK government never knew where they stood with him. At times he was 'anti-Soviet, at another anti-American and at other anti-UK'. Bevin said he had 'no sense of being pals with Dr Evatt'. He did acknowledge, however, that Evatt had been 'helpful' over Britain's response to the Berlin blockade. Chifley told Bevin that he had instructed Dr Evatt to prepare a press statement supporting the West's actions in Berlin. Chifley thanked Bevin for his comments and said this would remain between himself and Bevin, and that he would 'have matters out quite frankly' with Evatt when he returned to Australia.[125]

There is no record of Chifley's conversation with Evatt. However, in a letter to Attlee, who was ill, in which he expressed his sympathy, Chifley said he had spoken to Evatt before the foreign minister left for London in July and asked him to provide as much assistance as possible.[126] Apparently, Evatt became more accommodating in his dealings with Bevin and, as a consequence, the British government supported Evatt in his campaign to become president of the third session of the United Nation's General Assembly. Chifley was told in late July 1948 that the British would not only vote for Evatt, they would lobby for him as well. This they did, and Evatt was elected president.[127] Despite Chifley's evident unease regarding Evatt's abrasiveness in his dealings with Bevin and other members of the Attlee government, the prime minister was resolute in his support for Evatt in his role as president of the United Nations General Assembly. The Chifley government supported Evatt's action on Berlin,[128] when he called for a meeting of the leaders of the great powers to negotiate with the Soviet Union on lifting their blockade of Berlin and to advance the peace process. In doing so, Evatt had placed the Berlin emergency on the agenda of the General Assembly, despite the Attlee government's wish for it to remain within the Security Council.[129] Moreover, the Chifley government supported Evatt's concern that the 'rule of law' rather than the 'use of force' should prevail, in addition to the ongoing need for international arbitration through the United Nations.[130]

Chifley's Visit to Berlin

On 11 July 1948, during his trip to London, Chifley visited Berlin for a brief, hectic, eight-hour tour of the western sector, flying into the 'heart of the raging "cold war" … to get a first-hand impression of the situation in Berlin',[131] and to speak with German trade union and political leaders.[132] He was the first Allied leader to visit Germany since the Potsdam conference in July–August 1945.[133] While he was there, he saw more in eight hours than most would see in eight weeks,[134] meeting with British, US, French and Australian authorities in order to 'obtain first-hand information' and to 'gauge the atmosphere of the situation in the German capital'.[135] During his visit, Chifley declared his support for Britain's 'firm policy' on the Russian blockade of Berlin. His visit coincided with a 'record day in the Anglo-American airlift' and played a significant part in the propaganda effort the British employed to boost pro-British sentiment amongst Germans.[136]

There was a great deal of German interest in his visit and he 'deeply impressed Berlin Left-Wing supporters with his visit to trades union headquarters, close to the Soviet sector, in a car flaunting the Southern Cross flag'.[137] On arriving in Berlin, Chifley insisted on posing for a photograph with railwaymen's delegates when he was introduced to them, pointing out that he was once an engine-driver himself.[138] At union headquarters, he was welcomed as 'a champion of the peoples from down under' visiting Berliners 'in this besieged fortress'. His discussion with trade union leaders about problems impacting on Berlin lasted for almost an hour.[139] He told union leaders that the great aim for unions was to 'improve living conditions for union members and the whole population'. He congratulated the trade unions on their fight for freedom and 'expressed sympathy' with the activities of the politically independent trade unions in Berlin.[140]

Chifley also spoke with the US military commander, General Lucius D Clay, about the possibility of obtaining more displaced persons as immigrants to Australia.[141] As he said to the press on his return home, Chifley 'hoped there would be a substantial overall increase in the number of new settlers for Australia'.[142] The government had set a quota of 20 000 displaced persons to be accepted in 1948, but there was great concern that, because of a shortage of shipping, Australia had so far received only 4000. US authorities noted that the prime minister had 'recently appealed directly to President Truman to obtain additional shipping for this service, offering at the same time to admit a total of 200 000 DP's [displaced persons] as rapidly as possible'.[143]

During Chifley's visit to Berlin, the destruction he witnessed affected him profoundly and confirmed his fears that, as he stated in a speech he gave in parliament later that year, the scientific advances in warfare and weaponry meant that a future war would see the most 'appalling' loss of 'human life and property'. The 'nations of the world' needed to take every opportunity 'to avoid another catastrophe which, compared with the last war, would be 50 or 100 times as great'.[144] The fact that Chifley endorsed the Western allies' airlift into Berlin in no way repudiates his stance on the Cold War. He was firmly anti-communist and he made no secret of his opinion that 'communism as we see it in Russia' was another 'form of Fascism'. The Soviet Union was a 'dictatorship in which the people have no rights, and no voice in the appointment of their leaders'.[145] The Berlin blockade was an aggressive act by the Soviet Union that needed to be resisted by the Western allies.

Conclusion

On 2 September 1948, in Chifley's address to parliament, a little over seven weeks after his return from London, it appears that he had not changed his mind about the United States and the United Kingdom's Cold War view of the world. He continued to argue that, although the Soviet Union was prepared to go as far as possible to gain territorial, economic or ideological advantage, it was not capable of waging war against the military and industrial might of the United States.[146] Chifley accused members of the Menzies Opposition of blithely suggesting force could solve any problem; he advised Liberal MP, Percy Spender and others of his party, to consider the catastrophic impact of a third world war with the 'new forms of warfare' now in use. His government had been criticised by the Opposition for working hard to bring the nations of the world together to encourage peace. This was done, Chifley declared, not for the sake of politicians, 'who merely make speeches, but for the boys who have to go out and die for their country'. Chifley believed there was 'too much talk by people who themselves are not likely to be killed which encourages warfare and killing'. He added, 'every human being who had any love of the human race should try to achieve unity and understanding among the nations of the world'.[147]

It has been argued that, from October 1948, although 'differences and tensions remained,' Australian foreign policy regarding the potential threat posed by the Soviet Union aligned more with the policies of the United Kingdom.[148] Furthermore, the 'crucial role in the reversal of Australia's policy appears to have been played by Chifley'.[149] However, Chifley's speech in the foreign policy debate on 2 September 1948, and his later speech to the Australian Labor Party's federal executive on 11 May 1949, indicate that this is not so. Chifley continued to maintain his opposition to the British and United States Cold War 'framework for understanding change', in which the world was divided into two polarised camps, with world war imminent.[150] We can see in Chifley's speeches and in his response to the devastation inflicted on Berlin—'this once beautiful city'—a confirmation of his belief that war was to be avoided at all cost.[151] He believed military technology was so advanced that any escalation of conflict would lead to mutual destruction. The only way to achieve world peace was through the United Nations Organisation, in which member nations pledged to avoid the use of force, choosing to take collective action against those nations who violated that rule. Chifley's views on the Cold War were consistent with his internationalist principles, which were grounded in more than thirty years of study and involvement in international affairs and his interaction over many years with his network of advisers, many of whom shared his internationalist perspective.

Notes

1. Melvyn P Leffler, *A Preponderance of Power: National Security, the Truman Administration, and the Cold War*, Stanford University Press, Stanford, CA, c.1992, p. 2.
2. David Reynolds, *One World Divisible: A Global History Since 1945*, Penguin Books, London, 2000, p. 12.
3. Leffler, *A Preponderance of Power*, p. 2.
4. David S Painter and Melvyn P Leffler, 'Introduction: The International System and the Origins of the Cold War', in Melvyn P Leffler and David S Painter (eds), *Origins of the Cold War: An International History*, Routledge, London, 1994, p. 3.
5. Leffler, *A Preponderance of Power*, p. 5.
6. Reynolds, *One World Divisible*, pp. 12–13.
7. David Reynolds, 'Empire, Region, World: the International Context of Australian Foreign Policy since 1939', *Australian Journal of Politics and History*, vol. 51, no. 3, 2005, p. 350.
8. Reynolds, *One World Divisible*, p. 29.
9. ibid., p. 24.
10. ibid., p. 28.

11 Edwards with Pemberton, *Crises and Commitments*, p. 17.
12 Lee, *Search for Security*, p. 83.
13 Waters, *Empire Fractures*, p. 109.
14 ibid., p. 104.
15 ibid., p. 106.
16 ibid., pp. 120–121.
17 Reynolds, *One World Divisible*, p. 25.
18 Lee, *Search for Security*, p. 90.
19 Reynolds, *One World Divisible*, pp. 30–31.
20 Waters, *The Empire Fractures*, pp. 136.
21 ibid., p. 137; Reynolds, *One World Divisible*, p. 31.
22 Reynolds, *One World Divisible*, p. 31.
23 ibid.
24 Waters, *Empire Fractures*, p. 159.
25 Melvyn P Leffler, 'National Security and US Foreign Policy', in Leffler and Painter (eds), *Origins of the Cold War*, p. 18
26 David Lee, *Australia and the World in the Twentieth Century*, pp. 81–82.
27 Pitty and Leach, 'Australian Nationalism and Internationalism', p. 99.
28 Waters, *Empire Fractures*, pp. 109–110.
29 ibid., p. 111.
30 Lowe, *Menzies and the Great World Struggle*, p. 14.
31 Neville Meaney, 'Australia, the Great Powers and the Coming of the Cold War', *Australian Journal of Politics and History*, vol. 38, issue 3, 1992, p. 330.
32 'Address by the Prime Minister (Mr Chifley) to the Federal Executive of the Australian Labor Party', Canberra, 11 May 1949, in Weller (ed.), *Federal Executive Minutes 1915–1955*, p. 392.
33 Coombs, *Trial Balance*, p. 86.
34 *CDP*, HoR, 26 February 1948, p. 255.
35 Chifley, 'These Things are Really Worth Fighting For', speech to annual conference of the New South Wales branch of the ALP on 12 June 1948, in *Things Worth Fighting For*, p. 28.
36 *CPD*, HoR, 2 September 1948, p. 63.
37 ibid., p. 65.
38 ibid., pp. 63–64.
39 'Address by Prime Minister (Mr Chifley)', Canberra, 11 May 1949, in Weller (ed.), *Federal Executive Minutes 1915–1955*, p. 392.
40 Sean Scalmer, The Career of Class: Intellectuals and the Labour Movement 1942–56, PhD thesis, University of Sydney, 1997, p. 41.
41 Crisp, *Ben Chifley*, p. 192.
42 Scalmer, The Career of Class, p. 41.
43 'Address by Prime Minister (Mr Chifley)', Canberra, 11 May 1949, in Weller (ed.), *Federal Executive Minutes 1915–1955*, p. 392–393.
44 Lee, *Search for Security*, p. 83.
45 Top secret and personal message, Attlee to Chifley, 14 January 1948, pp. 1–2, NAA: A1838, TS78/7.
46 Top secret and personal message, Chifley to Attlee, 22 January 1948, p. 1, in ibid.

47 ibid., pp. 1–2.
48 ibid., p. 2.
49 ibid.
50 Joy Damousi, *Memory and Migration in the Shadow of War: Australia's Greek Immigrants After World War II and the Greek Civil War*, Cambridge University Press, Cambridge, UK, 2015, p. 80.
51 ibid., p. 78.
52 Edwards with Pemberton, *Crises and Commitments*, p. 17
53 Waters, *Empire Fractures*, p. 117.
54 ibid., pp. 154–155.
55 Top secret and personal message, Chifley to Attlee, 22 January 1948, p. 2.
56 ibid., p. 3.
57 ibid., pp. 3–4.
58 ibid., p. 4
59 ibid.
60 ibid., pp. 4–5.
61 ibid., p. 5.
62 Meaney, 'Dr HV Evatt and the United Nations: The Problem of Collective Security and Liberal Internationalism', in Cotton and Lee (eds), *Australia and the United Nations*, p. 56.
63 Waters, *Empire Fractures*, p. 111.
64 Meaney, 'Australia, the Great Powers and the Coming of the Cold War', p. 330.
65 *CPD*, HoR, 27 September 1950, p. 25.
66 Breen, 'J.B. Chifley', p. 239.
67 Cablegram 200, Chifley to Attlee, 28 July 1947, in Phillip Dorling (ed.), *DAFP, Volume XI: Indonesia 1947*, AGPS, Canberra, 1994, p. 167.
68 Copy of message to Chifley annotated 'Dated from London 2nd HC saw PM on 5th', in Chifley to Attlee, 10 February 1948, NAA: A1838, TS78/7.
69 Cable 76, United Kingdom High Commissioner in Australia to Commonwealth Relations Office, 7 February 1948, pp. 1–2, NAUK. FO 371/70189. I am very grateful to Chris Waters for sharing with me his copies of these documents, which are to be found in the National Archives of the United Kingdom (NAUK).
70 ibid., p. 3.
71 Attlee's message to Chifley is undated. It is included with Chifley's message to Attlee on 10 February 1948, p. 1, NAA: A1838, TS78/7.
72 Waters, *Empire Fractures*, p. 110.
73 Attlee to Chifley, n.d. p. 1, NAA: A1838, TS78/7.
74 ibid., pp. 1–2.
75 ibid., p. 2.
76 ibid., pp. 2–3.
77 ibid., p. 3.
78 PG Edwards, 'The Origins of the Cold War, 1947–1949', in Carl Bridge (ed.), *Munich to Vietnam: Australia's Relations with Britain and the United States since the 1930s*, Melbourne University Press, Melbourne, 1991, p. 76.

79 ibid., p. 74.
80 Waters, *Empire Fractures*, p. 113.
81 Top secret and personal message, Chifley to Attlee, 10 February 1948, pp. 1–2. NAA: A1838, TS78/7.
82 Edwards, 'The Origins of the Cold War', p. 86.
83 ibid., p. 76.
84 Letter, Top Secret and Personal, Patrick Duff to Machtig, Wellington, 5 March 1948, NAUK: PREM 8/734.
85 Breen, 'JB Chifley', p. 243.
86 Dunk, *They Also Serve*, p. 13.
87 ibid., p. 117.
88 ACT Research Group, 'Commonwealth Policy Co-ordination', p. 202.
89 Burton, 'Review of Ben Chifley: A Biography by LF Crisp', p. 96.
90 Burton, 'Indonesia: Unfinished Diplomacy', in Legge (ed.), *New Directions in Australian Foreign Policy*, p. 44.
91 Letter, Patrick Duff, UK High Commissioner in New Zealand to Machtig, Wellington, 5 March 1948, NAUK: PREM 8/734.
92 Letter, Dening to Machtig, 7 May 1948, NAUK: PREM 8/736.
93 Report of meeting signed by FK Roberts, 6 April 1948, NAUK: FO 800/444, Com/48/5.
94 Waters, *Empire Fractures*, p. 125
95 Record of conversation, signed by N Charles, 13 May 1948, NAUK: FO 371/70202A.
96 Letter, Top Secret and Personal, ME Dening to Machtig, 7 May 1948, NAUK: PREM 8/736.
97 Waters, *Empire Fractures*, p. 131.
98 Frank Bongiorno, 'John Beasley and the Postwar World', in Carl Bridge, Frank Bongiorno and David Lee (eds), *The High Commissioners: Australia's Representatives in the United Kingdom, 1910–2010*, Department of Foreign Affairs and Trade, Canberra, 2010, p. 121.
99 Minute, H McNeil to Bevin, 12 May 1948, NAUK: FO 371/70202A.
100 Waters, *Empire Fractures*, p. 131.
101 Cabinet Memorandum by the Secretary of State for Foreign Affairs, 'Review of Soviet Policy', 5 January 1948, C.P. (48) 7, p. 12, NAUK: PREM 8/1431 Part 1.
102 ibid., p. 9.
103 ibid., p. 10.
104 ibid., p. 13.
105 Waters, *Empire Fractures*, pp. 137–138.
106 'No Dreams in My Mission', *Herald*, (Melbourne, Vic.) 3 July 1948.
107 Waters, *Empire Fractures*, p. 138.
108 Minutes of Meetings with the Prime Minister of Australia, 8 July 1948, p. 1, NAUK: PREM 8/712E.
109 Lee, *Australia and the World in the Twentieth Century*, p. 50.
110 ibid., p. 82.
111 Coombs, *Trial Balance*, p. 150.
112 Day, *Chifley*, p. 473.

113 Minutes of Meetings with the Prime Minister of Australia, 8 July 1948, NAUK: PREM 8/712E, p. 2.
114 ibid., p. 3.
115 Waters, *Empire Fractures*, p. 138.
116 ibid., p. 129.
117 For a different view, see chapters three and four in David Horner, *The Spy Catchers: the Official History of ASIO: Volume One, 1949–1963*, Allen & Unwin, Sydney, 2014.
118 Waters, *Empire Fractures*, pp. 129–130.
119 ibid., p. 165.
120 Letter, Shedden to Chifley, [London], 1 July 1949, p. 4, NAA: A5954, 1795/3.
121 Letter, Chifley to Shedden, 15 July 1949, in ibid.
122 Letter, Shedden to Chifley, 7 September 1949, p. 2, in ibid.
123 Letter, Shedden to Gray, London, 30 June 1949, p. 1, in ibid.
124 Pamela Andre (ed.), *DAFP, Volume XVI: Beyond the Region 1948–49*, DFAT, Canberra, 2001, p. 470.
125 Minute by FK Roberts, 10 July 1948, Com/48/15, NAUK: FO 800/444.
126 Waters, *Empire Fractures*, p. 140.
127 ibid., p. 142.
128 ibid., p. 157.
129 ibid., p. 150.
130 ibid., p. 158.
131 '"We Must Hold On in Berlin"—Chifley', *Herald*, (Melbourne, Vic.), 13 July 1948.
132 *DDA*, No. 137, 18 July 1948, p. 4, NAA: B5459, 137.
133 'Chifley Sympathetic with Freedom of Berlin', *Canberra Times*, 13 July 1948.
134 'Chifley Says "Must Hold On: Australia, New Zealand Back Berlin Policy"', *Sydney Morning Herald*, 13 July 1948.
135 *DDA*, No. 137, pp. 7–8.
136 'Mr Chifley talks with Berliners: Supports British Policy', *Argus*, (Melbourne, Vic.), 13 July 1948.
137 'Mr Chifley talks with Berliners: Supports British Policy', *Argus*, (Melbourne, Vic.), 13 July 1948.
138 'Chifley Sympathetic with Freedom of Berlin'.
139 'Mr Chifley talks with Berliners'.
140 'Chifley Sympathetic with Freedom of Berlin'.
141 'Overseas Prices will Limit Dollar Imports', *Argus*, (Melbourne, Vic.), 19 July 1948.
142 'Chifley Home—"Hard Road" on Dollars', *Sydney Morning Herald*, 19 July 1948.
143 Cable, 'Policy Statement of the Department of State, Washington, August 18, 1948, *FRUS: 1948*, vol. VI, p. 3.
144 *CPD*, HoR, 2 September 1948, p. 64.
145 ibid., p. 67.
146 ibid., pp. 63 and 65.

147 ibid., pp. 63–64.
148 Edwards, 'The Origins of the Cold War', in Bridge (ed.), *Munich to Vietnam*, p. 84.
149 ibid., p. 86.
150 Lowe, *Menzies and the 'Great World Struggle'*, p. 14.
151 *DDA*, No. 137, commercial radio broadcast on 25 July 1948, p. 8; see also JB Chifley, 'Think and Act in Terms of the Nation', in *Things Worth Fighting For*, p. 171.

Part V
Conclusion

Autographed portrait of Prime Minister Ben Chifley, ca. 1946, courtesy National Library of Australia.

CHAPTER NINE
A Receptivity to 'New Ideas and to the Impact of New Conditions'

Chifley's government held power in an era of unprecedented new international institutions, new rules and new charters regulating international affairs and trade. The United Nations, the Bretton Woods institutions—the International Monetary Fund, the International Bank for Reconstruction and Development and the multilateral trade treaty, the General Agreement on Tariffs and Trade—and other international bodies, such as the South Pacific Commission and the North Atlantic Treaty Organisation, were just some of the institutions established in Chifley's era. Chifley, as prime minister, had to come to terms with, and deal with these new institutions and approaches to international relations. In the second half of the 1940s, the British Commonwealth also went through a period of modernisation and revival, which again called on heavy prime ministerial involvement. In this era of heightened international cooperation and conflict, Chifley was well equipped to lead Australia.

Chifley had long been 'an ardent advocate of all international organisations'.[1] Far from the traditional view of Chifley as a pipe-smoking prime minister who was only comfortable dealing with domestic issues, because world affairs were left to his External Affairs minister, Dr HV Evatt, this book has detailed his sophisticated understanding of international finance and trade and his active involvement in his government's foreign policy. Furthermore, Chifley drew upon a well-developed and clearly thought through concept of internationalism, which provided a coherent source for his government's policies and actions in international affairs. The origins of this internationalism can be traced to his lived experience: his rural background; his experience of economic depressions and world wars and his commitment to the labour movement and to the Australian Labor Party.

Growing up and living in a rural area like Bathurst, Chifley was well aware that Australia was dependent on world trade; because of this, he viewed the Australian economy within the context of the world economic system. Although not a pacifist, Chifley believed that war was to be avoided at all cost. He had consistently condemned the massive expenditure on World War I, in which 'a great reserve of wealth had been used up almost entirely for destructive purposes'.[2] Chifley's experience of world war and economic depression meant that he understood the need for fundamental changes in the global economic system to prevent future depressions and wars. The interdependence of the countries of the world was made very real to him. In Chifley's words, 'No one can live alone; we are all dependent on each other'.[3] His commitment to the labour movement was not confined to Australian workers, but included workers globally. He believed that economic stability needed to be established after World War II so that future generations could be assured of prosperity for all.[4] This could only be achieved by collaboration in international organisations and 'adherence to universal laws and institutions instead of the crude exercise of power relations'.[5] Chifley understood that no nation was self-sufficient or isolated; instead, nations were part of an international society and economy.

Chifley's speeches have been used extensively in this book, to demonstrate how his experiences and beliefs formed his view of the world in which he lived. Many of his speeches—in parliament, to constituent groups of the Australian Labor Party, and to local community groups—were printed verbatim in the Bathurst newspaper, the *National Advocate*. This local newspaper has provided an extraordinarily rich source of evidence that has been used to trace the evolution of Chifley's internationalism. Through studying Chifley's early speeches, we have seen that his interest in international affairs can be traced back to World War I. By the early 1930s he was a respected expert on international relations in his Bathurst community. It is also apparent that Chifley's internationalism had a very definite economic dimension.

The development of Chifley's expertise in international finance and economic policy during the inter-war years can be seen in his speeches in parliament, at political meetings and to local Bathurst groups. His ongoing interest in international affairs and the international monetary system is evident in his speeches to groups such as the Bathurst Rotarians and the Advance Bathurst League. He followed the many international conferences held in the inter-war years on finance and monetary policy, disarmament, reparations and war debts and kept up-to-date with all the latest reports published by the League of Nations. Chifley's expertise was further extended in his role as a commissioner on the Royal Commission into the Monetary and Banking System where his grasp of high finance was acknowledged, as were his leadership skills.

Chifley also understood that for a government to be able to implement policy, political solidarity was essential. As a member of the Scullin government—which had such high hopes when it came to office in the election of October 1929, but collapsed because of its own internal warring factions—Chifley knew the importance of loyalty, cohesion and solidarity in a political party. His bitter experience of the disunity that brought down the Scullin government meant that loyalty and solidarity to the Labor Party became a driving force in his later political life.

Chifley's experience of the Great Depression, his work as a commissioner on the Royal Commission into Australia's Monetary and Banking System, his own self-education in economics and finance, and the advice he received from the network of brilliant intellectuals and advisers he gathered around him, meant he developed a coherent view of the world economy. He understood that a rules-based international monetary system needed to be established to prevent a return to the economic chaos of the inter-war years. This led him to embark on a lengthy campaign to persuade his own party, and the nation, of the need to join the new post-war international economic institutions. In his effort to gain both caucus and cabinet support for the Australian government to ratify the Bretton Woods Agreement, Chifley proved to be a remarkable 'example of a political craftsman'.[6] In addition, his experience of two world wars meant that he was a staunch supporter of the United Nations on security and foreign policy issues.

Many previous accounts of Chifley have situated him within the domestic realm and have paid little attention to his interest in international affairs and the evolution of his internationalist world view. This book has shown that Chifley, together with HV Evatt and John Burton, were the three architects of Australia's foreign policy in the immediate post-war years. In many instances, especially in formulating Australia's foreign policy on Asia, Chifley, rather than Evatt, was the dominant force. In any differences in opinion between the prime minister and his minister for External Affairs, Chifley's 'vetoes were final'.[7] He had the 'capacity to rein Evatt in whenever he felt it necessary'.[8] Chifley kept in close contact with Australian diplomats, who were 'impressed by his grasp of complex issues and by his ability to give immediate answers to impromptu questions', but he took great pains not to undermine Evatt's authority as minister for External Affairs.[9]

Historians such as Christopher Waters and David Lee have acknowledged Chifley's deep involvement in his government's foreign policy, but the sources of Chifley's internationalism have not been explored.[10] Other historians, such as David Day, have situated him mainly within the domestic sphere, with most of his attention focused on the 'reconstruction' of post-war Australia.[11] James Curran, in part inspired by historian Neville Meaney's work in which 'British race patriotism' was central to Australia's self-image, argues that Australian prime ministers since 1901 had 'largely told the story of Australia as a white British enclave searching for security in an unfamiliar Asian-Pacific world'.[12] This is not so in the case of the Chifley government, which looked for security *within* its region, but not *from* its region. Like many of his generation, Chifley shared a sentimental attachment to Britain. This Britishness might well have been 'the dominant strand of Australian identity' in the 1940s,[13] but it is a mistake to use it as an over-arching categorisation to explain the efforts of a Labor leader such as Chifley to understand and negotiate

Australia's place in a post-war world in which internationalism, decolonisation and the Cold War took primacy over an older British world, which was in decline.

Chifley's internationalism was not just a form of Britishness: it was much more than this. Chifley condemned those European powers, such as the British in India, who had taken 'untold millions of wealth' which had 'flowed' out of India to Europe. The poverty and exploitation that existed in cities such as Calcutta made his 'blood boil', as he told 'Nugget' Coombs during their visit there in 1946.[14] Similarly, as he said in the House of Representatives on 2 September 1948, the many Europeans who went to Malaya went there for profit, 'not for love of the country'—a comment that infuriated the Menzies Opposition.[15] As Christopher Waters notes, there were 'profound differences in policy and attitude between the Labor and non-Labor parties' in the post-war period. These differences 'cannot be explained away as alternative manifestations of an identification with Britishness', differing only in the manner in which it was expressed.[16] David Lowe has also shown—in his study of conservative rhetoric—that in the Menzies Opposition's fierce criticism of the Chifley government's foreign policy, conservatives constantly accused Labor of abandoning 'the organic ideal of the Empire/Commonwealth and Australia's role therein'.[17]

Despite these charges of disloyalty to the Commonwealth ideal, Chifley and others thought that the Commonwealth could act as an example to the rest of the world. Nehru shared this view, although he had long fought the British in the struggle for India's independence. Both leaders understood that World War II had brought about a 'complete political and economic reorientation' in the world.[18] Chifley was a great admirer of Nehru, who 'exercised a deep influence on him'.[19] In Nehru, Chifley received inspiration and a validation of his own beliefs. Chifley believed that—and here he was very much in agreement with Nehru—nationalism, not communism, was the driving force of events in post-war Asia. Chifley was deeply disturbed at the West's support of corrupt and feudalistic forms of government in the crusade against communism.[20] Both Chifley and Nehru refused to accept the Anglo-American Cold War view of world affairs.[21]

Chifley was a key architect in the Australian government's bold new approach to a decolonising Asia. He refused to allow the Dutch to establish military and naval bases in Australia to support their attempt to reinstate their colonial empire in Indonesia. As acting minister for External Affairs, he referred the conflict between the Indonesian republicans and the Dutch to the United Nations. He supported a republican India in its desire to remain a member of the Commonwealth, and British government requests for Australian troops to be deployed in Malaya and Hong Kong in 1948 and 1949 were rejected. In addition, although it was a 'difficult' issue to support, as Chifley said in parliament, he had always advocated that the 'victorious nations should immediately commence the task of building up the economic strength' of ex-enemy countries.[22] This was a long-held belief of his.

At the 1946 Commonwealth Prime Ministers' conference, Chifley expressed concern at Allied policy towards Germany. He believed a policy of retribution was not the way to reconstruct the European economy. If this path was chosen, he said, it was inevitable that further conflicts would arise in the future.[23] Similarly, although public opinion towards Japan in the immediate post-war years was a retributive one, Chifley was concerned about the possibility of a resurgence of militarism if the Japanese economy did not recover. For that reason, he supported land reform and democratisation measures in Japan. He believed that economic recovery was vital to ensure post-war peace and prosperity in the world. A policy of revenge against former enemies would be counter-productive, leading to further international instability, a return to the disastrous inter-war period when world trade collapsed, resulting in the economic devastation of the Great Depression. These were all bold decisions, vehemently opposed by the Menzies Opposition and most of the Australian media.

As historian David Lowe has noted, the Chifley government was unique in its refusal to view the post-war world through the lens of Cold War politics, which divided the world into two polarised camps.[24] Unlike the Menzies Opposition, Chifley and his government refused to conflate the rise of Asian nationalist movements with communist insurgency. Chifley saw the dangers of a world divided into two power blocs. He rejected the simplistic notion that all the turmoil of the post-war years could be attributed to communism. As a result, he opposed the formation of the Western Union, Britain's 'anti-Soviet strategy for western Europe'.²⁵ Chifley believed that foreign policy should be based on justice and the 'permanent settlement of disputes' through the United Nations,²⁶ rather than 'policies of strategy and expedience',²⁷ which would only lead to ongoing conflict.²⁸ Chifley rejected the use of power politics, arguing that 'secret alliances' should be avoided.²⁹ Instead, he placed his trust in working through the United Nations on security and foreign policy issues, citing the Australian government's policy towards Indonesia as a successful demonstration of 'the value of standing by principle despite seemingly strategic or other doubtful interests'.³⁰ Because of these beliefs, Chifley refused to send Australian forces into colonial conflicts in Southeast Asia. In fact, Chifley's sentiments were very similar to those of political scientist, William Macmahon Ball, as expressed in *Nationalism and Communism in East Asia*, published in 1952.³¹ Ball, in particular, opposed the 'attempted imposition of the Cold War policy template' on nationalist movements that had local support, one example of which was the Indochina conflict.³² Ball was unconvinced that military force would contain these uprisings. Like Chifley, he was fiercely critical of how the West attempted to use 'Western puppets' whose regimes had no local support.³³

There was a shared understanding between Chifley and advisers such as Ball that European and British colonial power in Asia was in rapid decline, and that the Pacific War had brought enormous change to the region. As Chifley stated in his 'Report to the Nation' on 21 November 1948, Australia was 'directly concerned with the great region of Asia and the Far East'. But this was 'not the Asia of pre-war days', but an Asia in which newly independent states had been established. It was an 'Asia in which vigorous nationalism is bringing new changes almost every day'.³⁴ There was also a shared belief that the best way to defeat communism was through improved living conditions, not through military force; and a rejection of the Cold War framework through which change in Asia was viewed by the US and British governments.³⁵

Chifley was Australia's prime minister for a brief period, from 1945 to 1949, yet his significance goes far beyond that short period in office would suggest. Chifley's contribution to the wider national life lay in his 'belief in the emergent future', and his ability to see that momentous change was occurring in the post-war world—that the old colonial world was ending.[36] The comments of well-known international relations scholar JDB (Bruce) Miller are particularly apt here. Miller had studied economics part-time at the University of Sydney from 1939. After a brief period in military service, he worked at the Australian Broadcasting Service as a reporter at Parliament House, where he developed a high regard for both John Curtin and Ben Chifley.[37] Miller noted in his review of Crisp's biography of Chifley that the ex-train driver had an exceptional receptivity to 'new ideas and to the impact of new conditions'. According to Miller, Crisp had depicted the Chifley who was

> the one known both to his closest associates and to casual acquaintances: a man of great capacity and sympathy, capable of generating intense loyalty in those around him; commanding in his grasp of a Prime Minister's work, yet accessible to old friends and to anyone with a serious matter to bring before him.[38]

Miller added that Crisp had brought out Chifley's 'occasional rigidity and insensitivity to the tides of public opinion, his absorption in administration, his aspects of anti-intellectualism, the times when he veered towards sharp practice in the internal politics of the Labor movement'. And yet, Miller noted, there was 'more *wholeness* about him than about any of the other Prime Ministers; he was not a very complicated man, though he was a highly interesting one'.[39] Miller was pleased at 'seeing Chifley's fine character so well depicted'. He wondered at how Chifley was able to survive the 'morass of New South Wales politics in the 1920s and 30s, apparently unaffected in his morality and serene in his confidence in the Labor movement'. Miller wondered, too, 'at his breadth of outlook, in contrast with the narrowness and sectarianism of so many of his contemporaries'.[40]

Because of his receptiveness to 'new ideas and to the impact of new conditions',[41] and his rejection of 'ordinary petty … parish-pump' politics,[42] Chifley developed a far-sighted vision of Australia's future. This meant that he and his government took a bold new approach to Australian foreign policy. A policy driven by a belief in a global rules-based order built on principles of justice, equity and the permanent settlement of disputes through international collaboration, secured through the multilateral institutions of the United Nations. Economic security would be achieved through the implementation of the Bretton Woods Agreement, a new rules-based international economic order that would promote 'economic cooperation and collaboration' amongst the nations of the world.[43] These international organisations were 'designed to prevent the catastrophes that result from wars and financial and economic depressions'. In Chifley's words, through these organisations, 'we are engaging in a great human experiment'.[44]

Notes
1. *CPD*, HoR, 20 March 1947, p. 1002.
2. 'World Problems', *National Advocate* (Bathurst, NSW), 19 October 1932.
3. JB Chifley, 'They Think They Can Go Back to the Old Order: Well, They Cannot', speech to federal ALP conference, 30 September 1948, in *Things Worth Fighting For*, p. 38.
4. *CPD*, HoR, 20 March 1947, p. 1003.
5. Pitty and Leach, 'Australian Nationalism and Internationalism', p. 99.
6. Weller, *Cabinet Government in Australia, 1901–2006*, p. 80.
7. Edwards, *Prime Ministers and Diplomats*, p. 173.
8. Edwards with Pemberton, *Crises and Commitments*, p. 6.
9. Edwards, *Prime Ministers and Diplomats*, p. 173.
10. Waters, *Empire Fractures*, p. 113; Lee, *Search for Security*, p. 75.
11. Day, *Chifley*, p. 423.
12. Curran, *The Power of Speech*, p. 4.
13. Christopher Waters, 'Nationalism, Britishness and Australian History: The Meaney Thesis Revisited', *History Australia*, vol. 10, no. 3, 2013, p. 22.
14. Coombs, *Trial Balance*, p. 77.
15. *CPD*, HoR, 2 September 1948, p. 65.
16. Waters, 'Nationalism, Britishness and Australian History', p. 20.
17. David Lowe, 'Driving a Labor line: Conservative Constructions of Labor's Foreign Policy, 1944–49', in Lee and Waters (eds), *Evatt to Evans: The Labor Tradition in Australian Foreign Policy*, p. 63.
18. Chifley, 'Clear Cut Decisions', in *Things Worth Fighting For*, p. 369.
19. 'Leadership of Mr. Chifley—Strong Influence On Party', *Sydney Morning Herald*, 14 June 1951, p. 2.
20. *CPD*, HoR, 27 September 1950, p. 24.
21. Lowe, *Menzies and the Great World Struggle*, p. 14.
22. *CPD*, HoR, 2 September 1948, p. 63.
23. Minutes of Meetings of Dominion Prime Ministers London 1946, 9th Meeting, 1 May 1946, p. 3. NAA: A5954, 258/2.
24. Lowe, *Menzies and the 'Great World Struggle'*, p. 14.
25. Waters, *The Empire Fractures*, p. 109.
26. Top secret and personal message, Chifley to Attlee, 22 January 1948, p. 2, NAA: A1838, TS78/7.

27. ibid., p. 3.
28. ibid., p. 2.
29. ibid., p. 3.
30. ibid., p. 4.
31. W Macmahon Ball, *Nationalism and Communism in East Asia*, Melbourne University Press, Carlton, Victoria, 1952.
32. Cotton, *The Australian School of International Relations*, p. 181.
33. Ball, *Nationalism and Communism*, p. 203.
34. 'Asia and the Far East', Report to the Nation by the Prime Minister, No. 11, 21 November 1948, p. 1. NAA: A1838, 380/1/9.
35. Lowe, *Menzies and the 'Great World Struggle'*, p. 14.
36. Stargardt, 'Introduction', in *Things Worth Fighting For*, p. 9.
37. James Cotton, 'In Memorium: JDB Miller', *Australian Journal of International Affairs*, vol. 65, no. 2, 2011, p. 143.
38. JDB Miller, 'Reviews. *Ben Chifley: A Biography*. By LF Crisp', *Historical Studies: Australia and New Zealand*, vol. 10, no. 39, 1962, p. 381.
39. ibid.
40. ibid., p. 382.
41. ibid., p. 381.
42. *CPD*, HoR, 26 February 1948, p. 253.
43. Ann Capling, Australia and the Global Trade System: From Havana to Seattle, Cambridge University Press, UK, 2001, p. 2.
44. JB Chifley, 'Bretton Woods—A Great Human Experiment', in Things Worth Fighting For, p. 146.

Bibliography

PRIMARY SOURCES

Government Records (National Archives of Australia)
Cabinet Secretariat (CA 3)
A2700 Curtin, Forde and Chifley Ministries—folders of Cabinet minutes and agendas, 1941–49.
A2703 Curtin, Forde and Chifley Ministries—folders of Cabinet minutes, 1941–49.
A3264 Scullin Ministry—folders of typed copies of Cabinet minutes, 1929–1931.

Prime Minister's Department (CA 12)
A461   Correspondence files 1934–50.
M1455 Correspondence of Joseph Benedict Chifley as Prime Minister.

Department of the Treasury [I] (CA 11)
A571   Correspondence files

Department of External Affairs (CA 18)
A1066 Correspondence files, 1945.
A1067 Correspondence files, 1946.
A1068 Correspondence files, 1947.
A1838 Correspondence files, 1945–1948.

A1838   Correspondence files, 1948–
A1838   Correspondence files, 1948–1952.

Department of External Affairs, London (CA 1759)
A3317   Correspondence files, 1945–47.
A3318   Correspondence files, 1948–50.

Department of Defence [III] (CA 46)
A816   Correspondence files.
A5954   Records collected by Sir Frederick Shedden during his career with the Department of Defence.

War Cabinet Secretariat (CA 1468)
A2671   War Cabinet agenda files, 1939–46.
A2676   War Cabinet Minutes Without Agenda files, 1939–1946.

Department of Post-War Reconstruction, Central Office (CA49)
M2271   Folders of documentation collected by Arthur Tange (later Sir Arthur) as an Australian representative participating in United Nations and British Commonwealth negotiations concerned with post World War II economic and social reconstruction.

Department of Post-War Reconstruction, Central Office (CA 49)
A9790   Correspondence files.

Rural Reconstruction Commission (CA 245)
A6189   Correspondence relating to the preparation of Reports 1943–1948.

Department of Commerce and Agriculture (CA 48)
A606   Correspondence Files 'R' (Research and Reconstruction) Series.

Australian Legation, United States of America [Washington] (CA 1831)
A3300   Correspondence files, 1940–46.

Australian Embassy, Washington (CA 1817)
A3300   Correspondence files, 1946–48.

Australian Legation, Republic of China [Chungking/Nanking] (CA 1978)
A4144   Correspondence files 1941–1949.

Australian Commission, Malaya (CA 2950)
A4968   Correspondence files.

Australian Consulate-General, Bangkok, [Thailand] (CA 2783)
A5019   Correspondence files, 1948–1956.

National Archives of Australia (CA 8540)
B5459   Digest of [Commonwealth Government] decisions and announcements, and important speeches by the Prime Minister (The Rt Hon. John Curtin and the Rt Hon. JB Chifley).

Dr Herbert Cole Coombs (CP 119)
M448   Research material, drafts and papers directly associated with Dr Coombs' autobiography—'Trial Balance' (1981).

Secretary to Cabinet/Cabinet Secretariat [I] (CA 3)
A11099 Cabinet Notebooks Sep 25 Aug 1950–27 Nov 1995.

Government Records (The National Archives of the United Kingdom)
Foreign Office
FO 371   General Correspondence files.
FO 800/434-522 Bevin: Private Office papers.

Prime Minister's Office
PREM 8   Attlee's Private Office correspondence and papers, 1945–51.

Other British Government Papers
CAB 129   Cabinet memoranda, 1945–51.
CAB 130   Ad-Hoc Committees: General and miscellaneous series.

Published Official Records
Foreign Relations Records—Australia
Documents on Australian Foreign Policy 1937–49:
——*Volume VIII: 1945*, Hudson, WJ, and Way, Wendy (eds), Australian Government Publishing Service, Canberra, 1989.
——*Volume IX: January–June 1946*, Hudson, WJ, and Way, Wendy (eds), Australian Government Publishing Service, Canberra, 1991.
——*Volume X: July–December 1946*, Hudson, WJ, and Way, Wendy (eds), Australian Government Publishing Service, Canberra, 1993.
——*Volume XI: Indonesia 1947*, Dorling, Philip (ed.), Australian Government Publishing Service, Canberra, 1994.

——*Volume XII: 1947*, Hudson WJ, and Way, Wendy (eds), Australian Government Publishing Service, Canberra, 1995.
——*Volume XIII: Indonesia 1948*, Dorling, Philip, and Lee, David (eds), Australian Government Publishing Service, Canberra, 1996.
——*Volume XIV: The Commonwealth, Asia and the Pacific 1948–49*, Andre, Pamela (ed.), Department of Foreign Affairs and Trade, Canberra, 1998.
——*Volume XV: Indonesia 1949*, Lee, David (ed.), Department of Foreign Affairs and Trade, Canberra, 1998.
——*Volume XVI: Beyond the Region 1948–49*, Andre, Pamela (ed.), Department of Foreign Affairs and Trade, Canberra, 2001.
Soft cover volumes of *Documents on Australian Foreign Policy 1937–49* under the title of *Australia and Indonesia's Independence:*
——*Diplomasi: Australia and Indonesia's Independence, Documents 1947*, Dorling, Philip (ed.), Australian Government Publishing Service, Canberra, 1994.
——*Australia and Indonesia's Independence: The Renville Agreement, Documents 1948*, Dorling, Philip, and Lee, David (eds), Australian Government Publishing Service, Canberra, 1996.

Others—Australia
Commonwealth of Australia, *Royal Commission Appointed to Inquire into the Monetary and Banking Systems at Present in Operation in Australia, Minutes of Evidence*, vols. I and II, Commonwealth Government Printer, Canberra, 1936.
Commonwealth of Australia, *Report of the Royal Commission Appointed to Inquire into the Monetary and Banking Systems at Present in Operation in Australia*, Commonwealth Government Printer, Canberra, 1937.
Chifley, JB, *A Rural Policy for Post-War Australia*, Bureau of Agricultural Economics, Canberra, 1946.
Rural Reconstruction Commission, *Tenth Report. Commercial Policy in Relation to Agriculture*, Australian Government Printer, Canberra, 1946.

Foreign Relations Records—United States of America
United States Department of State, *Foreign Relations of the United States: Diplomatic Papers 1940. The Far East*, vol. IV, United States Government Printing Office, Washington, 1940. http://digital.library.wisc.edu/1711.dl/FRUS.FRUS1940v04 (accessed 8 November 2013).
——*Foreign Relations of the United States: Diplomatic Papers 1944. The British Commonwealth and Europe*, vol. III, United States Government Printing Office, Washington, 1944. http://digital.library.wisc.edu/1711.dl/FRUS.FRUS1944v03 (accessed 9 May 2013).
——*Foreign Relations of the United States: Diplomatic Papers 1945. The British Commonwealth, the Far East*, vol. VI. United States Government Printing Office, Washington, 1945. http://digital.library.wisc.edu/1711.dl/FRUS.FRUS1945v06 (accessed 8 November 2013).

———*Foreign Relations of the United States: Diplomatic Papers 1946. General: The United Nations*, vol. 1. United States Government Printing Office, Washington, 1946. http://digital.library.wisc.edu/1711.dl/FRUS. FRUS1946v01 (accessed 10 October 2014).
———*Foreign Relations of the United States: Diplomatic Papers 1948. The Far East and Australasia*, vol. VI. United States Government Printing Office, Washington, 1948. http://digital.library.wisc.edu/1711.dl/FRUS. FRUS1948v06 (accessed 3 May 2013).
———*Foreign Relations of the United States: Diplomatic Papers 1949. The Far East and Australasia*, vol. VII, part 1. United States Government Printing Office, Washington, 1949. http://digital.library.wisc.edu/1711.dl/FRUS. FRUS1949v07p1 (accessed 6 November 2013).
———*Foreign Relations of the United States: Diplomatic Papers 1949. The Far East and Australasia*, vol. VII, part 2. United States Government Printing Office, Washington, 1949. http://digital.library.wisc.edu/1711.dl/FRUS. FRUS1949v07p2 (accessed 3 May 2013).

National Library of Australia
Private Papers
Papers of William Macmahon Ball, National Library of Australia: MS 7851.
Reports of Harold Cox, National Library of Australia: MS 4554.
Papers of LF Crisp, National Library of Australia: MS 5243.
Papers of WD Forsyth, National Library of Australia: MS 5700.
Papers of Lyndhurst F Giblin, National Library of Australia: MS 366.
Papers of DK Rodgers, National Library of Australia: MS 1536.
Papers of EG Theodore, National Library of Australia: MS 7222.

Oral Histories
Burton, Dr John Wear—Interview by Michael J Wilson, 1995, National Library of Australia: ORAL TRC 2981/23.
Critchley, TK—Interview by Michael Wilson, 1993, National Library of Australia: ORAL TRC 2981/7.
Dedman, John Johnstone—Interview by Hazel de Berg, 1967, National Library of Australia: ORAL TRC 1/322–326.
Dunk, William—Interview by Mel Pratt, 1971, National Library of Australia: ORAL TRC 121/16.
Heydon, Peter—Interview by Mel Pratt, 1970, National Library of Australia: ORAL TRC 121/2.
Kirby, Richard—Interview by Margaret George, 1972, National Library of Australia: ORAL TRC 202.
Melville, Leslie—Interview by Alan Hodgart, 1973, National Library of Australia: ORAL TRC 182.
Reid, Alan—Interview by Mel Pratt, 1972–73, National Library of Australia: ORAL TRC 121/40.
Rodgers, Donald Kilgour—Interview by Mel Pratt, 1971, National Library of Australia: ORAL TRC 121/14.

Sawer, Geoffrey—Interview by Mel Pratt, 1971–1972, National Library of Australia: ORAL TRC 121/32.

University of Melbourne Archives
Private Papers
Papers of RM Crawford, University of Melbourne Archives, 91/113.

Film Australia
HC 'Nugget' Coombs—Interview by Robin Hughes, 22–24 January 1992, Film Australia transcript, unpaginated. http://www.australianbiography.gov.au/subjects/coombs/ (accessed 12 March 2011).

Parliamentary Records
Commonwealth Parliamentary Debates, House of Representatives, 1928–1951.

Published Primary Sources
Chifley, JB, 'Reconstruction After The War', *Public Administration*, vol. 111, no. 3, September 1941, pp. 103–108.

——'Planning for Peace: 1. Employment Chief Aim', *Sydney Morning Herald*, Wednesday, 1 December, 1943.

——'Planning the Peace: 11. International Co-operation', *Sydney Morning Herald*, Thursday, 2 December, 1943.

——'Planning For Peace: 111. Social Security Scheme', *Sydney Morning Herald*, Friday, 3 December, 1943.

Crawford, John G, *Australian Trade Policy 1942–1966: A Documentary History*, ANU Press, Canberra, 1968.

Guha, Ramachandra (ed.), *Makers of Modern India*, Belknap Press of Harvard University Press, Cambridge, MA, 2011.

Nehru, J, *Selected Works of Jawaharlal Nehru*, Second Series, Volume 7, S Gopal (ed.), Jawaharlal Nehru Memorial Fund, New Delhi, 1988.

——*Selected Works of Jawaharlal Nehru*, Second Series, Volume 8, S Gopal (ed.), Jawaharlal Nehru Memorial Fund, New Delhi, 1989.

——*Selected Works of Jawaharlal Nehru*, Second Series, Volume 9, S Gopal (ed.), Jawaharlal Nehru Memorial Fund, New Delhi, 1990.

——*Selected Works of Jawaharlal Nehru*, Second Series, Volume 10, S Gopal (ed.), Jawaharlal Nehru Memorial Fund, New Delhi, 1990.

——*Selected Works of Jawaharlal Nehru*, Second Series, Volume 11, S Gopal (ed.), Jawaharlal Nehru Memorial Fund, New Delhi, 1991.

Rix, Alan (ed.), *Intermittent Diplomat: The Japan and Batavia Diaries of W Macmahon Ball*, Melbourne University Press, Carlton, Victoria, 1988.

Shann, EOG, and Copland, DB (eds), *The Battle of the Plans: Documents Relating to the Premiers' Conference, May 25th to June 11th, 1931*, Angus and Robertson, Sydney, 1931.

Things Worth Fighting For: Speeches by Joseph Benedict Chifley, selected and arranged by AW Stargardt, Australian Labor Party, Melbourne, 1953.

Weller, Patrick (ed.), assisted by Beverley Lloyd, *Caucus Minutes 1901–1949: Minutes of the Meetings of the Federal Parliamentary Labor Party, Volume 3, 1932–1949*, Melbourne University Press, Carlton, Victoria, 1975.

Weller, Patrick, and Lloyd, Beverley, (eds), *Federal Executive Minutes 1915–1955: Minutes of the Federal Executive of the Australian Labor Party*, Melbourne University Press, Carlton, Victoria, 1978.

Memoirs

Coombs, HC, *Trial Balance*, Macmillan, Melbourne, 1981.

Denning, Warren, *James Scullin: Prime Minister of Australia 1929–1932*, with Introduction by Frank Moorhouse, Black Inc., Melbourne, 2000.

Hasluck, Paul, *Diplomatic Witness: Australian Foreign Affairs, 1941–1947*, Melbourne University Press, Carlton, Victoria, 1980.

Lyons, Dame Enid, *Among the Carrion Crows*, Rigby, Adelaide, 1972.

Speeches by Chifley

Speeches to Community Groups

Speech to the Bathurst Rotarians on 'War Reparations Problem' on 19 July 1932. Reported in *National Advocate*, (Bathurst, NSW), 20 July 1932.

Speech to the Advance Bathurst League on 'World Problems—Economics and Unemployment' on 18 October 1932. Reported in *National Advocate*, (Bathurst, NSW), 19 October 1932.

Speech to the Bathurst Methodist Men's Brotherhood on 'The Roosevelt Plan and What It Aims to Achieve', on 3 September 1933. Reported in *National Advocate*, (Bathurst, NSW), 4 September 1933.

Speech to the Bathurst Apex Club on 'The Banking Commission'. Reported in *National Advocate*, (Bathurst, NSW), 4 February 1938.

Speech to Bathurst Rotarians on 'The Banking Commission'. Reported in *National Advocate*, (Bathurst, NSW), 2 June 1938.

Speech to Bathurst Rotarians on 'Banking Commission —Mr JB Chifley's Views'. Reported in *National Advocate*, (Bathurst, NSW), 24 June 1938.

Speeches to Political Groups

Election speech in Richmond on 9 October 1929. Reported in *National Advocate*, (Bathurst, NSW), 10 October 1929.

Speech to ALP Macquarie District Assembly on 28 February 1931. Reported in *Sydney Morning Herald*, 3 March 1931.

Speech to Macquarie District Assembly on 27 April 1931. Reported in the *Sydney Morning Herald*, 28 April 1931.

Speech to the Bathurst federal ALP branch on 17 August 1931. Reported in the *National Advocate*, (Bathurst, NSW), 19 August 1931.

Public address in Lithgow on 21 August 1931. Reported in the *Sydney Morning Herald*, 22 August 1931.

Election campaign launch at Walshaw Hall in Bathurst on 1 December 1931. Reported in the *National Advocate*, (Bathurst, NSW), 2 December 1931.

Election speech in Portland on 4 December 1931. Reported in the *National Advocate*, (Bathurst, NSW), 5 December 1931.

Election speech in Penrith on 7 December 1931. Reported in the *National Advocate*, (Bathurst, NSW), 8 December 1931.

Election speech in Rockley on 15 December 1931. Reported in the *National Advocate*, (Bathurst, NSW), 16 December 1931.

Election eve speech in Bathurst on 18 December 1931. Reported in the *National Advocate*, (Bathurst, NSW), 19 December 1931.

Declaration of election result on 8 January 1932. Reported in the *National Advocate*, (Bathurst, NSW), 9 January 1932.

Speech at a re-union of the Bathurst branch of the Municipal and Shire Employees' Union on 'World Problems', on 17 December 1932. Reported in *National Advocate*, (Bathurst, NSW), 19 December 1932.

Speech to Bathurst federal ALP branch on 18 December 1933. Reported in *National Advocate*, (Bathurst, NSW), 19 December 1933.

Speech to Bathurst federal ALP branch on 'The Roosevelt Plan' on 15 March 1934. Reported in *National Advocate*, (Bathurst, NSW), 16 March 1934.

Speech to launch the Martin by-election campaign. Reported in *National Advocate*, (Bathurst, NSW), 30 June 1934.

Election campaign launch with radio broadcast on 9 August 1934. Reported in *Sydney Morning Herald*, 10 August 1934.

State policy speech on 23 April 1935 when Chifley contested the state seat of Auburn against the leader of the Opposition, JT Lang. Reported in *National Advocate*, (Bathurst, NSW), 24 April 1935.

Speech in support of Labor candidate, Alderman MJ Griffin, in Bathurst on 26 April 1935. Reported in *National Advocate*, (Bathurst, NSW), 27 April 1935.

Speech at a Bathurst Trades and Labor Council social to celebrate May Day. Reported in *National Advocate*, (Bathurst, NSW),1 May 1939.

Speech to Melbourne Trade Union Conference on 8 June 1944. Reported in *Sydney Morning Herald*, 9 June 1944.

Speech to the Lithgow Citizen's Committee on 15 July 1945. Reported in *Advertiser*, (Adelaide), 16 July 1945.

Speech to the Macquarie District Assembly on 15 July 1945. Reported in *Advertiser*, (Adelaide), 16 July 1945.

Notes to the Labor caucus on 4 March 1947. See 'Bretton Woods', Issued by the Prime Minister (Mr Chifley), n.d., in the papers of Dr HC Coombs, National Archives of Australia: M448, 120.

Speech to the annual conference of the New South Wales' branch of the ALP on 15 June 1947. 'This Is A Country Of Freedom Of Expression', in *Things Worth Fighting For: Speeches by Joseph Benedict Chifley*, selected and arranged by AW Stargardt, (ALP ed.), Melbourne, 1953, pp. 22–27.

Speech to the annual conference of the New South Wales' branch of the ALP on 12 June 1948. 'These Things are Really Worth Fighting For' in AW Stargardt (ed.) in *Things Worth Fighting For*, pp. 27–34.

Speech to the ALP triennial federal conference on 30 September 1948. 'They Think They Can Go Back to the Old Order: Well, They Cannot', in *Things Worth Fighting For*, pp. 34–38.

Address to the federal executive of the Australian Labor Party in Canberra on 11 May 1949 in Patrick Weller (ed.), *Federal Executive Minutes 1915–1955, Minutes of the Meetings of the Federal Executive of the Australian Labor Party*, Melbourne University Press, Carlton, Victoria, 1978, pp. 392–393.

Speech as Leader of the Opposition, in the Second Reading Debate on the Commonwealth Bank Bill on 28 March 1950. 'Big Business Always Hated the Commonwealth Bank' in *Things Worth Fighting For*, pp. 304–322.

Address to the federal conference of the Australian Labor Party in Canberra on 2 March 1951, 'Clear-Cut Decisions', in *Things Worth Fighting For*, pp. 369–371.

Speeches in the Australian Parliament, House of Representatives
Commonwealth Parliamentary Debates, House of Representatives, 1928–1951.

Contemporary Newspapers and Journals
Advertiser (Adelaide).
Age.
Argus.
Australian Quarterly.
Australian Worker.
Canberra Times.
Herald (Melbourne).
Morning Bulletin (Rockhampton, Queensland).
National Advocate (Bathurst, NSW).
Pacific Islands Monthly.
Round Table.
Sunday Tribune (Ambala, India).
Sydney Morning Herald.
West Australian.
Worker (Brisbane).

SECONDARY SOURCES
Books
Ahamed, Liaquat, *Lords of Finance: The Bankers who broke the World*, Penguin Press, New York, 2009.

Albinski, Henry S, *Australian Policies and Attitudes Toward China*, Princeton University Press, Princeton, New Jersey, 1965.

Andrews, EM, *A History of Australian Foreign Policy*, 2nd edn, Longman Cheshire, Melbourne, 1988.

Appleyard, RT, and Schedvin, CB (eds), *Australian Financiers: Biographical Essays*, Macmillan, South Melbourne, 1998.

Asian Relations: Being Report of the Proceedings and Documentation of the First Asian Relations Conference, New Delhi, March–April, 1947, Asian Relations Organization, New Delhi, 1948.

Ball, W Macmahon, *Japan: Enemy or Ally?* Cassell, Melbourne, 1948.

——*Nationalism and Communism in East Asia*, Melbourne University Press, Carlton, Victoria, 1952.

Beaumont, Joan, Waters, Christopher, Lowe, David, with Woodard, Garry (eds), *Ministers, Mandarins and Diplomats: Australian Foreign Policy Making 1941–1969*, Melbourne University Press, Carlton, Victoria, 2003.

Bell, Roger, *Unequal Allies: Australian-American Relations and the Pacific War*, Melbourne University Press, Carlton, Victoria, 1977.

Bennett, Jnr, Frank C, *The Return of the Exiles: Australia's Repatriation of the Indonesians, 1945–1947*, Monash Asia Institute, Monash University Press, Clayton, Victoria, 2003.

Bennett, Scott, *JB Chifley*, Oxford University Press, Melbourne, 1973.

Bolton, Geoffrey, *The Oxford History of Australia, Volume 5, 1942–1995: The Middle Way*, 2nd edn, Oxford University Press, Melbourne, 1996.

Brown, Judith M, *Nehru: A Political Life*, Yale University Press, New Haven, CT, 2003.

Butlin, S, and Schedvin, CB, *War Economy, 1942–45*, Australian War Memorial, Canberra, 1977.

Cain, Neville, *Economists and the Monetary Commission of 1936: Ideas and Circumstances*, Australian National University Working Papers in Economic History, No. 120, Canberra, 1988.

Campbell, DAS (ed.), *Post-War Reconstruction in Australia*, Australasian Publishing Co. Pty Ltd, in association with Australian Institute of Political Science, Sydney, 1944.

Capling, Ann, *Australia and the Global Trade System: From Havana to Seattle*, Cambridge University Press, UK, 2001.

Capling, Ann, Considine, Mark, and Crozier, Michael, *Australian Politics in the Global Era*, Longman, South Melbourne, 1998.

Chapman, Ivan, *Iven G Mackay Citizen and Soldier*, Melway Publishing, Melbourne, 1975.

Clark, Colin, *Australian Hopes and Fears*, Hollis & Carter, London, c1958.

Clavin, Patricia, *Securing the World Economy: The Reinvention of the League of Nations, 1920–1946*, Oxford University Press, Oxford, 2013.

Cockburn, Stewart, and Ellyard, David, *Oliphant: The Life and Times of Sir Mark Oliphant*, Axiom Books, Adelaide, 1981.

Connor, John, Stanley, Peter, and Yule, Peter, *The War at Home: The Centenary History of Australia and the Great War, Volume 4*, Oxford University Press, South Melbourne, 2015.

Coombs, HC, *Trial Balance*, Macmillan, South Melbourne, 1981.

Conway, Ed, *The Summit*, Abacus, London, 2014.

Copland, DB, *Inflation and Expansion: Essays on the Australian Economy*, FW Cheshire, Melbourne, 1951.

——(ed.), *Giblin: The Scholar and the Man*, FW Cheshire, Melbourne, 1960.

Cornish, Selwyn, *Sir Leslie Melville: An Interview*, Working Papers in Economic History, Working Paper No. 173, Australian National University, Canberra, June 1993.
——*The Evolution of Central Banking in Australia*, Reserve Bank of Australia, Sydney, 2010.
Cotton, James, *The Australian School of International Relations*, Palgrave Macmillan, New York, 2013.
Cotton, James, and Lee, David (eds), *Australia and the United Nations*, Department of Foreign Affairs and Trade, Barton, ACT, c2012.
Crisp, LF, *Ben Chifley: A Biography*, Longmans, London, n.d.
Crockett, Peter, *Evatt: A Life*, Oxford University Press, Oxford, 1993.
Curran, James, *The Power of Speech: Australian Prime Ministers Defining the National Image*, Melbourne University Press, Carlton, Victoria, 2004.
Damousi, Joy, *Memory and Migration in the Shadow of War: Australia's Greek Immigrants After World War II and the Greek Civil War*, Cambridge University Press, Cambridge, UK, 2015.
Davis, Steve, *Rise Like Lions: The Hijacking of Australian History*, Ginninderra Press, Charnwood, ACT, 2000.
Day, David, *Chifley*, HarperCollins, Pymble, NSW, 2001.
de Matos, Christine, *Imposing Peace and Prosperity: Australia, Social Justice and Labour Reform in Occupied Japan*, Australian Scholarly Publishing, North Melbourne, 2008.
Denning, Warren, *James Scullin*, Black Inc., Melbourne, 2000.
Dunk, William, *They Also Serve*, privately published, Canberra, 1974.
Dyster, Barrie, and Meredith, David, *Australia in the International Economy in the Twentieth Century*, Cambridge University Press, UK, 1990.
Edwards, John, *Curtin's Gift: Reinterpreting Australia's Greatest Prime Minister*, Allen & Unwin, Crows Nest, NSW, 2005.
Edwards, PG, *Prime Ministers and Diplomats: The Making of Australian Foreign Policy, 1901–1949*, Oxford University Press, Melbourne, 1983.
Edwards, Peter, with Pemberton, Gregory, *Crises and Commitments: The Politics and Diplomacy of Australia's Involvement in Southeast Asian Conflicts 1948–1965*, Allen & Unwin, North Sydney, 1992.
Eggleston, FW, *Reflections of an Australian Liberal*, FW Cheshire, Melbourne, 1953.
Ellis, Bob, and McLachlan, Robin, *A Local Man: A Play about Ben Chifley*, Currency Press, Sydney, 2005.
Evans, LT, and Miller, JDB (eds), *Policy and Practice; Essays in Honour of Sir John Crawford*, Australian National University Press, Sydney, 1987.
Faulkner, John, and Macintyre, Stuart (eds), *True Believers: The Story of the Federal Parliamentary Labor Party*, Allen & Unwin, Crows Nest, NSW, 2001.
Firth, Stewart, *Australia in International Politics: An Introduction to Australian Foreign Policy*, Allen & Unwin, St Leonards, NSW, 1999.
George, Margaret, *Australia and the Indonesian Revolution*, Melbourne University Press, Carlton, Victoria, 1980.
Gerster, Robin, *Travels in Atomic Sunshine: Australia and the Occupation of Japan*, Scribe, Carlton North, Victoria, 2008.

Gettleman, Marvin E (ed.), *Vietnam: History, Documents and Opinions on a Major World Crisis*, Penguin Books, Ringwood, Victoria, 1965.

Giblin, LF, *The Growth of a Central Bank: The Development of The Commonwealth Bank of Australia, 1924–1945*, Melbourne University Press, Carlton, Victoria, 1951.

Goldsworthy, David (ed.), *Facing North. A Century of Australian Engagement with Asia Volume 1: 1901 to the 1970s*, Melbourne University Press, Carlton South, Victoria, 2001.

Gopal, Sarvepalli, *Jawaharlal Nehru: A Biography*, (abridged edn), Oxford University Press, Delhi, 1993.

Grattan, Michelle (ed.), *Australian Prime Ministers*, New Holland, Sydney, 2000.

Greenwood, Gordon (ed.), with the assistance of Pamela Bray, *Approaches to Asia: Australian Postwar Policies and Attitudes*, McGraw-Hill, Sydney, 1974.

Groenewegen, Peter, and McFarlane, Bruce, *A History of Australian Economic Thought*, Routledge, London, 1990.

Gurry, Meg, *India: Australia's Neglected Neighbour? 1947–1996*, Centre for the Study of Australia-Asia Relations, Griffith, Queensland, 1996.

——*Australia and India: Mapping the Journey 1944–2014*, Melbourne University Press, Carlton, Victoria, 2015.

Hall, Peter A (ed.), *The Political Power of Economic Ideas: Keynesianism Across Nations*, Princeton University Press, New Jersey, 1989.

Harper, Marjorie, *Douglas Copland: Scholar, Economist, Diplomat*, Miegunyah Press, Carlton, Victoria, 2013.

Hasluck, Paul, *The Government and the People, 1942–45*, Australian War Memorial, Canberra, 1970.

Haylen, Leslie, *Blood on the Wattle: A Play of the Eureka Stockade*, with a Foreword by The Rt Hon. JB Chifley, Angus and Robertson, Sydney, 1948.

——*Twenty Years' Hard Labor*, Macmillan of Australia, South Melbourne, 1969.

Horner, David, *The Spy Catchers: The Official History of ASIO. Volume One, 1949–1963*, Allen & Unwin, Sydney, 2014.

Hudson, WH, *Australia and the New World Order: Evatt at San Francisco 1945*, Australian National University, Canberra, 1993.

Iriye, Akira, *Cultural Internationalism and World Order*, Johns Hopkins University Press, Baltimore, 1997.

Jones, Barry, *A Thinking Reed*, Allen & Unwin, Crows Nest, NSW, 2008.

Kennedy, David M, *Freedom from Fear: The American People in Depression and War, 1929–1945*, Oxford University Press, New York, 1999.

King, JE (ed.), *A Biographical Dictionary of Australian and New Zealand Economists*, Edward Elgar Publishing, Cheltenham, UK, c2007.

Kobayashi, Ai, *W Macmahon Ball: Politics for the People*, Australian Scholarly Publishing, North Melbourne, Victoria, 2013

Langmore, Dianne, *Prime Ministers' Wives: The Public and Private Lives of Ten Australian Women*, McPhee Gribble, Ringwood, Victoria, 1992.

Legge, John (ed.), *New Directions in Australian Foreign Policy: Australia and Indonesia 1945–50*, Monash Asia Institute, Clayton, Victoria, 1997.

Lee, David, *Search for Security: The Political Economy of Australia's Postwar Foreign and Defence Policy*, Allen & Unwin, St Leonards, NSW, 1995.
——*Australia and the World in the Twentieth Century*, Circa, Beaconsfield, Victoria, 2006.
——*Stanley Melbourne Bruce: Australian Internationalist*, Continuum, London, 2010.
Lee, David, and Waters, Christopher (eds), *Evatt to Evans: The Labor Tradition in Australian Foreign Policy*, Allen & Unwin, Sydney, 1997.
Leffler, Melvyn P, *A Preponderance of Power: National Security, the Truman Administration, and the Cold War*, Stanford University Press, Stanford, CA, c1992.
Leffler, Melvyn P, and Painter, David S (eds), *Origins of the Cold War: An International History*, Routledge, London, 1994.
Lowe, David (ed.), *Australia and the End of Empires: The Impact of Decolonisation in Australia's Near North 1945–1965*, Deakin University Press, Geelong, Victoria, 1996.
——*Menzies and the 'Great World Struggle': Australia's Cold War 1948–1954*, University of New South Wales Press, Sydney, 1999.
——*Australian Between Empires: The Life of Percy Spender*, Pickering & Chatto, London, 2010.
Love, Peter, *Labour and the Money Power: Australian Labour Populism 1890–1950*, Melbourne University Press, Carlton, Victoria, 1984.
McGarr, Paul M, *The Cold War in South Asia: Britain, the United States and the Indian Subcontinent 1945–1965*, Cambridge University Press, UK, 2013.
Macintyre, Stuart, *The Oxford History of Australia, Volume 4, 1901–1942*, Oxford University Press, Melbourne, 1986.
——*Australia's Boldest Experiment: War and Reconstruction in the 1940s*, Newsouth, Sydney, 2015.
McKercher, BJC, *Transition of Power: Britain's Loss of Global Pre-eminence to the United States, 1930–1945*, Cambridge University Press, New York, 1999.
McLean, Ian W, *Why Australia Prospered: The Shifting Sources of Economic Growth*, Princeton University Press, Princeton, New Jersey, 2013.
McMullin, Ross, *The Light on the Hill: The Australian Labor Party 1891–1991*, Oxford University Press, Melbourne, 1991.
Malloy, Sam (ed.), *Chifley Oral Project: A Collection of Oral History Interviews Focusing on the Lives of Ben and Elizabeth Chifley in Bathurst*, Funded by the National Council for the Centenary of Federation, 2002.
Meredith, David, and Dyster, Barrie, *Australia in the Global Economy: Continuity and Change*, Cambridge University Press, Cambridge, UK, 1999.
Millmow, Alex, *The Power of Economic Ideas: The Origins of Keynesian Macroeconomic Management in Interwar Australia 1929–39*, ANU E Press, Canberra, 2010.
Mills, RC, and Walker, Ronald E, *Money*, 7th edn, Angus and Robertson, Sydney, 1941.
Moore, RJ, *Making the New Commonwealth*, Claremont Press, Oxford, 1987.
Osborne, Milton, *Southeast Asia: An Introductory History*, 9th edn, Allen & Unwin, Crows Nest, NSW, 2004.

Osmond, Warren G, *Frederic Eggleston: An Intellectual in Australian Politics*, Allen & Unwin, North Sydney, 1985.
Pemberton, Gregory, *All the Way: Australia's Road to Vietnam*, Allen & Unwin, Sydney, 1987.
Raghavan, Srinath, *War and Peace in Modern India*, Palgrave Macmillan, Basingstoke, UK, 2010.
——*India's War: The Making of Modern South Asia 1939–1945*, Penguin Books, London, UK, 2017.
Renouf, Alan, *Let Justice be Done: The Foreign Policy of Dr HV Evatt*, University of Queensland Press, St Lucia, Queensland, c1983.
Reynolds, David, *One World Divisible: A Global History since 1945*, Penguin Books, London, 2000.
Rix, Alan, *Coming to Terms: The Politics of Australia's Trade with Japan 1945–57*, Allen & Unwin, Sydney, 1986.
Rose, Mavis, *Indonesia Free: A Political Biography of Mohammad Hatta*, Cornell Modern Indonesia Project, Cornell University, Ithaca, NY, 1987.
Rosecrance, RN, *Australian Diplomacy and Japan, 1945–1951*, Melbourne University Press, Parkville, Victoria, 1962.
Rowse, Tim, *Nugget Coombs: A Reforming Life*, Cambridge University Press, Cambridge, UK, 2002.
Ryan, Peter, *Brief Lives*, Duffy and Snellgrove, Potts Point, NSW, 2004.
Sands, Philippe, *Lawless World: Making and Breaking Global Rules*, Penguin Books, London, UK, 2006.
Schedvin, CB, *Australia and the Great Depression: A Study of Economic Development and Policy in the 1920s and 1930s*, Sydney University Press in association with Oxford University Press, Sydney, 1970.
——*In Reserve: Central Banking in Australia, 1945–75*, Allen & Unwin, St Leonards, NSW, 1992.
——*Emissaries of Trade: A History of the Australian Trade Commissioner Service*, Department of Foreign Affairs and Trade, Barton, ACT, 2008.
Sheridan, Tom, *Division of Labour: Industrial Relations in the Chifley Years 1945–1949*, Oxford University Press, Melbourne, 1989.
Sloan, Clyde, *A History of the Pharmaceutical Benefits Scheme 1947–1992*, Commonwealth of Australia, Australian Government Printing Service, 1995.
Sluga, Glenda, *Internationalism in the Age of Nationalism*, University of Pennsylvania Press, PA, 2013.
Smyth, Paul, *Australian Social Policy: The Keynesian Chapter*, UNSW Press, Sydney, 1994.
Souter, Gavin, *Acts of Parliament: A Narrative History of the Senate and the House of Representatives Commonwealth of Australia*, Melbourne University Press, Carlton, Victoria, 1988.
Spratt, Elwyn, *Eddie Ward: Firebrand of East Sydney*, Rigby, Adelaide, 1965.
Stargardt, AW, *Australia's Asian Policies: The History of a Debate 1839–1972*, The Institute of Asian Affairs in Hamburg, Germany, 1977.
Tennant, Kylie, *Evatt: Politics and Justice*, Angus and Robertson, Sydney, 1970.

Thompson, John, *Five to Remember*, Lansdowne, Melbourne, 1964.
Tosh, John, *The Pursuit of History: Aims, Methods, and New Directions in the Study of Modern History*, 3rd ed., Longman, London, 2002.
Ward, EE, *Land Reform in Japan 1946–1950, the Allied Role*, Nobunkyo, Tokyo, 1990.
Waters, Christopher, *The Empire Fractures: Anglo-Australian Conflict in the 1940s*, Australian Scholarly Publishing, Melbourne, 1995.
Weller, Patrick, *Australia's Mandarins: The Frank and the Fearless?* Allen & Unwin, Crows Nest, NSW, 2001.
——*Cabinet Government in Australia, 1901–2006: Practice, Principles, Performance*, UNSW Press, Sydney, 2007.
Whitington, Don, *The Rulers: Fifteen Years of the Liberals*, rev. edn, Cheshire-Lansdowne, Melbourne, 1965.
——*Twelfth Man?* Jacaranda Press, Milton, Queensland, 1972,
Whitwell, Greg, *The Treasury Line*, Allen & Unwin, Sydney, 1986.
Williamson, Philip, *Stanley Baldwin: Conservative Leadership and National Values*, Cambridge University Press, Cambridge, 1999.

Journal Articles and Book Chapters

ACT Regional Study Group, 'Commonwealth Policy Co-ordination', *Australian Journal of Public Administration* 14, 1955, pp. 193–213.
Bailey, KH, 'Dependent Areas of the Pacific: An Australian View', *Foreign Affairs*, vol. 24, no. 3, 1946, pp. 494–512.
Ball, W Macmahon, 'Preface', in WGK Duncan (ed.), *Australia's Foreign Policy*, Angus and Robertson, Sydney, 1938.
Beaumont, Joan, 'Making Australian Foreign Policy 1941–69, in Joan Beaumont, Christopher Waters, and David Lowe with Garry Woodard (eds), *Ministers, Mandarins and Diplomats: Australian Foreign Policy Making 1941–1969*, Melbourne University Press, Carlton, Victoria, 2003.
Bell, Roger, 'Testing the Open Door Thesis in Australia, 1941–1946', *Pacific Historical Review*, vol. 51, no. 3, 1982, pp. 283–311.
Beresford, M, and Kerr, P, 'A Turning Point for Australian Capitalism, 1942–52', in E Wheelright, and K Buckley (eds), *Essays in the Political Economy of Australian Capitalism, Volume 4*, Australia and New Zealand Book Company, Sydney, 1980.
Bhagavan, Manu, 'A New Hope: India, the United Nations and the Making of the Universal Declaration of Human Rights', *Modern Asian Studies*, vol. 44, no. 2, 2010, pp. 311–347.
Bolton, Geoffrey, 'Duncan Waterson: A Lapidary Historian', in Paul Ashton, and Bridget Griffen-Foley (eds), 'From the Frontier: Essays in Honour of Duncan Waterson', special joint issue of *Journal of Australian Studies*, no. 69, and *Australian Cultural History*, no. 20, 2001, pp. 9–16.
——'The Art of Australian Political Biography', in Tracey Arklay, John Nethercote, and John Wanna (eds), *Australian Political Lives: Chronicling Political Careers and Administrative Histories*, ANU E Press, Canberra, c2006.

Bongiorno, Frank, 'Commonwealthmen and Republicans: Dr HV Evatt, the Monarchy and India', *Australian Journal of Politics and History*, vol. 46, no. 1, 2000, pp. 33–55.

——'"British to the Bootstraps?" HV Evatt, JB Chifley and Australian Policy on Indian Membership of the Commonwealth, 1947–49', *Australian Historical Studies*, vol. 37, issue 125, 2005, pp. 18–39.

——'The Price of Nostalgia: Menzies, the "Liberal" Tradition and Australian Foreign Policy', *Australian Journal of Politics and History*, vol. 51, no. 3, 2005, pp. 400–417.

——'John Beasley and the Postwar World' in Carl Bridge, Frank Bongiorno, and David Lee (eds), *The High Commissioners: Australia's Representatives in the United Kingdom, 1910–2010*, Department of Foreign Affairs and Trade, Canberra, 2010.

——'Herbert Vere Evatt and British Justice: The Communist Party Referendum of 1951', *Australian Historical Studies*, vol. 44, no. 1, 2013, pp. 54–70.

Breen, Harold, 'JB Chifley', *Twentieth Century*, March 1974, pp. 226–245.

Brown, Nicholas, 'Review of Kim E Beazley's Father of the House and Ashley Hogan's Moving in the Open Daylight', in *History Australia*, vol. 6, no. 3, 2009, pp. 82.1–82.3.

Burton, JW, 'Review of Ben Chifley: A Biography, by LF Crisp', in *Bulletin of the Australian Society for the Study of Labour History*, no. 2, May, 1962, pp. 94–96.

——'Indonesia: Unfinished Diplomacy', in John Legge (ed.), *New Directions in Australian Foreign Policy: Australia and Indonesia 1945–50*, Monash Asia Institute, Clayton, Victoria, 1997.

Butlin, SJ, 'The Banking Commission's Report', *Australian Quarterly*, September 1937, pp. 40–50.

——'Richards Charles Mills', *Economic Record*, vol. 29, November, 1953, pp. 177–188.

Butlin, NG, and Gregory, RG, 'Trevor Winchester Swan 1918–1989', *Economic Record*, vol. 65, December, 1989, pp. 369–377.

Capling, Ann, 'The "Enfant Terrible": Australia and the Reconstruction of the Multilateral Trade System, 1946–8', *Australian Economic History Review*, vol. 40, no. 1, 2000, pp. 1–21.

Clavin, Patricia, and Wessels, Jens-Wilhelm, 'Another Golden Idol? The League of Nations' Gold Delegation and the Great Depression, 1929–1932', *International History Review*, vol. 26, no. 4, 2004, pp. 765–795.

'Commonwealth Relations: The Commonwealth Conference', *The Round Table: The Commonwealth Journal of International Affairs*, vol. 43, 1952, pp. 359–363.

Cotton, James, 'In Memorium: JDB Miller', *Australian Journal of International Affairs*, vol. 65, no. 2, 2011, pp. 143–147.

——'Australia in the League of Nations: Role, debates, presence', in James Cotton, and David Lee (eds), *Australia and the United Nations*, Department of Foreign Affairs and Trade, Barton, ACT, c2012.

Crawford, JG, 'Australia as a Pacific Power', in WGK Duncan (ed.), *Australia's Foreign Policy*, Angus and Robertson, Sydney, 1938.

Critchley, TK, 'View from the Good Offices Committee', in John Legge (ed.), *New Directions in Australian Foreign Policy: Australia and Indonesia 1945–50*, Monash Asia Institute, Clayton, Victoria, 1997.

Crozier-De Rosa, Sharon, and Lowe, David, 'Introduction: Nationalism and Transnationalism in Australian Historical Writing', *History Australia*, vol. 10, no. 3, 2013, pp. 7–11.

Darwin, John, 'Decolonisation and World Politics', in David Lowe (ed.), *Australia and the End of Empire: The Impact of Decolonisation in Australia's Near North, 1945–1965*, Deakin University Press, Geelong, Victoria, 1996.

Dedman, John J, 'The practical application of collective responsibility', *Politics*, vol. 3, no. 2, 1968, pp. 148–162.

Deery, Phillip, 'Communism, Security and the Cold War', *Journal of Australian Studies*, vol. 21, no. 54, 1997, pp. 162–175.

de Matos, Christine, 'Encouraging "Democracy" in a Cold War Climate: The Dual-Platform Policy Approach of Evatt and Labor Toward the Allied Occupation of Japan 1945–1949', *Pacific Economic Papers*, no. 313, March, 2001, pp. 1–30.

——'Diplomacy Interrupted?: Macmahon Ball, Evatt and Labor's Policies in Occupied Japan', *Australian Journal of Politics and History*, vol. 52, no. 2, 2006, pp. 188–201.

Dennis, Peter, 'Australia and Indonesia: The early years', in David Lowe (ed.), *Australia and the End of Empires: The Impact of Decolonisation in Australia's Near North 1945–1965*, Deakin University Press, Geelong, Victoria, 1996.

Dingman, Roger, 'The View from Down Under: Australia and Japan, 1945–1952', in Thomas W Burkman (ed.), *The Occupation of Japan: The International Context*, MacArthur Memorial Foundation, Norfolk, VA. 1984.

Drysdale, Peter, 'The Relationship with Japan: Despite the Vicissitudes', in Evans LT, and Miller, JDB (eds), *Policy and Practice: Essays in Honour of Sir John Crawford*, Australian National University Press, Sydney, 1987.

Dutton, David, 'An Alternate Course in Australian Foreign Policy 1943–50', *Australian Journal of Politics and History*, vol. 43, no. 2, 1997, pp. 153–167.

Dymock, Darryl, and Billett, Stephen, 'Skilling Australians: Lessons from World War II National Workforce Development Programs', *Australian Journal of Adult Learning*, vol. 50, no. 3, 2010, pp. 468–496.

Edwards, PG, 'On Assessing HV Evatt', *Historical Studies*, vol. 21, no. 83, 1984, pp. 258–269.

——'The Australian commitment to the Malayan emergency, 1948–1950', *Historical Studies*, vol. 22, no. 89, 1987, pp. 604–616.

——'The Origins of the Cold War', in Carl Bridge (ed.), *Munich to Vietnam: Australia's Relations with Britain and the United States since the 1930s*, Melbourne University Press, Carlton, Victoria, 1991.

Eichengreen, Barry, and Temin, Peter, 'The Gold Standard and the Great Depression', *Contemporary European History*, vol. 9, issue 2, 2000, pp. 183–207.

Eichengreen, Barry, and Uzan, Marc, 'The 1933 World Economic Conference as an Instance of Failed International Cooperation', in Peter B Evans, Harold K Jacobson, and Robert D Putnam (eds), *Double-Edged Diplomacy: International Bargaining and Domestic Politics*, University of California Press, Berkeley, CA, c1993.

Fettling, David, 'JB Chifley and the Indonesian Revolution, 1945–1949', *Australian Journal of Politics and History*, vol. 59, issue 4, 2013, pp. 517–531.

—— 'An Australian Response to Asian Decolonisation: Jawaharlal Nehru, John Burton and the New Delhi Conference of Non-Western Nations', *Australian Historical Studies*, vol. 45, issue 2, 2014, pp. 202–219.

Gifford, Peter, 'The Cold War across Asia', in David Goldsworthy (ed.), *Facing North. A Century of Australian Engagement with Asia Volume 1: 1901 to the 1970s*, Melbourne University Press, Carlton South, Victoria, 2001.

Harper, ND, 'Australian policy towards Japan', *Australian Outlook*, vol. 1, no. 4, 1947, pp. 14–24.

Henderson, Anne, 'Joseph Aloysius Lyons', in Michelle Gratten (ed.), *Australian Prime Ministers*, New Holland, Sydney, 2000.

Howard, Michael, 'The Curtin-Chifley Governments: an Ideal Collective Capitalist State?' in *A Century of Social Change*, Pluto Press, Leichhardt, NSW, 1992.

Iriye, Akira, 'The Transnational Turn', *Diplomatic History*, vol. 31, no. 3, 2007, pp. 373–376.

—— 'Environmental History and International History', *Diplomatic History*, vol. 24, no. 4, 2008, pp. 643–646.

Isaac, JE, 'The Macmahon Ball Mission November 1945', in John Legge (ed.), *New Directions in Australian Foreign Policy: Australia and Indonesia 1945–50*, Monash Asia Institute, Clayton, Victoria, 1997.

Johnson, C, 'Social Harmony and Australian Labour: The Role of Private Industry in the Curtin and Chifley Governments' Plans for Australian Economic Development', *Australian Journal of Politics and History*, vol. 32, no. 1, 1986, pp. 39–51.

Kennedy, KH, 'EG Theodore', in RT Appleyard and CB Schedvin (eds), *Australian Financiers: Biographical Essays*, Macmillan, South Melbourne, 1988.

Lee, David, 'Protecting the Sterling Area: The Chifley Government's Response to Multilateralism 1945–9', *Australian Journal of Political Science*, vol. 25, 1990, pp. 178–195.

—— 'The 1949 Federal Election: A Reinterpretation', *Australian Journal of Political Science*, vol. 29, no. 3, 1994, pp. 501–519.

—— 'Britain and Australia's Defence Policy, 1945–1949', *War and Society*, vol. 13, no. 1, 1995, pp. 61–80.

—— 'Indonesia's Independence', in David Goldsworthy (ed.), *Facing North. A Century of Australian Engagement with Asia Volume 1: 1901 to the 1970s*, Melbourne University Press, Carlton South, Victoria, 2001.

—— 'Australia and the Security Council', in James Cotton and David Lee (eds), *Australia and the United Nations*, Department of Foreign Affairs and Trade, Barton, ACT, c2012.

Leffler, Melvyn P, 'National Security and US Foreign Policy', in Melvyn P Leffler, and David S Painter (eds), *Origins of the Cold War: An International History*, Routledge, London, 1994.

Love, Peter, 'Frank Anstey and the Monetary Radicals' in RT Appleyard, and CB Schedvin (eds), *Australian Financiers: Biographical Essays*, Macmillan, South Melbourne, 1988.

Lowe, David, 'Driving a Labor Line: Conservative constructions of Labor's foreign policy, 1944–49', in David Lee, and Christopher Waters (eds), *Evatt to Evans: The Labor Tradition in Australian Foreign Policy*, Allen & Unwin, Sydney, 1997.

——'Brave New Liberal: Percy Spender', *Australian Journal of Politics and History*, vol. 51, no. 3, 2005, pp. 389–399.

——'Introduction', *Australian Journal of Politics and History*, vol. 51, no. 3, 2005, pp. 327–331.

McCooey, David, and Lowe, David, 'Autobiography in Australian Parliamentary First Speeches', *Biography*, vol. 33, no. 1, 2010, pp. 68–83.

Macintyre, Stuart, 'The Post-War Reconstruction Project', in Samuel Furphy (ed.), *The Seven Dwarfs and the Age of the Mandarins: Australian Government Administration in the Post-War Reconstruction Era*, Australian National University Press, Canberra, 2015.

Mackenzie, Hector, 'An Old Dominion and the New Commonwealth: Canadian Policy on the Question of India's Membership, 1947–49', *The Journal of Imperial and Commonwealth History*, vol. 27, no. 3, 1999, pp. 82–112.

McLean, David, 'Australia in the Cold War: A Historiographical Review', *The International History Review*, vol. 23, no. 2, 2001, pp. 299–321.

McMullin, Ross, 'Joseph Benedict Chifley', in Michelle Grattan (ed.), *Australian Prime Ministers*, New Holland, Sydney, 2000.

Maddox, Graham, and Battin, Tim, 'Australian Labor and the Socialist Tradition', *Australian Journal of Political Science*, vol. 26, July, 1991, pp. 189–196.

Martin, AW and Penny, Janet, 'The Rural Reconstruction Commission 1943–47', *Australian Journal of Politics and History*, vol. 29, no. 2, 1983, pp. 218–236.

Meaney, Neville, 'Australia, the Great Powers and the Coming of the Cold War', *Australian Journal of Politics and History*, vol. 38, issue 3, 1992, pp. 316–333.

——'Britishness and Australian Identity: The Problem of Nationalism in Australian History and Historiography', *Australian Historical Studies*, vol. 32, no. 116, 2001, pp. 76–90.

——'Dr HV Evatt and the United Nations: The Problem of Collective Security and Liberal Internationalism', in James Cotton and David Lee (eds), *Australia and the United Nations*, Department of Foreign Affairs and Trade, Barton, ACT, c2012.

Miller, JDB, 'Australian Public Opinion: The Bretton Woods Controversy', *The Australian Outlook*, vol. 1, issue 3, 1947, pp. 31–41.

——'Reviews. *Ben Chifley: A Biography*. By LF Crisp', in *Historical Studies: Australia and New Zealand*, vol. 10, no. 39, 1962, pp. 381–382.

——'The Man', in LT Evans and JDB Miller, (eds), *Policy and Practice; Essays in Honour of Sir John Crawford*, Australian National University Press, Sydney, 1987.

Millmow, Alex, 'The Power of Economic Ideas: Australian Economists in the Thirties', *History of Economics Review*, vol. 37, Winter, 2003, pp. 84–99.

——'Australian Economics in the Twentieth Century', *Cambridge Journal of Economics*, vol. 29, 2005, pp. 1011–1026.

Moravcsik, Andrew, 'Introduction: Integrating International and Domestic Theories of International Bargaining', in Peter B Evans, Harold K Jacobson, and Robert D Putnam (eds), *Double-Edged Diplomacy: International Bargaining and Domestic Politics*, University of California Press, Berkeley, CA, c1993.

Packer, Gerald, 'The Asian Relations Conference: The Group Discussions', *Australian Outlook*, vol. 1, no. 2, 1947, pp. 3–7.

Painter, David S, and Leffler, Melvyn P, 'Introduction: The International System and the Origins of the Cold War', in Melvyn P Leffler, and David S Painter (eds), *Origins of the Cold War: An International History*, Routledge, London, 1994.

Pemberton, Gregory, 'An Imperial Imagination: Explaining the Post-1945 Foreign Policy of Robert Gordon Menzies' in Frank Cain (ed.), *Menzies in Peace and War*, Allen & Unwin, Sydney 1997.

Pitty, Roderic, and Leach, Michael, 'Australian Nationalism and Internationalism', in Paul Boreham, Geoffrey Stokes, and Richard Hall (eds), *The Politics of Australian Society: Political Issues for the New Century*, 2nd edn, Pearson Education, Frenchs Forrest, NSW, 2004.

Reynolds, David, 'Empire, Region, World: The International Context of Australian Foreign Policy since 1939', *Australian Journal of Politics and History*, vol. 51, no. 3, 2005, pp. 346–358.

Rix, Alan, 'Macmahon Ball and the Allied Council for Japan: The Limits of an Australian Diplomacy under Evatt', *Australian Outlook*, vol. 42, no. 1, 1988, pp. 21–28.

Schaffer, BB, 'Review of LF Crisp, Ben Chifley: A Biography', in *Journal of Commonwealth Political Studies*, vol. 2, no. 2, 1963, pp. 172–173.

Schedvin, CB, 'Australia and Article VII-A Comment', *Australian Economic History Review*, vol. 18, no. 1, 1978, pp. 75–77.

'Sir John Crawford: Profile of a public servant and economist', *History of Economics Review*, no. 32, Summer, 2000, Supplement, pp. 18–30.

Smith, Shannon L, 'Towards Diplomatic Representation', in David Goldsworthy (ed.), *Facing North: A Century of Australian Engagement with Asia. Volume 1: 1901 to the 1970s*, Melbourne University Press, Carlton South, Victoria, 2001.

Stargardt, AW, 'Introduction', in *Things Worth Fighting For: Speeches by Joseph Benedict Chifley*, selected and arranged by AW Stargardt, (ALP ed), Melbourne, 1953.

——'The Emergence of the Asian System of Powers', *Modern Asian Studies*, vol. 23, no. 3, 1989, pp. 561–595.

Stargardt, Nicholas, 'Children and the Holocaust: An Interview with Nicholas Stargardt', *Limina Interview*, vol. 6, 2000, pp. 2–14.

Stephens, David., 'Three Labor Veterans Look Back', *Australian Quarterly*, vol. 46, no. 3, 1974, pp. 84–89.

——'The Effect of the Great Depression on the Federal Labor Governments, 1941–49', *Australian Journal of Politics and History*, vol. XXII, no. 2, 1976, pp. 258–270.

Stone, Julius, 'Peace Planning and the Atlantic Charter', *Australian Quarterly*, vol. 14, no. 2, 1942, pp. 5–22.

Suares, Julie, 'Engaging with Asia: The Chifley Government and the New Delhi Conferences of 1947 and 1949', *Australian Journal of Politics and History*, vol. 57, no. 4, 2011, pp. 495–510.

Tange, Arthur, 'Plans for the World Economy: Hopes and Reality in Wartime Canberra. A Personal Memoir', *Australian Journal of International Affairs*, vol. 50, no. 3, 1996, pp. 259–267.

Turnell, Sean, 'Australia's "Employment Approach" to International Postwar Reconstruction: Calling the Bluff of Multilateralism', *History of Economics Review*, no. 36, Summer, 2002, pp. 111–125.

Valentine, TJ, 'The Causes of the Depression in Australia', *Explorations in Economic History*, vol. 24, no. 1, 1987, pp. 43–62.

Waters, Christopher, 'Conflict with Britain in the 1940s' in David Lowe (ed.), *Australia and the End of Empires: The Impact of Decolonisation in Australia's Near North 1945–1965*, Deakin University Press, Geelong, Victoria, 1996.

——'Creating a Tradition: The Foreign Policy of the Curtin and Chifley Governments', in David Lee, and Christopher Waters (eds), *Evatt to Evans: The Labor Tradition in Australian Foreign Policy*, Allen & Unwin, St. Leonards, NSW, 1997.

——'War, Decolonization and Postwar Security', in David Goldsworthy (ed.), *Facing North: A Century of Australian Engagement with Asia. Volume 1: 1901 to the 1970s*, Melbourne University Press, Carlton South, Victoria, 2001.

——'Review of Wayne Reynolds, *Australia's Bid for the Atomic Bomb*, (2000)', in *Australian Journal of International Affairs*, vol. 56, no. 1, 2002, pp. 164–166.

——'The Great Debates: HV Evatt and the Department of External Affairs, 1941–49', in Joan Beaumont, Christopher Waters, and David Lowe, with Garry Woodard (eds), *Ministers, Mandarins and Diplomats: Australian Foreign Policy Making 1941–1969*, Melbourne University Press, Carlton, Victoria, 2003.

——'Nationalism, Britishness and Australian History: The Meaney Thesis Revisited', *History Australia*, vol. 10, no. 3, 2013, pp. 12–22.

Webb, Leicester, 'The Labour Party and the Future', review of *Things Worth Fighting For: Speeches by Joseph Benedict Chifley*, selected and arranged by AW Stargardt, in *Australian Quarterly*, vol. 25, issue 1, 1953, pp.122–127.

Williams, DB, 'Contributions to Agricultural Economics' in LT Evans and JDB Miller (eds), *Policy and Practice: Essays in Honour of Sir John Crawford*, Australian National University Press, Sydney, 1987.

Woodard, Garry, 'Macmahon Ball's Goodwill Mission to Asia 1948', *Australian Journal of International Affairs*, vol. 49, no. 1, 1995, pp. 129–134.

Yule, Peter, 'Part 1: Economy', in John Connor, Peter Stanley and Peter Yule (eds), *The War at Home: The Centenary History of Australia and the Great War, Volume 4*, Oxford University Press, South Melbourne, 2015.

Australian Dictionary of Biography

Bennett, Scott, 'Crisp, Leslie Finlay (Fin) (1917–1984)', in *Australian Dictionary of Biography*, Volume 17, Melbourne University Press, Carlton, Victoria, 2006, pp. 269–270.

Blaazer, DP, 'Breen, Harold Patrick (1893–1966)', *Australian Dictionary of Biography*, National Centre of Biography, Australian National University, http://adb.anu.edu.au/biography/breen-harold-patrick-9574/text16869 (accessed 5 April 2013).

Farquarson, John, 'Melville, Sir Leslie Galfried (1902–2002)', Obituaries Australia, National Centre of Biography, Australian National University. http://oa.anu.edu.au/obituary/Melville-sir-leslie-galfried-720/text721 (accessed 11 May 2014).

Groenewegen, PD, 'Mills, Richard Charles (1886–1952)', *Australian Dictionary of Biography*, Volume 10, Melbourne University Press, Carlton, Victoria, 1986, pp. 517–519.

Holt, Stephen, 'Reid, Alan Douglas (1914–1987)', *Australian Dictionary of Biography*, National Centre of Biography, Australian National University. http://adb.anu.edu.au/biography/reid-alan-douglas-14435 (accessed 11 May 2014).

Kingsland, Richard, 'Mighell, Sir Norman Rupert (1894–1955)', *Australian Dictionary of Biography*, Volume 15, Melbourne University Press, Carlton, Victoria, 2000, pp. 366–367.

Miller, JDB 'Crawford, Sir John Grenfell (Jack) (1910–1984)', *Australian Dictionary of Biography*, National Centre of Biography, Australian National University, http://adb.anu.edu.au/biography/Crawford-sir-john-grenfell-jack-1391/text22223 (accessed 7 March 2012).

Nairn, Bede, 'Lang, John Thomas (Jack) (1876–1975)', *Australian Dictionary of Biography*, Volume 9, Melbourne University Press, Carlton, Victoria, pp. 661–666.

Osmond, Warren, 'Eggleston, Sir Frederic William (1875–1954)', *Australian Dictionary of Biography*, National Centre of Biography, Australian National University, http://adb.anu.edu.au/biography/eggleston-sir-frederic-william-344/text10409 (accessed 20 January 2014).

Richardson, Jack E, 'Bailey, Sir Kenneth Hamilton (1898–1972)', *Australian Dictionary of Biography*, Volume 13, Melbourne University Press, Carlton, Victoria, 1993, pp. 89–90.

Richardson, Peter, 'Robinson, William Sydney (1876–1963), *Australian Dictionary of Biography*, National Centre of Biography, Australian National University. http://adb.anu.edu.au/biography/robinson-william-sydney-8247/text14441 (accessed 3 October 2014).

Spaull, Andrew, 'Dedman, John Johnstone (1896–1973)', *Australian Dictionary of Biography*, Volume 13, Melbourne University Press, Carlton, Victoria, 1993, pp. 606–607.

Waterson, DB, 'Chifley, Joseph Benedict (Ben) (1885–1951)', *Australian Dictionary of Biography*, Volume 13, Melbourne University Press, Carlton, Victoria, 1993, pp. 412–420.
Wilson, Roland, 'Brigden, James Bristock (Jim) (1887–1950), *Australian Dictionary of Biography*, National Centre of Biography, Australian National University, http://adb.anu.edu.au/biography/brigden-james-bristock-jum-5358/text9061 (accessed 11 May 2014).

Theses

Boyd, Jodie, Conservative Discourse at the Time of the Korean War, 1950–52, PhD thesis, Deakin University, 2005.
Dutton, David H, Australian Foreign Policy towards Korea 1943–1950, BA (Hons) thesis, Macquarie University, 1994.
Kuruppu, Nihal Randolph, An Indian Perspective of the Relationship Between India and Australia, 1947 to 1975: Personalities and Policies, Peaks and Troughs, PhD thesis, Victoria University of Technology, 2000.
Martin, Stephen, Labor and Financial Deregulation: The Hawke/Keating Governments, Banking and New Labor, PhD thesis, University of Wollongong, 1999.
Robinson, Marcus Lawrence, Economists and Politicians: The Influence of Economic Ideas upon Labor Politicians and Governments. 1931–1949, PhD thesis, Australian National University, Canberra, 1986.
Scalmer, Sean, The Career of Class: Intellectuals and the Labour Movement 1942–56, PhD thesis, University of Sydney, 1997.
Sutherlin, Kim, The Struggle for Central Banking in Australia: The Royal Commission of 1935–1937 on the Monetary and Banking Sectors, BEc Hons Thesis, ANU, 1980.
Turnell, Sean, Monetary Reformers, Amateur Idealists and Keynesian Crusaders: Australian Economists' International Advocacy, 1925–1950, PhD thesis, Macquarie University, 1999.

Websites

Day, David, Speech at the National Biography Award Day of Discussion, 23 March 2002. www.sl.nsw.gov.au/about/awards/doc/sessw.pdf (accessed 19 July 2010).
Menzies, The Rt Hon. RG, 'The First Smuts Memorial Lecture', at the University of Cambridge, 16 May 1960, p. 5. http://pmtranscripts.dpmc.gov.au/browse.php?did=183 (accessed 21 June 2014).

The online journal, *Economic Roundup* is published by the Australian Treasury. It can be accessed at: https://treasury.gov.au/?s=Economic+Roundup
Gruen, David, and Clark, Colin, 'What Have We Learnt? The Great Depression in Australia from the Perspective of Today', *Economic Roundup*, Issue 4, 2009, pp. 27–50.
Hawkins, John, 'SM Bruce: The Businessman as Treasurer', *Economic Roundup*, Issue 3, 2009, pp. 71–83.

——'Earle Page: An Active Treasurer', *Economic Roundup*, Issue 4, 2009, pp. 55–67.
——'Ted Theodore: The Proto-Keynesian', *Economic Roundup*, Issue 1, 2010, pp. 91–110.
——'James Scullin: Depression Treasurer', *Economic Roundup*, Issue 2, 2010, pp. 109–116.
——'Menzies: Treasurer in Transition to War', *Economic Roundup*, Issue 1, 2011, pp. 53–58.
——'Percy Spender: An Early Keynesian', *Economic Roundup*, Issue 2, 2011, pp. 149–156.
——'Ben Chifley: The True Believer', *Economic Roundup*, Issue 3, 2011, pp. 103–150.
Henry, Ken, Kissack, Adam, Parkinson, Martin, Peterson, Alice and Taylor, Karen, 'Australia and the International Finance Architecture—60 years on', *Economic Roundup*, Spring, 2003, pp. 69–88.

Index

Pages with illustrations are indicated in **bold** *type.*

Abbott, Joseph Palmer 95, 97
Aersson, Baron Van 147
Alexander, Albert Victor 260
Allied Council for Japan (ACJ) 213–14, 227, 228, 230–1, 232
ALP see Labor Party, Australian
Amalgamated Worker's Association of North Queensland 81
American Banker's Association 126
anti-colonialism see colonialism, end of
arbitration, Chifley's belief in 22, 34, 85, 87, 104, 162–3, 201, 250, 262
Arbitration Court, federal 73, 103–4
arms trade 248, 252
Asia, Chifley's early tour of 35, 144–6
Asia, post-colonial 143–180
   anti-colonialism 143, 171–2, 194, 199, 201–2, 277
   Australian foreign policy 141–210, 258, 276
   Britain and 143, 144, 149, 150, 159, 160–1, 166, 191, 184, 227, 231, 258, 279
   changes in region 152–4, 158–62, 169, 194–204
   Chifley's interest in and knowledge of 11, 18–19, 20, 40, 48, 144–6, 158–9, 160,168–9, 170–2, 183–4, 186–9, 190–1, 192, 194–204, 244
   colonialism *see* colonialism
   communism 11, 18–19, 60, 155, 158–9, 160–1, 162, 163, 165–6, 167, 169, 171, 172, 186, 187,195–6, 197, 198, 201–2, 227, 234, 242, 244, 258, 277, 278, 279
   corrupt regimes 162, 163–6, 169, 198, 277
   decolonisation 20, 153–5, 158, 169, 277–8
   economic conditions and security 159, 196, 197
   independence 5, 40, 143, 144, 146, 148, 157, 161, 167, 169, 170, 171, 172, 181, 193, 199, 202, 231, 258, 277
   intelligence on 153–5
   nationalism in 143–4, 154–5, 157–62, 165–6, 168–9, 182, 258, 278, 279

unrest in 194–204
see also India; Indonesia; Japan; Vietnam
Asian Relations Conference New Delhi (1947) 154, 158, 182–3, 198–9
ASIO (Australian Security Intelligence Organisation) 39
Atlantic Charter 41, 199–200, 219
Attlee, Clement, and his government 16, 25, 50, 188, 189–90, **211**, 214–15, 257, 258
   Indonesia 149, 155, 156, 188–9
   India 184, 185, 186, 188, 189–90
   and Chifley on the Western Union proposal 242–56
   Chifley's 1948 London visit 259–62
Australian Federated Union of Locomotive Enginemen (AFULE) 33, 47
Australian Institute of International Affairs (AIIA) 153, 154, 158
Australian Institute of Political Science (AIPS) 153, 158, 221
Australian Labor Party *see* Labor Party, Australian
Australian National University 39, 52
'Australian School' of international relations 23

Ball, William Macmahon 23, 220, 279
   Allied Council for Japan 213, 227–31, 232
   Indonesian mission 150–3, 158, 171, 198–9, 227
   mission to Southeast and East Asia 154, 157–158, 169, 198–9
Bank Interest Bill (1931) 82
banks and banking 40, 100, 225
   Chifley on 80–1, 99–102
   Great Depression 80–1, 82–83
   independent central 77–8, 95, 97
   see also central banks; Commonwealth Bank
Banking Act 37
Beasley, John (Jack) 78, 85, 96, 256
Bell, Roger 115–116

Beaumont, Joan 170
Bevin, Ernest 25, 241, 242, 256, 259, 260, 261–2
Bhagavan, Manu 199–200, 201
Blakeley, Arthur 52
Bolton, Geoffrey 8, 145, 146
Bongiorno, Frank 188, 190–1, 193
Breen, Harold 10, 54–5
   on Chifley 254–5
Bretton Woods Agreement
   achieving ratification in Australia 117–135, 276
   benefits for Australia 124–9
   Chifley's caucus speech 25, 123–9
   Chifley's support for 22–3, 115–17, 123–35, 273, 276, 281
   delegation, Australian 116, 118–119, 125–6, 128
   institutions created by 113, 114–15, 118, 119, 124–5, 129, 134, 273
   invitation 114–115, 118
   limitations created 127
   opposition 118, 119, 120–9, 130, 134–5
   purpose 92, 114–15, 124–5, 126–7, 131
   ratification, Australia's 9, 24, 39–40, 117, 120–3
   withdrawal, possibility of 128
   see also International Monetary Fund (IMF); International Bank for Reconstruction and Development (IBRD); International Trade Organisation (ITO)
Brigden, James 82, 119–20, 133
Britain
   and Asia 143, 144, 149, 150, 159, 160–1, 166, 191, 184, 197–9, 227, 231, 258, 279
   Australia and 75–6, 79, 150–1, 159–62, 168, 214, 215
   Chifley government and 25, 39, 150, 151, 159–61, 218, 242, 244, 214–15, 222, 245–65, 276–7, 278–9

Cold War 20, 25, 159, 160, 197–9, 234, 239–40, 241, 242, 244–59, 276–7, 278–9
communism 159, 161, 195, 241, 242, 245, 246–7, 278–9
consultation with Australia 246, 248, 251, 253, 257
divergence of policy with Australia 25, 147, 159–61, 215, 218, 222, 227, 231, 242, 244, 245–50, 251–2, 256, 257–9, 264–5, 278–9
imperialism and empire 86, 143, 144, 145, 149, 159, 161, 181, 188, 189, 192, 202, 227, 231, 258, 260, 277–8, 279
and India 5, 86–7, 181, 182, 184–92, 193, 195
and Indonesia 149, 150–3, 155–6, 157, 188–9
inter-war years 75–6, 87, 89
Japan peace settlement 213, 214–15, 222, 227–8, 231–2, 233
and Nehru 185, 186, 188–9, 190, 201–2, 203
Pacific 248–9, 191
post-war economy 132, 215, 239, 243, 258, 259
Soviet Union and 159, 241, 242, 244–5, 246, 247–8, 251–2, 253, 258–9, 262
trade 41–2, 75–6, 89–90, 219–20, 260
United States and 41–2, 89, 118, 184, 199, 214, 215, 233–4, 239–40, 241, 242, 245, 246, 253, 256, 264, 265
see also Atlantic Charter; Attlee, Clement, and his government; Commonwealth, British; conferences; Prime Ministers' Conference, Commonwealth (London, 1949); Western Union
British Medical Association 38–9
Brown, Harry 119
Brown, Judith M 192
Bruce, Stanley Melbourne 73, 77, 90

Bruce–Page government 73–4, 76, 103–4, 119
Burma 144, 160, 169, 195
Burton, Herbert, 220
Burton, John 10, 14, 59–60, 88, 145, 149–50, 151, 158, 172, 183, 202–3, 233, 245–6, 252–3, 254, 257, 276
on Chifley 255–6
Byrnes, James F 251

Calwell, Arthur 118, 121, 122
Canada 89, 185, 186, 187, 188, 189, 192, 214, 241, 260
Casey, Richard 96
Central Reserve Bank Bill (1930) 77–8
central reserve banks 76, 77–8, 93
in Australia 77–8, 95, 97, 101
Commonwealth Bank as 37–8, 77, 78
Ceylon 144, 169, 189, 192
Chiang Kai-Shek 165, 169
Chifley, Ben, life and character 6, 17, 24, 31–69, **211**, **271**
childhood 3, 32–3, 41, 225–6
core beliefs 15, 16, 74–5, 79, 83–4, 104, 201
death 6–7
descriptions and opinions of 4–5, 7, 8–12, 23, 52, 53–7, 58–9, 60–61, 96, 117–118, 204, 219, 221, 254, 255–6, 280
education 32, 35, 51, 52–4, 86–7, 93, 97–8, 275–6
employment, non-political 33, 34, 35, 36, 86
family 15, 31, 32, 41, 225
health 6–7, 17, 259
home 35, **71**, 86
inter-war years 24, 33–5, 74–5, 86–103, 275, 74–5, 86–103, 135–6, 144–6, 202, 215–16, 275–6
marriage 33–4
personal life 31–8
personal papers, lack of 12–14
receptivity to new ideas 280–1

religion 33–4, 59
see also Chifley, Ben, government;
  Chifley, Ben, political career;
  influences on Chifley;
  internationalism, Chifley's;
  internationalism, Chifley's
  economic; inter-war years;
  peace; Royal Commission into
  the Monetary and Banking
  Systems in Operation in
  Australia (1935–37); war
Chifley, Ben, government 13, 39,
  45–6, 120–1, 162
  advisers 10, 23, 45, 51, 55–6,
    61–2, 116, 143, 157, 219, 220–1,
    255
  aims, post-war 214–15
  appointment of public servants
    58–61
  Asian policy 11, 24, 144, 171,
    186–7
  Britain and 151, 159–61, 242, 244,
    214–15, 245–65
  development, post-war 39–40, 52
  disunity/unity 24, 39–40, 118,
    120–3, 125, 127, 130, 134–5
  domestic policy 38–9, 40
  economic security 21, 23, 50, 114,
    116–17, 123–4, 132–3, 135, 181,
    230, 281
  economy *see* economy, Australian
  employment 115–117, 118, 122–3,
    126–7, 128
  foreign policy *see* foreign policy,
    Chifley government's
  India policy 6, 7–8, 167, 181,
    181–4, 185–92, 194
  Indonesia policy 146–53, 155, 248,
    255, 279
  inflation 39–50
  Japan policy 221, 222–5, 228–31,
    278
  liberal internationalism 11–12,
    21–2, 51, 60, 258
  migration 39, 47–8, 202–3, 259,
    263

military commitment 50, 51,
  149–50, 152, 153, 159–62, 232,
  278, 279
security, Australian 21, 39, 50, 112,
  114, 116–17, 123–4, 149, 151,
  214, 217, 242, 249, 251, 258–9,
  260–1, 276–7
Soviet Union 160–1, 163, 169, 197,
  234, 243, 248, 249–50, 253, 257,
  258–9, 260–1, 264–5, 279
trade, expansion of 116–117, 118,
  182–3
United States and 10, 20, 25, 53,
  117, 159, 166, 199, 214, 215,
  219–20, 222, 232–3, 243, 246,
  248, 249–50, 253, 256, 258–9,
  260–1, 264
White Australia Policy 202–3
see also Bretton Woods
  Agreement; Cold War; Cold War,
  Chifley and; Commonwealth,
  British; economy, Australian;
  foreign policy, Australian; India;
  Indonesia; internationalism;
  Japan Peace Settlement; trade;
  Western Union proposal
Chifley, Ben, political career 31–69
  assistant treasurer 34–5, 87, 98
  Curtin government 20, 31–2, 36–8,
    42, 61–2, 103
  Defence, minister for 34, 36, 60–1,
    80, 87
  election of 34–5, 36, 39, 40–1, 61,
    73–4, 120–1, 215
  election loss 35, 47, 162
  Mandated Territories, minister for
    34, 61
  Opposition, in 4–5, 9, 16, 17, 18,
    20, 24, 40–41, 53, 57–8, 61, 136,
    144, 145, 162–9, 170, 215, 226–7,
    278
  Post-war Reconstruction, minister
    for 8, 10, 37, 42–3, 58, 60, 182,
    221
  prime minister 4–5, 7, 8, 10, 12,
    19, 20, 23, 24, 31, 38–41, 45,
    51, 52, 53–4, 56–8, 62, 74–5, 98,

104, 120, 121–2, 129–30, 131–2, 135–6, 145, 146, 148, 150–3, 155, 154–62, 165, 166, 170, 172–3, 182, 183–4, 186, 187, 188, 190–1, 194, 196, 198, 203–4, 217–18, 219, 221, 227, 250, 251, 253–6, 259, 263, 273, 276–7, 279–80
  Scullin government 20, 34–5, 36, 47, 60–1, 86, 95
  treasurer 4, 18, 19, 23, 24, 31–2, 36–8, 51, 53–4, 55, 56–62, 74–5, 103, 104, 159, 219, 255
  see also Chifley, Ben; Chifley, Ben, government; Royal Commission into the Monetary and Banking Systems in Operation in Australia (1935–37)
Chifley, Elizabeth (nee McKenzie, JBC's wife) 33–4, 86
Chifley, Mary Anne (Chifley's mother) 31
Chifley, Patrick (Chifley's father) 15, 31, 41, 225
  Chifley, Patrick (Chifley's grandfather) 32, 41, 225–6
China 86, 143, 144, 154, 160, 165–6, 168, 195, 214, 227, 248
Churchill, Winston 41–42, 199–200, 219, 240
Clay, Lucius D 263
Cold War 162, 239–70
  Asia 159–62, 258, 277, 278–9
  balance of power 239–40, 241–2, 243
  Britain 20, 25, 159, 160, 234, 239–40, 241, 242, 244–59, 258, 276–7, 278–9
  communism, fear of 232, 233, 234, 240–2, 244, 245, 246, 251–2, 258–9, 264, 277, 278–9
  development of 159–60, 239–40
  power politics 196, 221, 242, 258, 279
  United States and Japan 231–4
  see also Cold War, Chifley and; communism; Soviet Union; United States; Western Union proposal
Cold War, Chifley and
  attitude to 7–8, 20, 25, 168–9, 201–2, 205, 232–3, 242–4, 246–7, 250, 253–6, 258, 264–5, 277, 278–9
  communism 244, 245, 246, 247, 251, 258–9, 264–5
  divergence of policy with Britain 242, 244, 245–50, 251–2, 256, 257–9
  internationalism 246, 265
  justice, focus on 246, 247–8
  London visit (1948) 259–62
  Pacific, commitment to 248, 249, 258
  peace, promoting 264–5
  power politics, dislike of 7–8, 21–2, 196, 242, 247–8, 279
  security, post-war Australia 242, 249, 258
  view of Soviet Union 243, 248–9, 250, 258–9, 264
  view of Soviet Union vs United States 242, 243, 248–9, 250, 258–9, 264
  view of United States 243, 250, 258–9, 264
  war, prospect of 159, 232–3, 242, 243, 249, 250, 251–2, 253, 258–9, 264
  Western Union proposal 242, 245–50, 252–6, 278–9
  see also communism; peace; war
collaboration, international 42, 51, 93, 104, 124, 126–7, 128, 130, 134–5, 192, 194, 234–5, 274, 280–1
colonialism, end of 18, 20, 22, 25, 40, 48, 143–4, 145, 154, 157, 158, 186, 196, 197, 199, 201–2
  Chifley's view of 145–6, 161, 168–9, 171–2, 186, 199, 202, 258, 278, 279–80
  Asia 143–80
  India 181–210

see also Asia, post-war; India; Indonesia; Netherlands, the
Commonwealth Bank
   central bank 37–8, 77, 78, 101, 123
   Great Depression 74, 76, 77–8, 81–83, 85
Commonwealth, British
   Australia 191, 192, 193, 251
   Chifley on 190, 194, 233, 277
   communism 196, 241
   India's membership 182, 183, 184–92, 193–4, 204, 277, 278
   Japan peace settlement 213–14, 227–8, 232,
   military aspects 195–6, 278, 279
   Nehru on 195–8, 277
   policies 6, 144, 159–60, 194–7
   post-war changes 192, 193, 194–204, 241, 252, 273–4
   Western Union 241, 245, 252
   see also Britain; conferences; Prime Ministers' Conference, Commonwealth (London, 1946); Prime Ministers' Conference, Commonwealth (London, 1949); Western Union proposal
Commonwealth Reconstruction Training Scheme (CRTS) 37, 52
communism
   Asia 11, 18–19, 60, 155, 158–9, 160–1, 162, 163, 165–6, 167, 169, 171, 172, 186, 187,195–6, 197, 198, 201–2, 227, 234, 242, 244, 258, 277, 278, 279
   Chifley government 11–12
   Chifley's view 60, 148, 158–9, 163, 166, 171–2, 186–7, 196, 197, 198, 200, 201–2, 226–7, 232–3, 244, 246, 247, 251, 258–9, 264, 278–9
   Europe 240–2, 245, 246–8, 251–2, 264, 278–9
   fear of 232, 233, 234, 240–2, 244, 245, 246, 251–2, 258–9, 264, 277, 278–9
   Menzies Opposition 40–1, 50, 155, 160–1, 166, 244

post-war instability 11–12, 158, 159–60, 195–6, 202, 232, 258, 277
see also Cold War; Soviet Union; United States of America; Western Union
Communist Dissolution Bill 40
conferences, international
   Commonwealth (Imperial) 9, 25, 40, 52, 89–90, 172–3, 183–94, 196, 198, 202, 203, 204, 216–17, 243, 278,
   inter-war years 86–90, 93, 114, 119–20, 133, 135, 275
   post-war 9, 39–40, 58, 153–4, 182–3
   see also Bretton Woods Agreement
Coombs, HC 'Nugget' 35, 58–9, 61, 62, 97, 98, 104, 116, 114–15, 182, 217–18, 229, 243, 277
cooperation, international 20, 183, 199, 203–4
   Chifley's support for 47, 77, 92, 104, 113–114, 125, 133–4, 135, 159, 204, 273, 201
   see also Bretton Woods Agreement; United Nations
Copland, Douglas 78, 35, 55, 61, 78, 83, 88, 103, 119, 165, 220, 233
Cornish, Selwyn 49, 120
Cotton, James 23, 113, 152–3
Council of Foreign Ministers, Moscow (1945) 213, 214, 240–1
Country Party 40, 95, 96
Crawford, John Grenfell (Jack) 60, 104, 131, 134, 220–221, 229
Crawford, Max 16, 17, 22, 30, 220
Cripps, Sir Stafford 189, 203, 259
Crisp, Leslie Finlay (Fin) 8–9, 10–11, 13–14, 32–3, 44, 54, 61, 97, 98, 103, 122, 129, 131, 134, 144, 145, 146, 162, 198, 200–1, 203–4, 225, 280
Critchley, Tom 145, 156, 171
Crocker, Walter 204
Crockett, Peter 145
Curtin, John 9, 10, 23, 38, 45–6, 73, 83, 115, 280

see also Curtin, John, government;
  Curtin, John, Opposition
Curtin, John government 10, 13,
  45–6, 143
  advisers 23, 45, 143, 220–1
  Chifley in 20, 31–2, 36–8, 42, 61–2,
    103
  foreign policy 45
  social services 36–7
  see also Chifley, Ben, political
    career
Curtin, John, Opposition 215

Day, David 8, 9, 12, 32, 215, 216, 276
Dedman, John 13, 56, 120, 146, 166,
  186–7
Debt Conversion Agreement Bill 83
de Matos, Christine 222–3
democracy, Chifley's belief in 132,
  198, 222, 224, 234, 244, 278
Dening, Esler 150, 256–7
Denning, Warren 77
Dennis, Peter 11, 146–7
depression
  appropriate government policy
    for 94, 99, 101
  1890s 31, 48, 100
  see also Great Depression;
    influences on Chifley:
    depressions
Depression, Great *see* Great
  Depression
disarmament conferences 87, 87–8
Dutch, the *see* Netherlands, the
Dingman, Roger 216, 222
Dixon, Sir Owen 6
Duff, Patrick 254, 256
Dunk, William 55–6, 255

economic system, international *see*
  financial and monetary system,
  international
economics and finance
  Chifley's interest in/knowledge
    of 8, 9, 19, 24, 35, 36, 55, 74–5,
    80–1, 86–7, 88, 89, 93, 94, 97–9,
    103–4, 113–114, 275–6

Keynesian 35, 59–60, 82, 87, 97–98,
  99, 119, 218
economy, Australian 74, 220
  Chifley government 9, 11–12, 22,
    29–40, 41, 49–50, 74–5, 114, 117,
    122–3, 147, 274
  Depression 78–9, 80, 82,
  employment 37, 19, 115–117, 118,
    122–3, 126–7, 128
  national income 125–6
  post-war 39–40, 114–18, 147,
    259–60
  see also Chifley, Ben, government;
    Great Depression; trade
economy, 1940s world 41, 113–140,
  274, 278
  Bretton Woods Agreement
    115–129
  conferences 87, 88–95
  International Monetary
    Agreements Bill (1947) 129–135
  inter-war years 75–6, 87, 88–95,
    218
  need for change 88–95, 104,
    114–15
  new global system 21, 25, 31,
    39–40, 114–118, 119, 129–30,
    132, 134, 273, 275–6, 277, 281
  1940s 113–140, 231, 243, 274
  see also Atlantic Charter; Bretton
    Woods Agreement; financial
    and monetary system,
    international; trade
Edwards, Peter 12, 170, 252–3, 254
Eggleston, Frederic W 23, 45–6, 131,
  143, 157, 220
  on JBC 45, 46
Evatt, Herbert Vere (Doc) 145, 200,
  211
  Chifley and 10, 40, 170, 190–1,
    201, 232–3, 247, 251, 254, 256–7,
    261–2, 273–4, 275–6
  Asia 172, 276
  Bevin and 256–7, 261–2
  communism 50, 60
  foreign affairs 10, 25–6, 160, 170,
    254, 258, 273–4, 276

Index 313

India 182, 185–6, 187, 188, 190, 191
Indonesia 146–7, 148–9, 153, 170
United Nations 201, 242, 260–1, 262
Western Union 245, 247, 256–7

Far Eastern Commission 214, 229
Fellers, Bonner 231–2
Fettling, David 11, 170
Fiduciary Notes Bill (1931) 82
Financial and Economic Advisory Committee 61
financial and monetary system, international 9, 24, 74, 79–81, 83–4, 88–9, 90, 91–2, 93, 104, 114–15, 118, 129–30, 132, 135, 259–60, 275–6
  see also Bretton Woods Agreement; gold standard; international Monetary Fund (IMF)
foreign policy, Chifley government's 10, 11–12, 19–23, 49–50, 116–117, 135–6, 148, 150–3, 154–62, 181–4, 185–6, 190–1, 192, 201–2, 242–4, 245–8, 276–9
  Asia 141–210, 258, 276
  economic dimension 21, 218–19
  Chifley's influence 8, 10–12, 18, 24–5, 26, 162–70, 171–3, 183–4, 190–1, 192, 215, 223, 227–8, 242, 245–8, 253–6, 257, 260, 274, 276–9, 280
  India policy 6, 7–8, 167, 181, 181–4, 185–9, 190, 192, 194
  Indonesia policy 11, 145, 146–53, 155–6, 248, 255, 279
  Japan policy 215–21, 222–5, 228–31, 258, 278
  liberal internationalism 11–12, 21–2, 51, 60, 258–9
  post-war reconstruction rather than retribution 216, 217, 218–19, 223, 274, 278
  see also Britain; Commonwealth, British; Cold War; Pacific and Asia-Pacific; peace; war
four freedoms 123–4

France 89, 152, 168, 170, 214, 226, 241, 245, 246, 252
Franco 246
Fraser, Peter 189, 191, 195, 256
future, Chifley's focus on 7, 11, 18–19, 20, 22–3, 36, 37, 39, 50–1, 60, 101, 114, 130, 131–2, 133, 152, 167, 170, 182–3, 194, 196, 214, 217, 221, 223, 224, 229, 243, 248, 264, 274, 278, 279–80, 280–1
Gandhi, Mohandas Karamchand (Mahatma) 5, 6, 7, 86
General Agreement on Tariffs and Trade (GATT) 119, 120, 134, 273
Genoa financial conference (1922) 77
George, Margaret 145
Germany, post-war 50–1, 217, 241, 245, 262–4, 278
  Berlin blockade 241, 262, 263
  Chifley on 50–1, 218–19
  Chifley visit to post-war Berlin 50–1, 262–4, 265
  peace settlement 240–1, 278
  trade unions 263–4
Gerster, Robin 223
Giblin, Eilean 55
Giblin, LF 35, 55, 61, 83, 119, 220
Gibson, Sir Robert 74, 77–8, 81, 82–3, 95, 99
Gold Delegation (1932) 90–2, 93
gold standard 76, 82, 85, 91–2
goodwill mission to Southeast and East Asia 157–58
Great Britain *see* Britain
Great Depression 240
  Australian banks 78, 80–1, 85, 95, 101–2
  Australian economy 49, 74–6, 77–9, 80, 82, 84–5
  Australian trade 22, 75–6, 77–8, 79–80, 84, 93, 218, 278
  Commonwealth Bank 74, 76, 77–8, 81–83, 85, 95, 99, 101, 103
  debt, government 36, 74, 76, 78, 79–81, 83, 85, 99
  effect on Chifley 22, 31, 41, 48–9, 73–112

global economy 75–6, 89, 218
government policy 34–5
Lang Plan 79–81
monetary policy 76, 82
preferential trade, imperial 89–90
Premiers' Plan 83–6
Theodore's Reflationist Plan 81–3
unemployment 40, 76, 85, 95, 113, 114
Wall Street crash 74, 75, 77, 81, 117
Greece 245, 246–8, 250, 252
Groenewegen, Peter 103
Gurry, Meg 183, 201, 205

Hartnett, Laurence 39
Hasluck, Paul, on Chifley 57
Hatta, Mohammad 143–4, 151, 155–6
Hodgson, William R 213–14
Hong Kong 159, 195, 258, 278
Hughes, William Morris 'Billy' 4

Imperial Economic Conference, Ottawa (1932) 89–90
India 154, 168, 169, 195, 201, 214, 277
   Australian policy 6, 7–8, 167, 181, 181–4, 185–9, 190, 192, 194
   Britain and 184, 185–6, 188–90
   Chifley and 5–6, 7, 7–8, 40, 155, 167, 183–4, 186–9, 190–1, 192, 194, 196, 197, 277
   civil disobedience 86–7
   Cold War 7–8
   Commonwealth membership 40, 182, 183, 184–92, 193, 204, 277
   communism 171, 195, 196
   economic development 197–8
   Evatt on 185–6, 187, 188, 190
   foreign policy 201–2
   independence 144, 181–2, 277
   nationalism 86–7, 182, 277
   Prime Ministers' Conference, Commonwealth (London, 1949) 183, 184–92
   reciprocal citizenship 186, 187
   United States and 184
   see also Nehru, Pandit Jawaharlal
Indian Council of World Affairs (ICWA) 153–4
Indochina *see* Vietnam
Indonesia
   Australian military 149–50, 152, 153
   Britain and 149, 150–3, 155, 156, 157, 188–9
   Chifley response to nationalism 11, 145, 146–53, 155, 155–6
   communism 148, 156, 160, 197
   Dutch in 188–9, 196
   Dutch military offensives 144, 145, 147, 155–7
   importance to Australia 152–3
   independence 157
   intelligence on 150–3
   nationalist movement 11, 40, 60, 143–4, 149, 151–152, 155, 170–1, 258
   New Delhi Conference on (1949) 60, 157, 172, 182–3, 255
   United Nations 145, 151, 152, 155, 156–7, 170–1, 255, 278
   United States and 151–2, 155, 157
influences on Chifley 14, 19, 22–3, 24, 31, 35, 104, 131, 201, 274–6
   Asia, early tour of 35, 144–6, 202
   depressions, economic 22, 31, 41, 48–9, 77, 48–9, 74–5, 76, 100–1, 103, 131, 135, 274, 275–6
   intellectual 23, 31, 51–62, 219–21
   labour movement 31, 43–45, 53, 280
   rural background 9, 19, 24, 25, 31, 41–3, 62, 225–6, 274
   world wars 31, 48, 50–1, 103–4, 113,131, 161–2, 274
   trade union movement 19, 31, 44, 45, 46–47, 62, 145–6, 224–5, 262–3
International Bank for Reconstruction and Development (IBRD) 115, 119, 124, 125, 126, 129, 134, 273

international economic and monetary system *see* financial and monetary system, international
International Monetary Agreements Bill (1947) 129–135
International Monetary Fund (IMF) 114–15, 116, 118, 119, 120, 124, 125–6, 129, 134, 260, 273
International Trade Organisation (ITO) 115, 119, 134
internationalism, Chifley's
 commitment to 8, 9, 19–23, 33, 41–42, 131–4, 132, 191, 204, 276
 evolution of 12, 19, 20, 22, 24, 74–5, 93–4, 274, 275, 276–7
 rules-based 19–20, 31, 41–42, 31, 62, 104, 116, 131, 163, 172, 200, 221, 273–4, 275–6, 280–1, 275
internationalism, economic, Chifley's interest in 8–9, 21, 22, 23, 24, 25, 41, 42–43, 47–8, 113, 133–4, 274
 origins of 74–5
inter-war years
 Chifley 24, 33–5, 74–5, 86–104, 135–6, 202, 215–16, 275–6
 Chifley's Asian trip 35, 144–6
 conferences 87–90, 275
 world economy 75–6, 87, 88–95, 218
 see also Great Depression
Iriye, Akira 20, 47, 133, 134–5
iron curtain 240
Isaac, JE 150–1
isolationism 80, 122, 124, 133, 199, 223
Italy 89, 226–7, 245, 252

Japan peace settlement 25, 213–238
 Allied Occupation 213–214, 233
 Australian attitudes to 219–221, 222–3
 Australian forces in 213, 231
 Australian role 213–15, 222–3, 224, 227–31
 Chifley government policy 215, 223–5

 Chifley's attitude to 215–19, 225–7, 234, 278
 Chifley's visit 50–1, 217–18
 Cold War and 231–4, 258
 Commonwealth Occupation Forces 213
 democratisation 222, 234, 278
 economic recovery 216, 217, 218–19, 223–5, 230, 234, 278
 land reform 222, 225–31, 278
 militarism of Japan 217, 218, 223, 224, 231, 234, 278
 Soviet Union and 231
 US policy and the Cold War 231–4
 variance from British policy 218, 231
Jensen, JK 36
Joyce, AC 61–2

Kashmir 6, 188
Kennnan, George F 240
Kirby, Sir Richard 144–5, 155
Kobayashi, Ai 228
Korea (North and South) 18–19, 144, 159, 162–5

Labor Party, Australian 45–8, 73, 102–3, 130, 163, 215, 244, 251, 277
 Chifley's membership and role 8, 12, 14, 20, 24, 25, 32, 34–5, 43, 45–48, 85, 94, 101, 115–16, 117–18, 121–3, 164, 226, 244, 245–6, 274, 276–7, 280
 communism 40–1
 isolationism 122–3, 124
 unity/disunity 9, 16, 17, 24, 35, 39–40, 58–9, 78–80, 83–4, 96, 117, 120–3, 125, 127, 130, 134–5, 275
 see also Bretton Woods Agreement; Chifley, Ben; Chifley, Ben, government; Chifley, Ben, political career; Cold War; Curtin, John, government; foreign policy, Australia's; Great Depression; Scullin, James, government; Western Union proposal

316 *Index*

labour movement 48, 53, 78, 96, 163
  Chifley commitment to 16, 17, 24, 31, 38, 43–8, 262–3, 274, 280
  support for United Nations 162, 200
land reform, Chifley on 226–7
Lang, JT (Jack) 35, 44, 47, 78–81, 85, 96, 130, 134, 135
Lang Plan 79–81
League of Nations 20, 87–8, 90–2, 93, 199, 275
  see also United Nations
Lee, David 8–9, 11, 21, 49, 77, 170, 276
Lewis, Essington 36
Limekilns 32, 41, 225
Listowel, Lord 186–7
Lowe, David 11–12, 15, 21–2, 160, 201, 277, 278
Lyons, Joseph 55, 78, 79, 95, 96, 219
Lyons government 96, 102–3, 104, 219–220
Lyons, Enid 55, 96

MacArthur, Douglas 213, 214, 228, 229, 230–2
Machtig, Sir Eric 254
Mackay, Sir Iven 181–2, 202
Mackie, Jamie 145
Mao Zedong 165–6
Maritime Industries Bill 73
Malaya 144, 151, 159, 160–1, 168, 195, 258, 277, 278
Marshall, George C 240, 241
Marshall Plan 240, 241, 250
McCallum, John 154
McFarlane, SG (Misery Mac) 62, 116
McFarlane, Bruce 103
McIntosh, Alister 254
McKell, WJ 39
McLean, Ian W 80, 225
McMullin, Ross 9–10
McNeil, Hector 257–8
McVey, Daniel 119
Meaney, Neville 10, 248–9, 276
Melville, LG (Leslie) 35, 61, 78, 81, 82, 83, 90, 98, 116, 118–120, 125–6

Menzies, RG 49, 51
  on Chifley 7, 53, 194
Menzies government 40, 49, 193, 261
  Asia 166
  banking reform 103
  communism and the Labor Party 40–1
  economy 49
  foreign policy 45, 162, 166, 167–8
  India 167, 197
  United Nations 162
Menzies Opposition 50, 130
  Asian nationalism 155, 160, 172, 182–3, 204, 277, 278
  bank privatisation 40, 103
  colonialism 157, 161, 193–4, 277
  communism 40–1, 50, 155, 160–1, 166, 244,
  foreign policy 157, 160, 172, 264, 277, 278
  India 155, 157, 172, 182, 186, 189, 193–4, 204
  Indonesia 157, 147–8, 155, 157, 172
  International Monetary Agreements Bill (1947) 130
  military commitments, Australian 147–8
  National Health Service Act 38–9
  prospect of war 50, 264
Mighell, Sir Norman 204
military commitment, Australian 50, 149–50, 152, 153, 159–61, 167, 278
Miller, JDB (Bruce) 122–3, 280
Millmow, Alex 82, 97
Mills, Richard Charles 35, 95, 96–7, 98, 119
monarchy, Chifley on 188
Money Power ideology 78, 118, 122, 130, 132
Moodie, Colin 202
Mook, HJ Van 151
Moore, RJ 194
Mountbatten, Lord Louis 150, 152
Napier, John Mellis 95, 97, 98
National Advocate 14–15, 35, 41, 73–4, 86–7, 88, 92, 102, 274–5

national health scheme 38–9
National Health Services Act 38–9
nationalism
　Asia 143–4, 154–5, 157–62, 165–6, 168–9, 182, 258, 278, 279
　dangers of 113, 118
Nationalist Party 73–4, 77, 79
Nehru, Pandit Jawaharlal 86, **141**, 154, 181–210, 244
　Britain and 185, 186, 188–9, 201–2
　Chifley and 7–8, 9, 162, 168, 171, 184, 194–204, 244, 277
　Chifley's view of 5–6, 24–25, 167
　Cold War 167, 244, 277
　Commonwealth, view of 195–8, 199
　Commonwealth membership, India's 184–6, 188–9, 190, 191–2, 199, 204
　communism, view of 196, 197, 198, 201–2, 277
　economic change, need for 201–2
　on Indonesia 157
　London Declaration 191–2
　New Delhi Conference (1949) 157, 172, 183
　Prime Ministers' Conference, Commonwealth (London, 1949) 172–3, 184–5, 188–9, 190, 191, 192, 194–204
　influence on Chifley 198–9
　support for United Nations 183, 199–201, 203
　White Australia policy 202–3
　see also India
Netherlands East Indies *see* Indonesia
Netherlands, the 214
　Australian military 149–50, 152, 153
　Australia's refusal of Dutch troops 147–50, 277–8
　Indonesia and 144, 146, 152
　Indonesian nationalism 144, 145, 147, 155–7
　military offensives in Indonesia 144, 145, 147, 155–7

United Nations 145, 151, 152, 155, 156–7, 170–1, 255, 278
New Delhi Conference on Indonesia (1949) 60, 157, 172, 182–3, 255
New South Wales Industrial Court 33
New South Wales Land Act 41, 225
New Zealand 36, 88, 126, 185, 189, 190, 191, 192, 195, 213, 214, 217, 254, 256, 257
Niemeyer, Sir Otto 130
Nixon, Edwin Van-der-vord 95, 97
Noel-Baker, Philip John 189, 259
North Atlantic Treaty Organisation (NATO) 241, 273

Ogura, Takekazu 228
Oliphant, Mark 52
Opposition, Chifley in federal *see* Chifley, political career

Pacific and Asia–Pacific region
　Britain and 242, 248–9
　cooperation 6
　development 20, 42–3, 182–3
　engagement with, Australia's 6, 7, 18, 23, 45, 61, 151–2, 157, 160, 216, 217, 220–1, 224, 248, 249, 252, 258
　security in 149, 196, 214, 215, 217, 221, 224, 233, 234, 242, 248, 249, 258, 276
　trade 42–4, 60, 182–3, 221
　war in the 19–20, 216, 279
　see also Asia; Japan; trade
Packer, Gerald 154
Page, Earle 95
Pakistan 6, 144, 169, 188, 189, 192, 195, 202
Patel, Vallabhbhai 185
peace
　Chifley on 5–6, 7–8, 19, 22, 23, 25, 42, 47, 51, 87–8, 113, 114, 127, 129–34, 163, 183, 192, 213–14, 215–16, 217–18, 224–5, 240–1, 248, 265, 278
　economic development/security 7–8, 21, 22, 25, 42, 127, 129–30,

131–5, 149, 157, 192, 200, 204–5, 215–16, 217–18, 278
internationalism 19, 20–1, 23, 47, 51, 113, 114, 129–30, 163, 170, 183–4, 200, 264,
  trade and 21, 22–23, 113
  see also Japan peace settlement; war
Pearson, Lester 189, 192, 193
Pharmaceutical Benefits Act 38
Pharmaceutical Benefits Scheme (PBS) 38
Philippines 144, 195, 214
Phillips, JG (Jock) 97, 98
Pitt, Henry Arthur 95–6, 98
Plimsoll, James 229
Potsdam conference 213, 215, 217, 232, 263
  exclusion of Australia 214–15
power politics 20–2, 196, 221, 242, 247–8, 258, 279
Premiers' Plan 34, 79, 83–6, 93, 119
Prime Ministers' Conference, Commonwealth (London, 1946), Chifley at 52, 216–17, 243, 278
Prime Ministers' Conference, Commonwealth (London, 1949) 9, 52, 183–208
  activities 189–92
  Chifley at 25, 40, 183–4, 186–9, 190–1, 192, 203, 204, 244
  Chifley and Nehru 172–3, 183–200, 191, 192, 194–204
  convergence of views 194–202, 204, 205
  delegates 189–90
  divergence of views 202–3
  London Declaration 191–2
  Nehru at 172–3, 184–5, 188–9, 190, 191, 192, 194–204
  opposition to London Declaration 193–4
  preparations for 185, 186–9
  proposal for 184–6
  views of Asian unrest 194–204
  see also Nehru, Pandit Jawaharlal

prosperity, Australian 18, 41, 38, 39, 41, 42, 47, 75, 80, 84, 85, 90, 104, 114, 115, 131–2, 135, 216
  land reform 225–6
prosperity, world 19, 21–2, 25, 41, 47, 79, 92, 93, 114, 115, 131–2, 133–4, 204, 215, 216, 217, 218, 219, 274, 278
public servants 56–61, 62

Qantas Empire Airways Act 38

Reddaway, W Brian 220
Reid, Alan 53, 57, 122
Renouf, Alan 170
Reparations Conference, Lausanne (1932) 88–9, 135
Rix, Alan 228, 229
Robertson, HCH 213
Robinson, Marcus 12
Robinson, WS 82, 168
Rodgers, Don 55, 219
Roosevelt, Franklin Delano 41–42, 94, 114–15, 123–4, 199, 219, 231–2, 240
Rosecrance, Richard N 223
Royal Commission into the Monetary and Banking Systems in Operation in Australia (1935–37) 24, 35, 95–103
  banks and banking 99–101
  central bank 99–100, 101
  Chifley a member of 94, 96, 97–8, 275
  Chifley opinion of 100–2
  members 95–6
  minority report 101, 102
  recommendations 102–3
  report 99–102
rules-based international order, Chifley's belief in 19–20, 104, 116, 221, 275–6, 280–1
Rural Policy for Post-War Australia, A 42
Rusk, Dean 260–1

Sahni, JN 3–7
  interview with JBC 4, 5–6, 7
St Laurent, Louis Stephen 187, 189
Schedvin, CB 78, 96, 115
Scullin, James 34, 44, 79
Scullin, James, government 34, 44, 47, 73–4 77–9, 95, 104
  Chifley in 20, 34–5, 36, 47, 60–1, 86, 95
  disunity 47, 74, 78–9, 275
  fall of 77, 85–6, 145
  Great Depression, response to 74, 76, 77–85, 99, 102–103
  Lang Plan 78, 79–81
  Premiers' Plan, deflationist 34, 79, 83–6, 93
  Theodore's reflationist plan 79, 81–3, 93
  royal commission into banking 95, 99, 102–3
  see also Great Depression
security, Australian economic 21, 23, 50, 114, 116, 117, 123–4, 132–3,135, 230, 281
Shann, EOG 35, 83, 103
Shaw, Patrick 164–5, 213, 232, 233
Shedden, Frederick 261
Sheridan, Tom 10
Shipping Act 38
Singapore 144, 151
Sluga, Glenda 20, 48
Smuts, Jan 193–4
Snowy Mountains Hydro-Electric Power Act 39
social justice 21–2, 117, 144, 146, 168–9, 222
South Africa 186, 188, 189
South Pacific Commission 273
Soviet Union
  and Asia 86, 155, 159, 163, 165, 166, 169, 197, 231–4, 258
  Australia and 160–1, 169, 233–4, 249, 258, 260–1, 264–5
  Berlin blockade 241, 262, 263
  Bretton Woods institutions 126
  Britain and 159, 241, 242, 244–5, 246, 247–8, 251–2, 253, 258–9, 262
  Chifley on 163, 169, 197, 234, 243, 248, 249–50, 253, 257, 258–9, 264, 279
  Cold War 232, 239–40, 244–5, 249, 250, 263
  distrust of 154–5, 232, 233
  economy and power, post-war 239, 243, 249–50, 259, 264
  Europe 152, 159, 165, 166, 240, 242, 243, 244–5, 244, 245, 247–8, 251–2, 257, 279
  expansion 197, 233–4, 240, 241–2, 243, 245, 247, 251–2, 264
  fear of 159, 232, 240–2, 246, 247, 249–50
  Japan 214, 231–2
  prospect of war 50, 232, 233, 239, 240, 242–3, 248, 249–50, 253, 258–9, 264
  United Nations and 163, 241, 242, 248, 250, 260–1
  United States and 159, 231–3, 239–40, 241–2, 243, 247, 248, 250
  see also communism; Cold War; United States of America; Western Union proposal
Spain 245, 246, 252
Spender, Sir Percy 50, 54, 146, 160–1, 166, 264
Spratt, Elwyn 123
Stalin, Joseph 240
Stargadt, AW 1, 15, 16–18, 46, 171
Stephens, David 49–50
Sukarno 143–4, 149, 151
  see also Indonesia

Tange, Arthur 58, 116–17, 118–19
Taylor Card System 34
Theodore, EG 34, 77, 79, 81–3, 86, 88, 93, 98, 102, 203
Tracy, Ray 53–4
trade 6, 7–8, 21–3, 41–3, 80, 116–117, 118, 126, 127–8, 182–3

Asia–Pacific, Australia with 42–4, 60, 182–3, 221
Australia–Japan 219–20, 228, 229–30
Australia–United States 219–20
Australian dependence on 9, 22, 41, 42, 75–76, 79, 80, 84, 89, 120, 122, 125–7, 259, 274
Britain 41–2, 75–6, 89–90, 219–20, 260
expansion/promotion 41–3, 60, 113, 114–15, 117, 118, 126–7, 219, 259
Great Depression 22, 75–6, 77–8, 79–80, 84, 93, 218, 278
Lyons trade diversion policy 219–20
post-war system 12, 19, 41–2, 132, 134, 219
preferential 89–90
see also Atlantic Charter; Bretton Woods Agreement; peace
Trade and Employment Organisation, membership of 127–8
trade union movement 19, 31, 33, 44, 45, 46–47, 62, 145–6, 224–5, 262–3
Truman, Harry 240, 263

United Australia Party 79, 85, 95, 96, 219
United Nations Organisation 18, 20–1, 22, 113, 116, 124, 126–7, 129–30, 163–4, 165, 166
Australia and 10, 151, 156–7, 159, 260–1, 262
Chifley, Cold War and 242, 250, 265, 279
Chifley's support for 6, 10, 21–2, 51, 124, 126–8, 129–30, 159, 162–3, 165–6, 170, 172, 199, 200–1, 221, 242, 247, 248, 249, 250, 262, 265, 273, 276, 279, 280–1
Good Offices Committee on the Indonesian Question 145, 155

India 6, 183
Nehru's support for 183, 199–201, 203
Security Council 6, 155, 156–7, 170, 172, 255, 262
Soviet Union and 163, 241, 242, 248, 250, 260–1
United Nations 145, 151, 152, 155, 156–7, 170–1, 172, 255, 278
see also Bretton Woods Agreement
United States of America 34, 40, 41–2, 52, 144, 167–8,
Asia and 151–2, 155, 157, 159, 162, 164–6, 167–8, 233–4
Australia and 10, 25, 117, 159, 166, 214, 246, 219–20, 222, 232–3, 249, 260–1
Britain and 41–2, 89, 118, 184, 199, 214, 215, 233–4, 239–40, 241, 242, 245, 246, 253, 256, 264, 265
Chifley and 10, 20, 53, 199, 215, 243, 246, 248, 249–50, 253, 256, 258–9, 264
Cold War 157, 159, 199, 231–3, 239–40, 241–2, 244–5, 249, 264, 265
communism 231–3, 240, 241–2
Europe 157, 241, 243, 248, 249
Great Depression 240
India 184
international reform 89, 119, 120, 126, 128–9, 199–200
isolationism 124
Japan 214, 215, 222, 230–4
Pacific 248–9
post-war power 133, 154, 239, 241–2
post-war power compared with Soviet Union 239, 241–2, 243, 249–50, 259, 264
prospect of war 50, 232, 233, 239, 240, 242–3, 248, 249–50, 253, 258–9, 264
security information with Australia, embargo on sharing 260–1

Soviet Union and 159, 231–3, 239–40, 241–2, 247, 248, 250
Wall Street crash 74, 75, 77, 81, 117
see also Atlantic Charter; Bretton Woods Agreement; Cold War; communism; Great Depression; Japan peace settlement; Soviet Union
university funding 39, 52, 53
USSR *see* Soviet Union

Vietnam (Indochina) 144, 160, 165–8, 170, 171, 195, 196, 258, 279

Walker, E Ronald 97, 119
Wall Street crash 74, 75, 77, 81, 117
war
  avoiding 8, 21, 41, 50–1, 113, 159, 163, 171, 172, 192, 196, 215–219, 224–5, 228–9, 234, 262, 263–4, 265, 274
  Chifley's attitude to 8, 49, 50–1, 88–9, 149, 264, 274
  costs 18–19, 49, 51, 88, 132, 161–2, 218, 263–4, 274
  debt, Chifley on 76, 87, 88–9, 93, 161–2, 167, 215–216, 275
  economic causes of 131–2
  economic development and preventing 159, 171, 215–16
  prospect of during Cold War 50, 232, 233, 239, 240, 242–3, 248, 249–50, 253, 258–9, 264
  reconstruction rather than retribution 216, 217, 218–19, 223, 274, 278
  recovery from 50–1, 215–19, 231, 278
  see also peace; Word War I; World War II
Ward, Eddie 96, 118, 120–1, 122, 123, 125, 127, 130

Ward, Eric E 227, 228, 230, 231–2
Warner, Denis 164
Waters, Christopher 11, 12, 21–2, 222, 249, 253, 260–1, 276, 277
Waterson, DB 10, 144–5
Webb, Leicester 16
Weller, Patrick 117–18, 120
West, Hilton 15, 74
Western Union proposal 25, 159, 242, 244–57
  Attlee's proposal 244–5
  Attlee's response to Chifley 250–2
  Chifley, Evatt and Dening 256–7, 261–2
  Chifley meeting with Bevin 261–2
  Chifley on 245–50, 252–6, 278–9
  Chifley's visit to London 244, 259–62
  Commonwealth support sought 245
Wheat Stabilisation Act 38
Wheeler, Fred 116, 118
White Australia policy 47–8, 202–3
Williams, Edward J 250–1, 257
Williamson, Phillip 15
Wilson, Roland 57, 119
Women's International league for Peace and Freedom 87–8
World Disarmament Conference, League of Nations (1932) 87–8
World Monetary and Economic Conference (1933) 92–4, 114, 119, 135
World War I 75-6, 103–4, 218, 274
  see also Great Depression; war
World War II 19–20, 125, 263–4, 279
  see also Germany; Japan Peace Settlement; war

Yates, Edwin 83–4